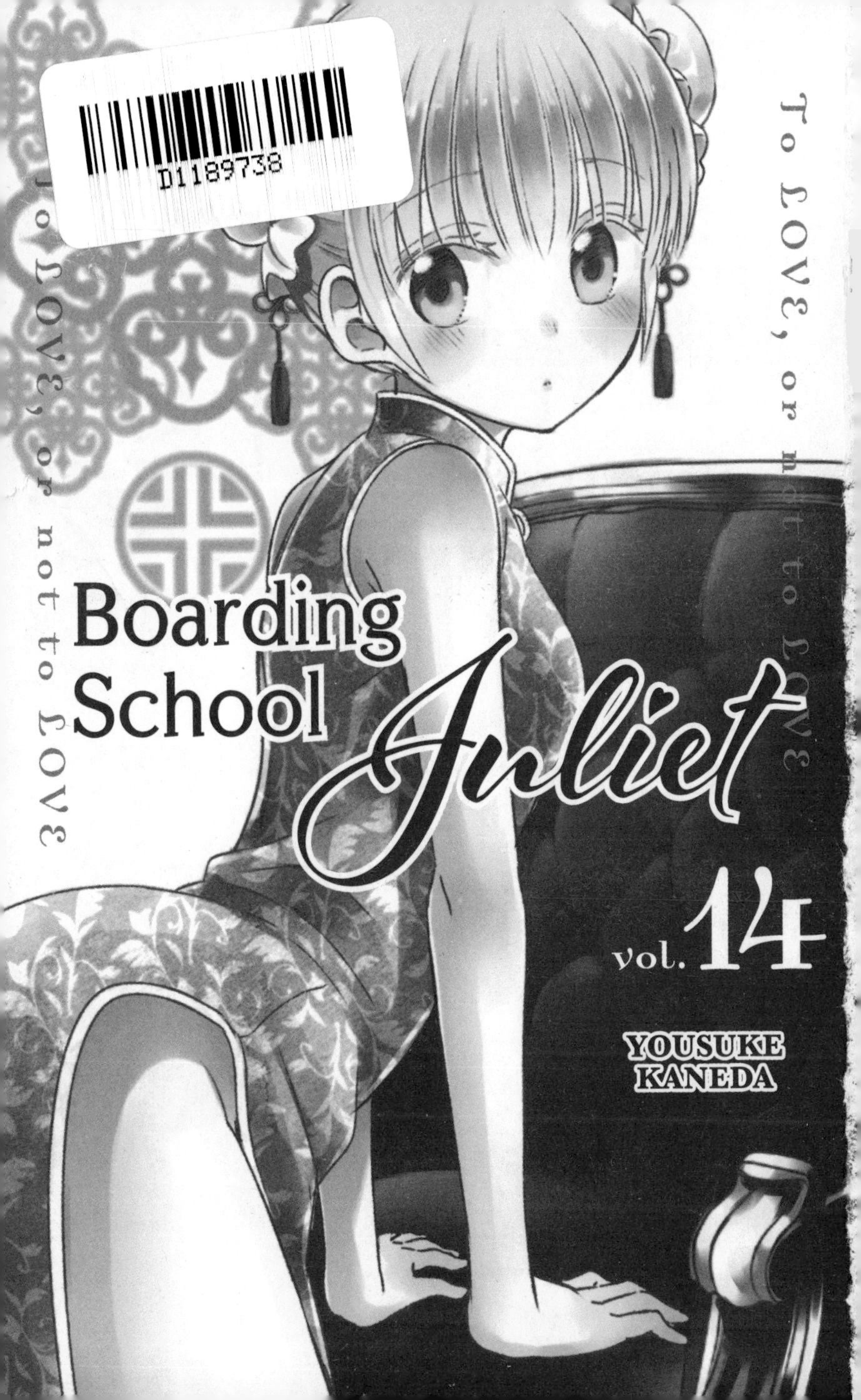
To LOVE, or not to LOVE
To LOVE, or not to LOVE
Boarding School
Juliet
vol. 14
YOUSUKE KANEDA

# THE PLAYERS

character

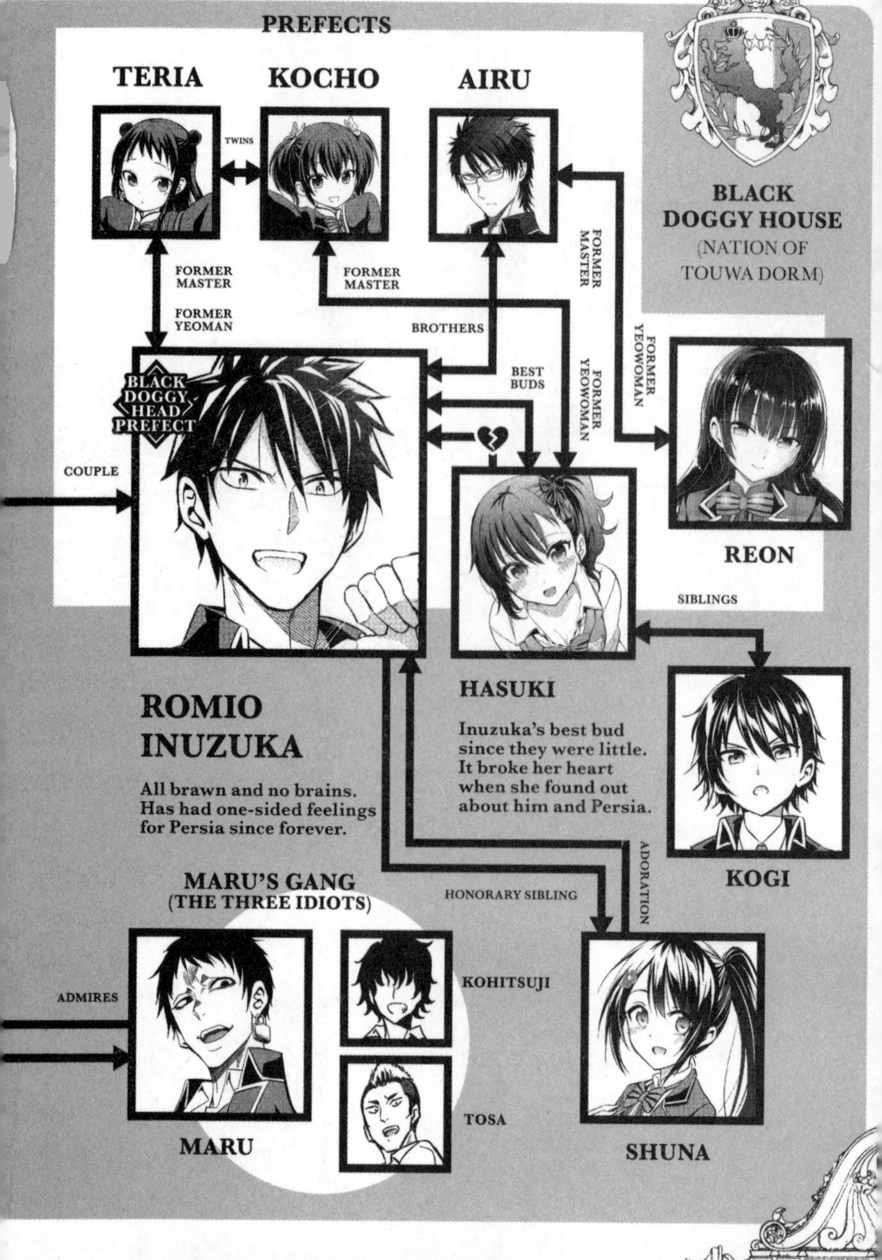
PREFECTS
TERIA
KOCHO
AIRU
TWINS
FORMER MASTER
FORMER YEOMAN
FORMER MASTER
BROTHERS
FORMER MASTER
FORMER YEOWOMAN
BEST BUDS
FORMER YEOWOMAN
BLACK DOGGY HOUSE
(NATION OF TOUWA DORM)
BLACK DOGGY HEAD PREFECT
COUPLE
REON
SIBLINGS
ROMIO INUZUKA
All brawn and no brains. Has had one-sided feelings for Persia since forever.
HASUKI
Inuzuka's best bud since they were little. It broke her heart when she found out about him and Persia.
KOGI
ADORATION
HONORARY SIBLING
MARU'S GANG
(THE THREE IDIOTS)
ADMIRES
KOHITSUJI
TOSA
MARU
SHUNA

# BOARDING SCHOOL JULIET

*To LOVE, or not to LOVE*

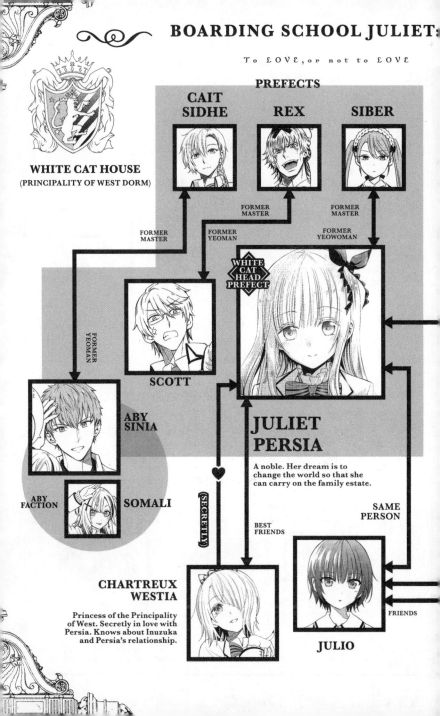

**PREFECTS**

**CAIT SIDHE**

**REX**

**SIBER**

**WHITE CAT HOUSE**
(PRINCIPALITY OF WEST DORM)

FORMER MASTER

FORMER MASTER

FORMER YEOMAN

FORMER MASTER

FORMER YEOWOMAN

**WHITE CAT HEAD PREFECT**

FORMER YEOMAN

**SCOTT**

**ABY SINIA**

**JULIET PERSIA**

A noble. Her dream is to change the world so that she can carry on the family estate.

**ABY FACTION**

**SOMALI**

(SECRETLY)

BEST FRIENDS

SAME PERSON

**CHARTREUX WESTIA**

Princess of the Principality of West. Secretly in love with Persia. Knows about Inuzuka and Persia's relationship.

FRIENDS

**JULIO**

# contents

## story

At boarding school Dahlia Academy, attended by students from two
feuding countries, one first-year longs for a forbidden love. His name:
Romio Inuzuka, leader of the Black Doggy House first-years. The apple
of his eye: Juliet Persia, leader of the White Cat House first-years. It all
begins when Inuzuka confesses his feelings to her. This is Inuzuka and
Persia's star-crossed, secret love story...

Now second-years, Inuzuka and Persia have been elected head
prefects. In an unexpected twist after the Election Day showdown, the
whole school now knows about their secret relationship! Moreover, the
new prefects' meetings are plagued by discord...and what's more,
the old prefects are standing in their way?!

# ACT 95: ROMIO & THE UPPERCLASSMEN III

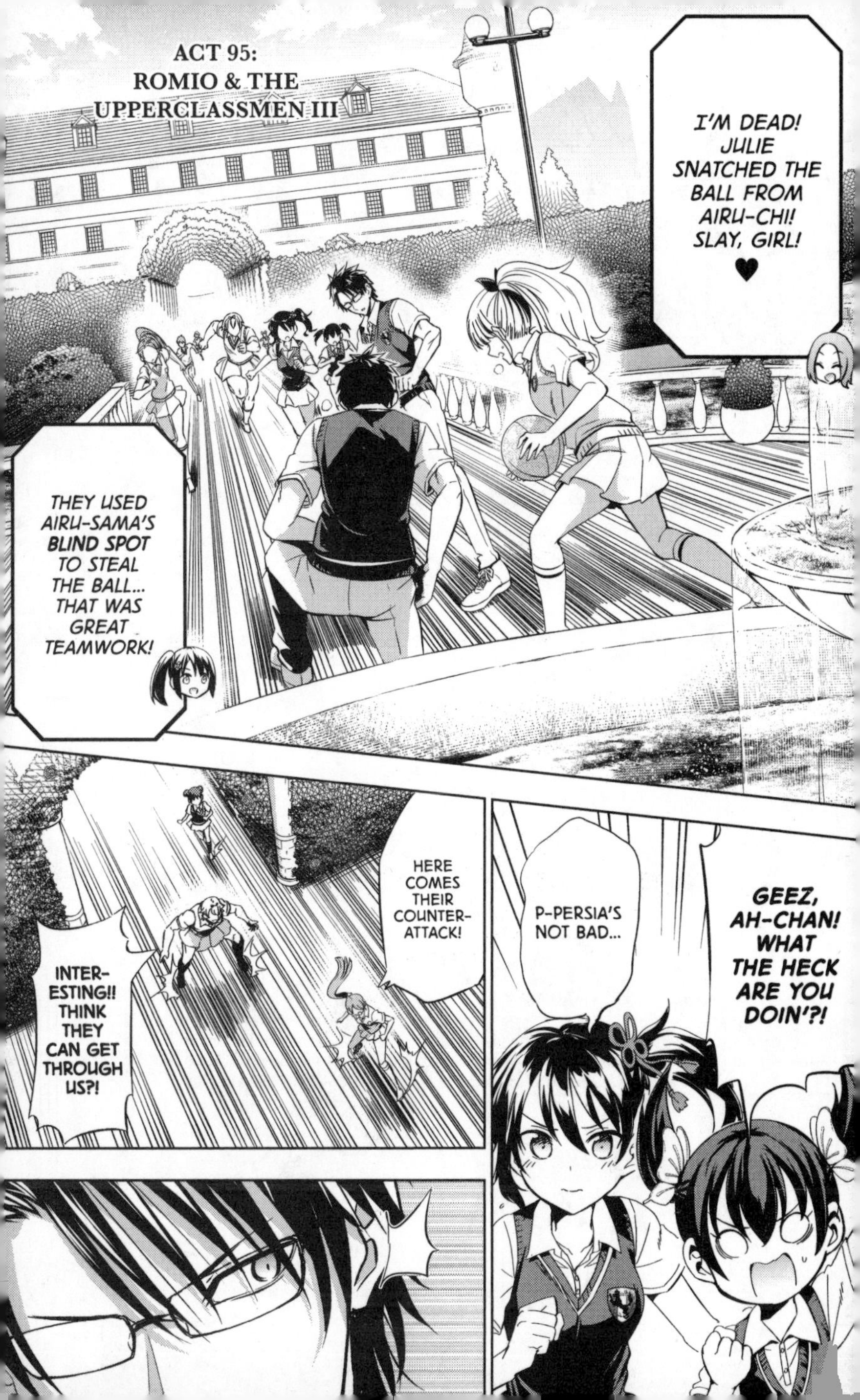
I'M DEAD! JULIE SNATCHED THE BALL FROM AIRU-CHI! SLAY, GIRL! ♥
THEY USED AIRU-SAMA'S BLIND SPOT TO STEAL THE BALL... THAT WAS GREAT TEAMWORK!
GEEZ, AH-CHAN! WHAT THE HECK ARE YOU DOIN'?!
P-PERSIA'S NOT BAD...
HERE COMES THEIR COUNTER-ATTACK!
INTERESTING!! THINK THEY CAN GET THROUGH US?!

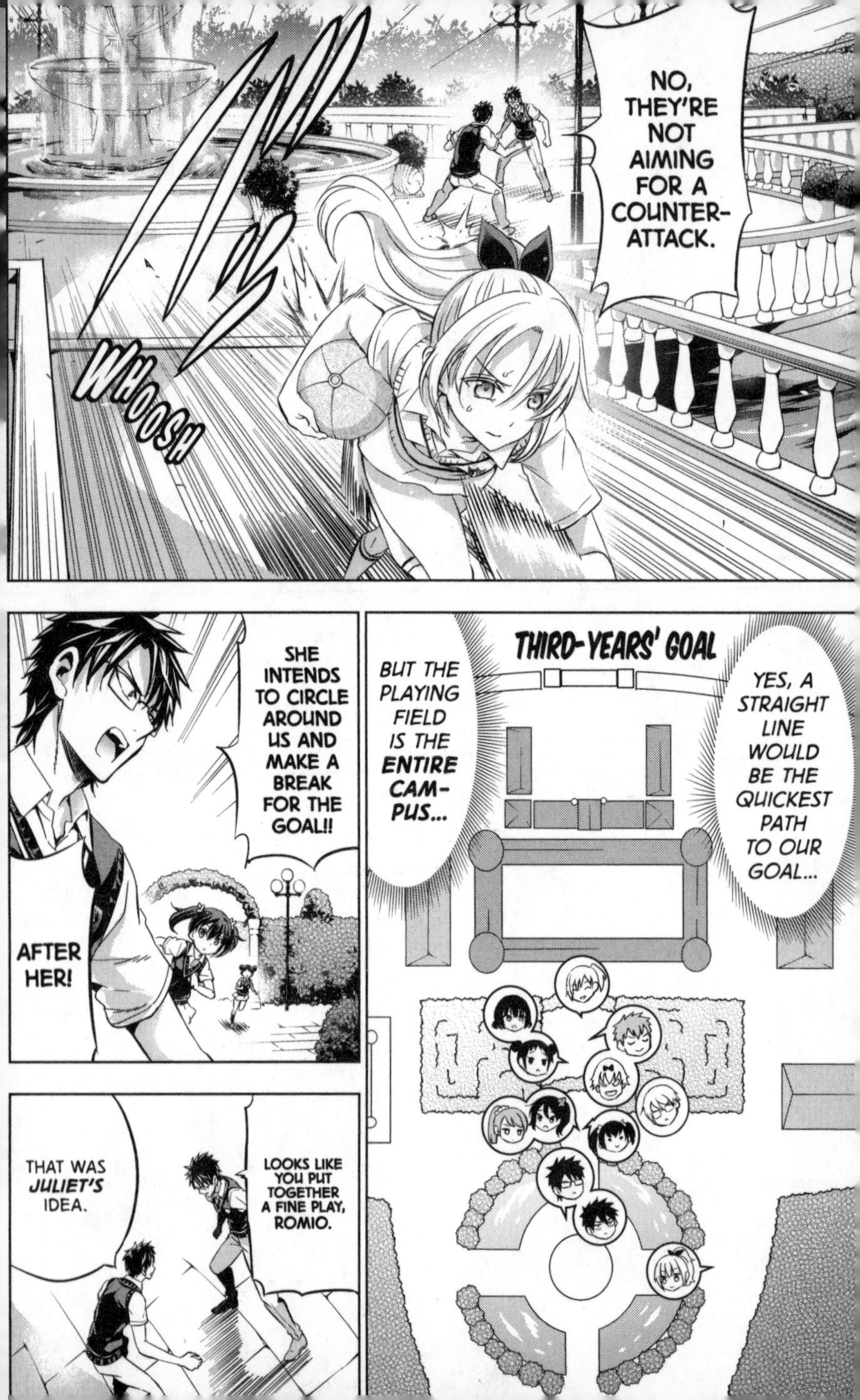
NO, THEY'RE NOT AIMING FOR A COUNTER-ATTACK.
WHOOSH
THIRD-YEARS' GOAL
YES, A STRAIGHT LINE WOULD BE THE QUICKEST PATH TO OUR GOAL...
BUT THE PLAYING FIELD IS THE ENTIRE CAM-PUS...
SHE INTENDS TO CIRCLE AROUND US AND MAKE A BREAK FOR THE GOAL!!
AFTER HER!
LOOKS LIKE YOU PUT TOGETHER A FINE PLAY, ROMIO.
THAT WAS JULIET'S IDEA.

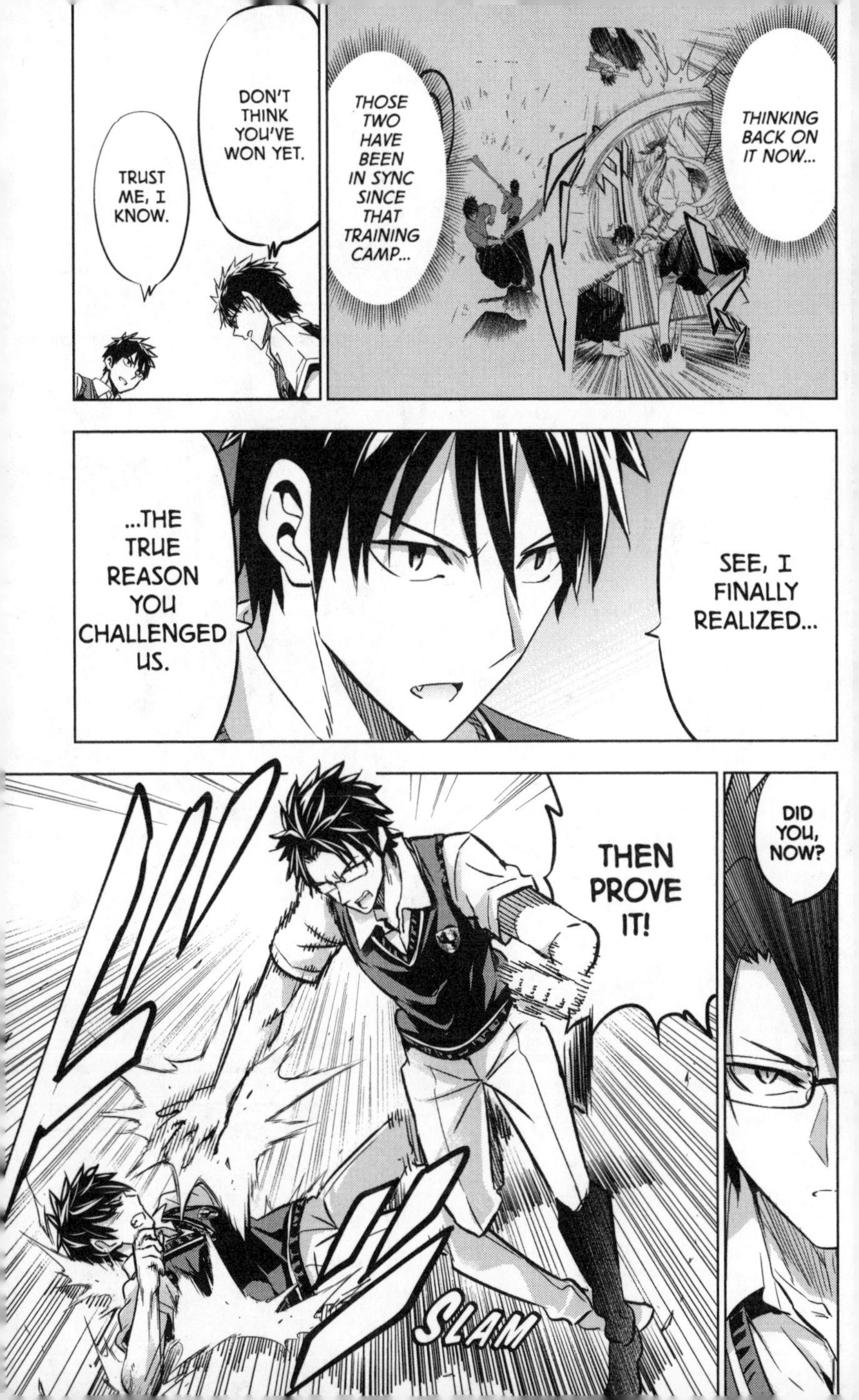
THINKING BACK ON IT NOW...
THOSE TWO HAVE BEEN IN SYNC SINCE THAT TRAINING CAMP...
DON'T THINK YOU'VE WON YET.
TRUST ME, I KNOW.
SEE, I FINALLY REALIZED...
...THE TRUE REASON YOU CHALLENGED US.
DID YOU, NOW?
THEN PROVE IT!
SLAM

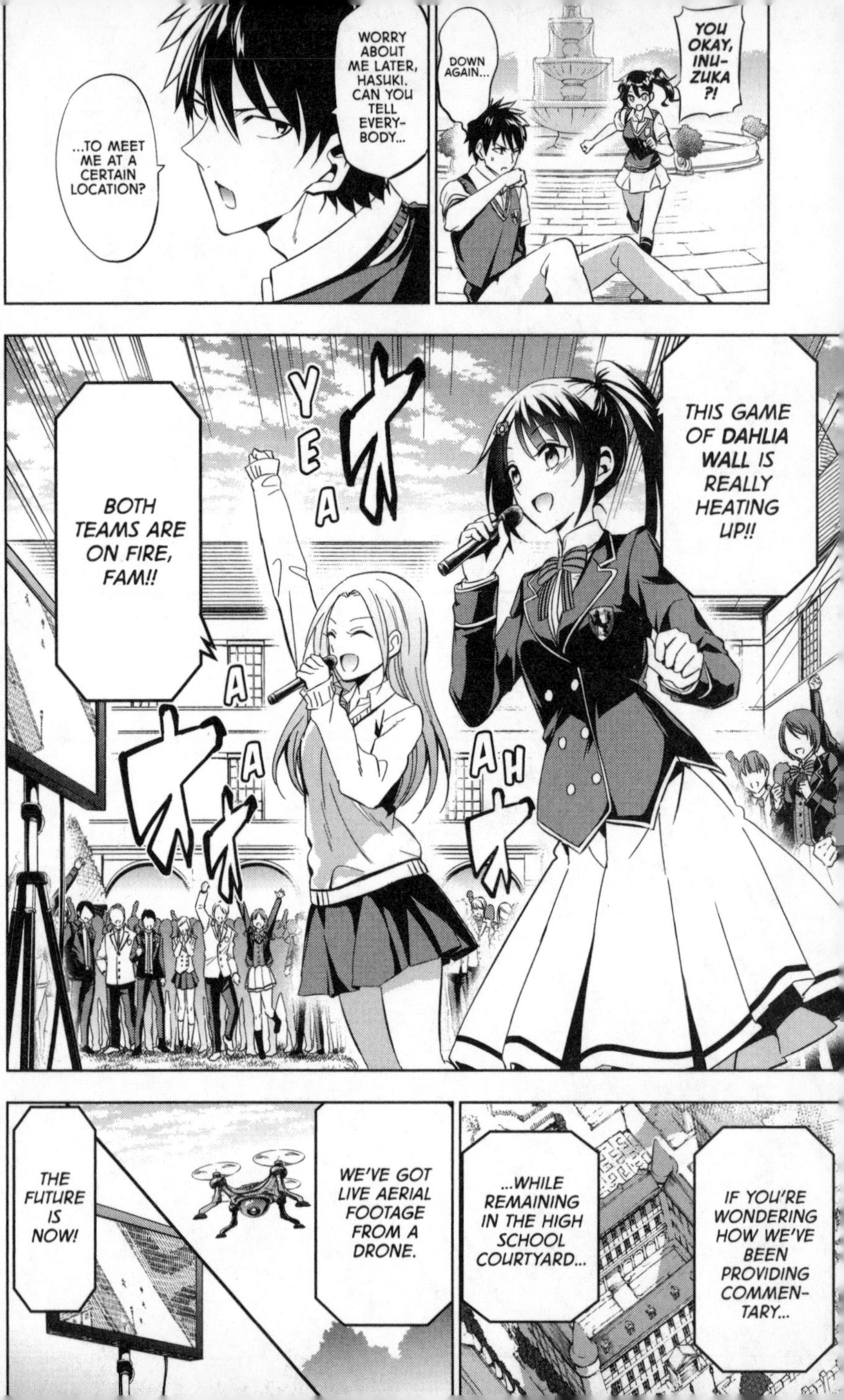
YOU OKAY, INUZUKA?!
DOWN AGAIN...
WORRY ABOUT ME LATER, HASUKI. CAN YOU TELL EVERYBODY...
...TO MEET ME AT A CERTAIN LOCATION?
THIS GAME OF DAHLIA WALL IS REALLY HEATING UP!!
YEA
AH
BOTH TEAMS ARE ON FIRE, FAM!!
AA
IF YOU'RE WONDERING HOW WE'VE BEEN PROVIDING COMMENTARY...
...WHILE REMAINING IN THE HIGH SCHOOL COURTYARD...
WE'VE GOT LIVE AERIAL FOOTAGE FROM A DRONE.
THE FUTURE IS NOW!

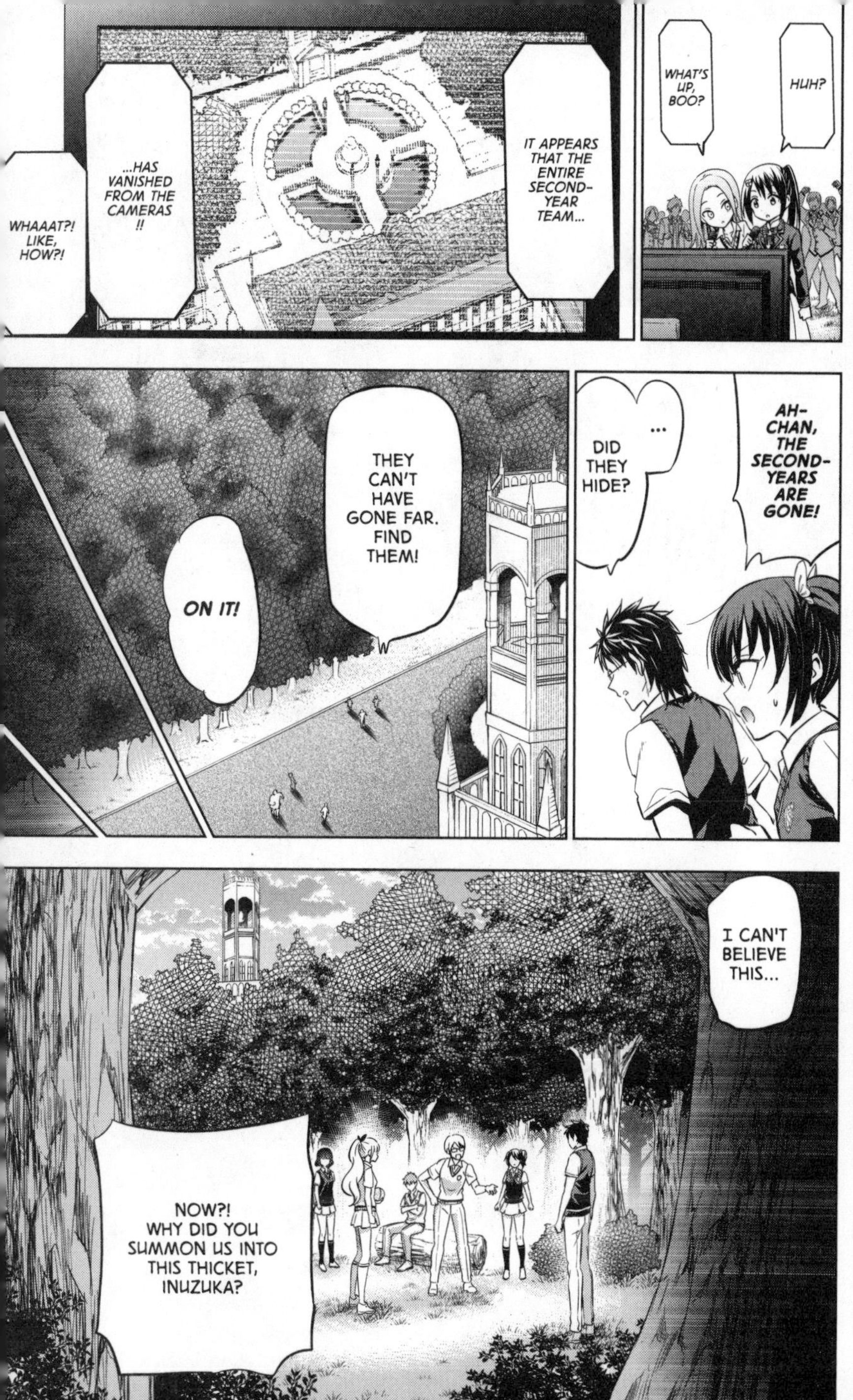
HUH?
WHAT'S UP, BOO?
IT APPEARS THAT THE ENTIRE SECOND-YEAR TEAM...
...HAS VANISHED FROM THE CAMERAS !!
WHAAAT?! LIKE, HOW?!
AH-CHAN, THE SECOND-YEARS ARE GONE!
... DID THEY HIDE?
THEY CAN'T HAVE GONE FAR. FIND THEM!
ON IT!
I CAN'T BELIEVE THIS...
NOW?! WHY DID YOU SUMMON US INTO THIS THICKET, INUZUKA?

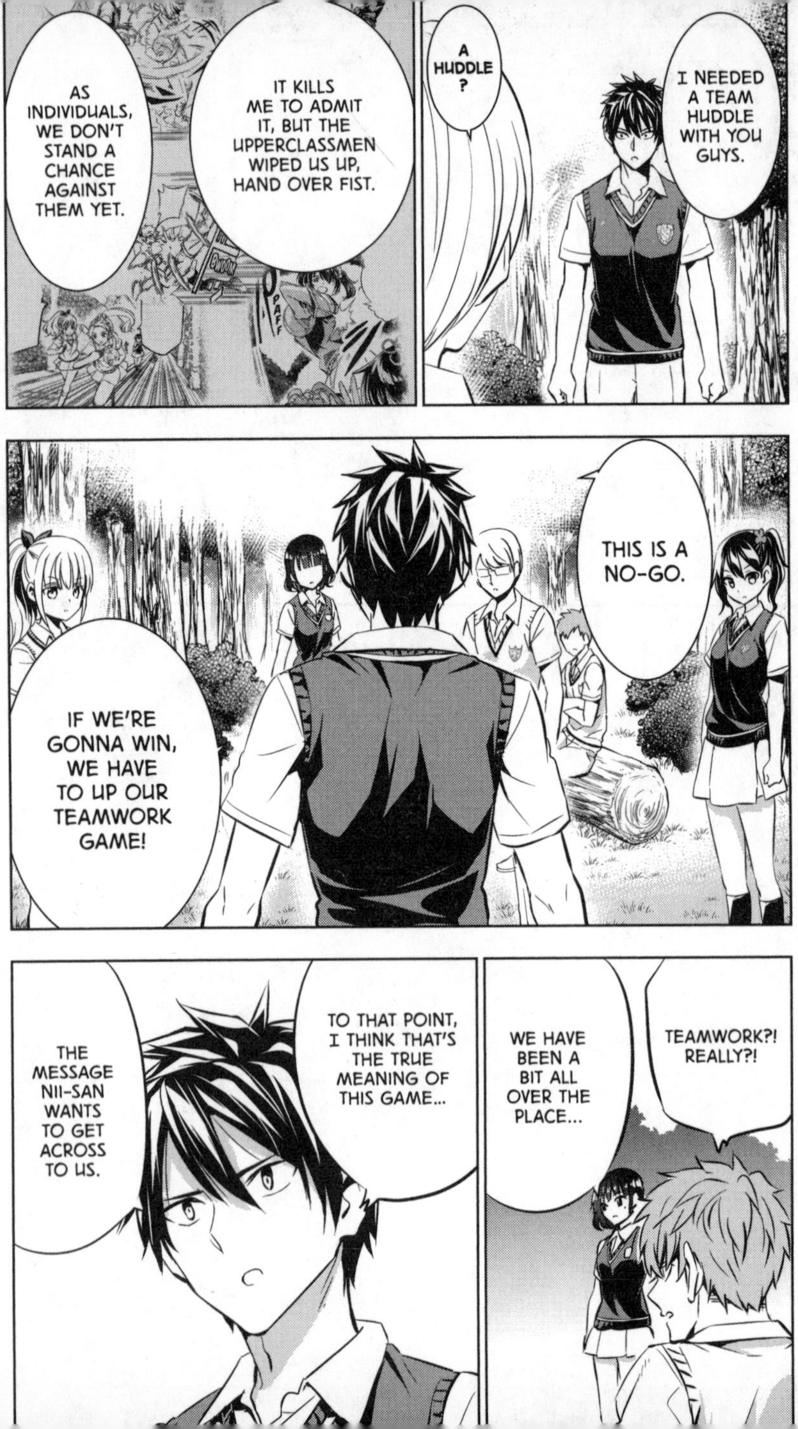
I NEEDED A TEAM HUDDLE WITH YOU GUYS.
A HUDDLE?
IT KILLS ME TO ADMIT IT, BUT THE UPPERCLASSMEN WIPED US UP, HAND OVER FIST.
AS INDIVIDUALS, WE DON'T STAND A CHANCE AGAINST THEM YET.
THIS IS A NO-GO.
IF WE'RE GONNA WIN, WE HAVE TO UP OUR TEAMWORK GAME!
TEAMWORK?! REALLY?!
WE HAVE BEEN A BIT ALL OVER THE PLACE...
TO THAT POINT, I THINK THAT'S THE TRUE MEANING OF THIS GAME...
THE MESSAGE NII-SAN WANTS TO GET ACROSS TO US.

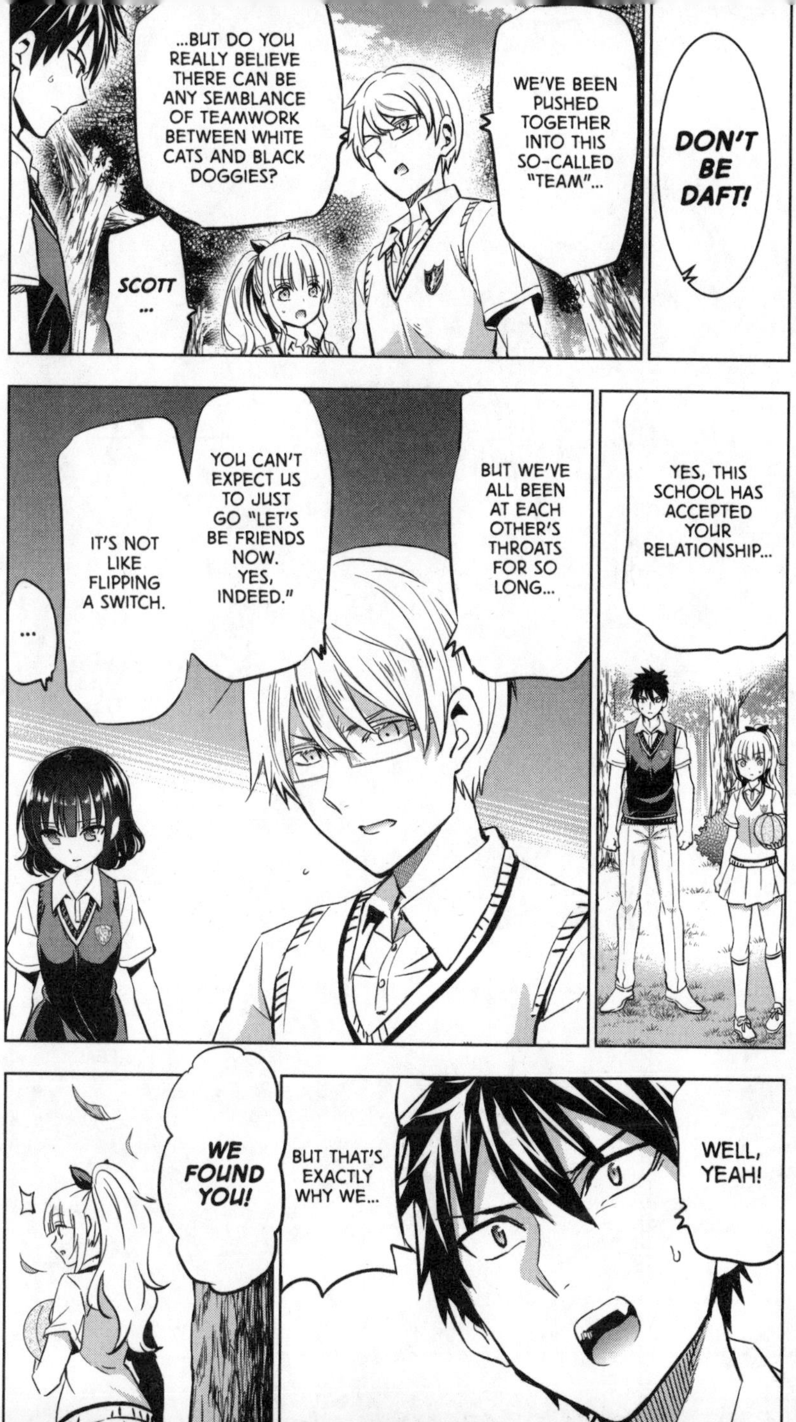

DON'T BE DAFT!
WE'VE BEEN PUSHED TOGETHER INTO THIS SO-CALLED "TEAM"...
...BUT DO YOU REALLY BELIEVE THERE CAN BE ANY SEMBLANCE OF TEAMWORK BETWEEN WHITE CATS AND BLACK DOGGIES?
SCOTT ...
YES, THIS SCHOOL HAS ACCEPTED YOUR RELATIONSHIP...
BUT WE'VE ALL BEEN AT EACH OTHER'S THROATS FOR SO LONG...
YOU CAN'T EXPECT US TO JUST GO "LET'S BE FRIENDS NOW. YES, INDEED."
IT'S NOT LIKE FLIPPING A SWITCH.
...
WELL, YEAH!
BUT THAT'S EXACTLY WHY WE...
WE FOUND YOU!

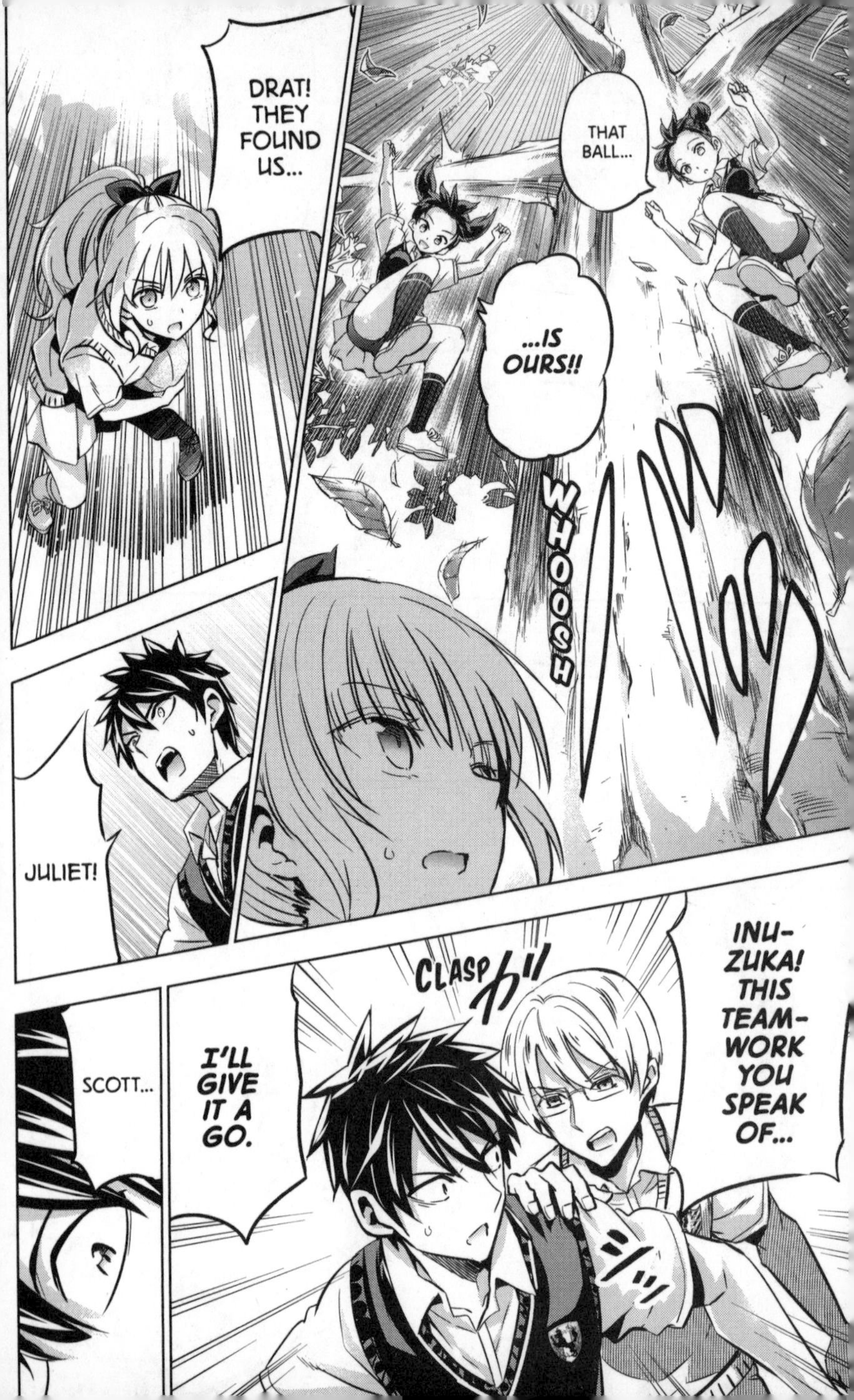
THAT BALL...
...IS OURS!!
WHOOOSH
DRAT! THEY FOUND US...
JULIET!
INU-ZUKA! THIS TEAM-WORK YOU SPEAK OF...
CLASP
I'LL GIVE IT A GO.
SCOTT...

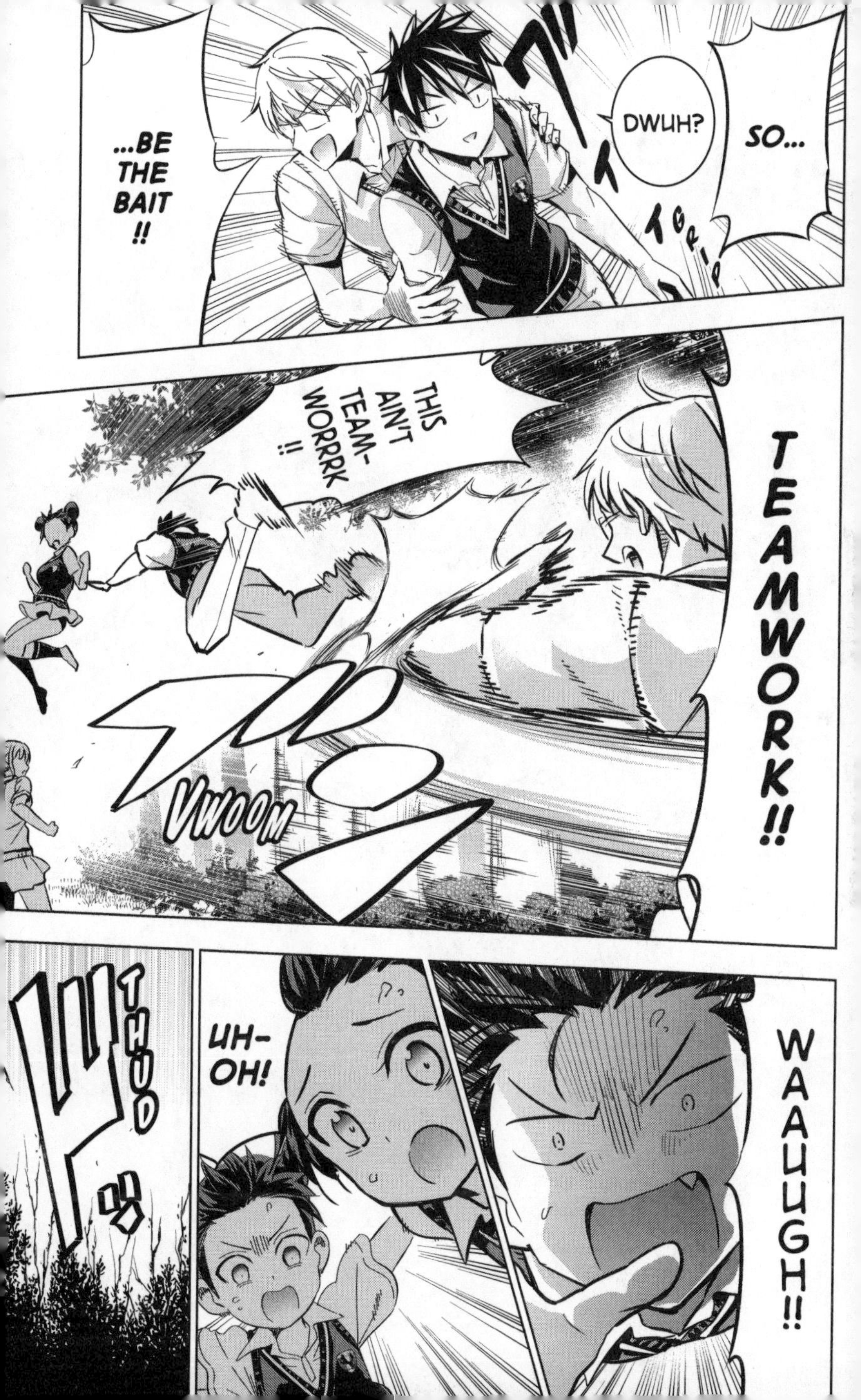
SO...
DWUH?
TRIP
...BE THE BAIT!!
TEAMWORK!!
THIS AIN'T TEAM-WORRRK!!
VWOOM
WAAAUGH!!
UH-OH!
THUD

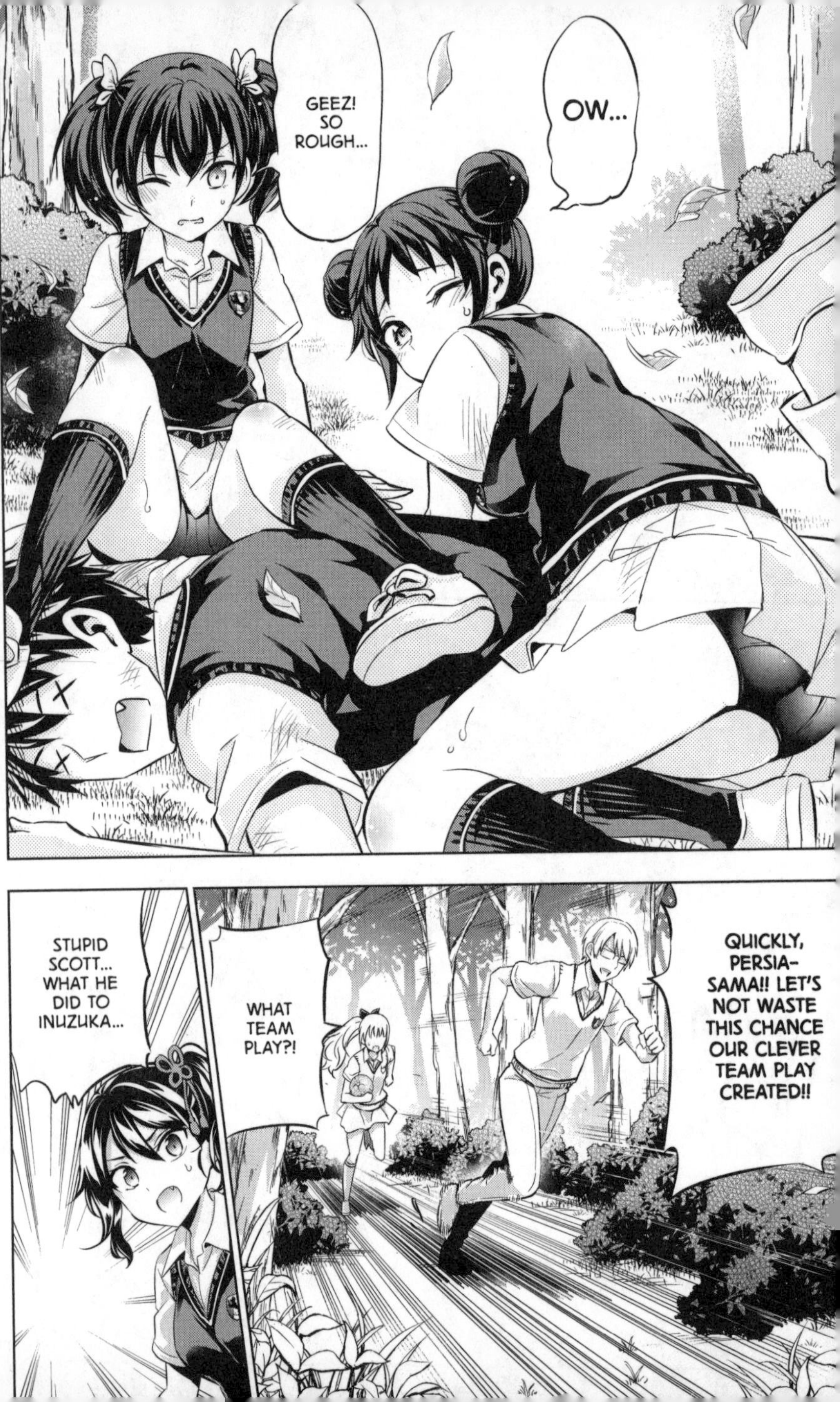
OW...
GEEZ! SO ROUGH...
QUICKLY, PERSIA-SAMA!! LET'S NOT WASTE THIS CHANCE OUR CLEVER TEAM PLAY CREATED!!
WHAT TEAM PLAY?!
STUPID SCOTT... WHAT HE DID TO INUZUKA...

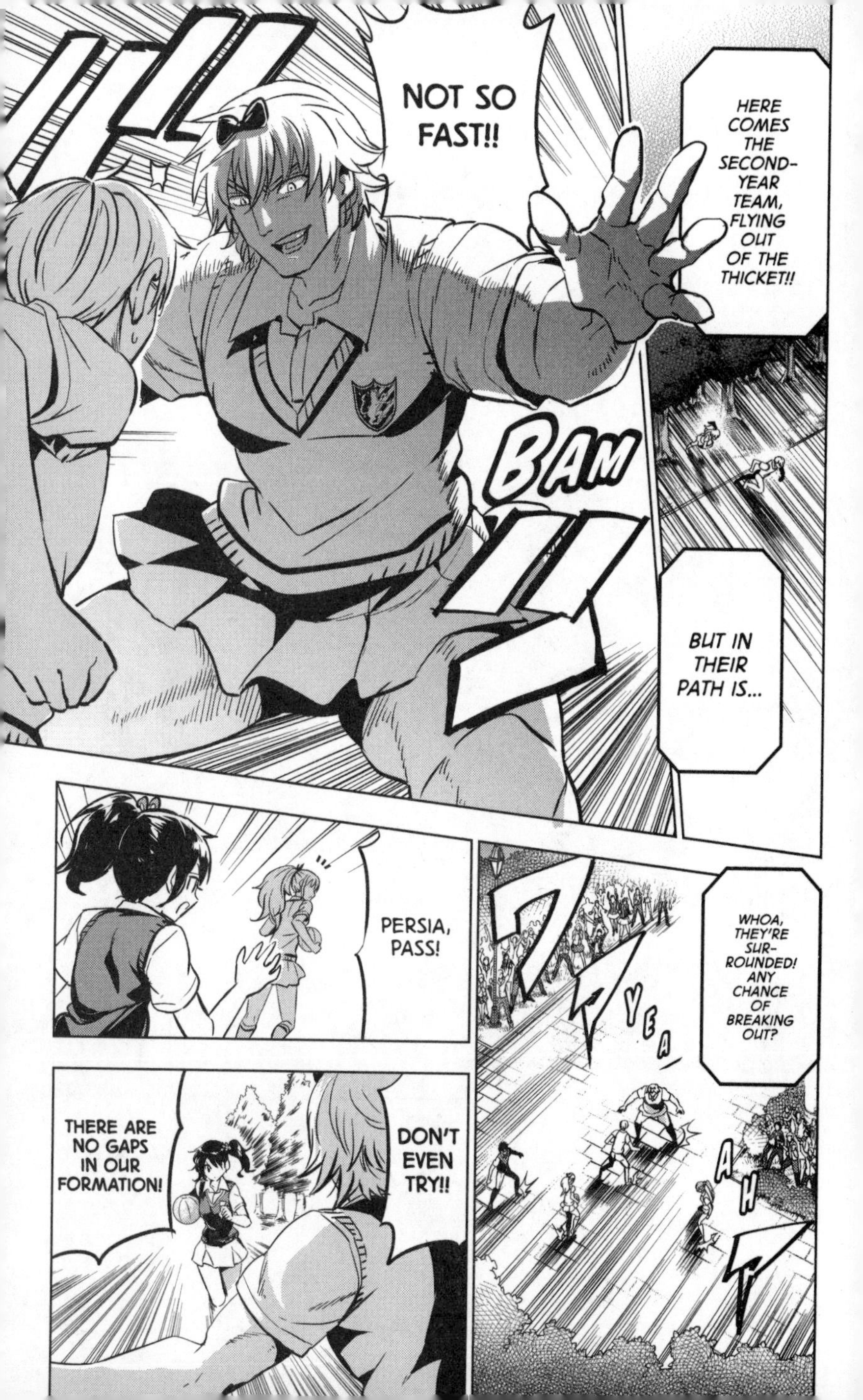
HERE COMES THE SECOND-YEAR TEAM, FLYING OUT OF THE THICKET!!
BUT IN THEIR PATH IS...
NOT SO FAST!!
BAM
WHOA, THEY'RE SUR-ROUNDED! ANY CHANCE OF BREAKING OUT?
YEA
AH
PERSIA, PASS!
DON'T EVEN TRY!!
THERE ARE NO GAPS IN OUR FORMATION!

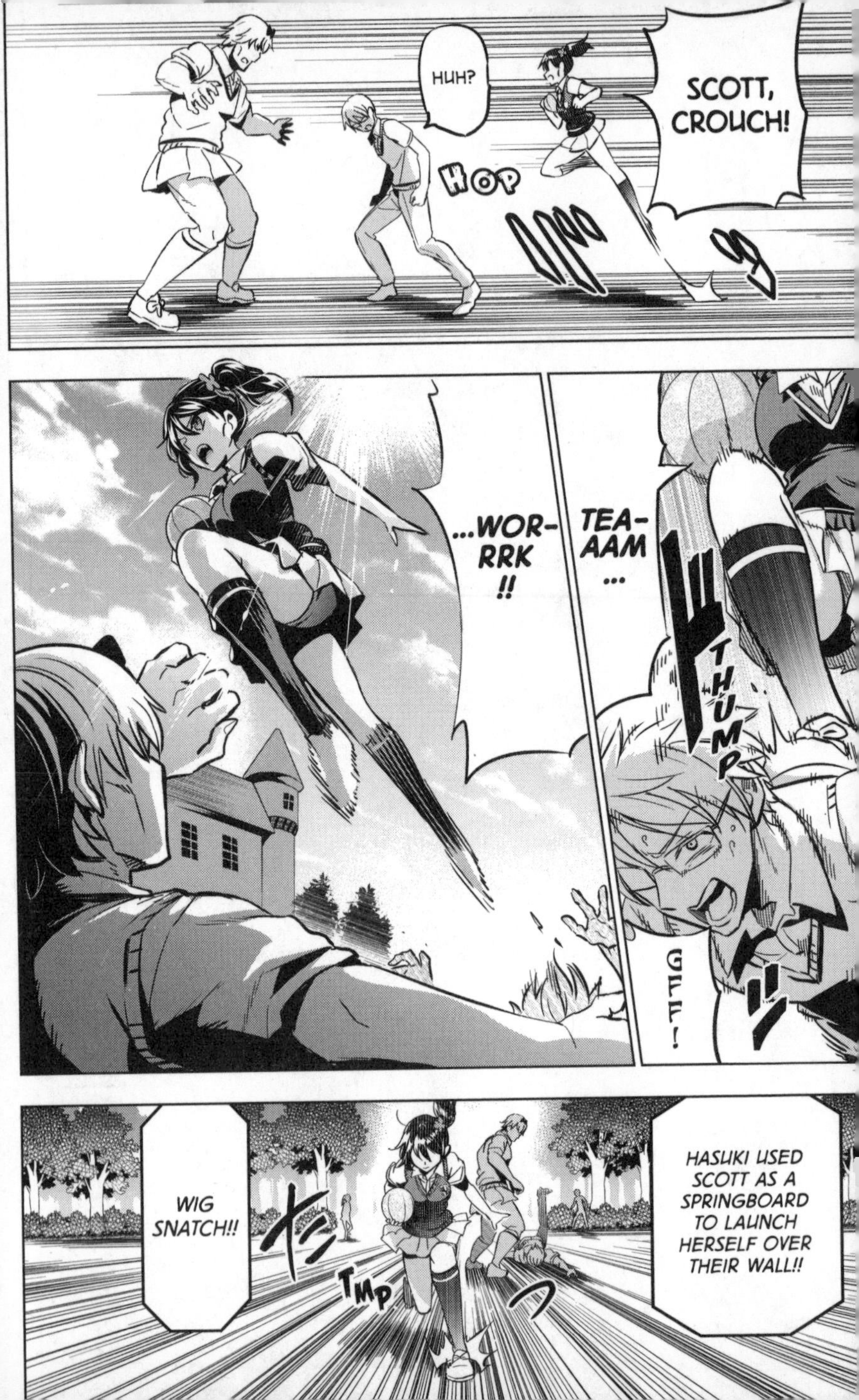
SCOTT, CROUCH!
HOP
HUH?
TEA-AAM ...
THUMP
GLL!
...WOR-RRK !!
HASUKI USED SCOTT AS A SPRINGBOARD TO LAUNCH HERSELF OVER THEIR WALL!!
TMP
WIG SNATCH!!

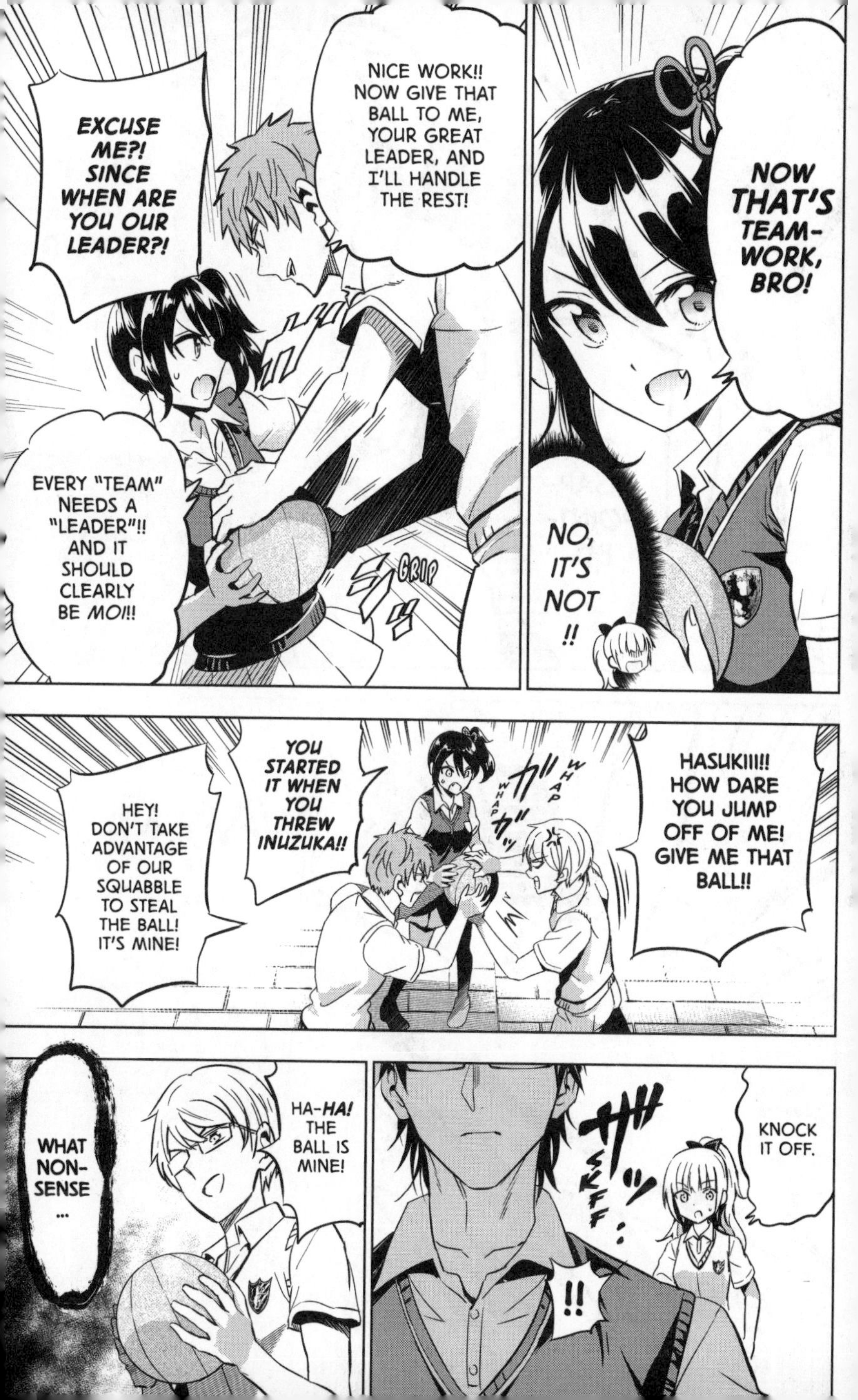
NOW THAT'S TEAM-WORK, BRO!
NO, IT'S NOT !!
NICE WORK!! NOW GIVE THAT BALL TO ME, YOUR GREAT LEADER, AND I'LL HANDLE THE REST!
EXCUSE ME?! SINCE WHEN ARE YOU OUR LEADER?!
EVERY "TEAM" NEEDS A "LEADER"!! AND IT SHOULD CLEARLY BE *MOI*!!
GRIP
HASUKIIII!! HOW DARE YOU JUMP OFF OF ME! GIVE ME THAT BALL!!
WHAP
WHAP
YOU STARTED IT WHEN YOU THREW INUZUKA!!
HEY! DON'T TAKE ADVANTAGE OF OUR SQUABBLE TO STEAL THE BALL! IT'S MINE!
KNOCK IT OFF.
SKFF
!!
HA-*HA!* THE BALL IS MINE!
WHAT NON-SENSE ...

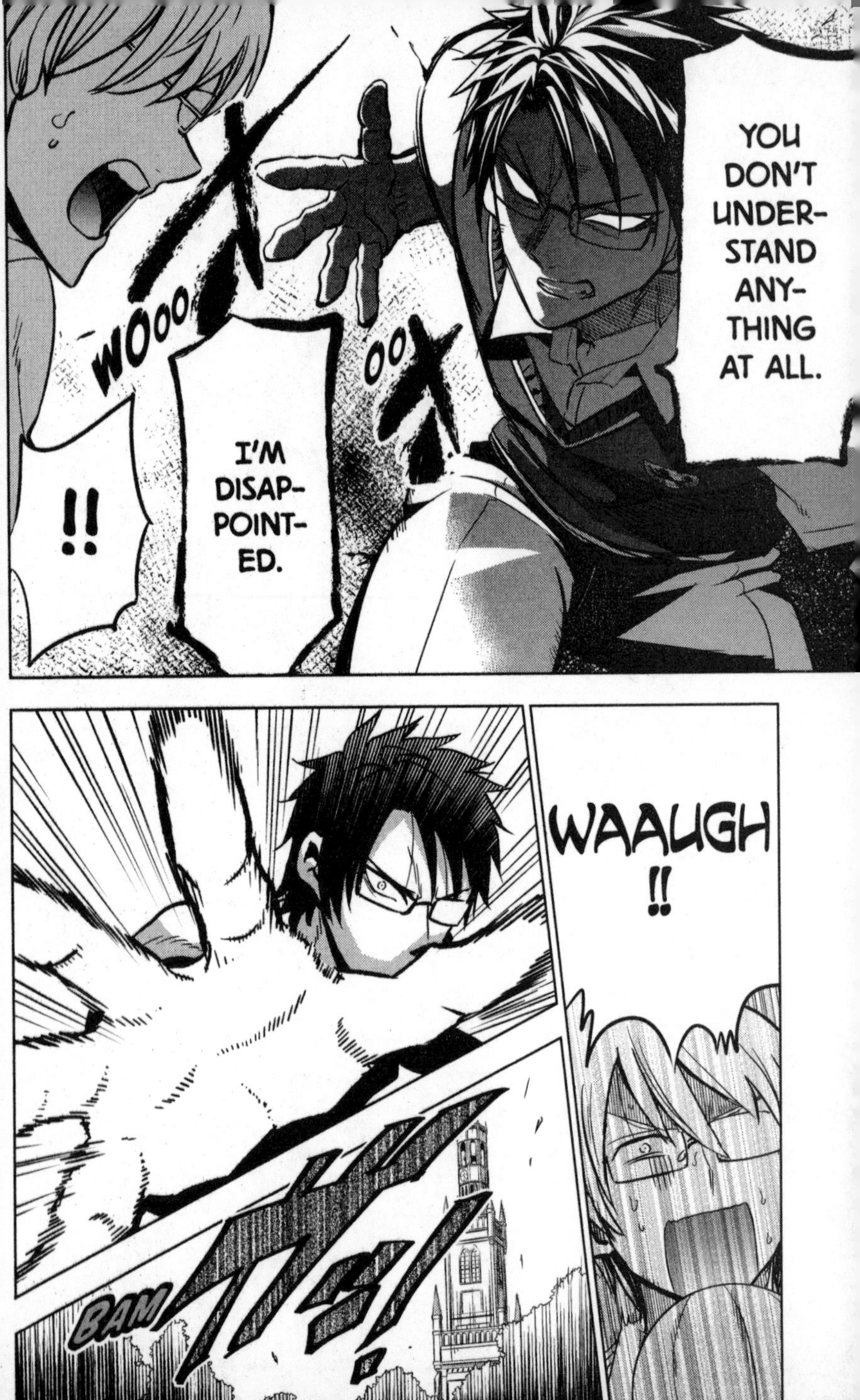
YOU DON'T UNDER-STAND ANY-THING AT ALL.
WOOO
OO
I'M DISAP-POINT-ED.
!!
WAAUGH !!
BAM

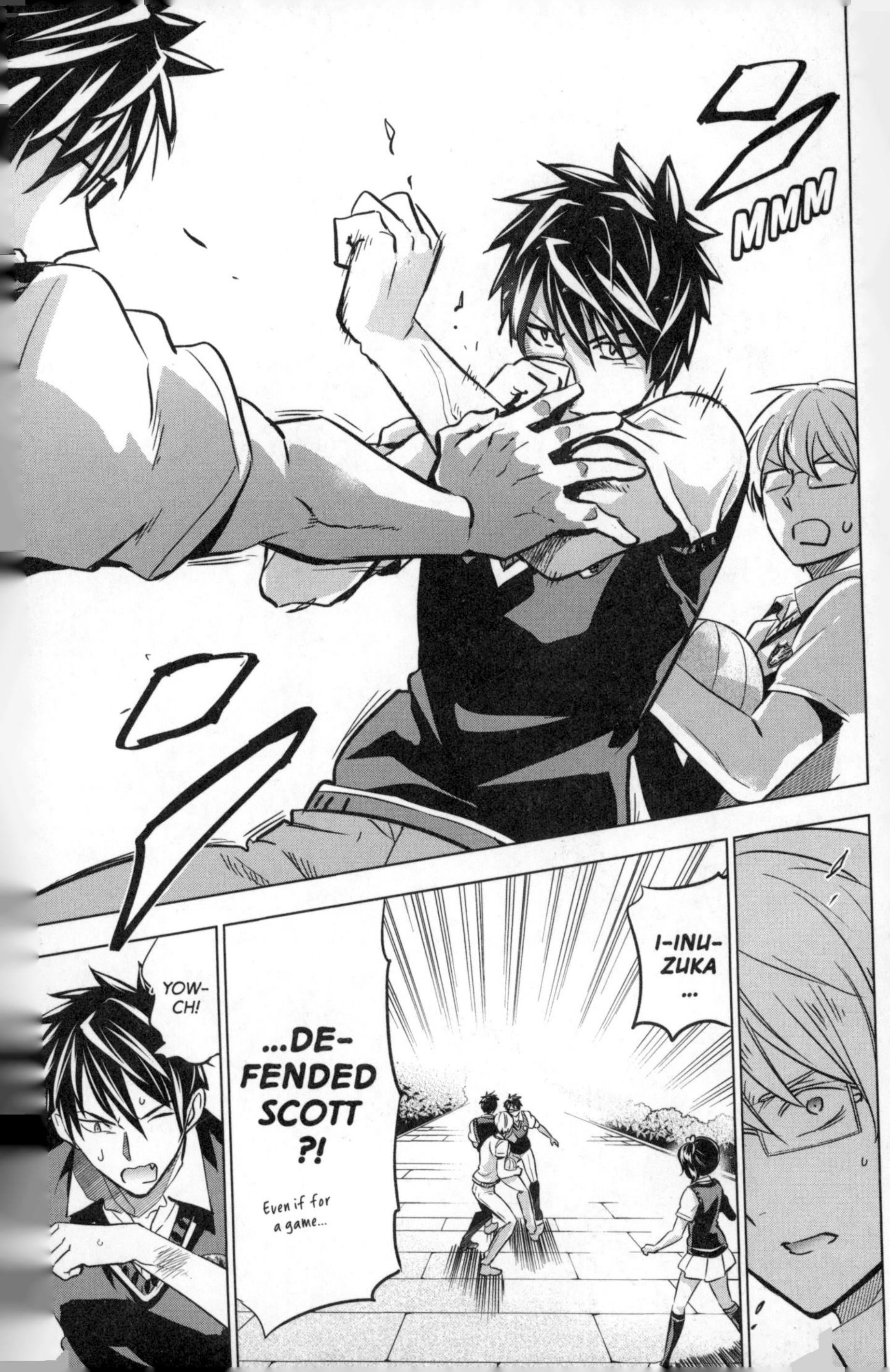
MMM
I-INU-ZUKA...
...DE-FENDED SCOTT?!
Even if for a game...
YOW-CH!

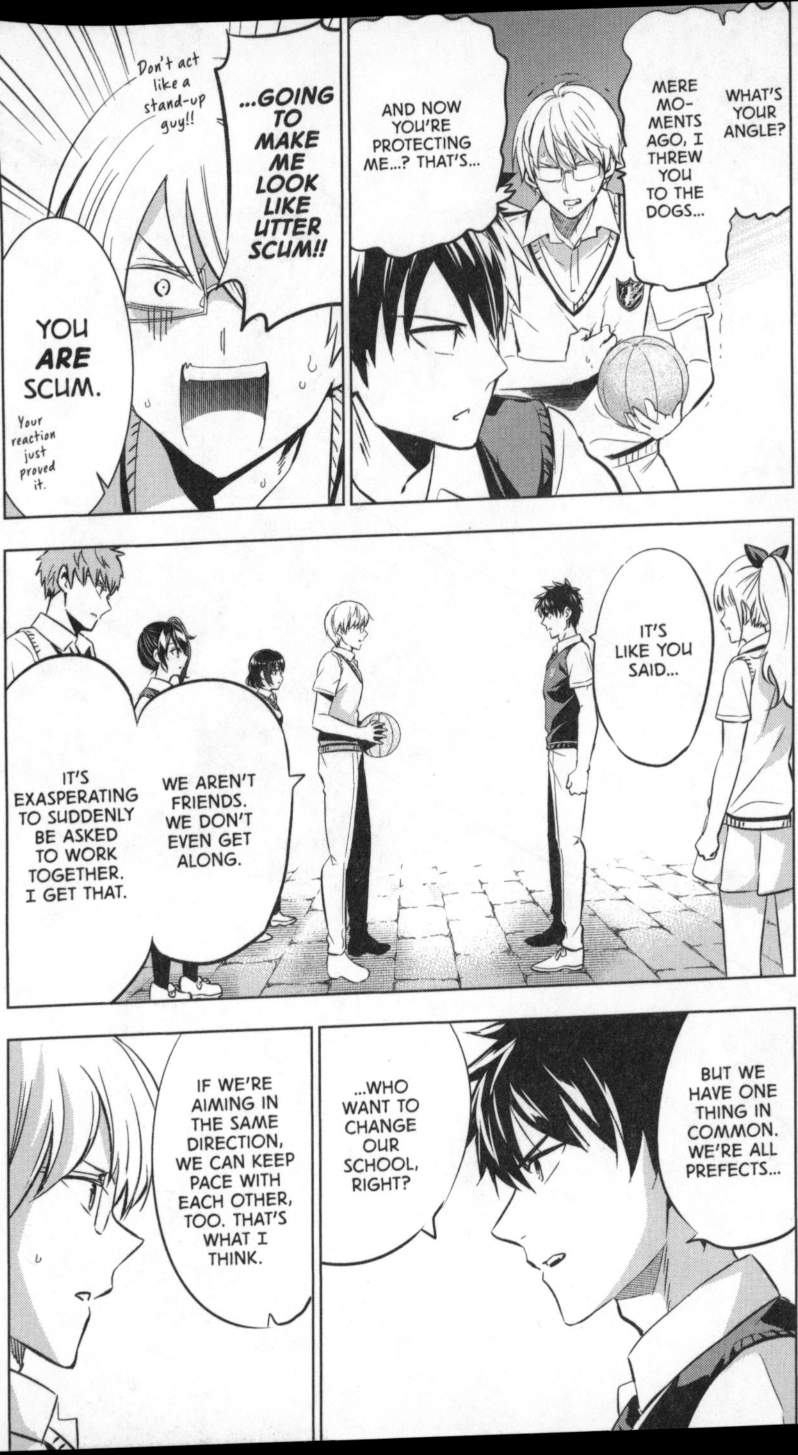
WHAT'S YOUR ANGLE?
MERE MOMENTS AGO, I THREW YOU TO THE DOGS...
AND NOW YOU'RE PROTECTING ME...? THAT'S...
...GOING TO MAKE ME LOOK LIKE UTTER SCUM!!
Don't act like a stand-up guy!!
YOU ARE SCUM.
Your reaction just proved it.
IT'S LIKE YOU SAID...
WE AREN'T FRIENDS. WE DON'T EVEN GET ALONG.
IT'S EXASPERATING TO SUDDENLY BE ASKED TO WORK TOGETHER. I GET THAT.
BUT WE HAVE ONE THING IN COMMON. WE'RE ALL PREFECTS...
...WHO WANT TO CHANGE OUR SCHOOL, RIGHT?
IF WE'RE AIMING IN THE SAME DIRECTION, WE CAN KEEP PACE WITH EACH OTHER, TOO. THAT'S WHAT I THINK.

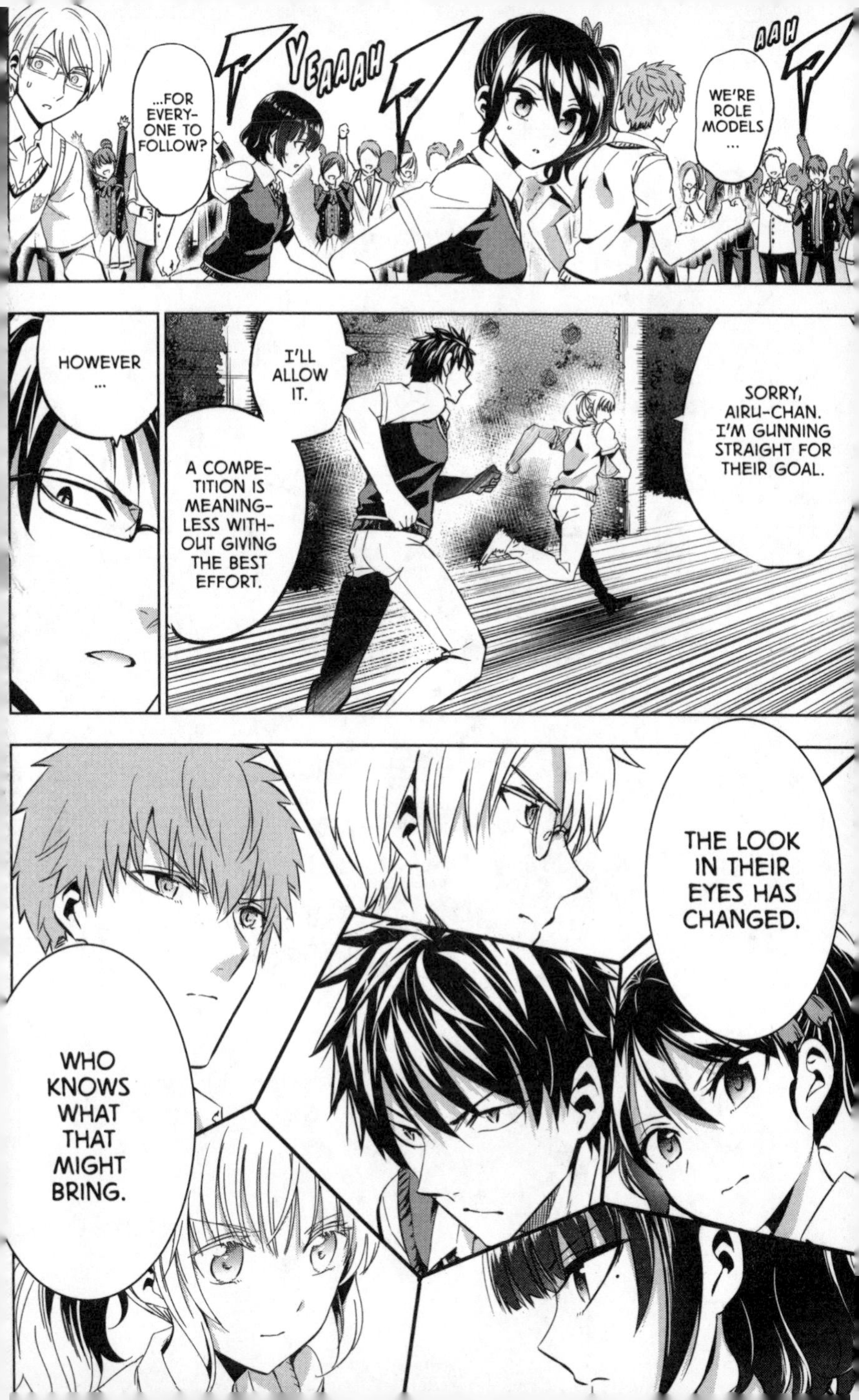
AAH
WE'RE ROLE MODELS ...
YEAAAH
...FOR EVERYONE TO FOLLOW?
SORRY, AIRU-CHAN. I'M GUNNING STRAIGHT FOR THEIR GOAL.
I'LL ALLOW IT.
A COMPETITION IS MEANINGLESS WITHOUT GIVING THE BEST EFFORT.
HOWEVER ...
THE LOOK IN THEIR EYES HAS CHANGED.
WHO KNOWS WHAT THAT MIGHT BRING.

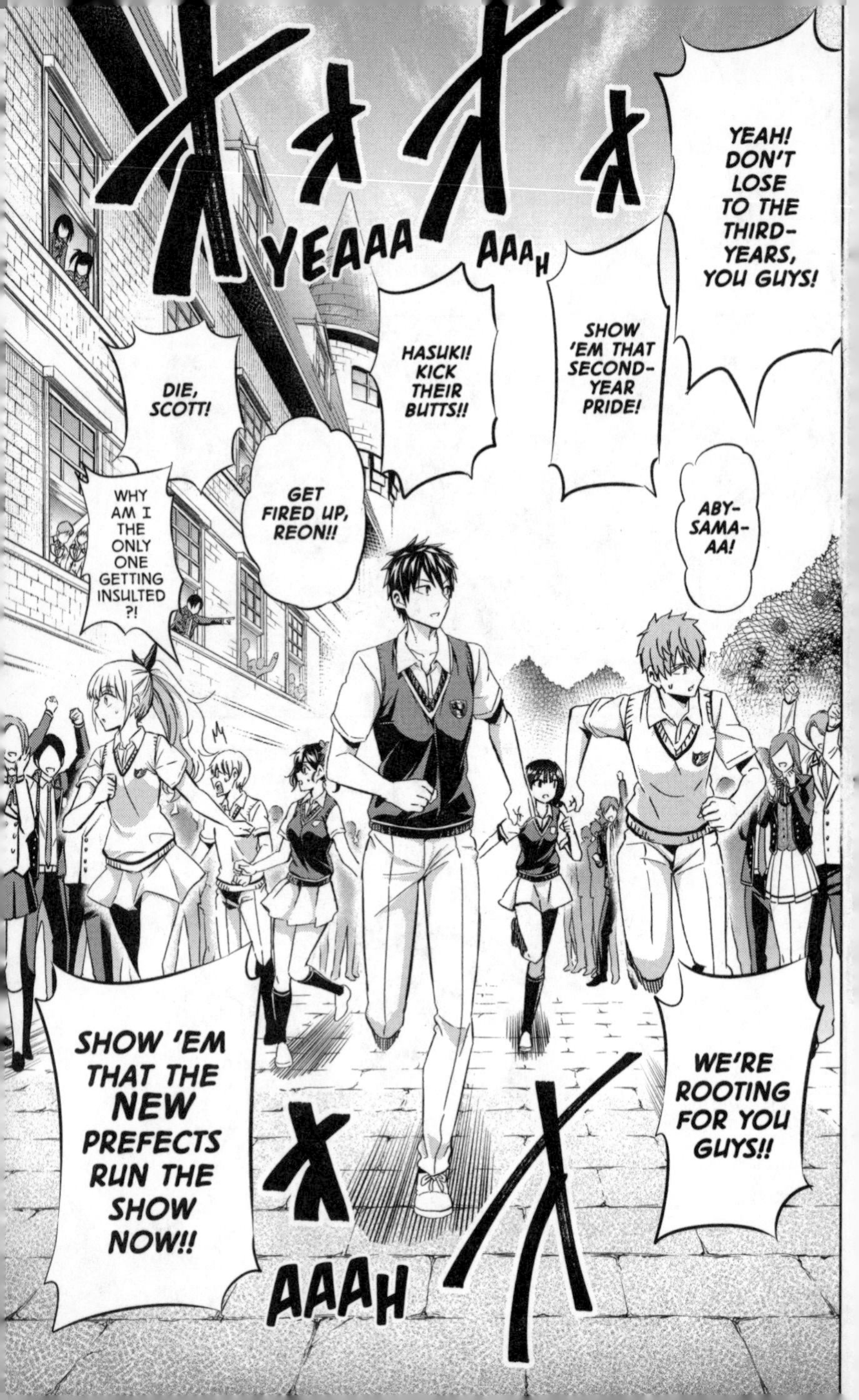
YEAH! DON'T LOSE TO THE THIRD-YEARS, YOU GUYS!
YEAAA AAAH
SHOW 'EM THAT SECOND-YEAR PRIDE!
HASUKI! KICK THEIR BUTTS!!
DIE, SCOTT!
ABY-SAMA-AA!
GET FIRED UP, REON!!
WHY AM I THE ONLY ONE GETTING INSULTED?!
WE'RE ROOTING FOR YOU GUYS!!
SHOW 'EM THAT THE NEW PREFECTS RUN THE SHOW NOW!!
AAAH

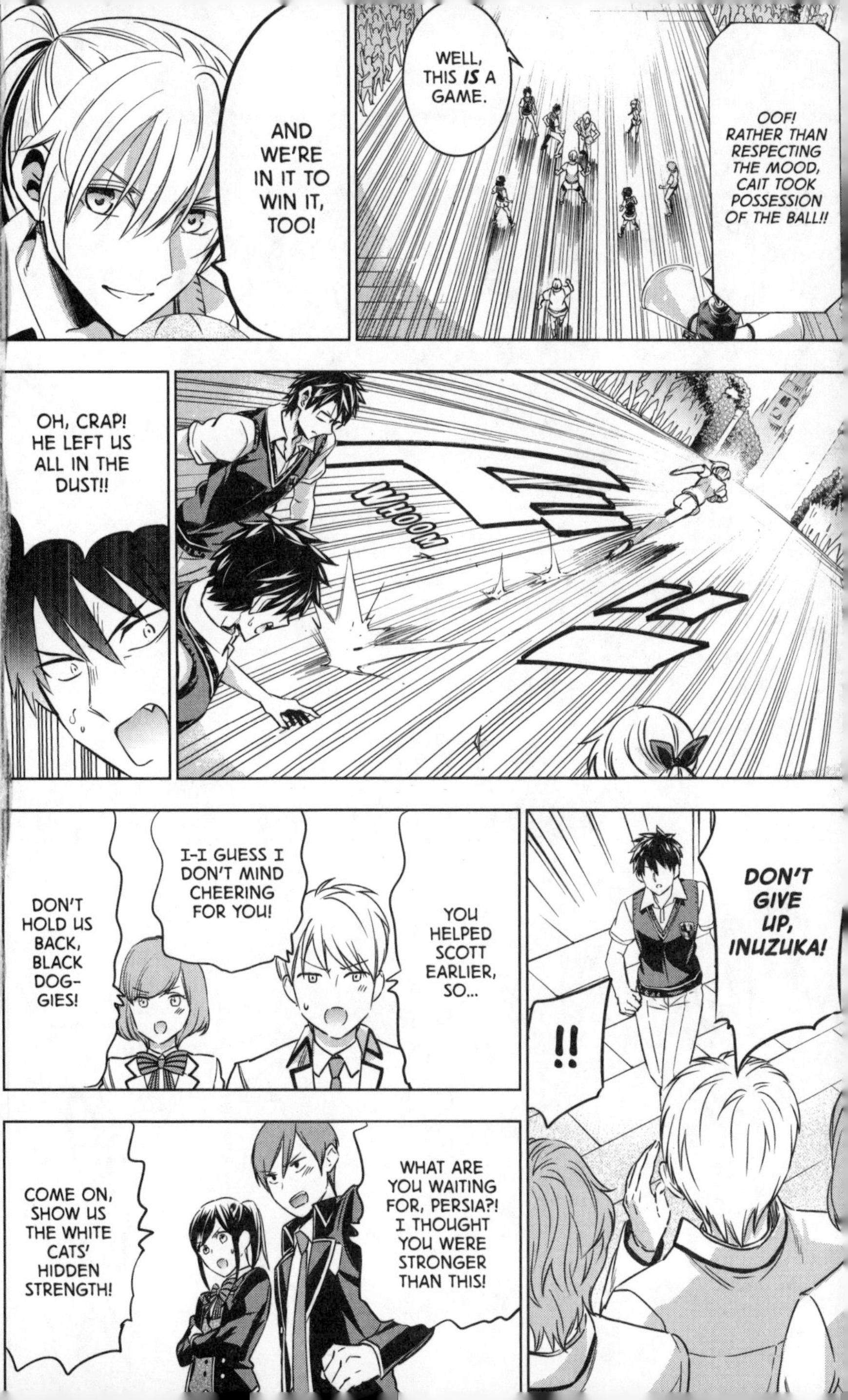
OOF! RATHER THAN RESPECTING THE MOOD, CAIT TOOK POSSESSION OF THE BALL!!
WELL, THIS IS A GAME.
AND WE'RE IN IT TO WIN IT, TOO!
WHOOM
OH, CRAP! HE LEFT US ALL IN THE DUST!!
DON'T GIVE UP, INUZUKA!
!!
YOU HELPED SCOTT EARLIER, SO...
I-I GUESS I DON'T MIND CHEERING FOR YOU!
DON'T HOLD US BACK, BLACK DOG-GIES!
WHAT ARE YOU WAITING FOR, PERSIA?! I THOUGHT YOU WERE STRONGER THAN THIS!
COME ON, SHOW US THE WHITE CATS' HIDDEN STRENGTH!

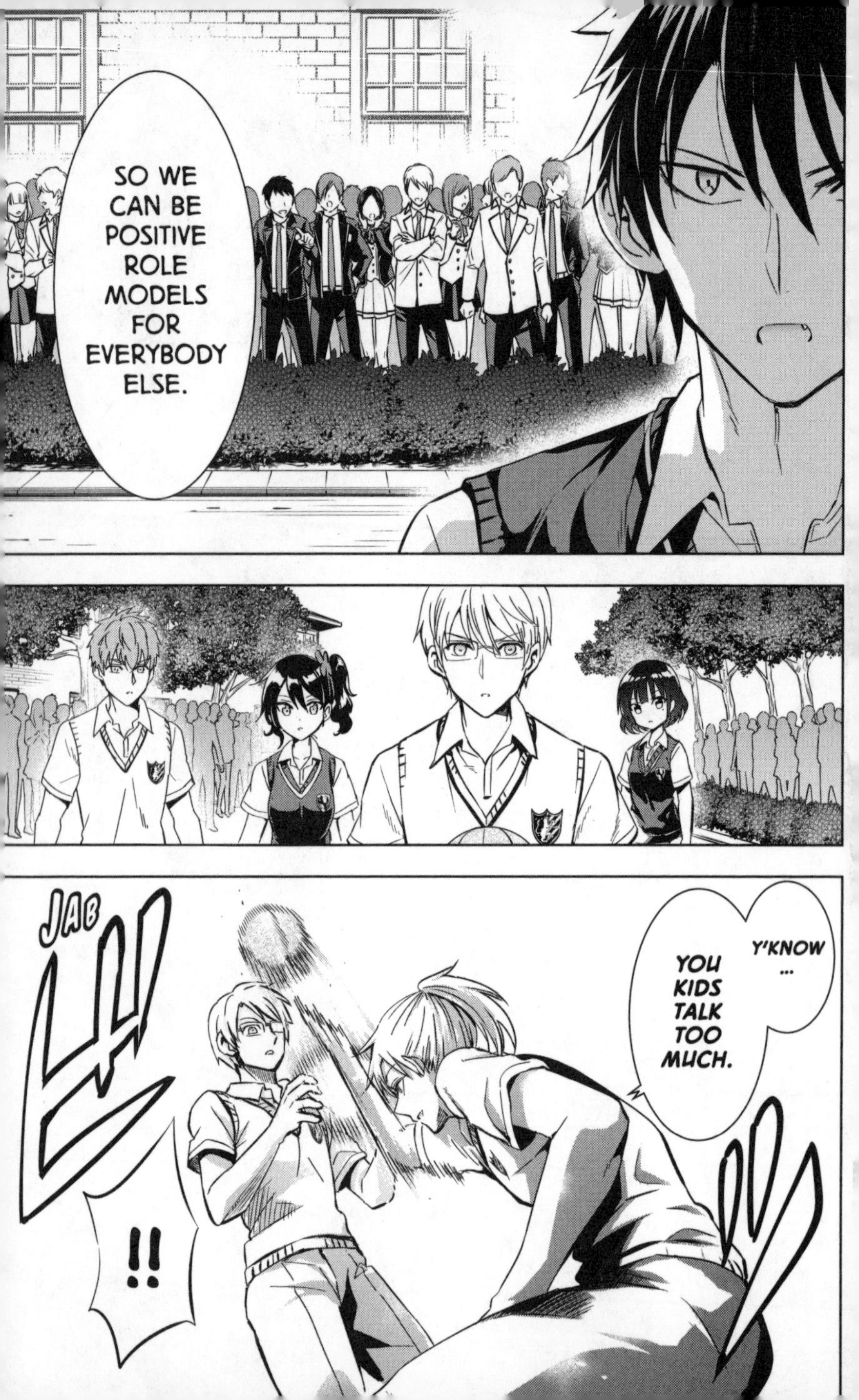
SO WE CAN BE POSITIVE ROLE MODELS FOR EVERYBODY ELSE.
Y'KNOW ...
YOU KIDS TALK TOO MUCH.
JAB
!!

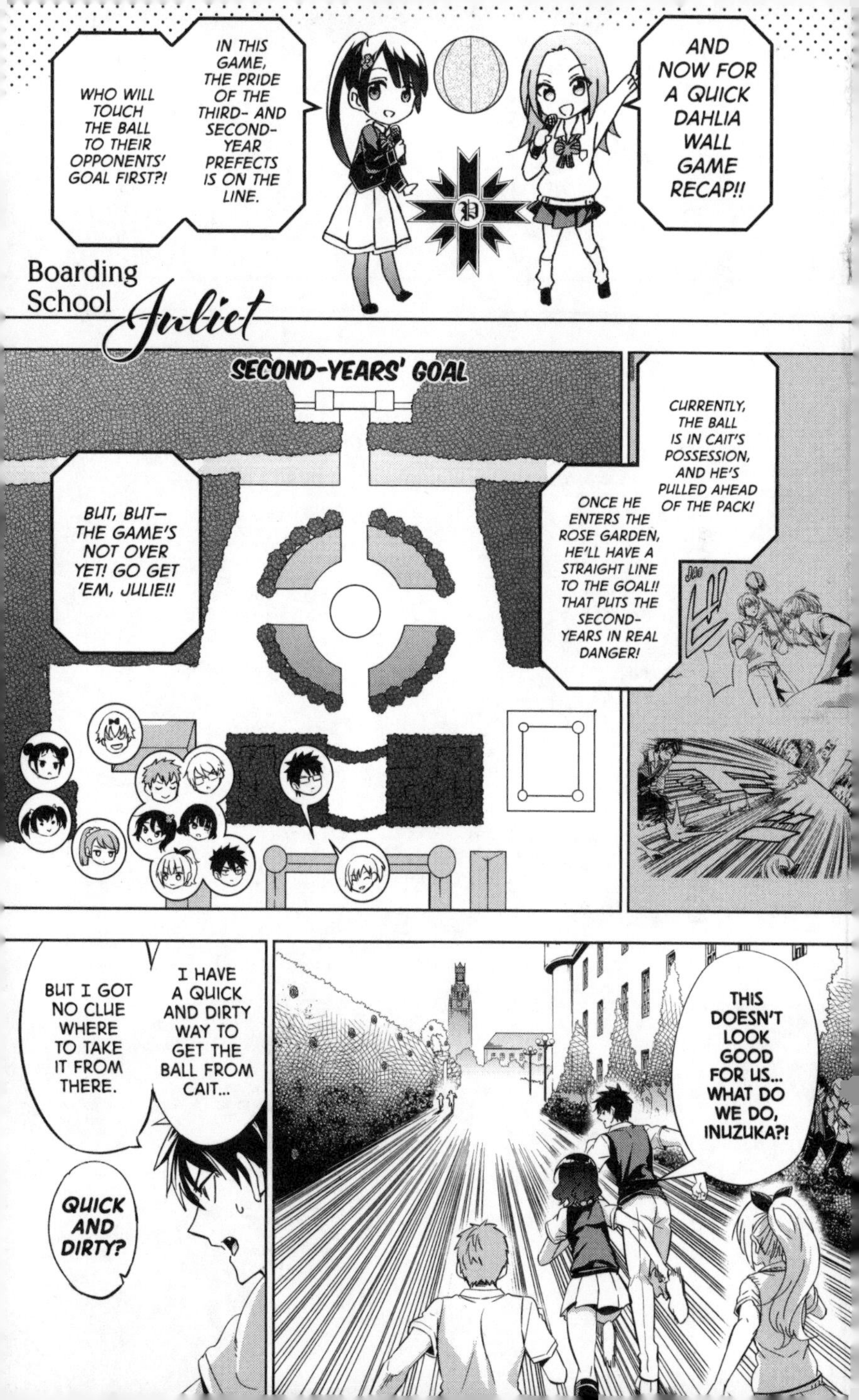
AND NOW FOR A QUICK DAHLIA WALL GAME RECAP!!
IN THIS GAME, THE PRIDE OF THE THIRD- AND SECOND-YEAR PREFECTS IS ON THE LINE.
WHO WILL TOUCH THE BALL TO THEIR OPPONENTS' GOAL FIRST?!
Boarding School Juliet
CURRENTLY, THE BALL IS IN CAIT'S POSSESSION, AND HE'S PULLED AHEAD OF THE PACK!
ONCE HE ENTERS THE ROSE GARDEN, HE'LL HAVE A STRAIGHT LINE TO THE GOAL!! THAT PUTS THE SECOND-YEARS IN REAL DANGER!
SECOND-YEARS' GOAL
BUT, BUT— THE GAME'S NOT OVER YET! GO GET 'EM, JULIE!!
THIS DOESN'T LOOK GOOD FOR US... WHAT DO WE DO, INUZUKA?!
I HAVE A QUICK AND DIRTY WAY TO GET THE BALL FROM CAIT...
BUT I GOT NO CLUE WHERE TO TAKE IT FROM THERE.
QUICK AND DIRTY?

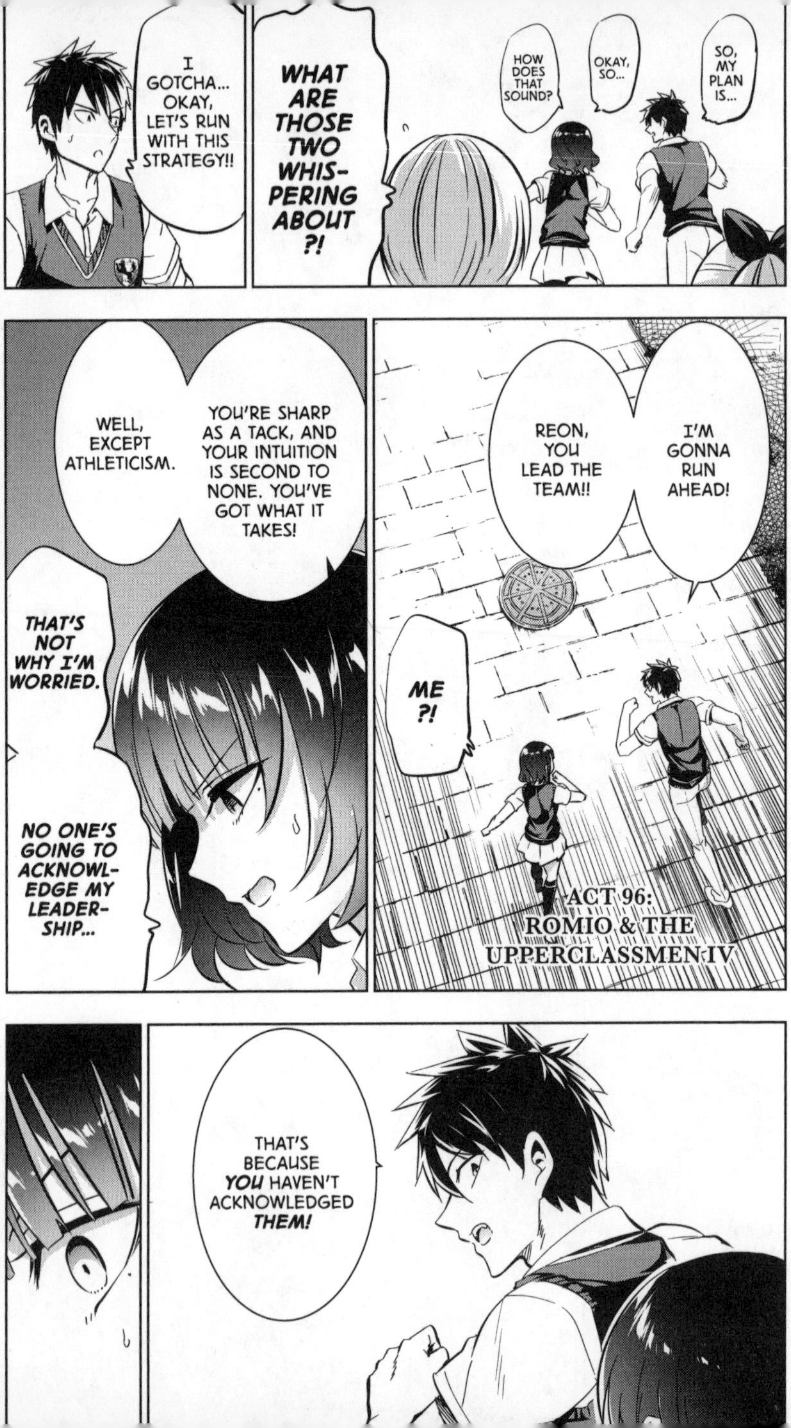
SO, MY PLAN IS...
OKAY, SO...
HOW DOES THAT SOUND?
WHAT ARE THOSE TWO WHISPERING ABOUT?!
I GOTCHA... OKAY, LET'S RUN WITH THIS STRATEGY!!
I'M GONNA RUN AHEAD!
REON, YOU LEAD THE TEAM!!
ME?!
ACT 96: ROMIO & THE UPPERCLASSMEN IV
YOU'RE SHARP AS A TACK, AND YOUR INTUITION IS SECOND TO NONE. YOU'VE GOT WHAT IT TAKES!
WELL, EXCEPT ATHLETICISM.
THAT'S NOT WHY I'M WORRIED.
NO ONE'S GOING TO ACKNOWLEDGE MY LEADERSHIP...
THAT'S BECAUSE YOU HAVEN'T ACKNOWLEDGED THEM!

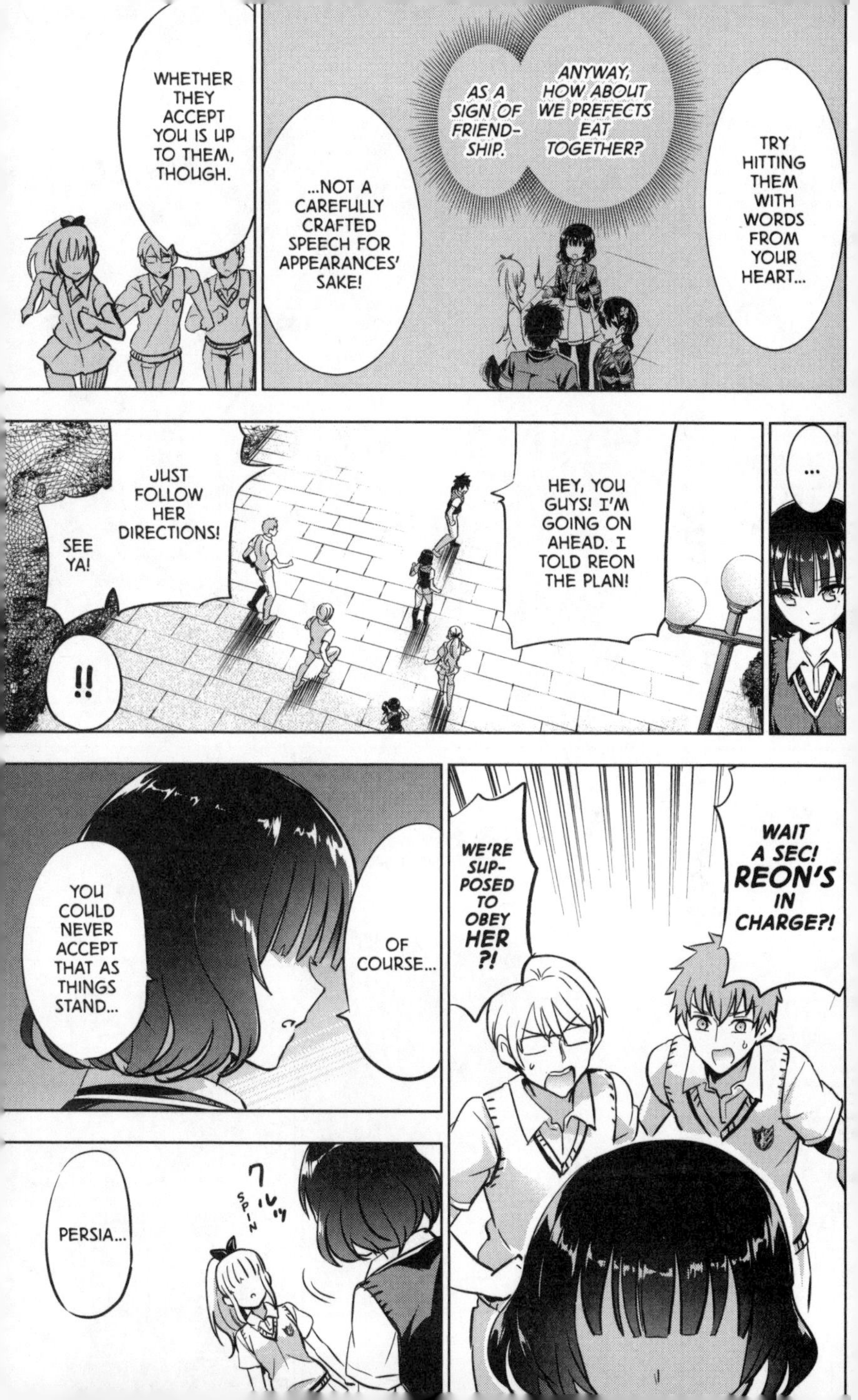
TRY HITTING THEM WITH WORDS FROM YOUR HEART...
ANYWAY, HOW ABOUT WE PREFECTS EAT TOGETHER?
AS A SIGN OF FRIEND-SHIP.
...NOT A CAREFULLY CRAFTED SPEECH FOR APPEARANCES' SAKE!
WHETHER THEY ACCEPT YOU IS UP TO THEM, THOUGH.
...
HEY, YOU GUYS! I'M GOING ON AHEAD. I TOLD REON THE PLAN!
JUST FOLLOW HER DIRECTIONS!
SEE YA!
!!
WAIT A SEC! REON'S IN CHARGE?!
WE'RE SUP-POSED TO OBEY HER?!
OF COURSE...
YOU COULD NEVER ACCEPT THAT AS THINGS STAND...
SPIN
PERSIA...

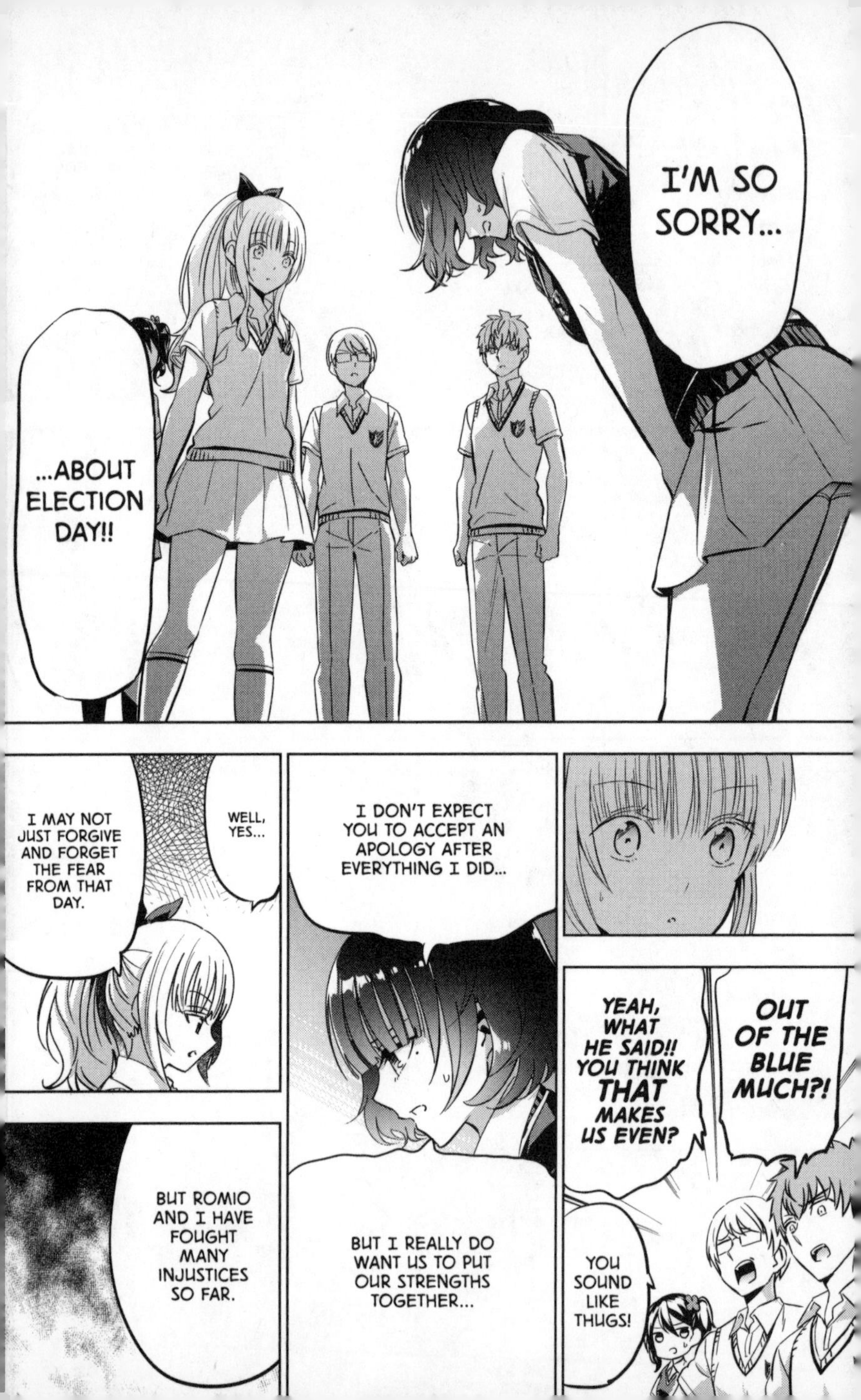
I'M SO SORRY...
...ABOUT ELECTION DAY!!
OUT OF THE BLUE MUCH?!
YEAH, WHAT HE SAID!! YOU THINK THAT MAKES US EVEN?
YOU SOUND LIKE THUGS!
I DON'T EXPECT YOU TO ACCEPT AN APOLOGY AFTER EVERYTHING I DID...
BUT I REALLY DO WANT US TO PUT OUR STRENGTHS TOGETHER...
WELL, YES...
I MAY NOT JUST FORGIVE AND FORGET THE FEAR FROM THAT DAY.
BUT ROMIO AND I HAVE FOUGHT MANY INJUSTICES SO FAR.

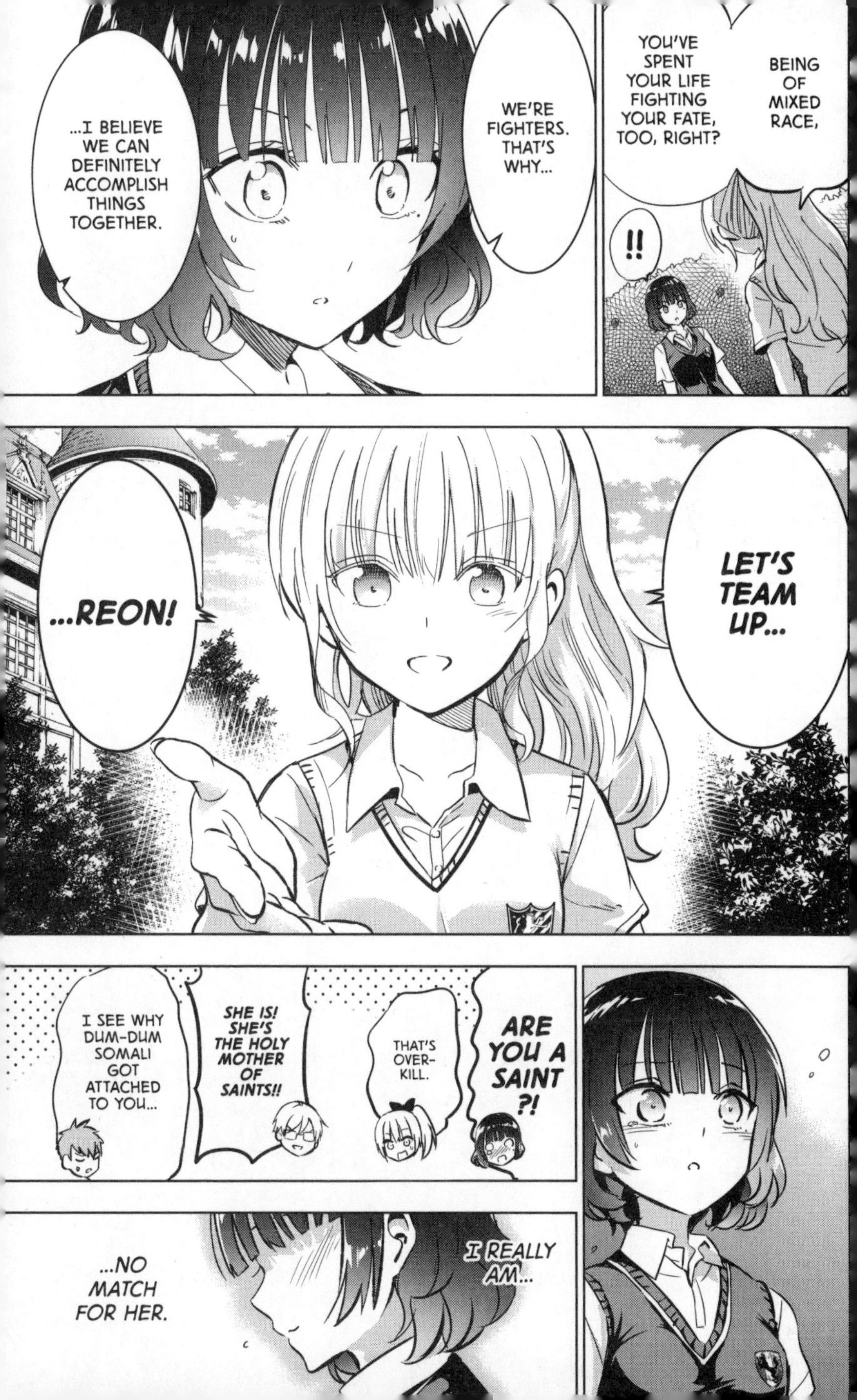
BEING OF MIXED RACE,
YOU'VE SPENT YOUR LIFE FIGHTING YOUR FATE, TOO, RIGHT?
!!
WE'RE FIGHTERS. THAT'S WHY...
...I BELIEVE WE CAN DEFINITELY ACCOMPLISH THINGS TOGETHER.
LET'S TEAM UP...
...REON!
ARE YOU A SAINT?!
THAT'S OVER-KILL.
SHE IS! SHE'S THE HOLY MOTHER OF SAINTS!!
I SEE WHY DUM-DUM SOMALI GOT ATTACHED TO YOU...
I REALLY AM...
...NO MATCH FOR HER.

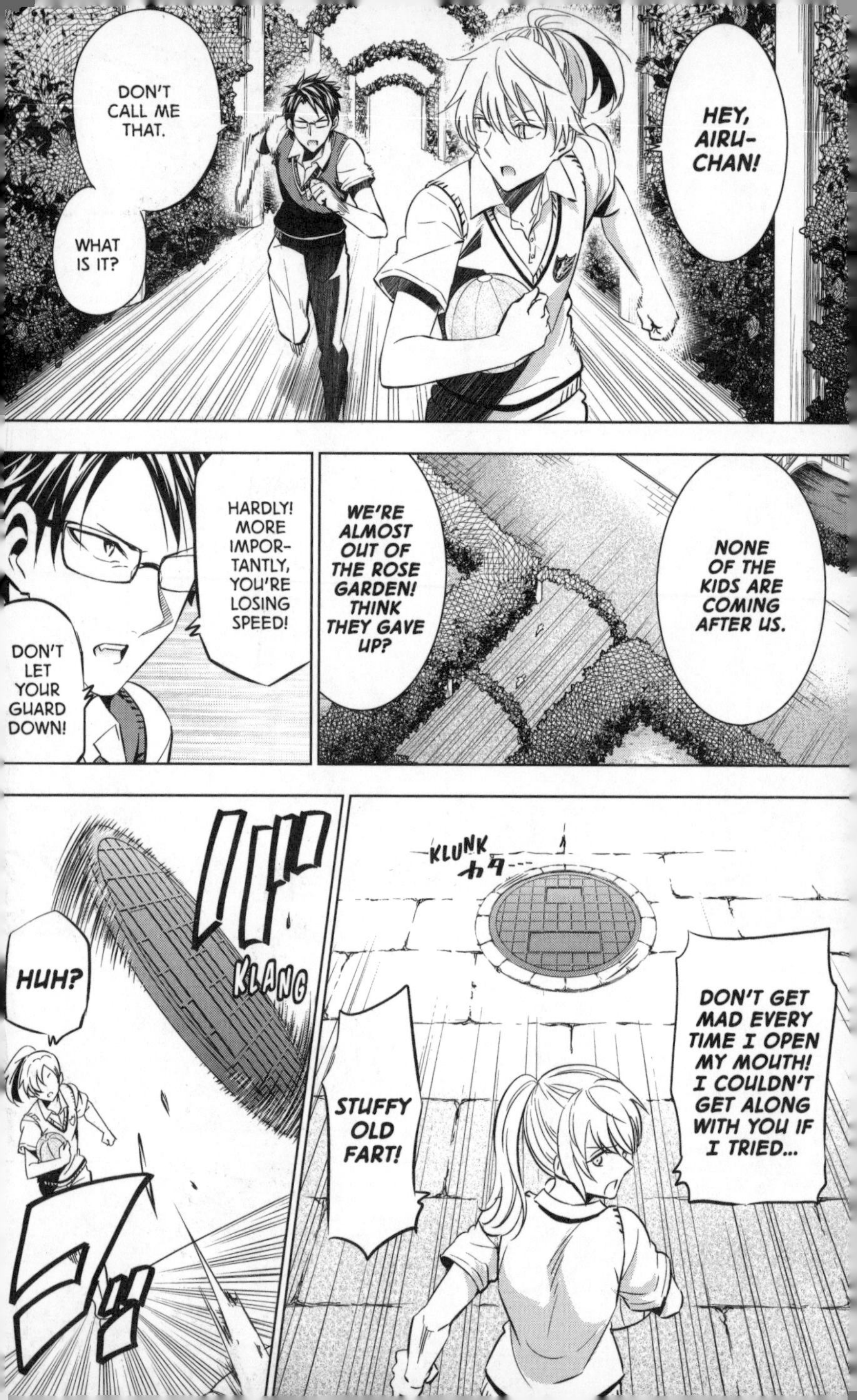
HEY, AIRU-CHAN!
DON'T CALL ME THAT.
WHAT IS IT?
NONE OF THE KIDS ARE COMING AFTER US.
WE'RE ALMOST OUT OF THE ROSE GARDEN! THINK THEY GAVE UP?
HARDLY! MORE IMPORTANTLY, YOU'RE LOSING SPEED!
DON'T LET YOUR GUARD DOWN!
KLUNK
カタ
DON'T GET MAD EVERY TIME I OPEN MY MOUTH! I COULDN'T GET ALONG WITH YOU IF I TRIED...
STUFFY OLD FART!
KLANG
HUH?

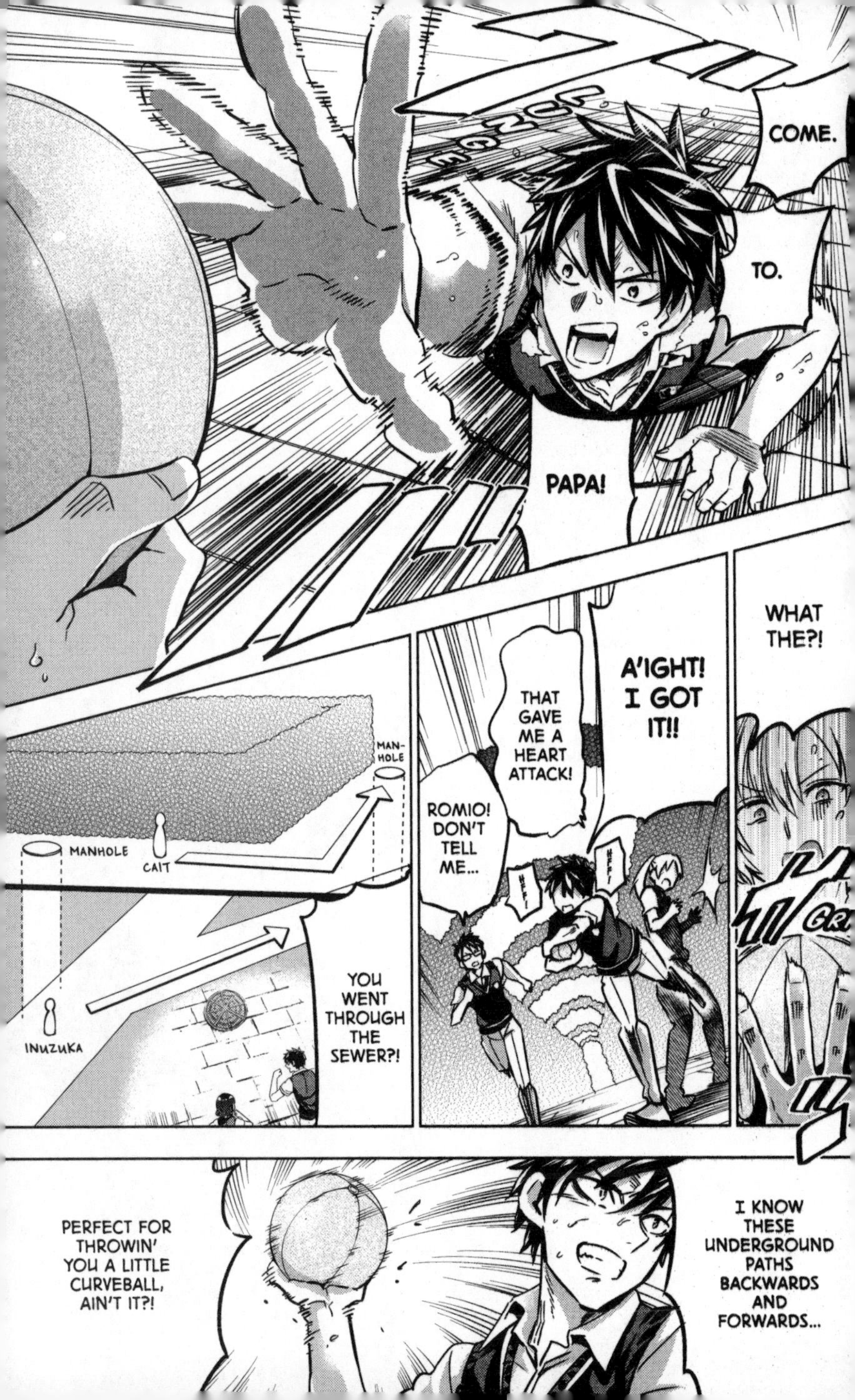
COME.
TO.
PAPA!
LUNGE
WHAT THE?!
A'IGHT! I GOT IT!!
THAT GAVE ME A HEART ATTACK!
ROMIO! DON'T TELL ME...
MAN-HOLE
MANHOLE
CAIT
INUZUKA
YOU WENT THROUGH THE SEWER?!
I KNOW THESE UNDERGROUND PATHS BACKWARDS AND FORWARDS...
PERFECT FOR THROWIN' YOU A LITTLE CURVEBALL, AIN'T IT?!

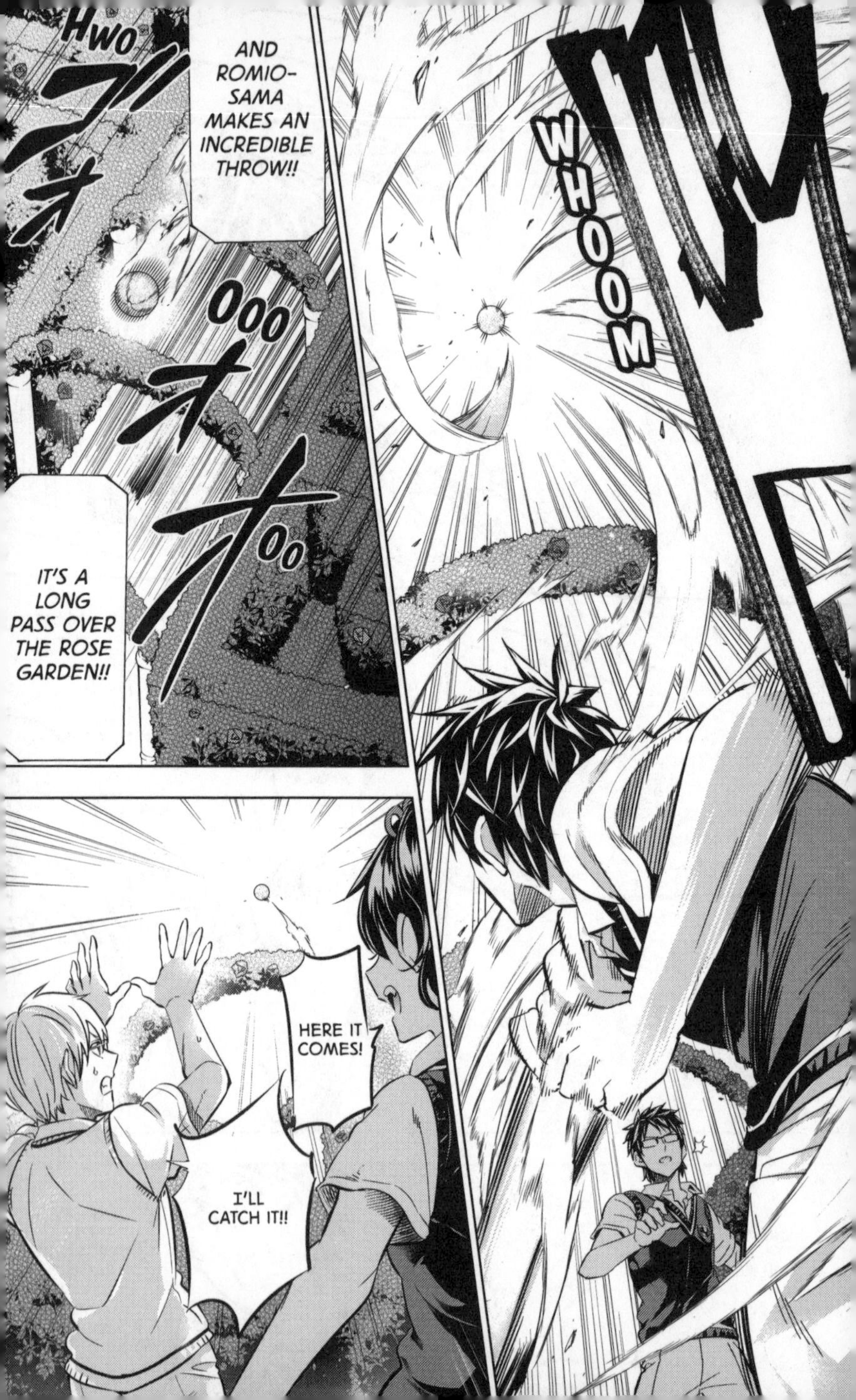
WHOOOM
AND ROMIO-SAMA MAKES AN INCREDIBLE THROW!!
HWO
OOO
OO
IT'S A LONG PASS OVER THE ROSE GARDEN!!
HERE IT COMES!
I'LL CATCH IT!!

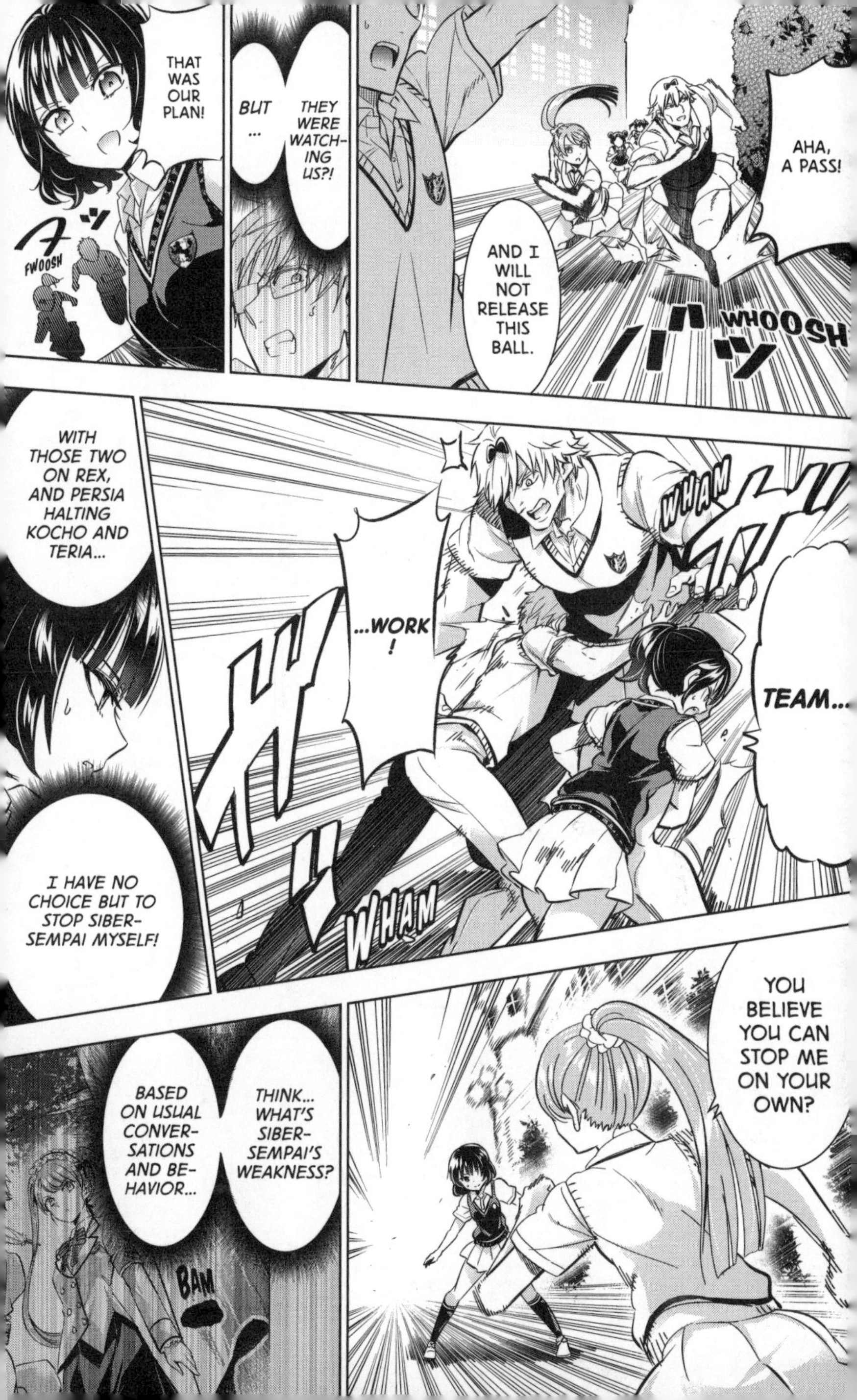
AHA, A PASS!
WHOOSH
AND I WILL NOT RELEASE THIS BALL.
THEY WERE WATCHING-ING US?!
BUT ...
THAT WAS OUR PLAN!
FWOOSH
TEAM...
...WORK!
WHAM
WHAM
WITH THOSE TWO ON REX, AND PERSIA HALTING KOCHO AND TERIA...
I HAVE NO CHOICE BUT TO STOP SIBER-SEMPAI MYSELF!
YOU BELIEVE YOU CAN STOP ME ON YOUR OWN?
THINK... WHAT'S SIBER-SEMPAI'S WEAKNESS?
BASED ON USUAL CONVER-SATIONS AND BE-HAVIOR...
BAM

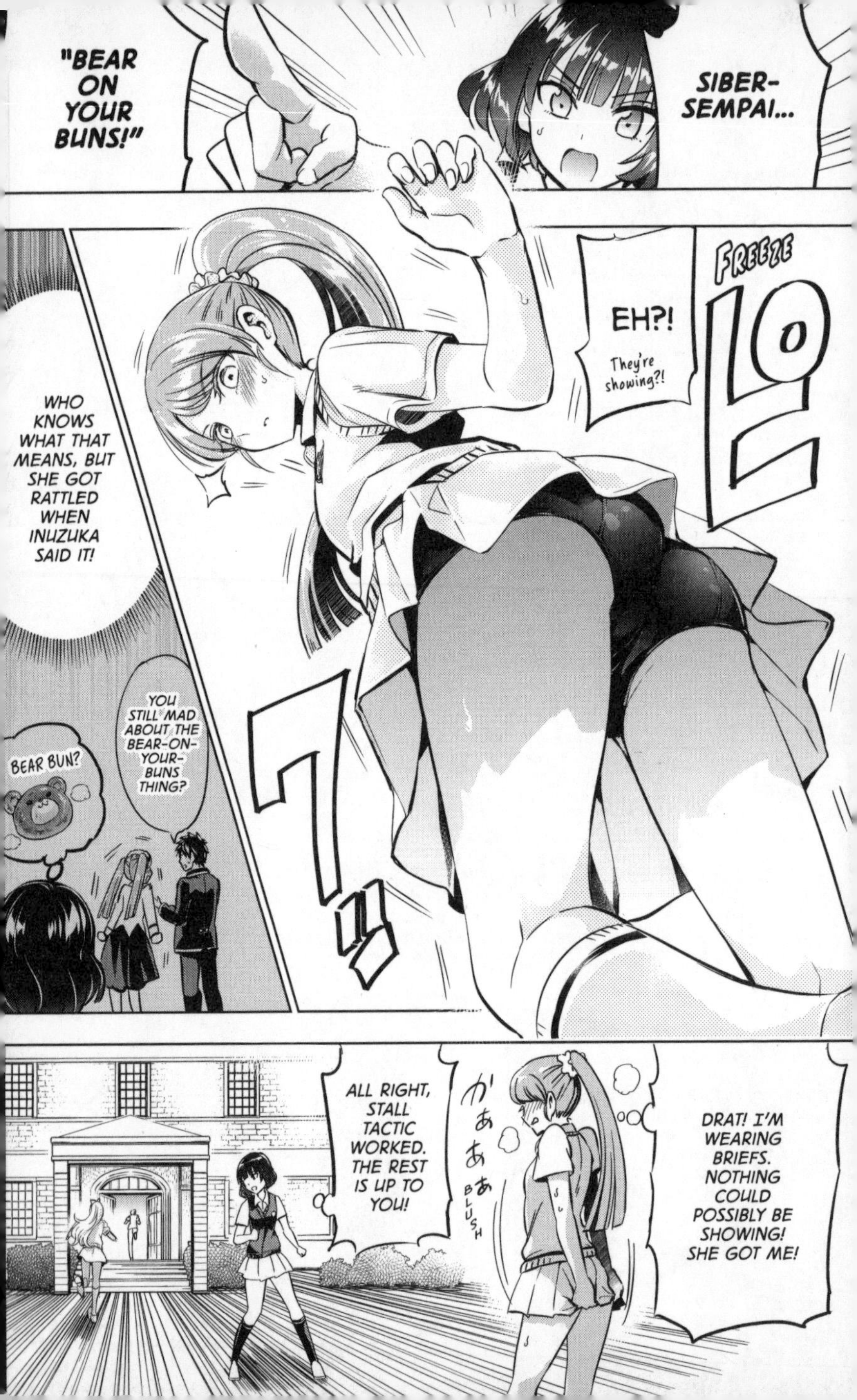
SIBER-SEMPAI...
"BEAR ON YOUR BUNS!"
FREEZE
EH?!
They're showing?!
WHO KNOWS WHAT THAT MEANS, BUT SHE GOT RATTLED WHEN INUZUKA SAID IT!
YOU STILL MAD ABOUT THE BEAR-ON-YOUR-BUNS THING?
BEAR BUN?
DRAT! I'M WEARING BRIEFS. NOTHING COULD POSSIBLY BE SHOWING! SHE GOT ME!
かあああ
BLUSH
ALL RIGHT, STALL TACTIC WORKED. THE REST IS UP TO YOU!

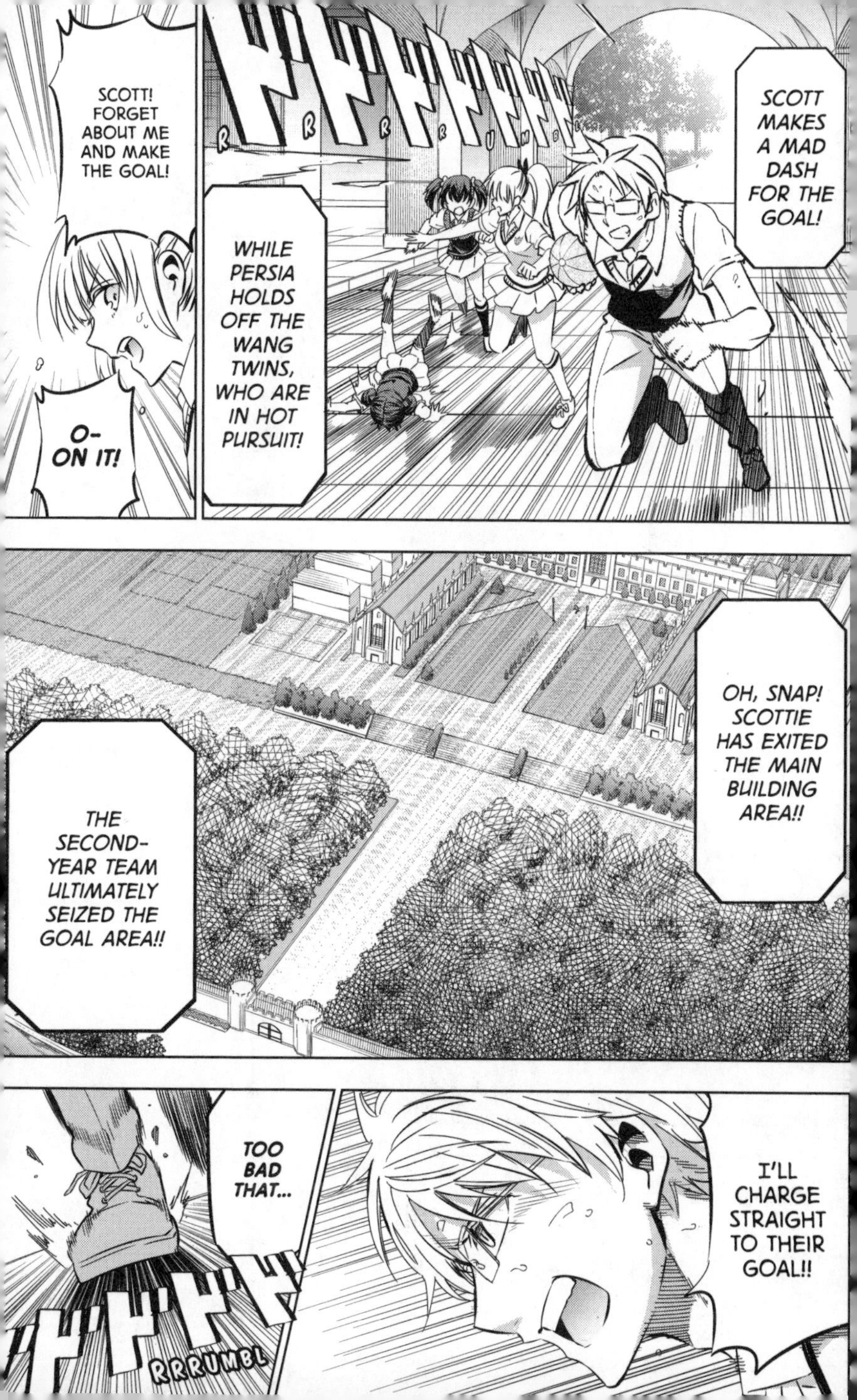
SCOTT MAKES A MAD DASH FOR THE GOAL!
RRRRRUMBL
WHILE PERSIA HOLDS OFF THE WANG TWINS, WHO ARE IN HOT PURSUIT!
SCOTT! FORGET ABOUT ME AND MAKE THE GOAL!
O- ON IT!
OH, SNAP! SCOTTIE HAS EXITED THE MAIN BUILDING AREA!!
THE SECOND-YEAR TEAM ULTIMATELY SEIZED THE GOAL AREA!!
I'LL CHARGE STRAIGHT TO THEIR GOAL!!
TOO BAD THAT...
RRRUMBL

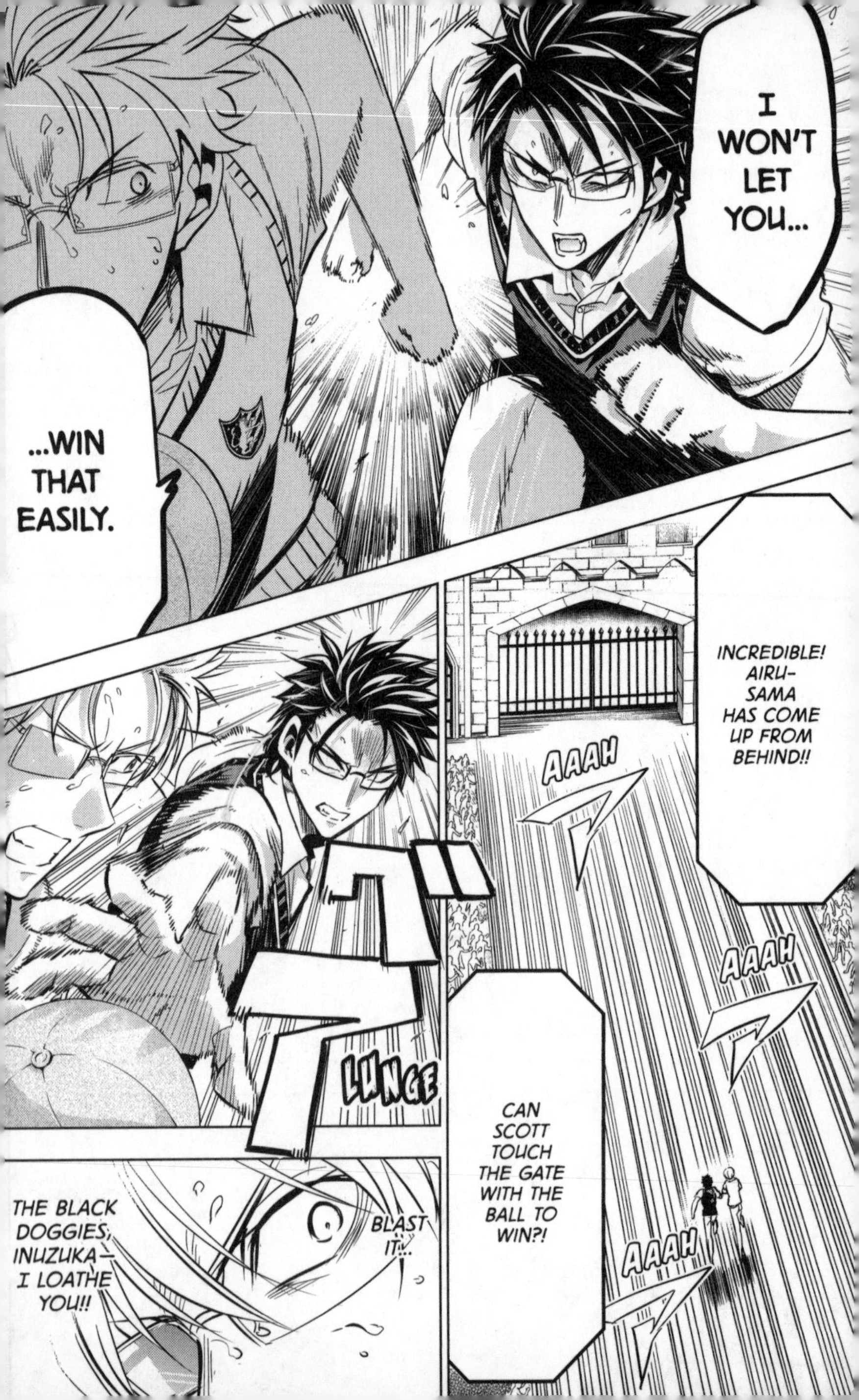
I WON'T LET YOU...
...WIN THAT EASILY.
INCREDIBLE! AIRU-SAMA HAS COME UP FROM BEHIND!!
AAAH
AAAH
CAN SCOTT TOUCH THE GATE WITH THE BALL TO WIN?!
AAAH
LUNGE
BLAST IT...
THE BLACK DOGGIES, INUZUKA— I LOATHE YOU!!

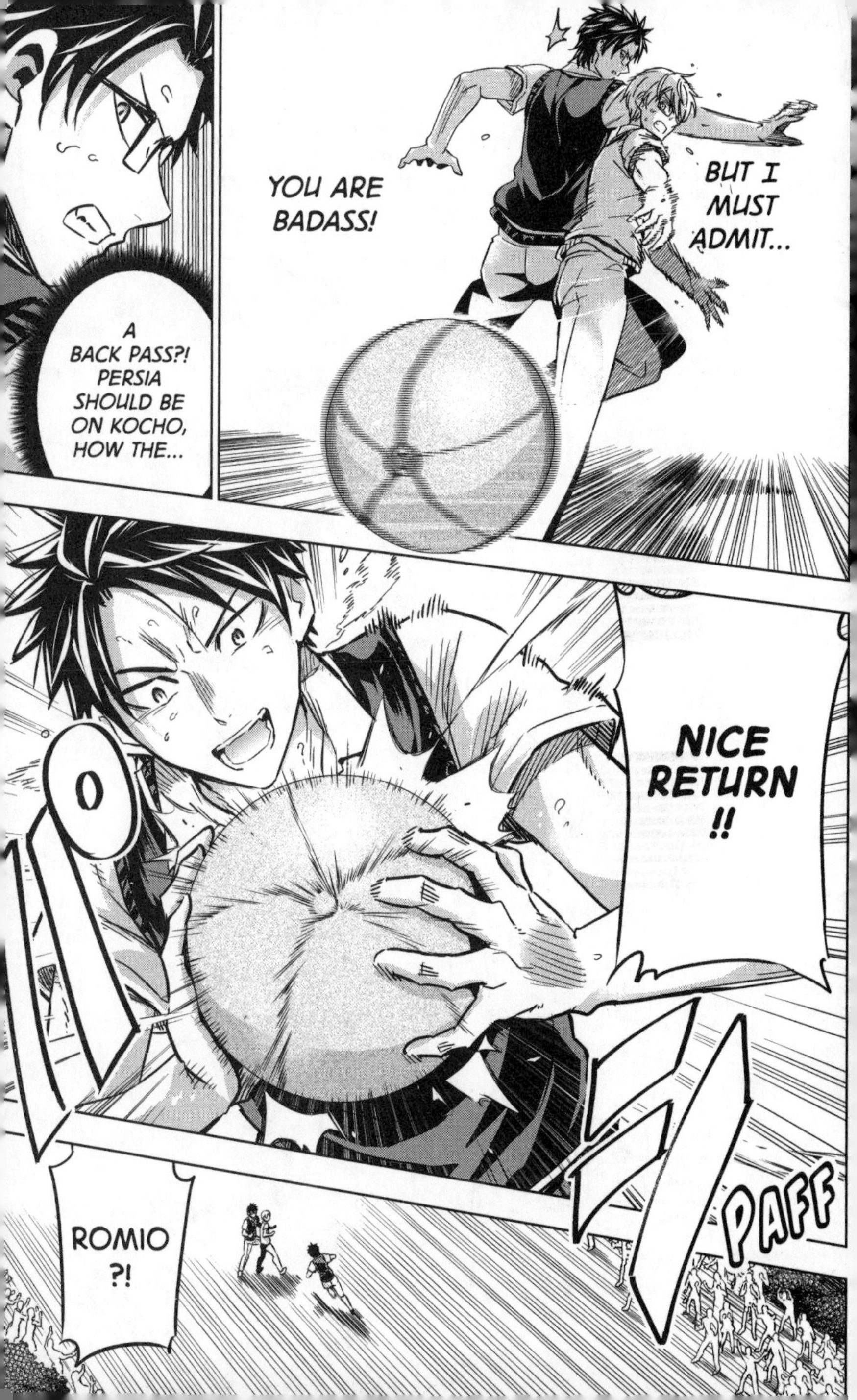
BUT I MUST ADMIT...
YOU ARE BADASS!
A BACK PASS?! PERSIA SHOULD BE ON KOCHO, HOW THE...
NICE RETURN !!
O
PAFF
ROMIO ?!

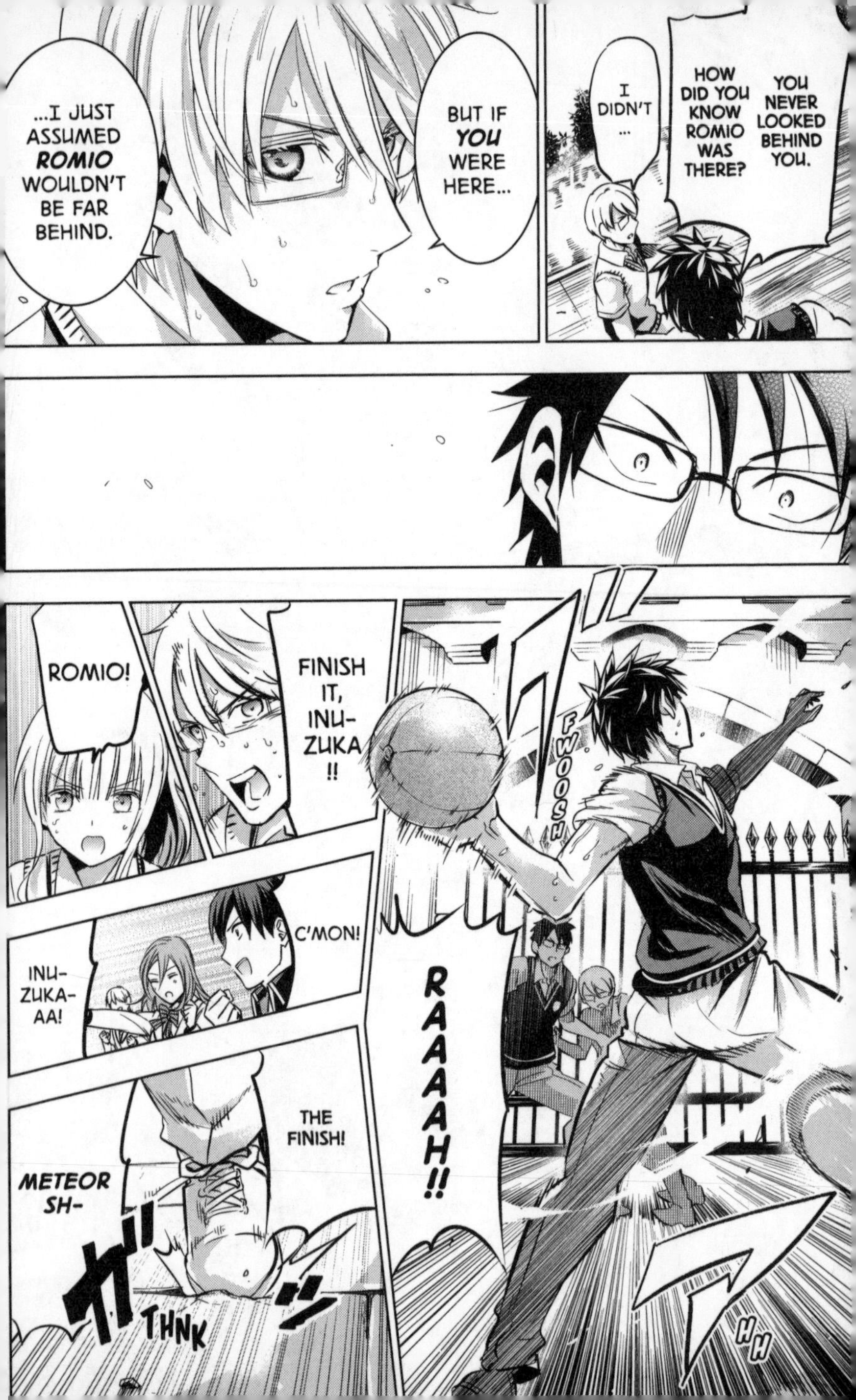
YOU NEVER LOOKED BEHIND YOU.
HOW DID YOU KNOW ROMIO WAS THERE?
I DIDN'T ...
BUT IF YOU WERE HERE...
...I JUST ASSUMED ROMIO WOULDN'T BE FAR BEHIND.
FWOOSH
RAAAAAH!!
HH
FINISH IT, INU-ZUKA!!
ROMIO!
C'MON!
INU-ZUKA-AA!
THE FINISH!
METEOR SH-
THNK

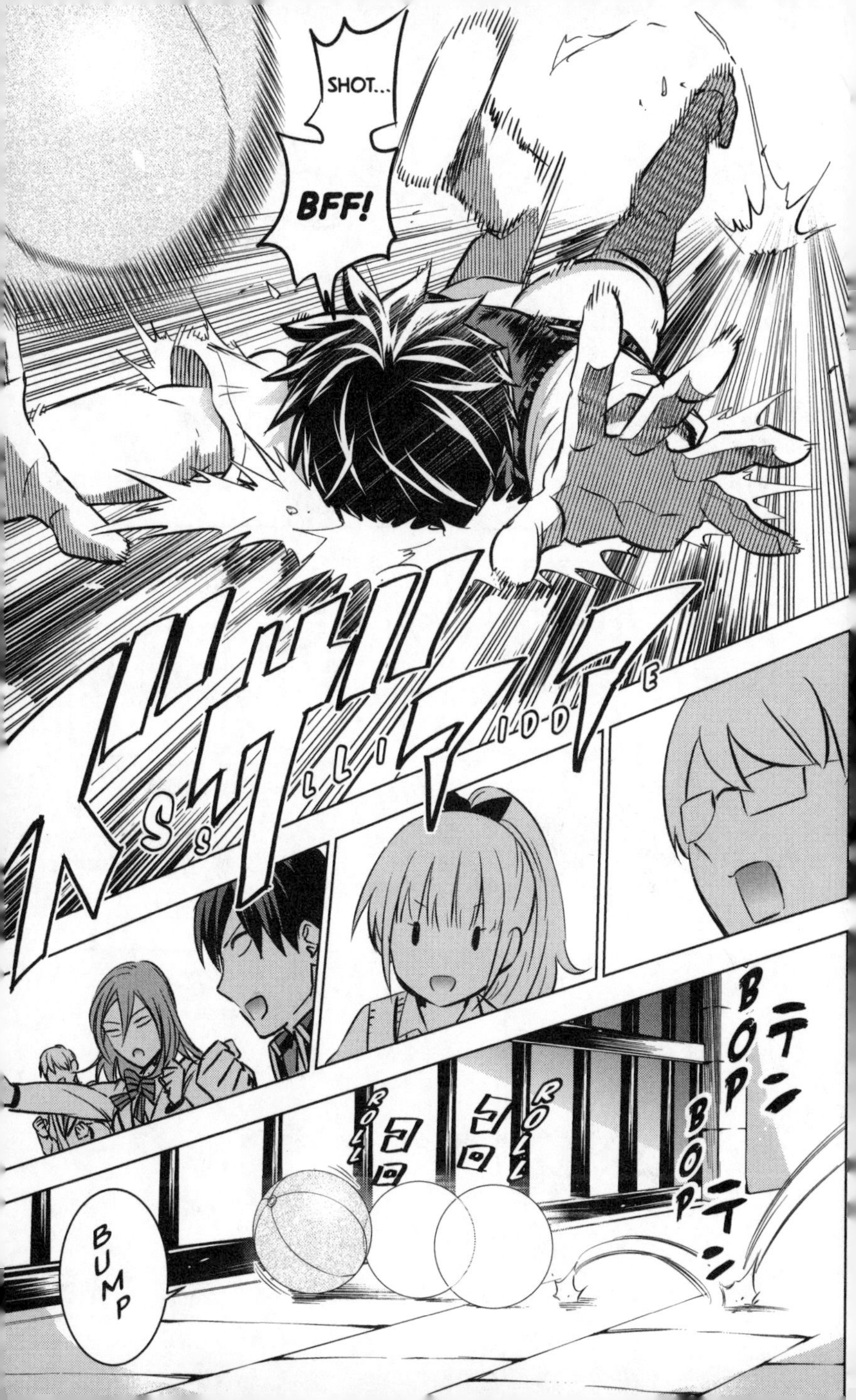
SHOT...
BFF!
SSLLIDDDE
BOP BOP
テン テン
ROLL ROLL
ゴロ ゴロ
BUMP

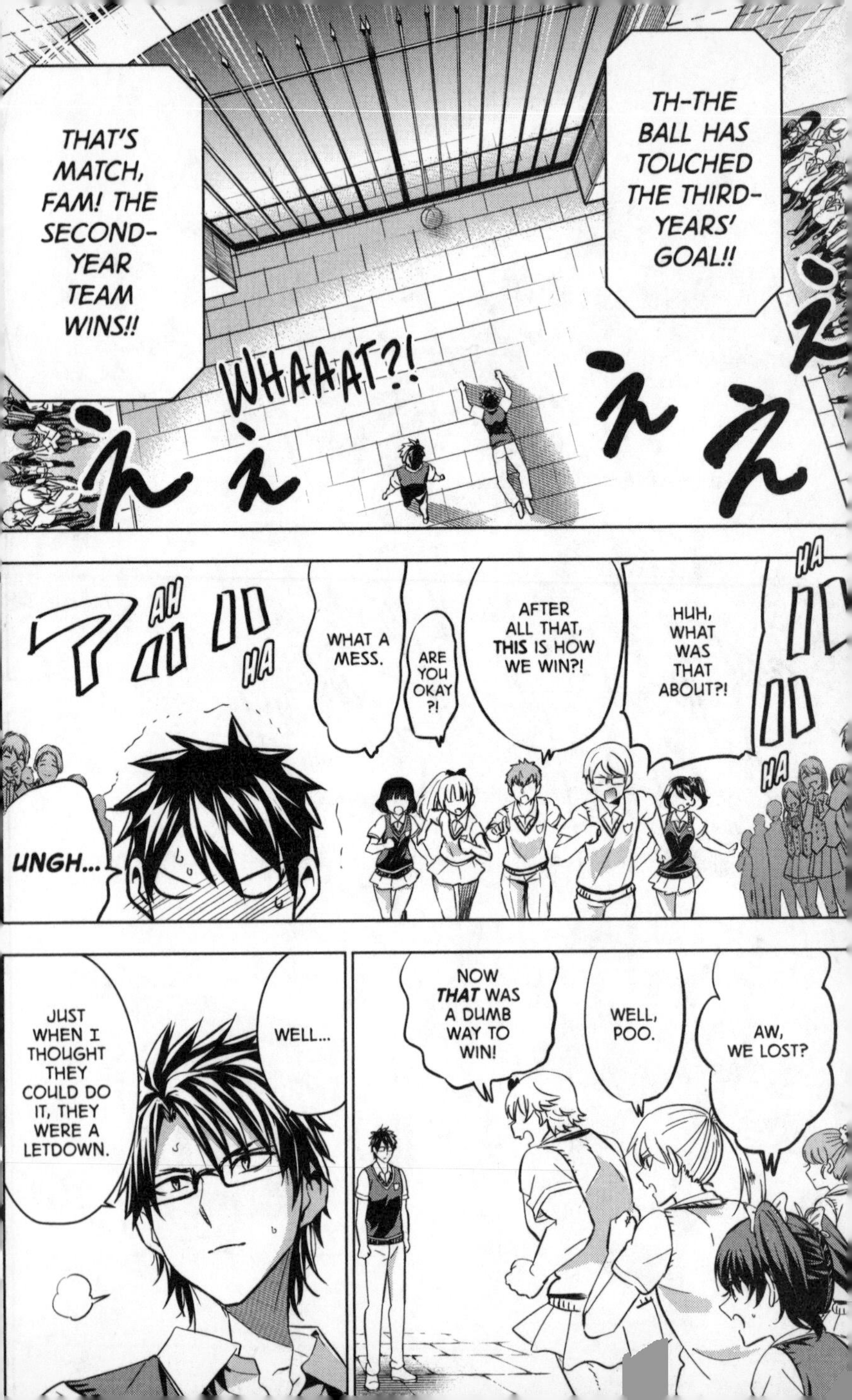
TH-THE BALL HAS TOUCHED THE THIRD-YEARS' GOAL!!
THAT'S MATCH, FAM! THE SECOND-YEAR TEAM WINS!!
WHAAAT?!
HA HA HA
HUH, WHAT WAS THAT ABOUT?!
AFTER ALL THAT, THIS IS HOW WE WIN?!
ARE YOU OKAY ?!
WHAT A MESS.
AH HA
UNGH...
AW, WE LOST?
WELL, POO.
NOW THAT WAS A DUMB WAY TO WIN!
WELL...
JUST WHEN I THOUGHT THEY COULD DO IT, THEY WERE A LETDOWN.

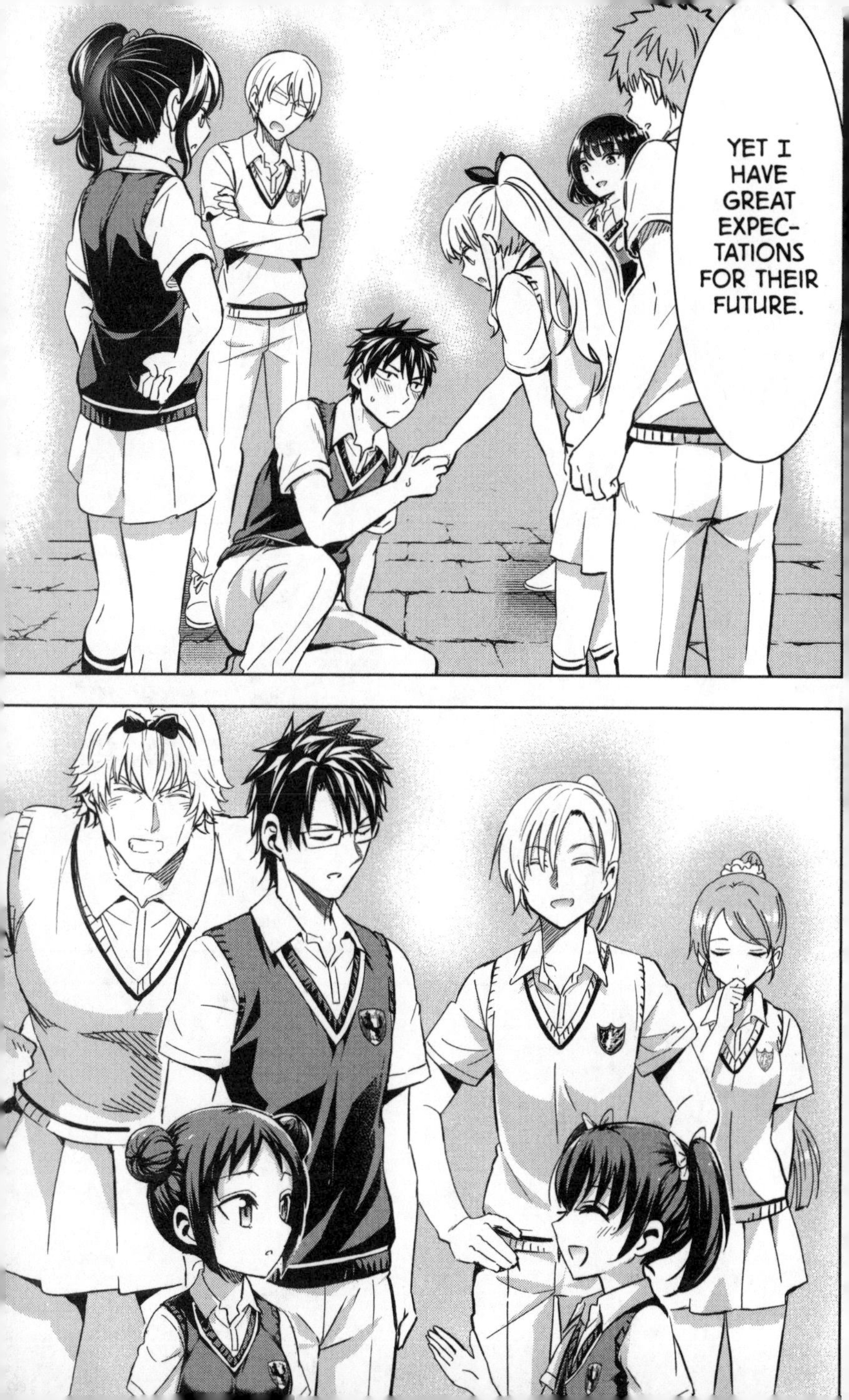
YET I HAVE GREAT EXPECTATIONS FOR THEIR FUTURE.

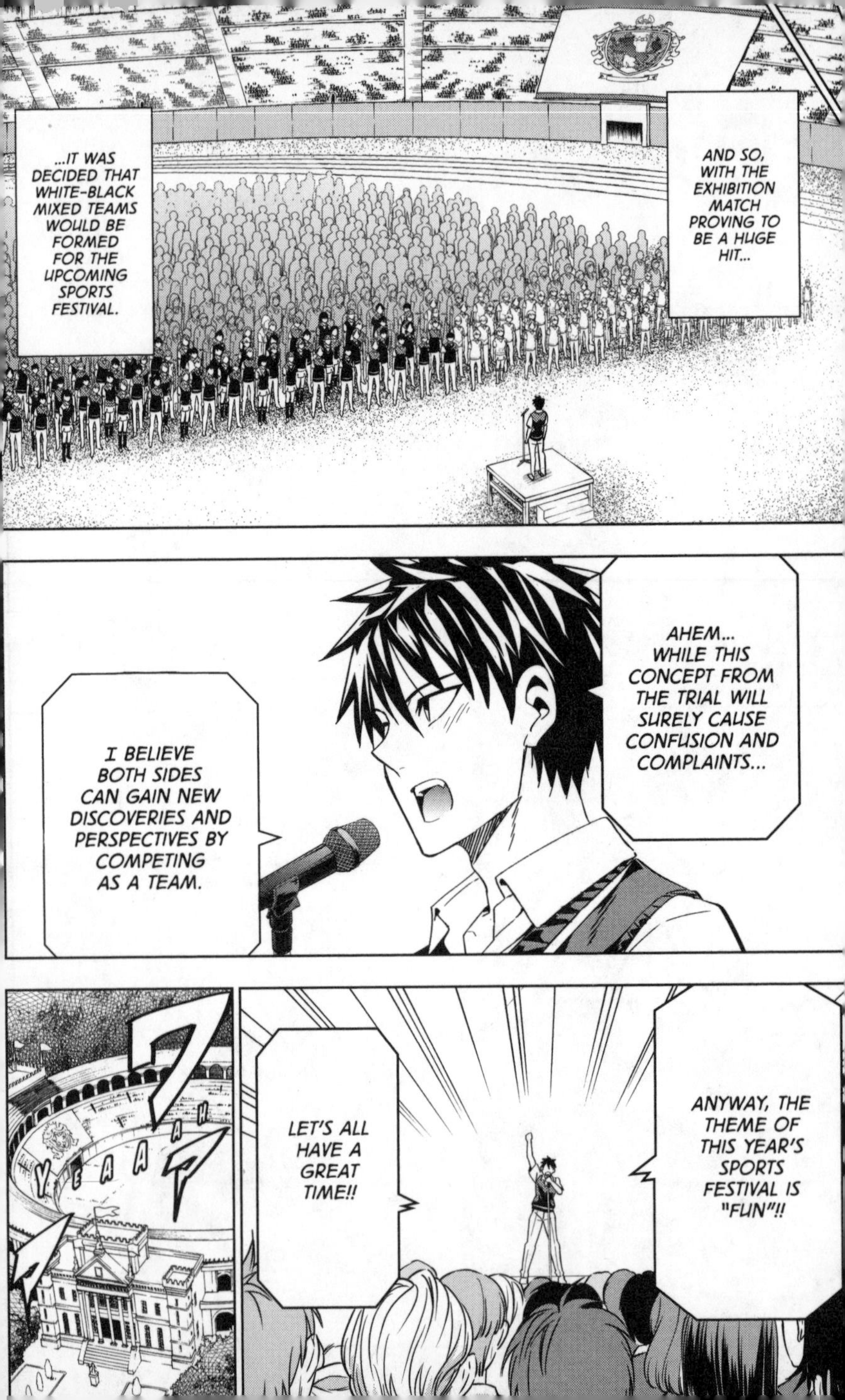
AND SO, WITH THE EXHIBITION MATCH PROVING TO BE A HUGE HIT...
...IT WAS DECIDED THAT WHITE-BLACK MIXED TEAMS WOULD BE FORMED FOR THE UPCOMING SPORTS FESTIVAL.
AHEM... WHILE THIS CONCEPT FROM THE TRIAL WILL SURELY CAUSE CONFUSION AND COMPLAINTS...
I BELIEVE BOTH SIDES CAN GAIN NEW DISCOVERIES AND PERSPECTIVES BY COMPETING AS A TEAM.
ANYWAY, THE THEME OF THIS YEAR'S SPORTS FESTIVAL IS "FUN"!!
LET'S ALL HAVE A GREAT TIME!!
YEAAAH

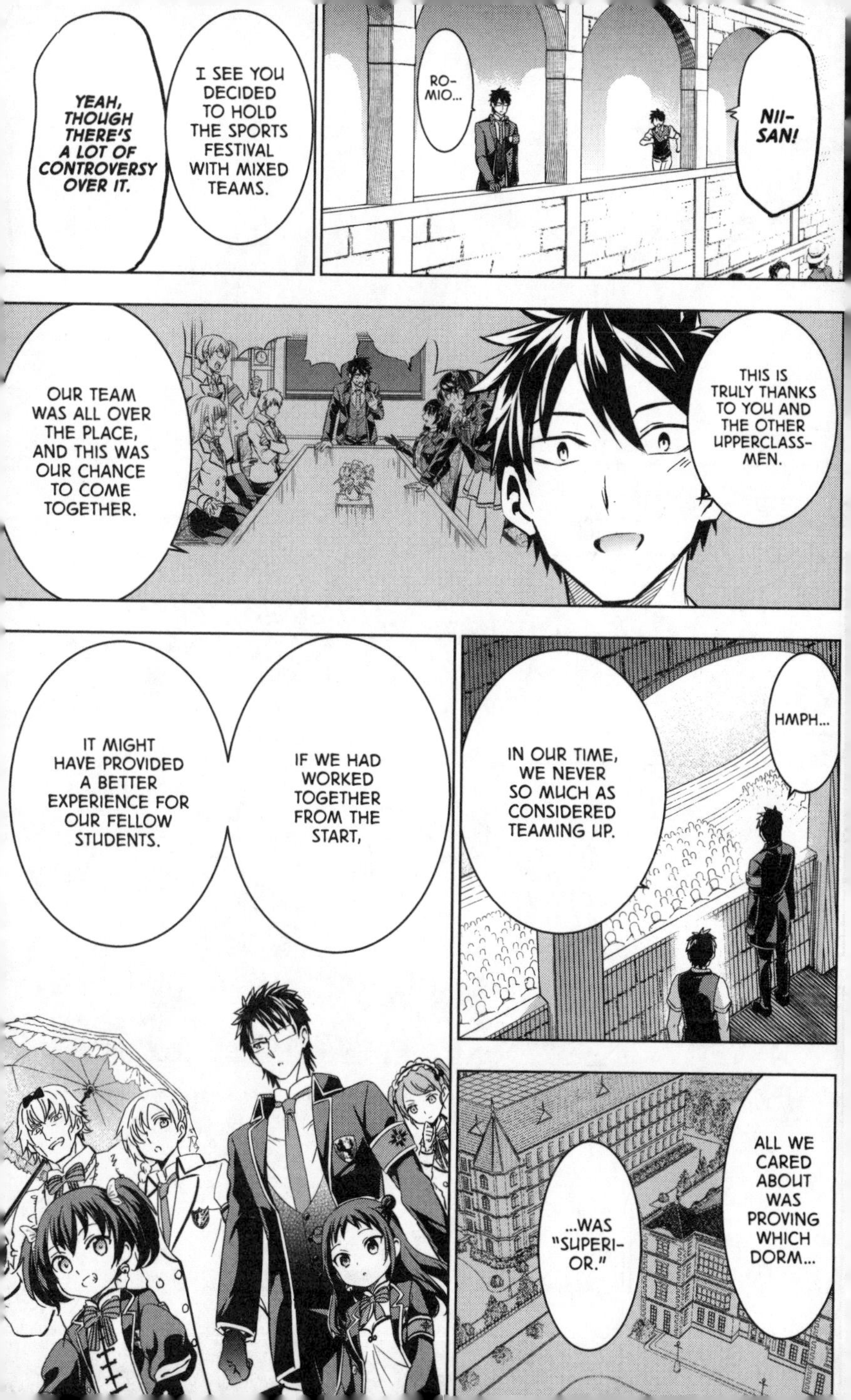
NII-SAN!
RO-MIO...
I SEE YOU DECIDED TO HOLD THE SPORTS FESTIVAL WITH MIXED TEAMS.
YEAH, THOUGH THERE'S A LOT OF CONTROVERSY OVER IT.
THIS IS TRULY THANKS TO YOU AND THE OTHER UPPERCLASS-MEN.
OUR TEAM WAS ALL OVER THE PLACE, AND THIS WAS OUR CHANCE TO COME TOGETHER.
HMPH...
IN OUR TIME, WE NEVER SO MUCH AS CONSIDERED TEAMING UP.
ALL WE CARED ABOUT WAS PROVING WHICH DORM...
...WAS "SUPERI-OR."
IF WE HAD WORKED TOGETHER FROM THE START,
IT MIGHT HAVE PROVIDED A BETTER EXPERIENCE FOR OUR FELLOW STUDENTS.

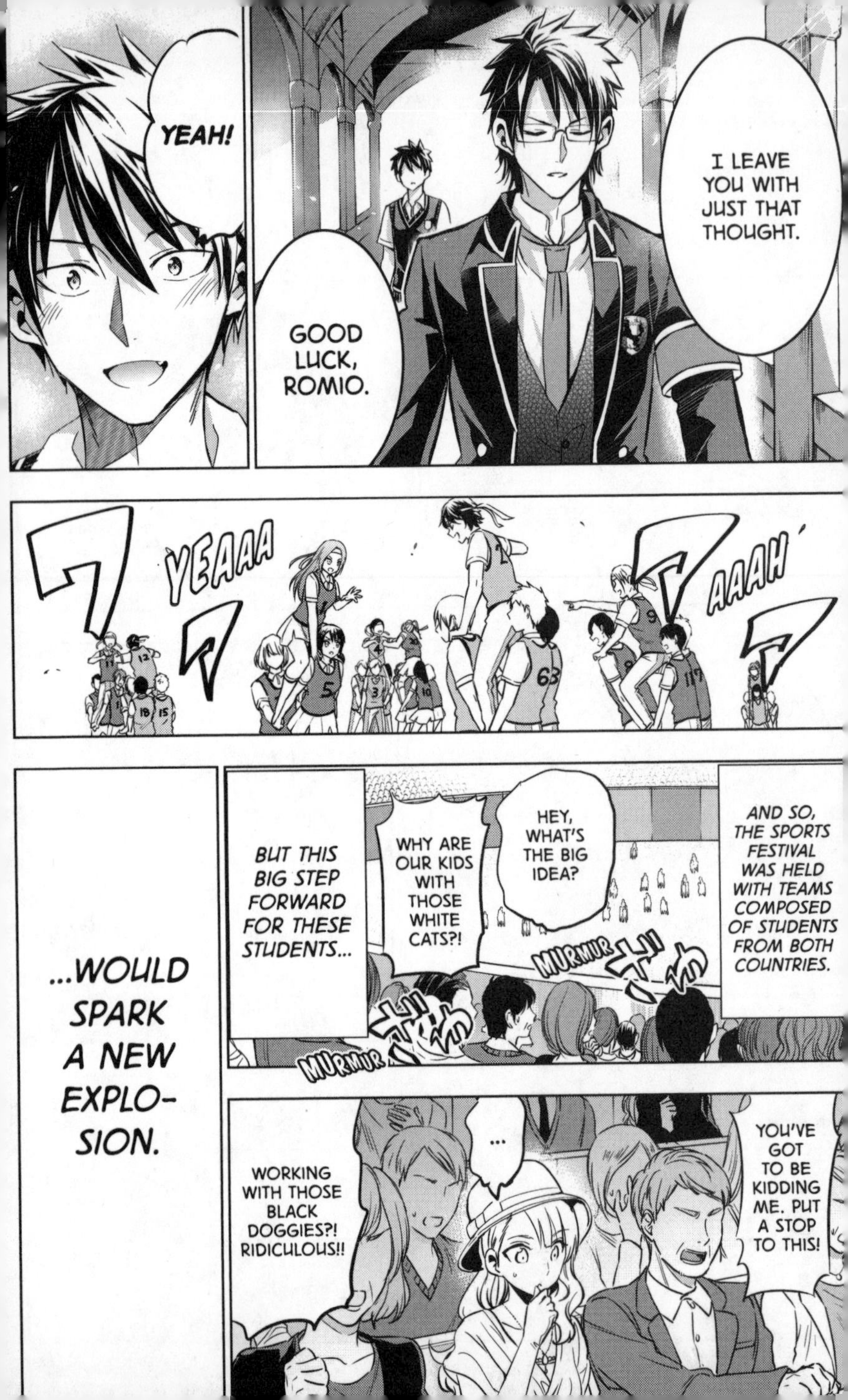
I LEAVE YOU WITH JUST THAT THOUGHT.
GOOD LUCK, ROMIO.
YEAH!
AAAH
YEAAA
AND SO, THE SPORTS FESTIVAL WAS HELD WITH TEAMS COMPOSED OF STUDENTS FROM BOTH COUNTRIES.
HEY, WHAT'S THE BIG IDEA?
MURMUR
WHY ARE OUR KIDS WITH THOSE WHITE CATS?!
BUT THIS BIG STEP FORWARD FOR THESE STUDENTS...
MURMUR
YOU'VE GOT TO BE KIDDING ME. PUT A STOP TO THIS!
...
WORKING WITH THOSE BLACK DOGGIES?! RIDICULOUS!!
...WOULD SPARK A NEW EXPLOSION.

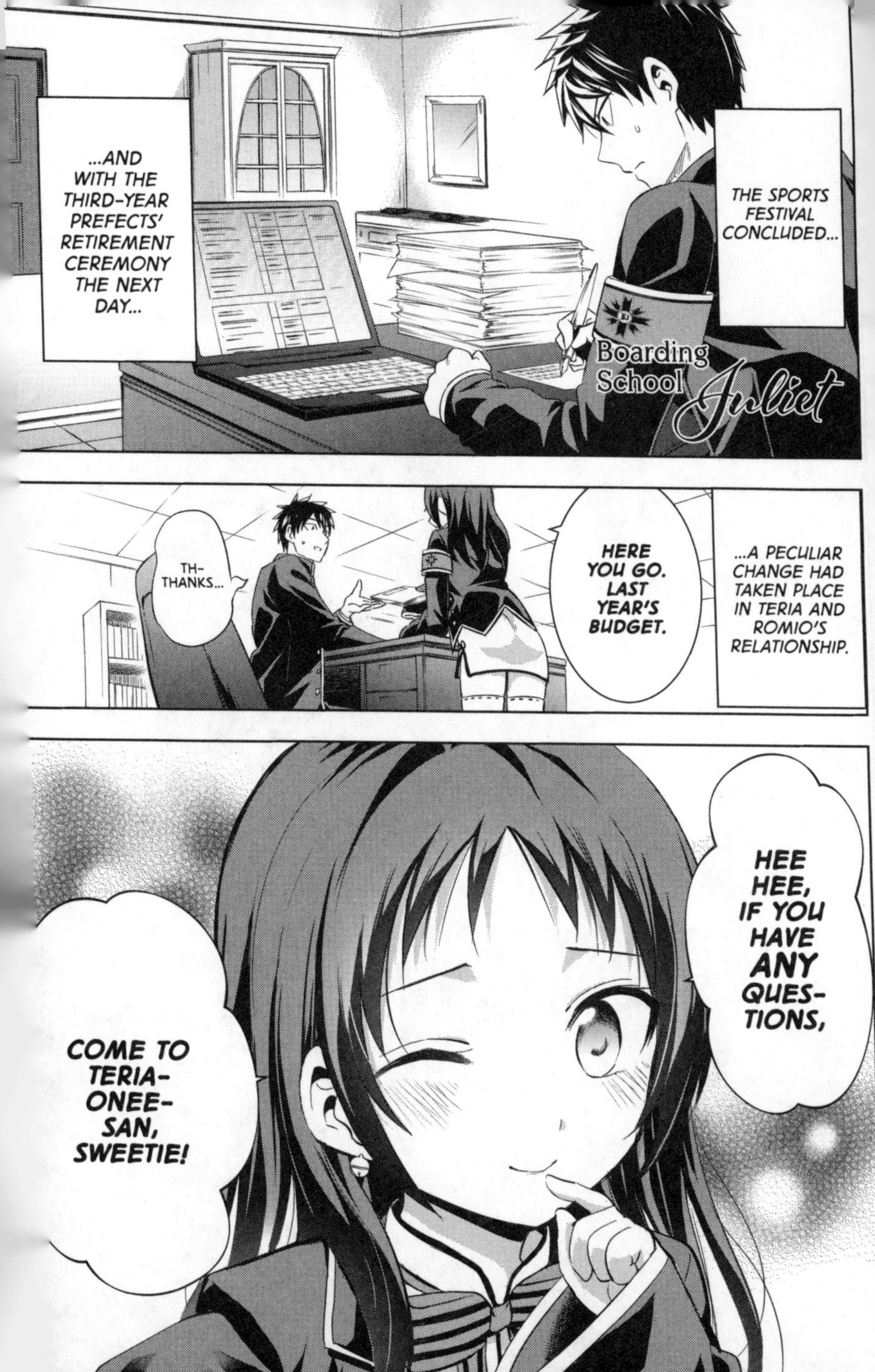
THE SPORTS FESTIVAL CONCLUDED...
...AND WITH THE THIRD-YEAR PREFECTS' RETIREMENT CEREMONY THE NEXT DAY...
Boarding School Juliet
...A PECULIAR CHANGE HAD TAKEN PLACE IN TERIA AND ROMIO'S RELATIONSHIP.
HERE YOU GO. LAST YEAR'S BUDGET.
TH-THANKS...
HEE HEE, IF YOU HAVE ANY QUESTIONS,
COME TO TERIA-ONEE-SAN, SWEETIE!

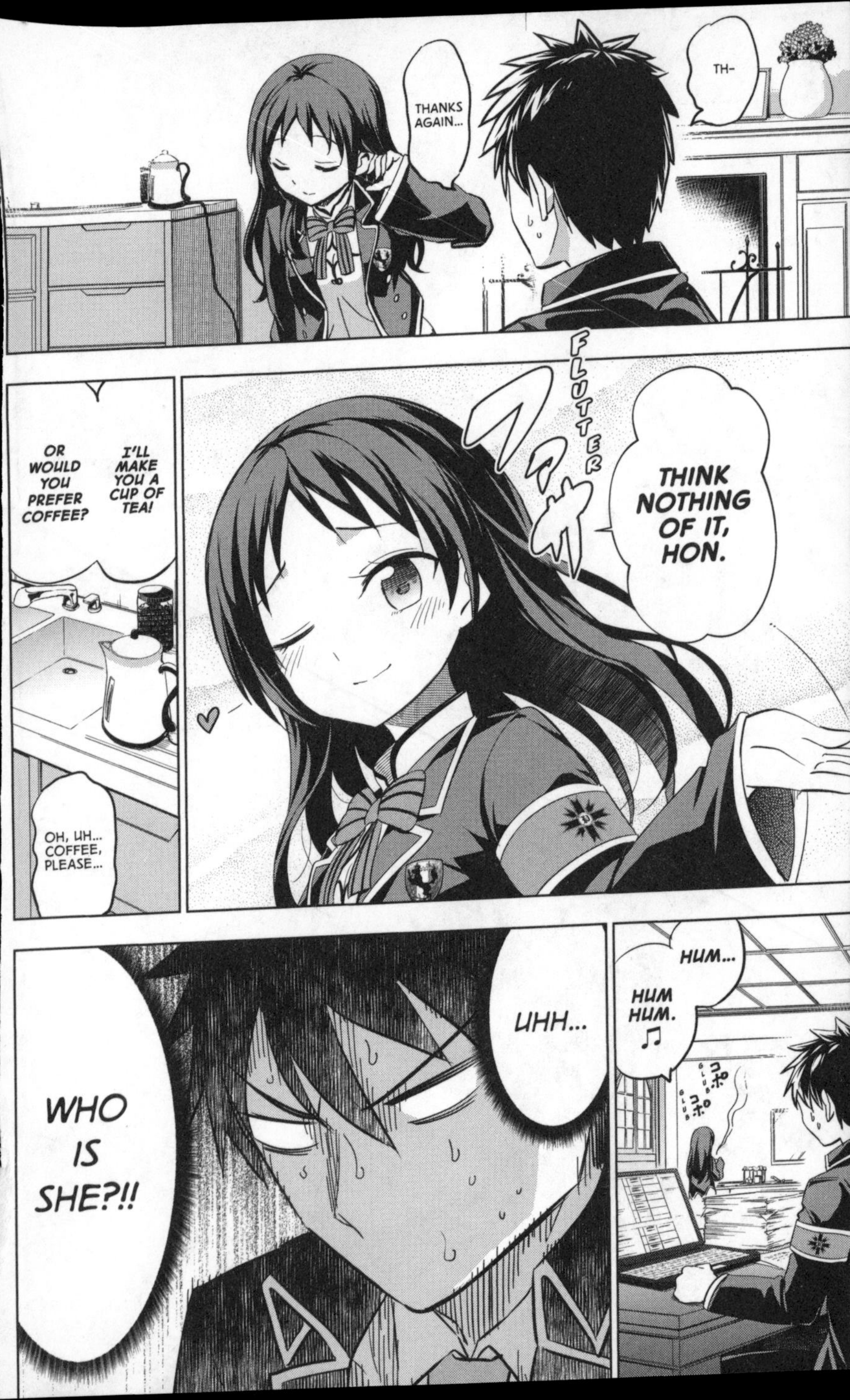
TH-
THANKS AGAIN...
FLUTTER
THINK NOTHING OF IT, HON.
I'LL MAKE YOU A CUP OF TEA!
OR WOULD YOU PREFER COFFEE?
OH, UH... COFFEE, PLEASE...
HUM...
HUM HUM. ♫
GLUB GLUB
UHH...
WHO IS SHE?!!

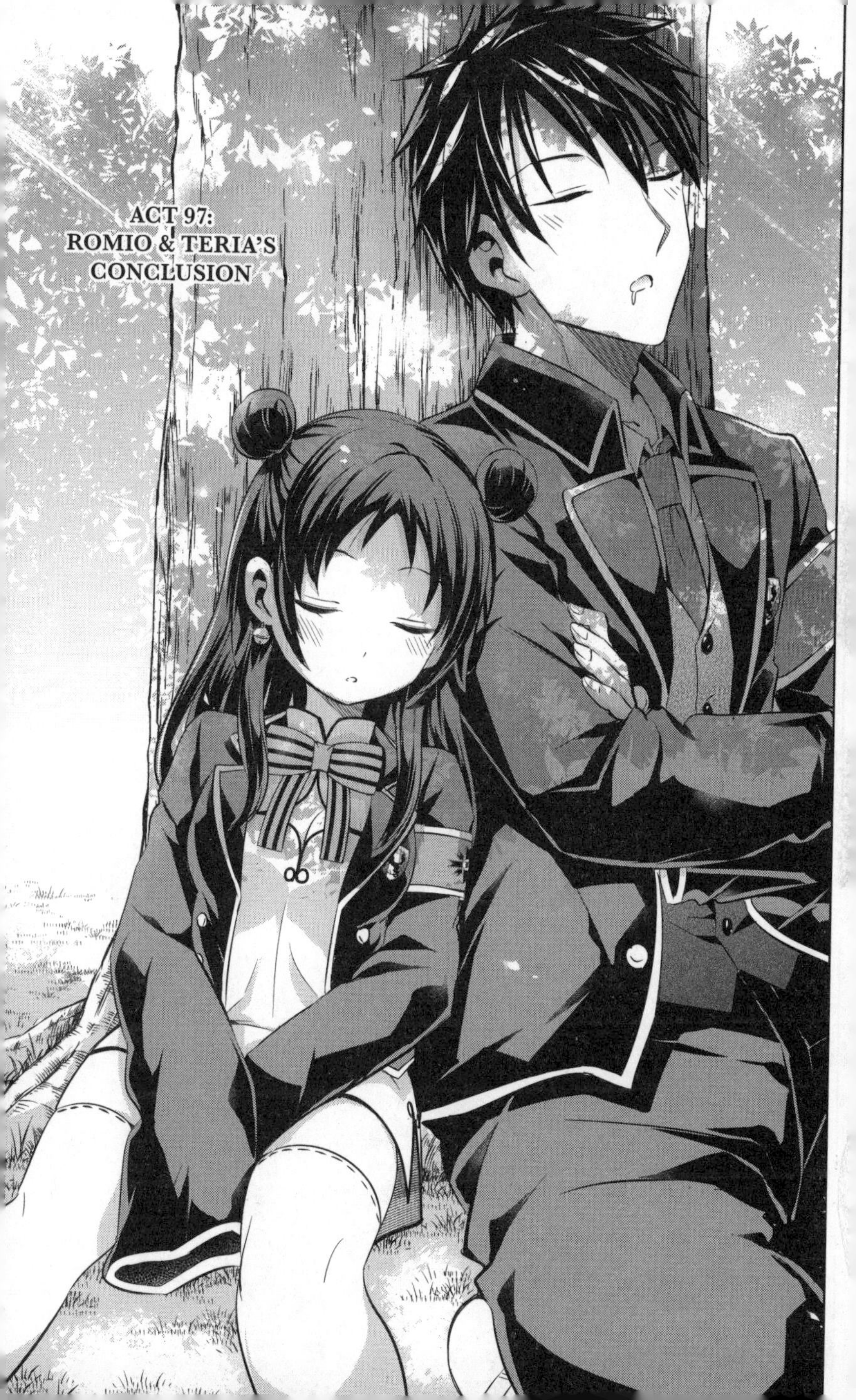
ACT 97:
ROMIO & TERIA'S
CONCLUSION

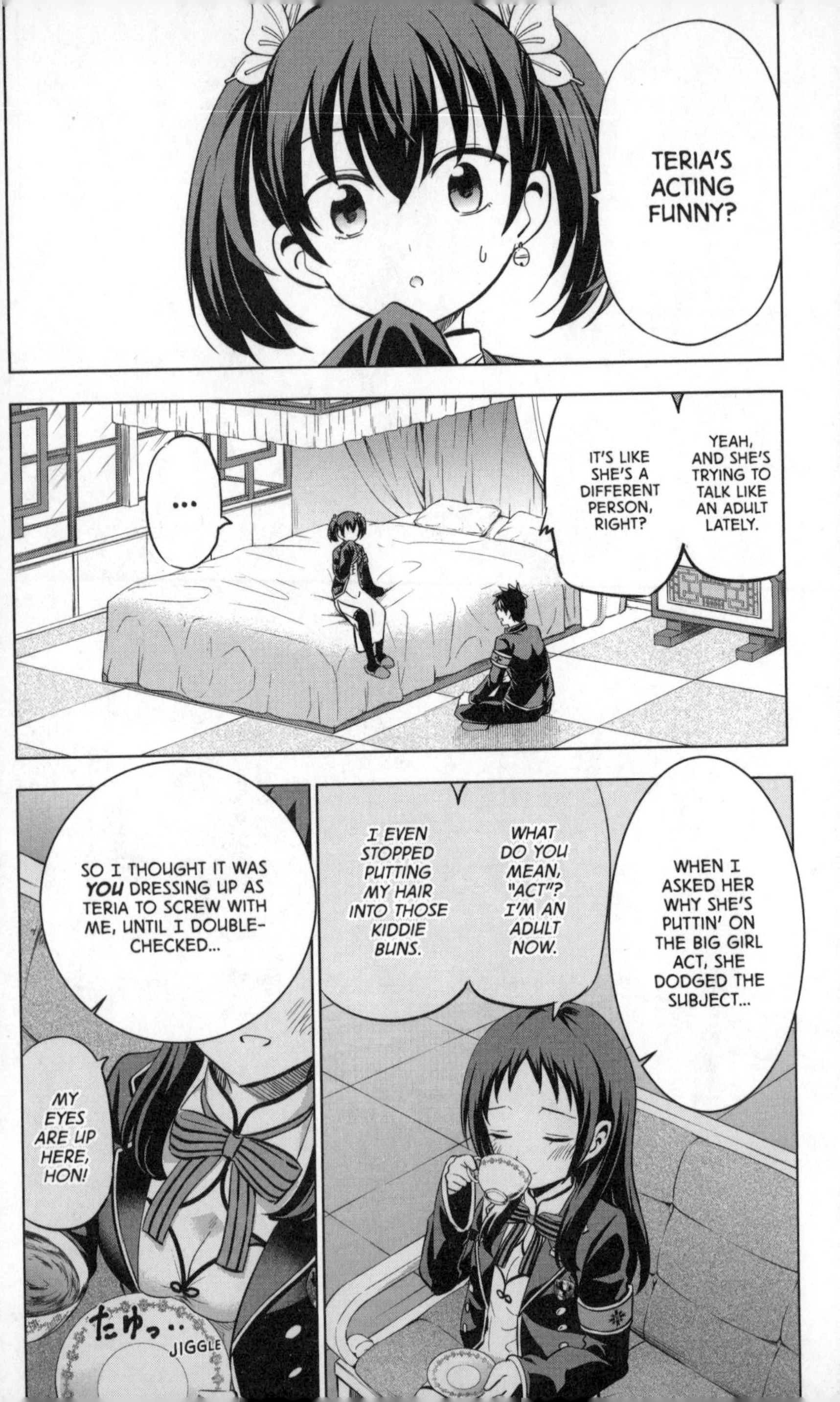
TERIA'S ACTING FUNNY?
YEAH, AND SHE'S TRYING TO TALK LIKE AN ADULT LATELY.
IT'S LIKE SHE'S A DIFFERENT PERSON, RIGHT?
...
WHEN I ASKED HER WHY SHE'S PUTTIN' ON THE BIG GIRL ACT, SHE DODGED THE SUBJECT...
WHAT DO YOU MEAN, "ACT"? I'M AN ADULT NOW.
I EVEN STOPPED PUTTING MY HAIR INTO THOSE KIDDIE BUNS.
SO I THOUGHT IT WAS YOU DRESSING UP AS TERIA TO SCREW WITH ME, UNTIL I DOUBLE-CHECKED...
MY EYES ARE UP HERE, HON!
たゆっ‥
JIGGLE

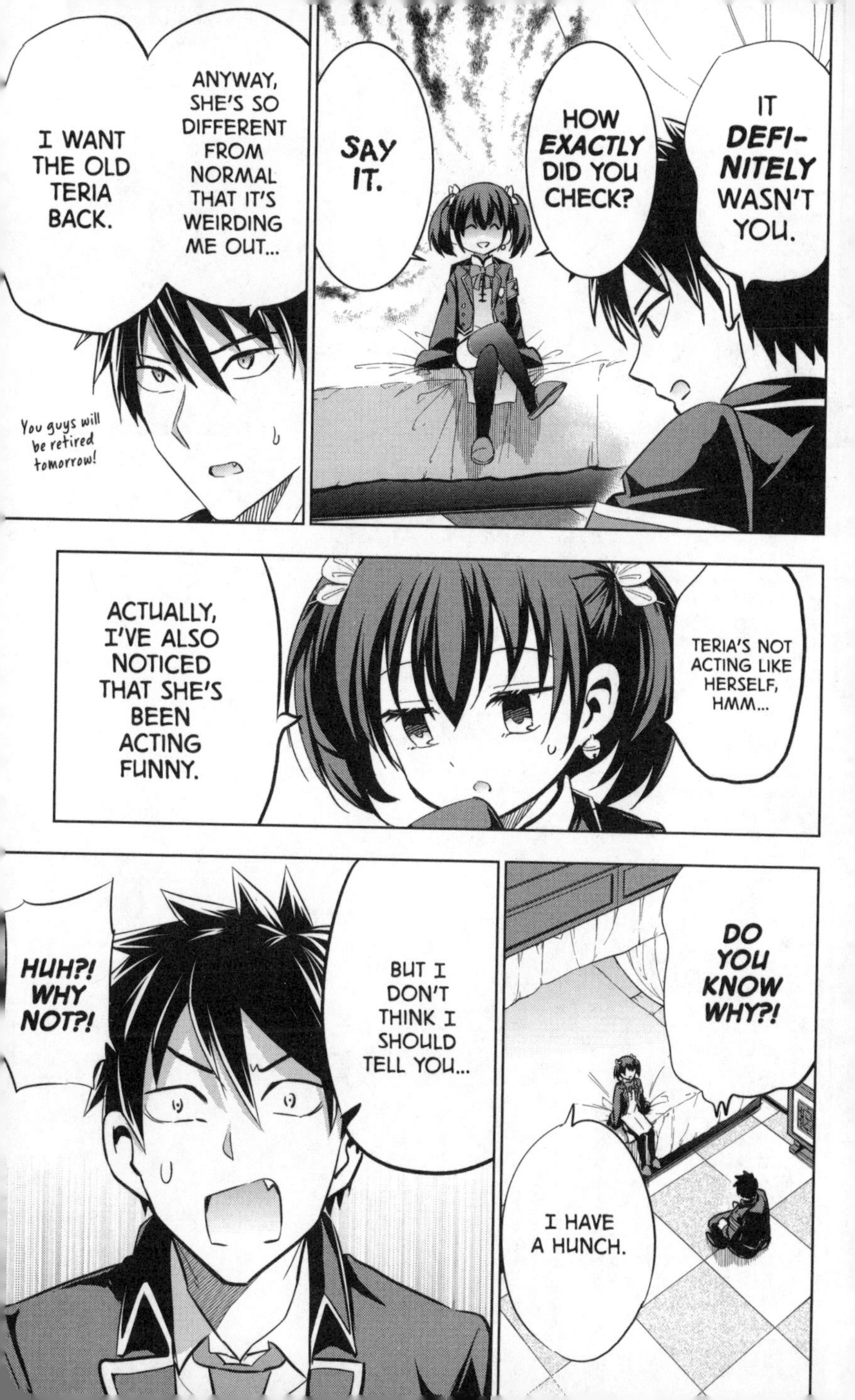
IT DEFINITELY WASN'T YOU.
HOW EXACTLY DID YOU CHECK?
SAY IT.
ANYWAY, SHE'S SO DIFFERENT FROM NORMAL THAT IT'S WEIRDING ME OUT...
I WANT THE OLD TERIA BACK.
You guys will be retired tomorrow!
TERIA'S NOT ACTING LIKE HERSELF, HMM...
ACTUALLY, I'VE ALSO NOTICED THAT SHE'S BEEN ACTING FUNNY.
DO YOU KNOW WHY?!
I HAVE A HUNCH.
BUT I DON'T THINK I SHOULD TELL YOU...
HUH?! WHY NOT?!

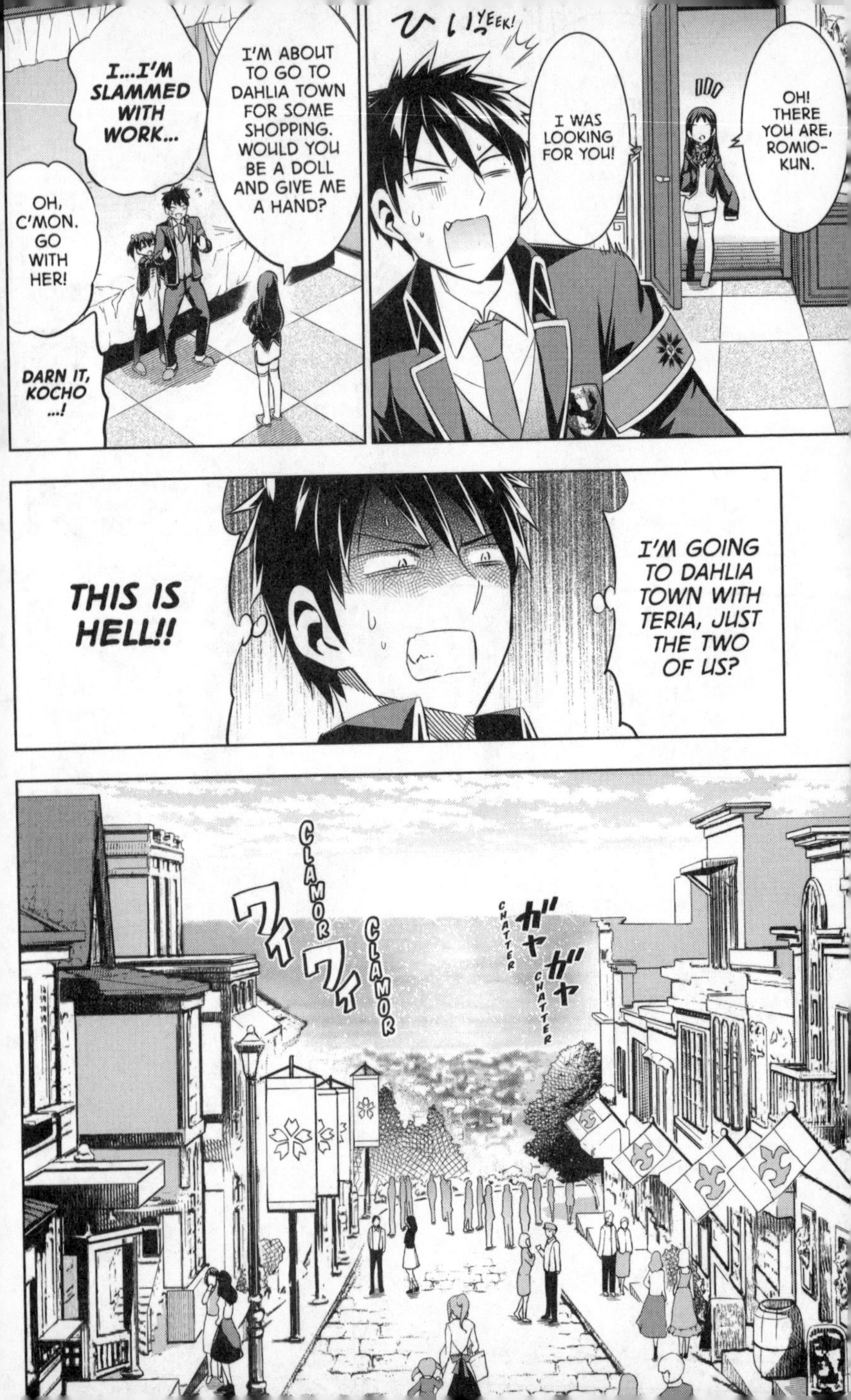
OH! THERE YOU ARE, ROMIO-KUN.
I WAS LOOKING FOR YOU!
ひいっ YEEK!
I'M ABOUT TO GO TO DAHLIA TOWN FOR SOME SHOPPING. WOULD YOU BE A DOLL AND GIVE ME A HAND?
I...I'M SLAMMED WITH WORK...
OH, C'MON. GO WITH HER!
DARN IT, KOCHO ...!
I'M GOING TO DAHLIA TOWN WITH TERIA, JUST THE TWO OF US?
THIS IS HELL!!
ガヤ CHATTER
ガヤ CHATTER
ワイ CLAMOR
ワイ CLAMOR

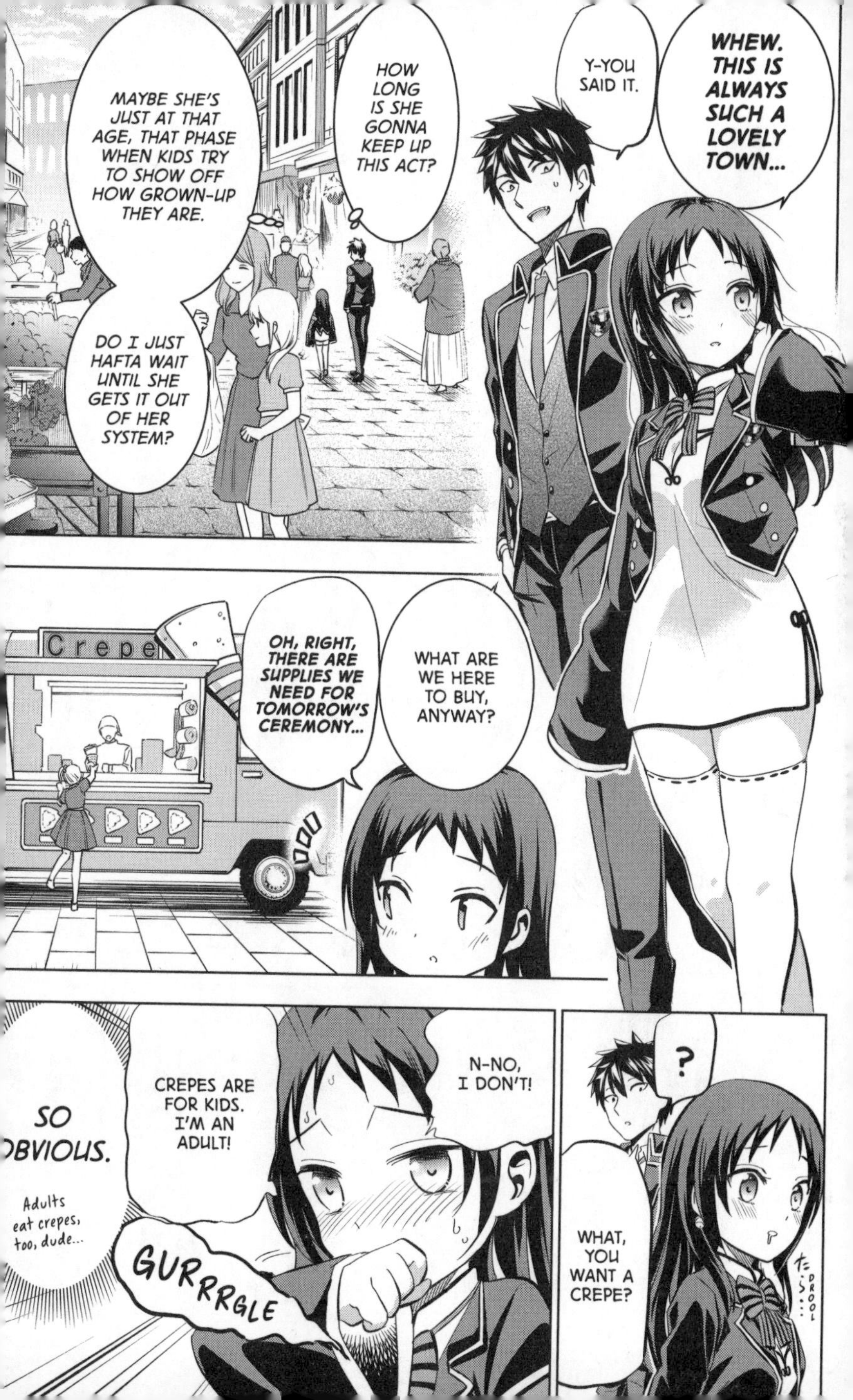
WHEW. THIS IS ALWAYS SUCH A LOVELY TOWN...
Y-YOU SAID IT.
HOW LONG IS SHE GONNA KEEP UP THIS ACT?
MAYBE SHE'S JUST AT THAT AGE, THAT PHASE WHEN KIDS TRY TO SHOW OFF HOW GROWN-UP THEY ARE.
DO I JUST HAFTA WAIT UNTIL SHE GETS IT OUT OF HER SYSTEM?
WHAT ARE WE HERE TO BUY, ANYWAY?
OH, RIGHT, THERE ARE SUPPLIES WE NEED FOR TOMORROW'S CEREMONY...
Crepe
?
WHAT, YOU WANT A CREPE?
DROOL
N-NO, I DON'T!
CREPES ARE FOR KIDS. I'M AN ADULT!
GURRRGLE
SO
BVIOUS.
Adults eat crepes, too, dude...

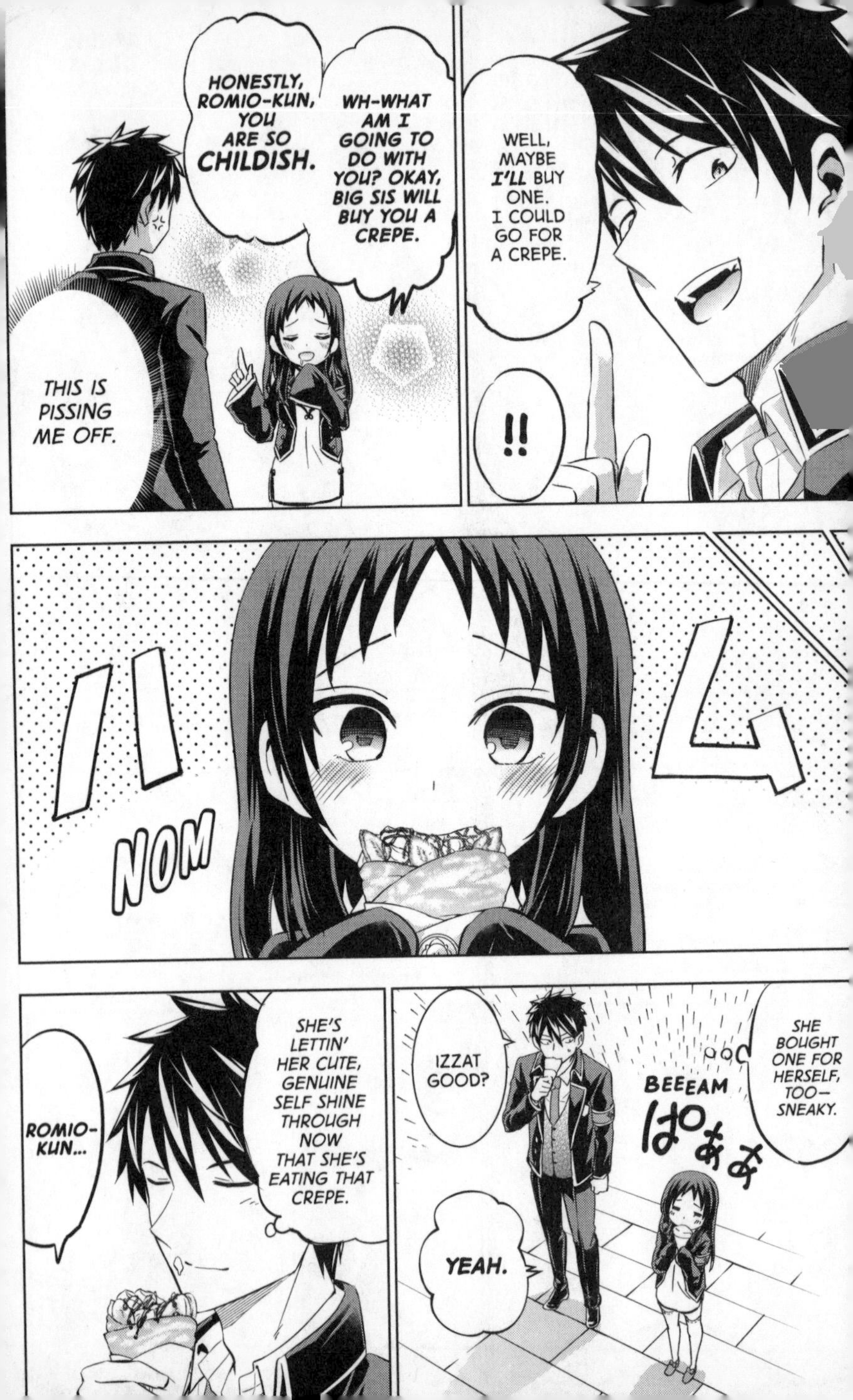
WELL, MAYBE I'LL BUY ONE. I COULD GO FOR A CREPE.
!!
WH-WHAT AM I GOING TO DO WITH YOU? OKAY, BIG SIS WILL BUY YOU A CREPE.
HONESTLY, ROMIO-KUN, YOU ARE SO CHILDISH.
THIS IS PISSING ME OFF.
ハム
NOM
SHE BOUGHT ONE FOR HERSELF, TOO—SNEAKY.
BEEEAM
ぱあぁ
IZZAT GOOD?
YEAH.
SHE'S LETTIN' HER CUTE, GENUINE SELF SHINE THROUGH NOW THAT SHE'S EATING THAT CREPE.
ROMIO-KUN...

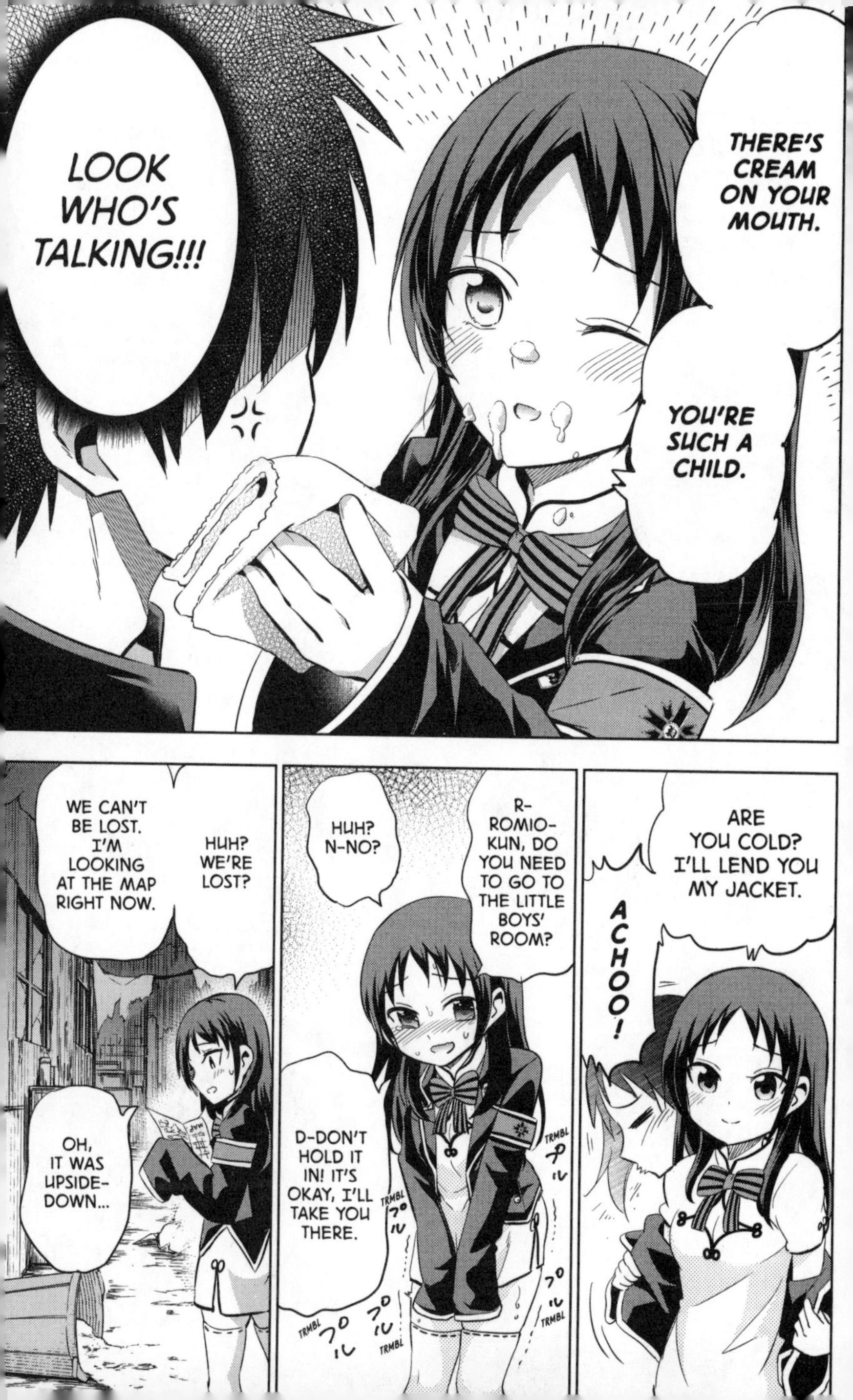
THERE'S CREAM ON YOUR MOUTH.
YOU'RE SUCH A CHILD.
LOOK WHO'S TALKING!!!
ARE YOU COLD? I'LL LEND YOU MY JACKET.
ACHOO!
R-ROMIO-KUN, DO YOU NEED TO GO TO THE LITTLE BOYS' ROOM?
HUH? N-NO?
TRMBL
D-DON'T HOLD IT IN! IT'S OKAY, I'LL TAKE YOU THERE.
TRMBL
TRMBL
TRMBL
TRMBL
HUH? WE'RE LOST?
WE CAN'T BE LOST. I'M LOOKING AT THE MAP RIGHT NOW.
OH, IT WAS UPSIDE-DOWN...

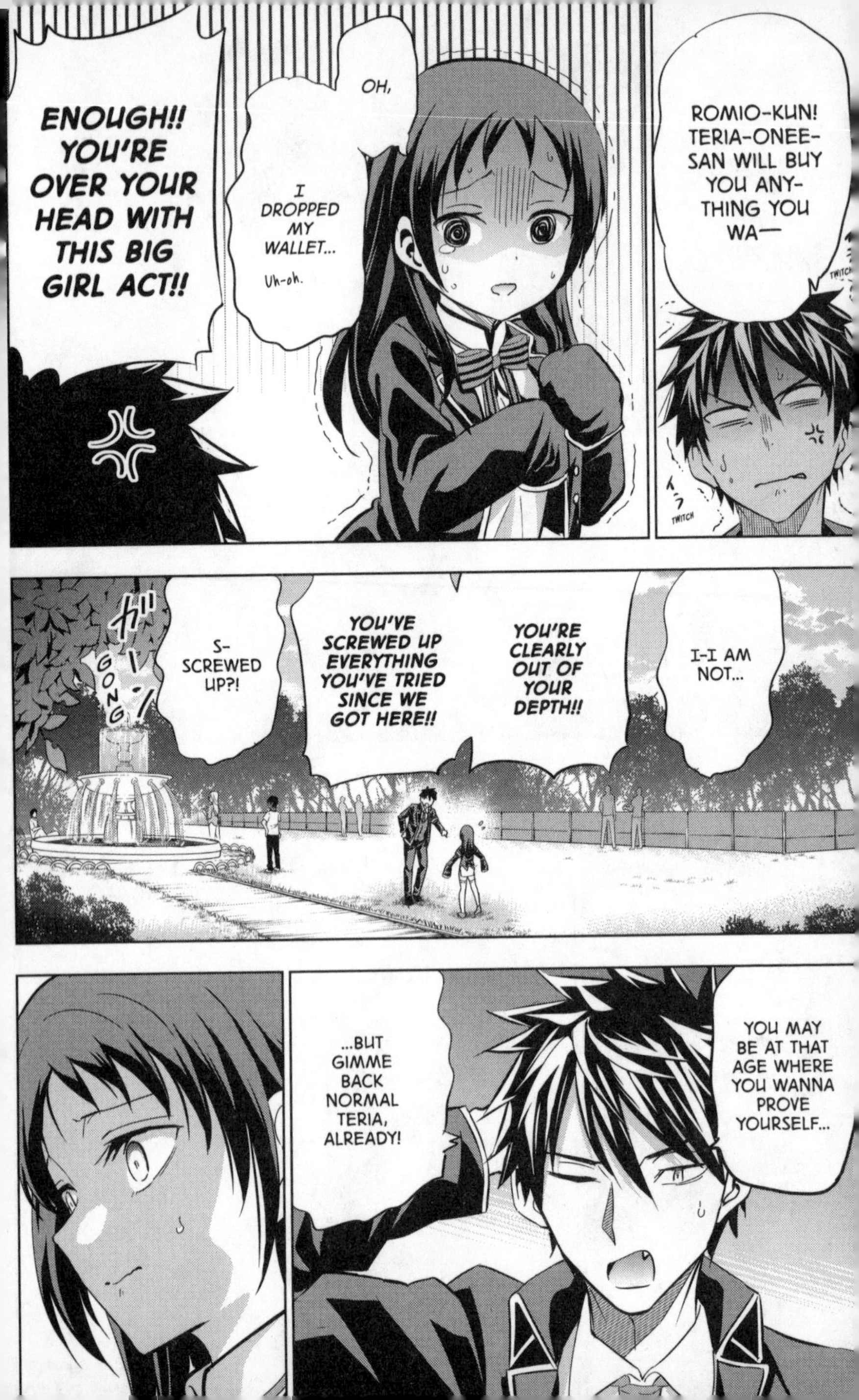
ROMIO-KUN! TERIA-ONEE-SAN WILL BUY YOU ANY-THING YOU WA—
TWITCH
TWITCH
OH,
I DROPPED MY WALLET...
Uh-oh.
ENOUGH!! YOU'RE OVER YOUR HEAD WITH THIS BIG GIRL ACT!!
I-I AM NOT...
YOU'RE CLEARLY OUT OF YOUR DEPTH!!
YOU'VE SCREWED UP EVERYTHING YOU'VE TRIED SINCE WE GOT HERE!!
S-SCREWED UP?!
GONG
YOU MAY BE AT THAT AGE WHERE YOU WANNA PROVE YOURSELF...
...BUT GIMME BACK NORMAL TERIA, ALREADY!

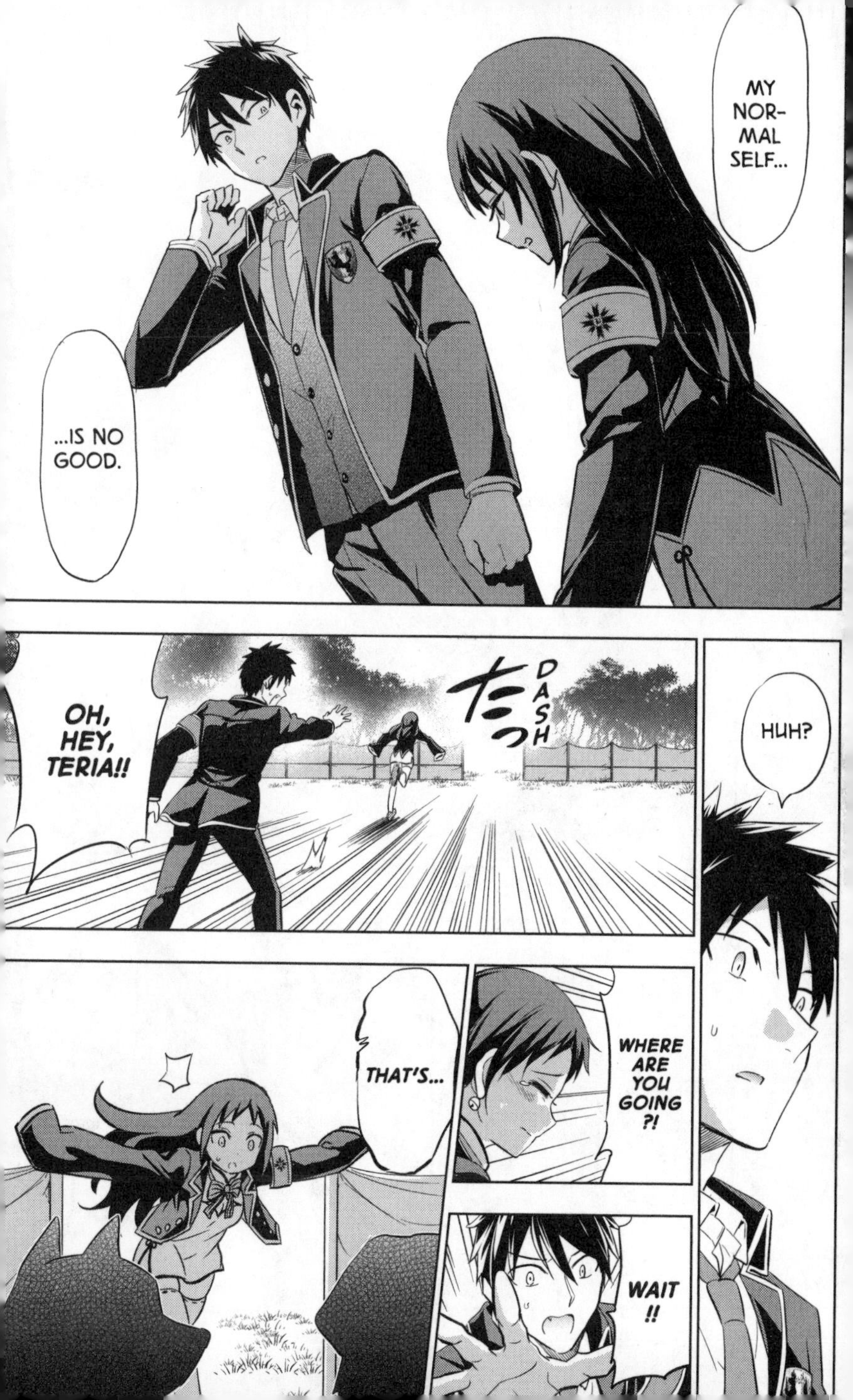
MY NOR-
MAL
SELF...
...IS NO
GOOD.
HUH?
OH,
HEY,
TERIA!!
DASH
WHERE
ARE
YOU
GOING
?!
WAIT
!!
THAT'S...

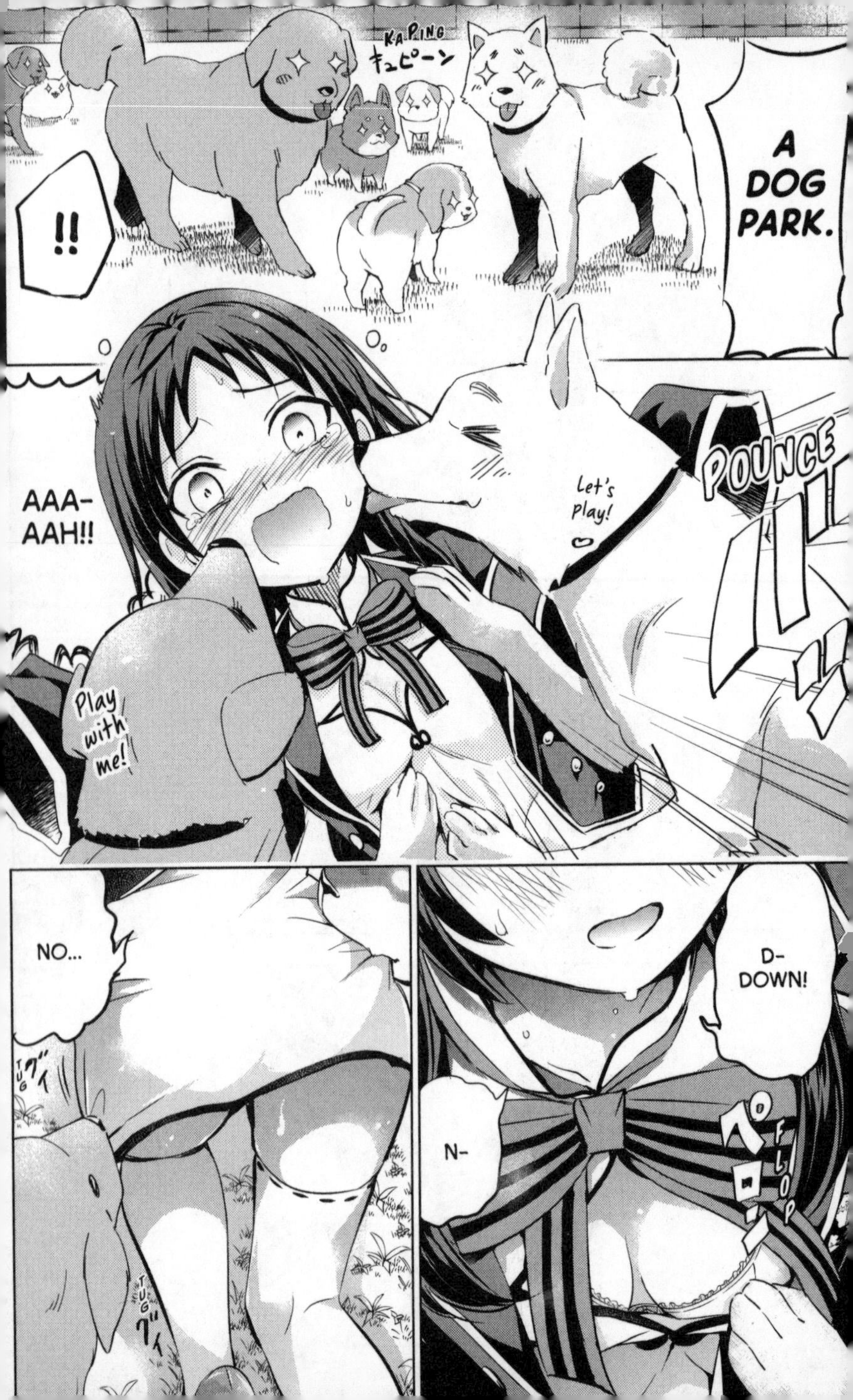

A DOG PARK.
KA-PING
キュピーン
!!
POUNCE
Let's play!
AAA-AAH!!
Play with me!
D-DOWN!
FLOP
ペロー
N-
NO...
TUG
グイ
TUG
グイ

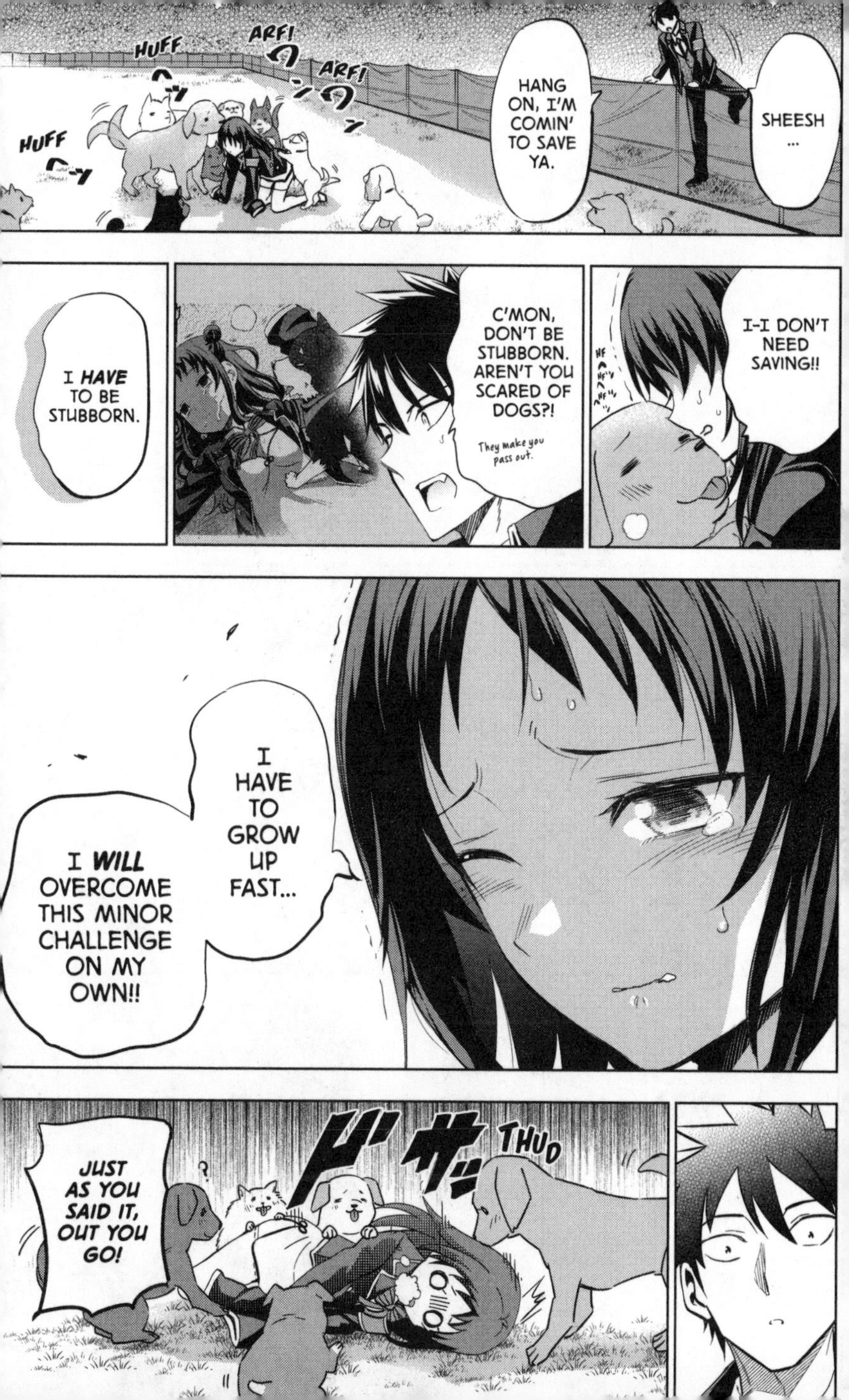
SHEESH ...
HANG ON, I'M COMIN' TO SAVE YA.
ARF!
ARF!
HUFF
HUFF
I-I DON'T NEED SAVING!!
HF HF HF
C'MON, DON'T BE STUBBORN. AREN'T YOU SCARED OF DOGS?!
They make you pass out.
I *HAVE* TO BE STUBBORN.
I HAVE TO GROW UP FAST...
I *WILL* OVERCOME THIS MINOR CHALLENGE ON MY OWN!!
THUD
JUST AS YOU SAID IT, OUT YOU GO!

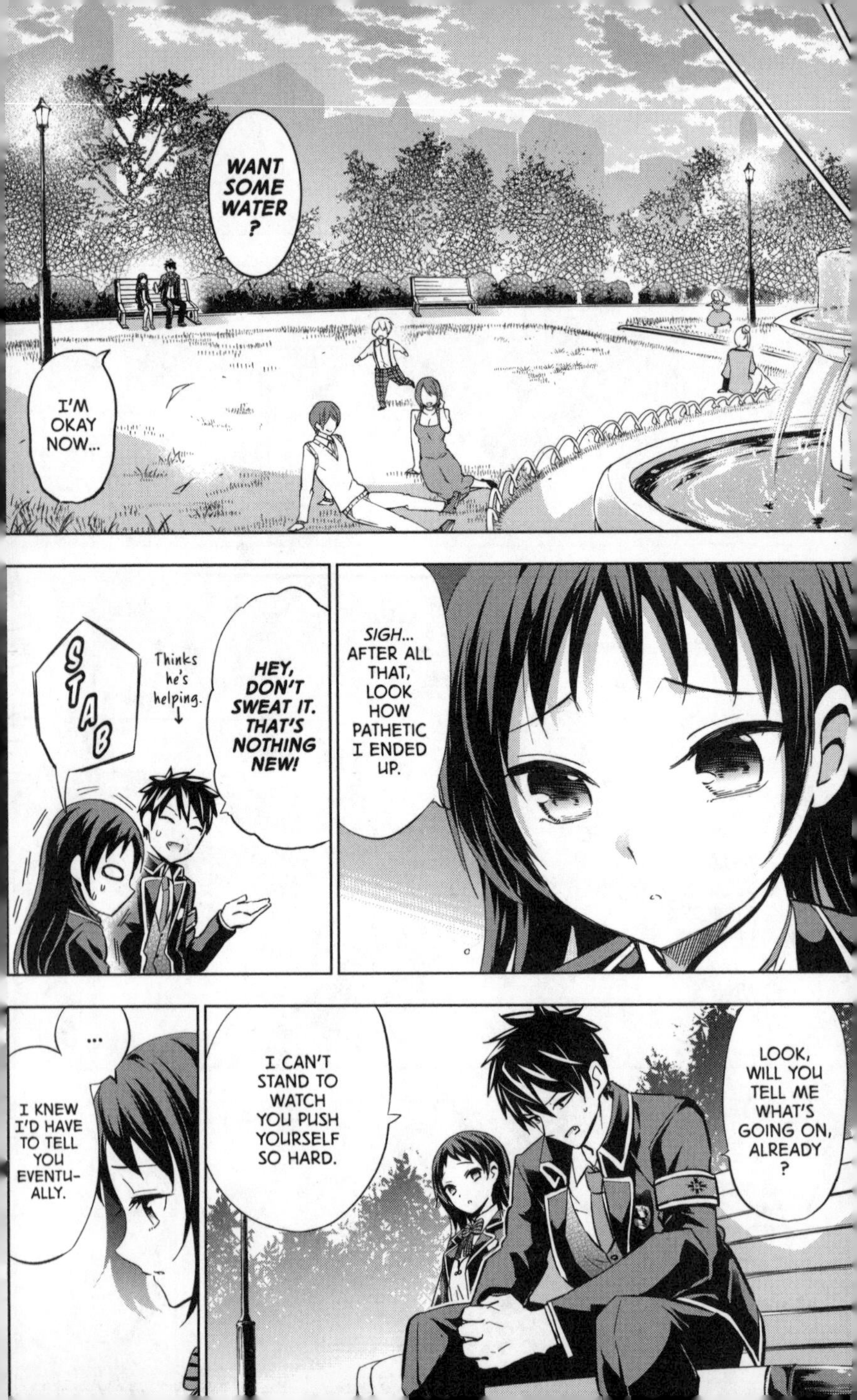
WANT SOME WATER?
I'M OKAY NOW...
SIGH... AFTER ALL THAT, LOOK HOW PATHETIC I ENDED UP.
HEY, DON'T SWEAT IT. THAT'S NOTHING NEW!
Thinks he's helping.
STAB
LOOK, WILL YOU TELL ME WHAT'S GOING ON, ALREADY?
I CAN'T STAND TO WATCH YOU PUSH YOURSELF SO HARD.
...
I KNEW I'D HAVE TO TELL YOU EVENTU-ALLY.

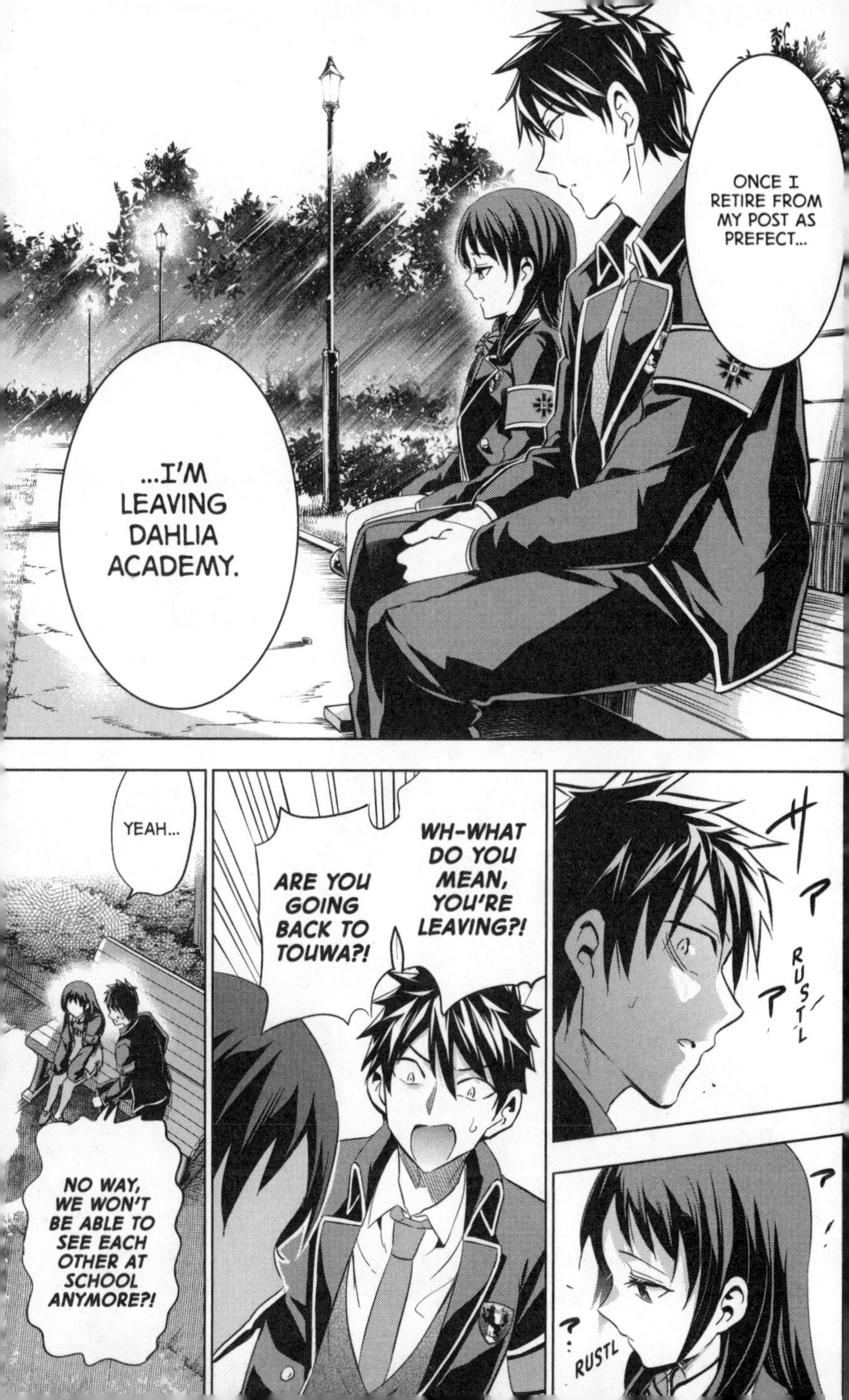
ONCE I RETIRE FROM MY POST AS PREFECT...
...I'M LEAVING DAHLIA ACADEMY.
RUSTL
RUSTL
WH-WHAT DO YOU MEAN, YOU'RE LEAVING?!
ARE YOU GOING BACK TO TOUWA?!
YEAH...
NO WAY, WE WON'T BE ABLE TO SEE EACH OTHER AT SCHOOL ANYMORE?!

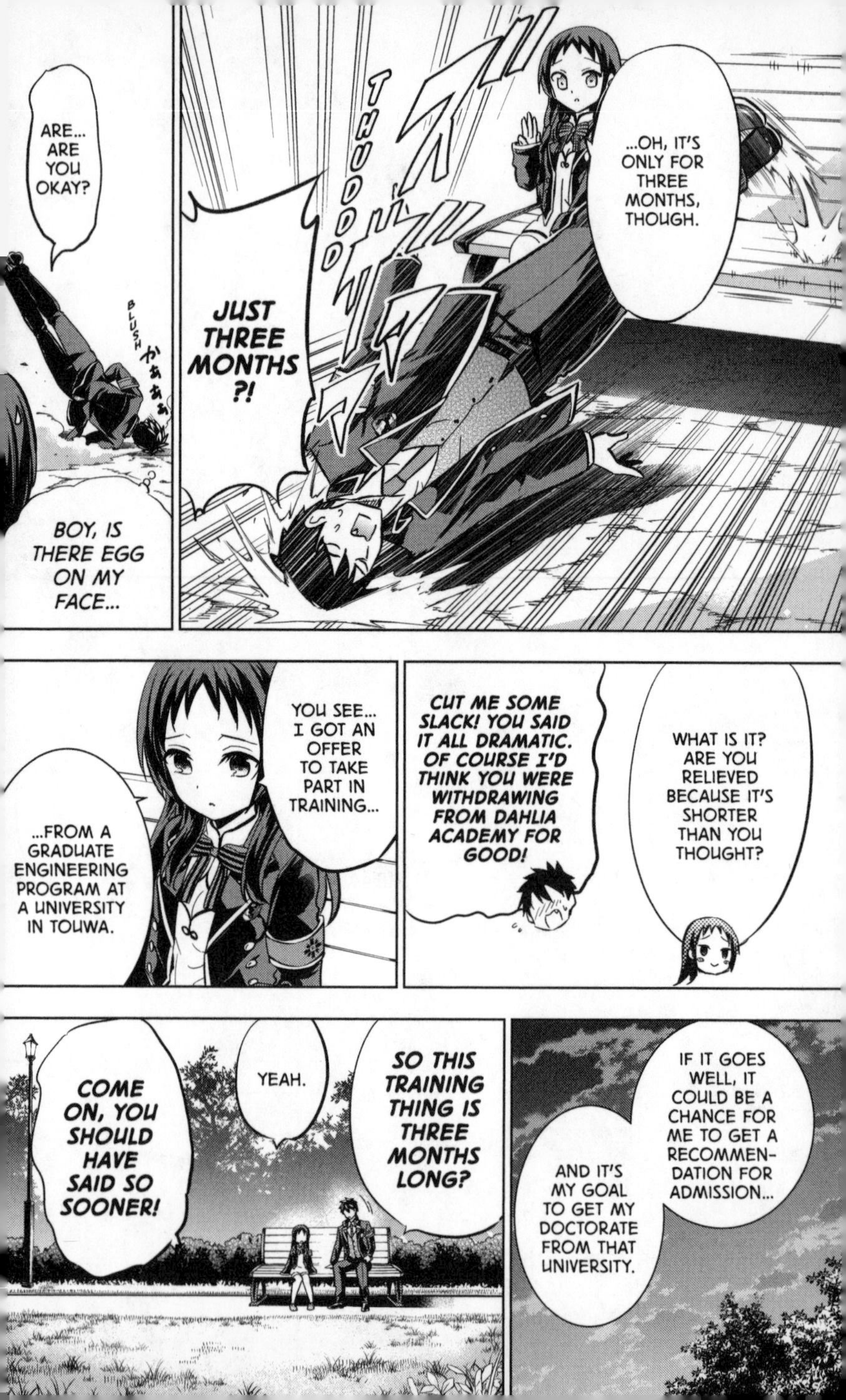
...OH, IT'S ONLY FOR THREE MONTHS, THOUGH.
THUDDDD
JUST THREE MONTHS ?!
ARE... ARE YOU OKAY?
BLUSH
BOY, IS THERE EGG ON MY FACE...
WHAT IS IT? ARE YOU RELIEVED BECAUSE IT'S SHORTER THAN YOU THOUGHT?
CUT ME SOME SLACK! YOU SAID IT ALL DRAMATIC. OF COURSE I'D THINK YOU WERE WITHDRAWING FROM DAHLIA ACADEMY FOR GOOD!
YOU SEE... I GOT AN OFFER TO TAKE PART IN TRAINING...
...FROM A GRADUATE ENGINEERING PROGRAM AT A UNIVERSITY IN TOUWA.
IF IT GOES WELL, IT COULD BE A CHANCE FOR ME TO GET A RECOMMEN-DATION FOR ADMISSION...
AND IT'S MY GOAL TO GET MY DOCTORATE FROM THAT UNIVERSITY.
SO THIS TRAINING THING IS THREE MONTHS LONG?
YEAH.
COME ON, YOU SHOULD HAVE SAID SO SOONER!

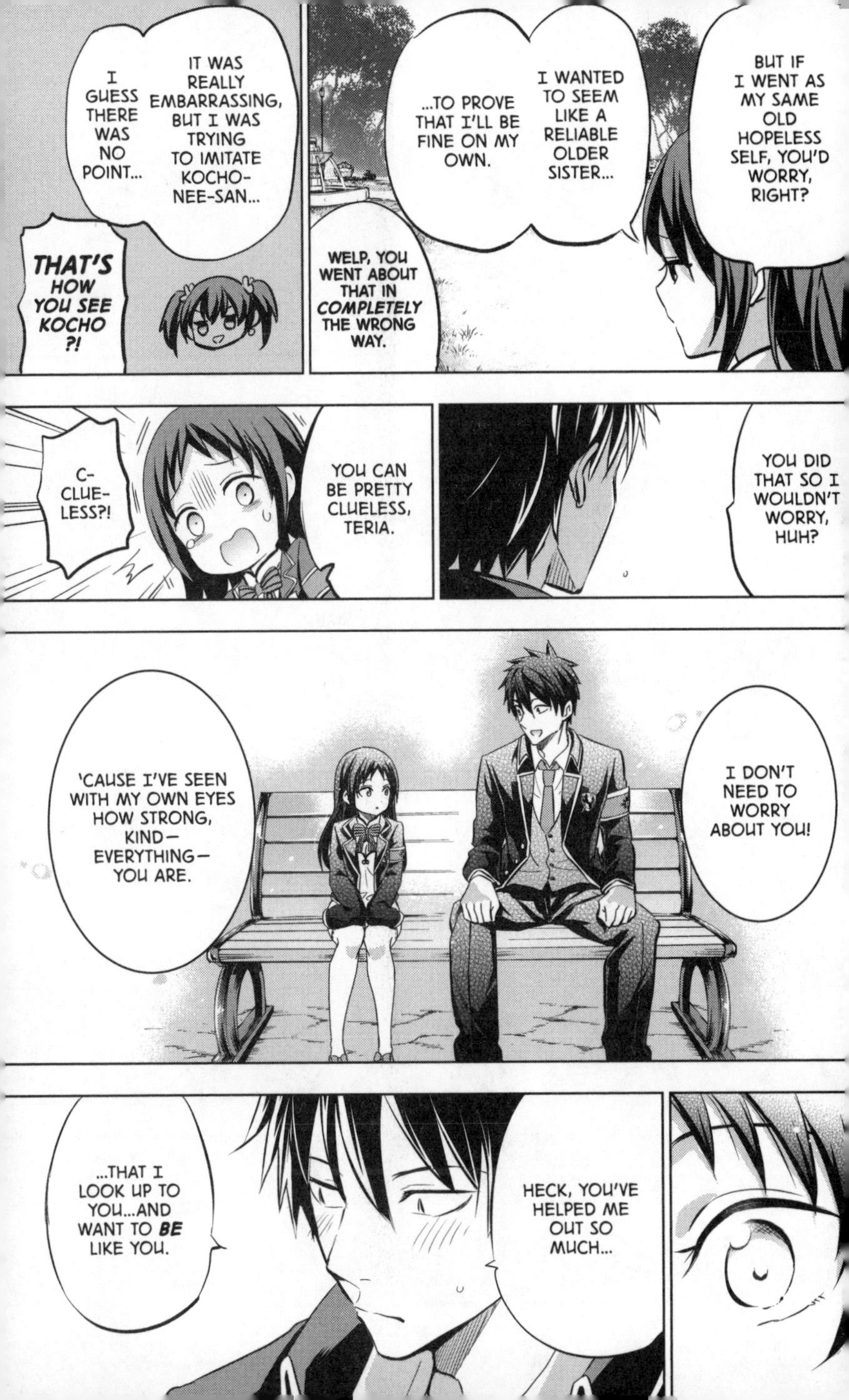
BUT IF I WENT AS MY SAME OLD HOPELESS SELF, YOU'D WORRY, RIGHT?
I WANTED TO SEEM LIKE A RELIABLE OLDER SISTER...
...TO PROVE THAT I'LL BE FINE ON MY OWN.
WELP, YOU WENT ABOUT THAT IN *COMPLETELY* THE WRONG WAY.
IT WAS REALLY EMBARRASSING, BUT I WAS TRYING TO IMITATE KOCHO-NEE-SAN...
I GUESS THERE WAS NO POINT...
***THAT'S** HOW YOU SEE KOCHO ?!*
YOU DID THAT SO I WOULDN'T WORRY, HUH?
YOU CAN BE PRETTY CLUELESS, TERIA.
C-CLUELESS?!
I DON'T NEED TO WORRY ABOUT YOU!
'CAUSE I'VE SEEN WITH MY OWN EYES HOW STRONG, KIND—EVERYTHING—YOU ARE.
HECK, YOU'VE HELPED ME OUT SO MUCH...
...THAT I LOOK UP TO YOU...AND WANT TO ***BE*** LIKE YOU.

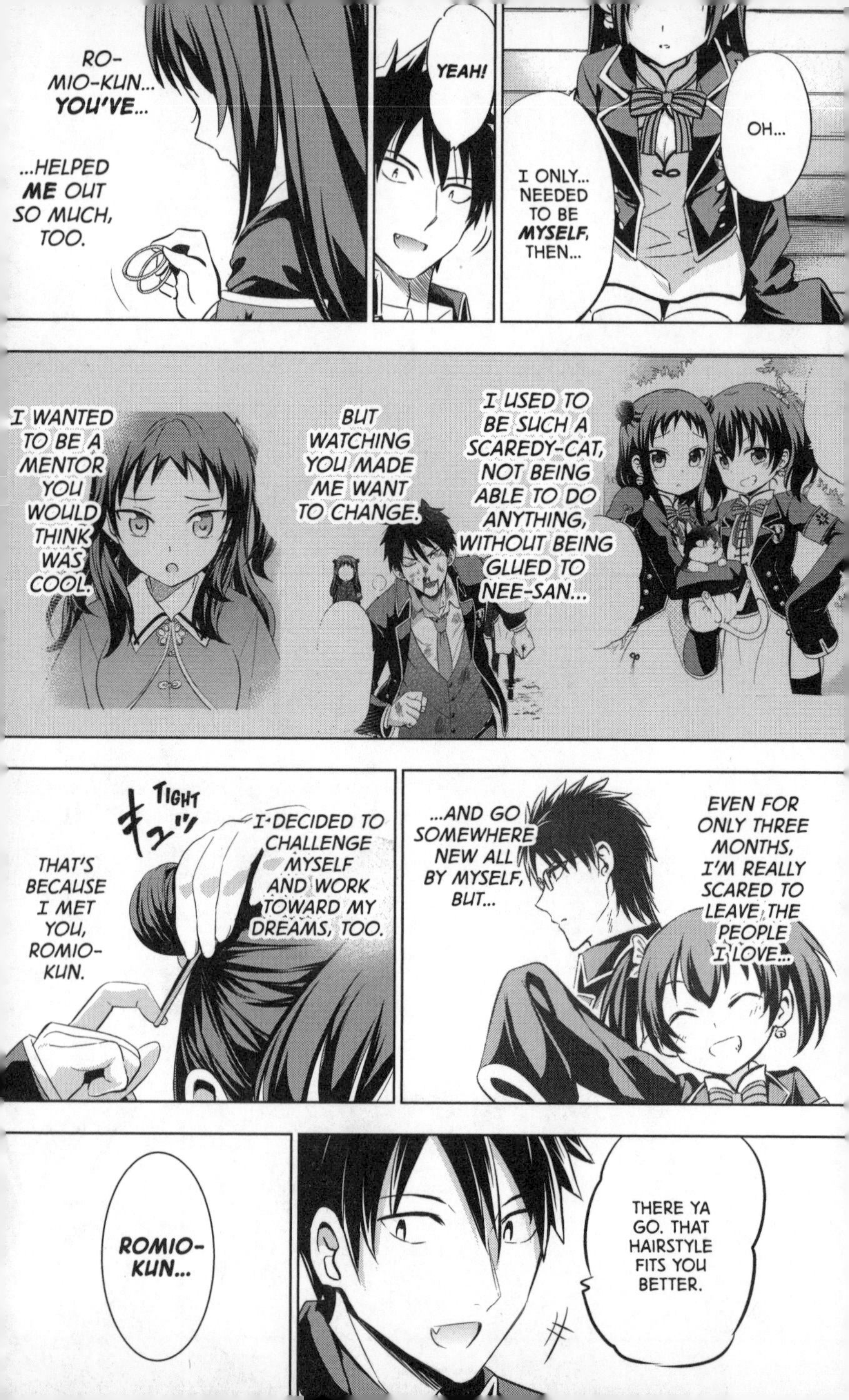
OH...
I ONLY... NEEDED TO BE MYSELF, THEN...
YEAH!
RO-MIO-KUN... YOU'VE...
...HELPED ME OUT SO MUCH, TOO.
I USED TO BE SUCH A SCAREDY-CAT, NOT BEING ABLE TO DO ANYTHING, WITHOUT BEING GLUED TO NEE-SAN...
BUT WATCHING YOU MADE ME WANT TO CHANGE.
I WANTED TO BE A MENTOR YOU WOULD THINK WAS COOL.
EVEN FOR ONLY THREE MONTHS, I'M REALLY SCARED TO LEAVE THE PEOPLE I LOVE...
...AND GO SOMEWHERE NEW ALL BY MYSELF, BUT...
I DECIDED TO CHALLENGE MYSELF AND WORK TOWARD MY DREAMS, TOO.
TIGHT
THAT'S BECAUSE I MET YOU, ROMIO-KUN.
THERE YA GO. THAT HAIRSTYLE FITS YOU BETTER.
ROMIO-KUN...

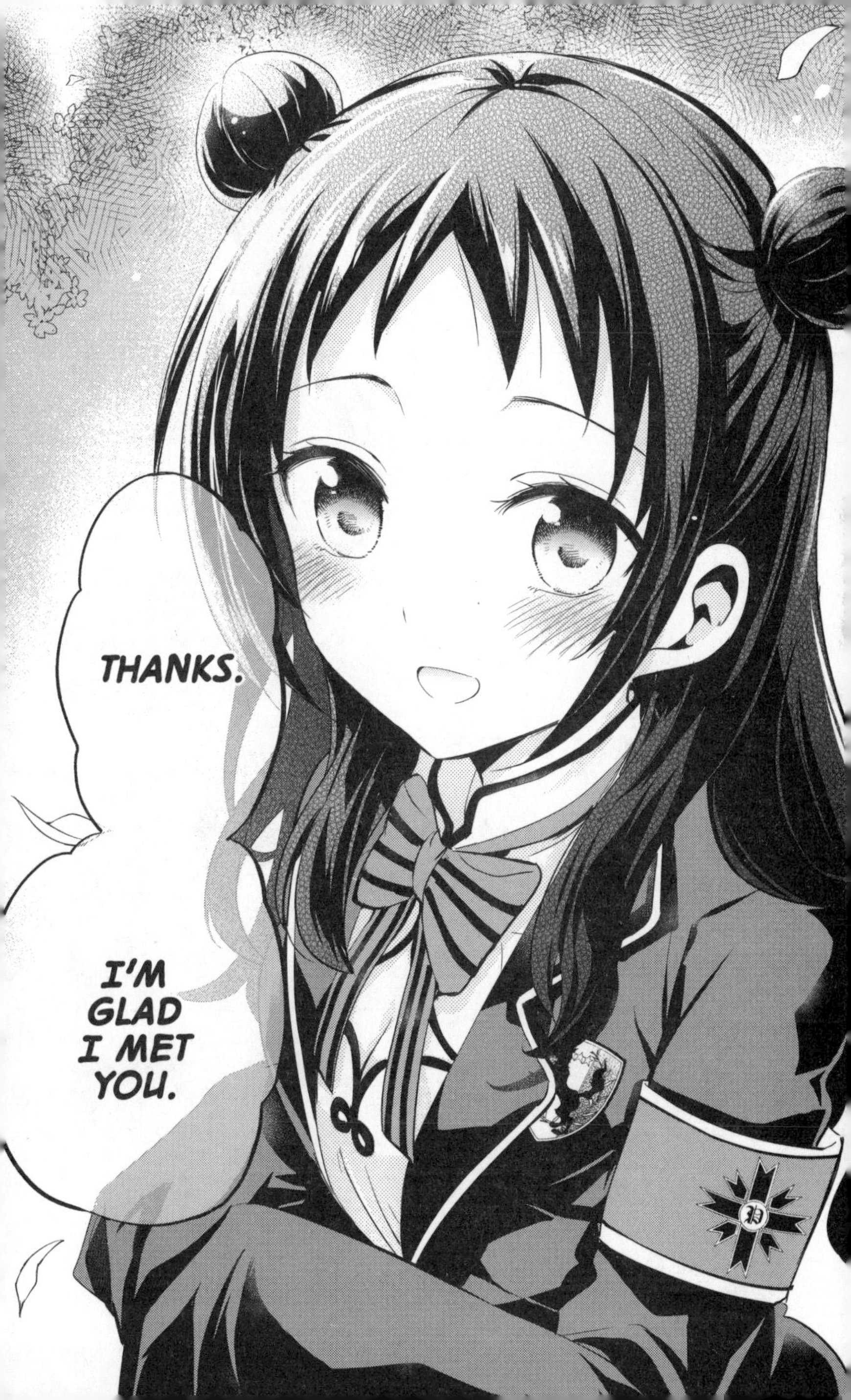
THANKS.
I'M GLAD I MET YOU.

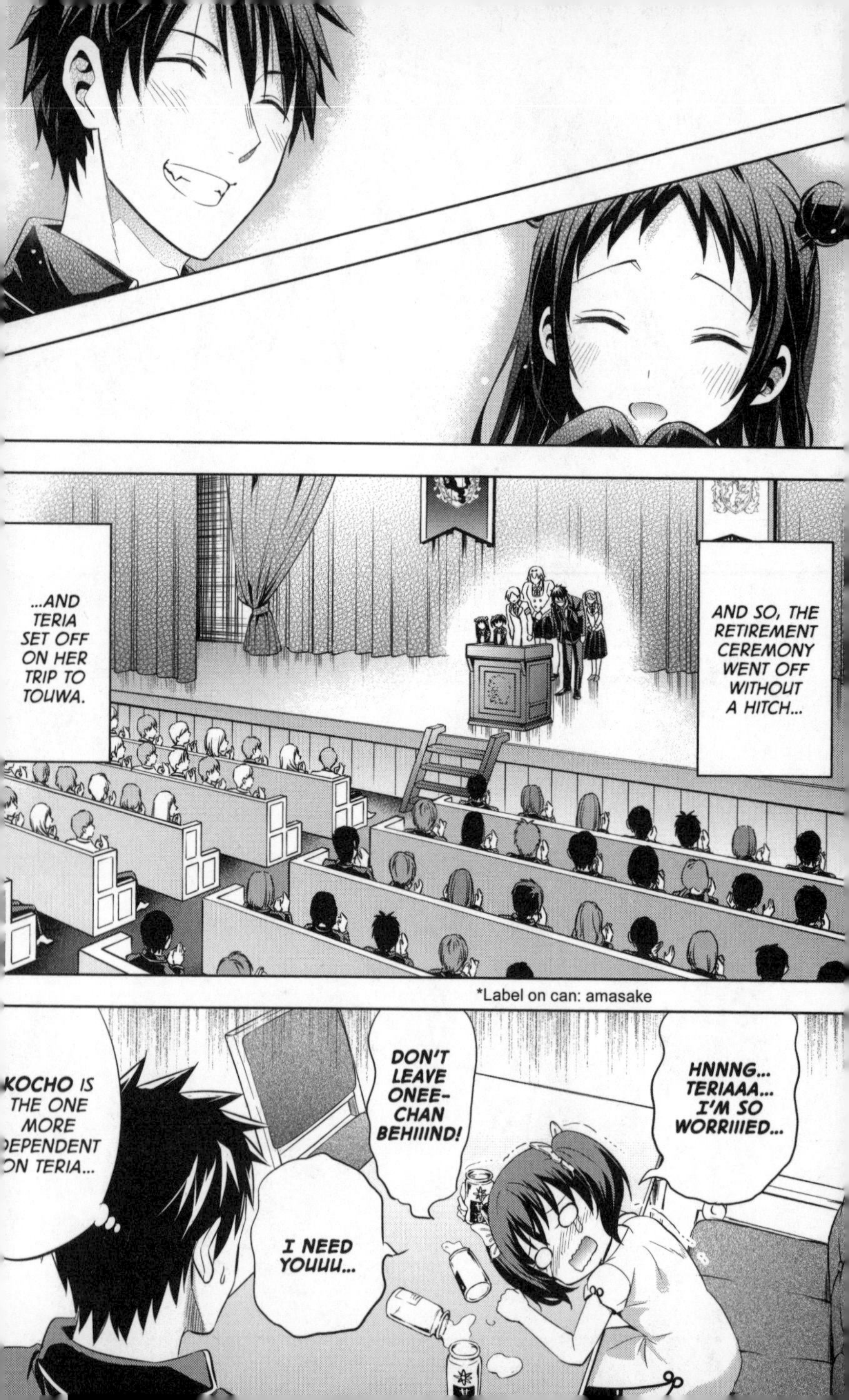
AND SO, THE RETIREMENT CEREMONY WENT OFF WITHOUT A HITCH...
...AND TERIA SET OFF ON HER TRIP TO TOUWA.
*Label on can: amasake
HNNNG... TERIAAA... I'M SO WORRIIIED...
DON'T LEAVE ONEE-CHAN BEHIIIND!
I NEED YOUUU...
KOCHO IS THE ONE MORE DEPENDENT ON TERIA...

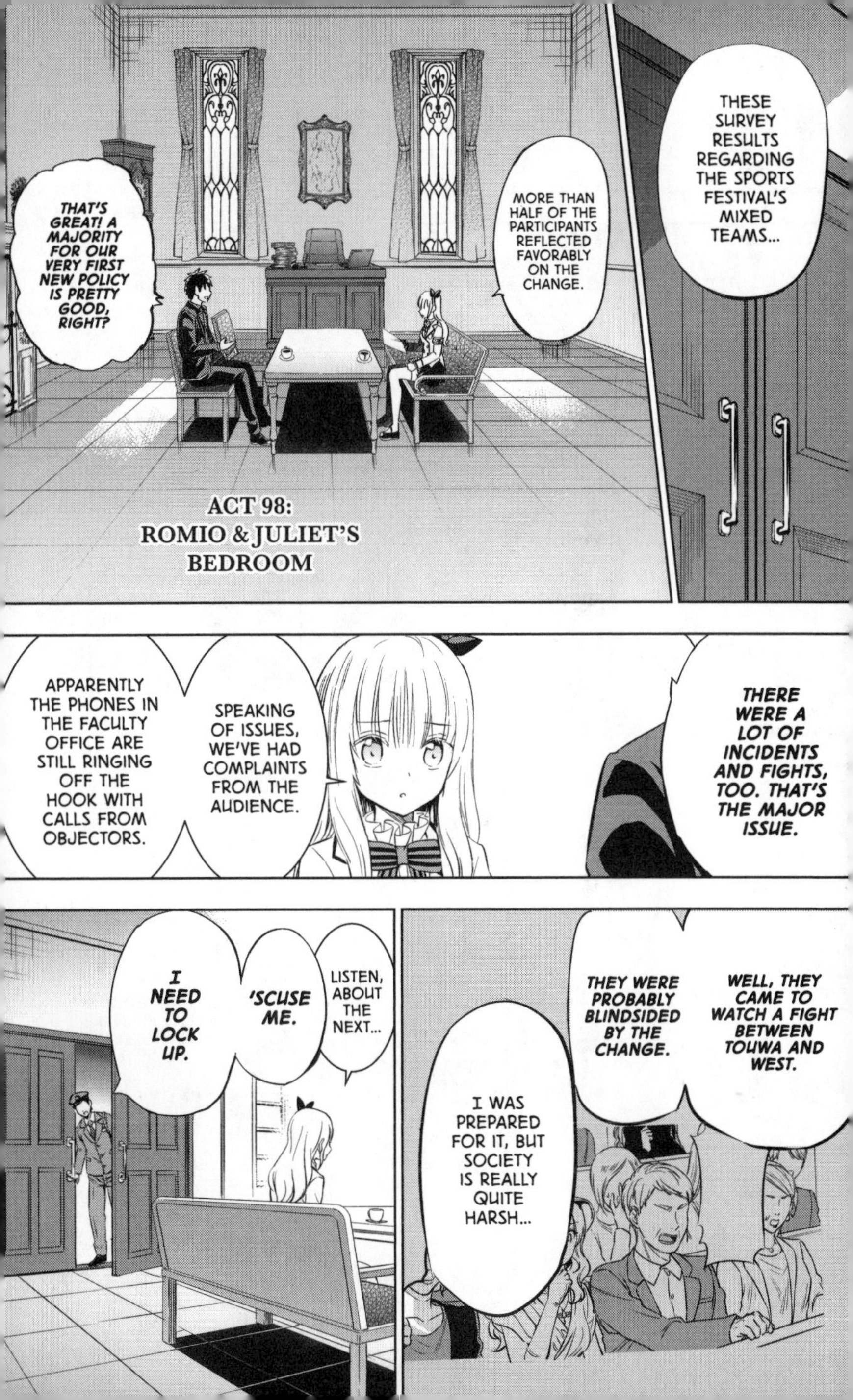
THESE SURVEY RESULTS REGARDING THE SPORTS FESTIVAL'S MIXED TEAMS...
MORE THAN HALF OF THE PARTICIPANTS REFLECTED FAVORABLY ON THE CHANGE.
THAT'S GREAT! A MAJORITY FOR OUR VERY FIRST NEW POLICY IS PRETTY GOOD, RIGHT?
ACT 98: ROMIO & JULIET'S BEDROOM
THERE WERE A LOT OF INCIDENTS AND FIGHTS, TOO. THAT'S THE MAJOR ISSUE.
SPEAKING OF ISSUES, WE'VE HAD COMPLAINTS FROM THE AUDIENCE.
APPARENTLY THE PHONES IN THE FACULTY OFFICE ARE STILL RINGING OFF THE HOOK WITH CALLS FROM OBJECTORS.
WELL, THEY CAME TO WATCH A FIGHT BETWEEN TOUWA AND WEST.
THEY WERE PROBABLY BLINDSIDED BY THE CHANGE.
I WAS PREPARED FOR IT, BUT SOCIETY IS REALLY QUITE HARSH...
LISTEN, ABOUT THE NEXT...
'SCUSE ME.
I NEED TO LOCK UP.

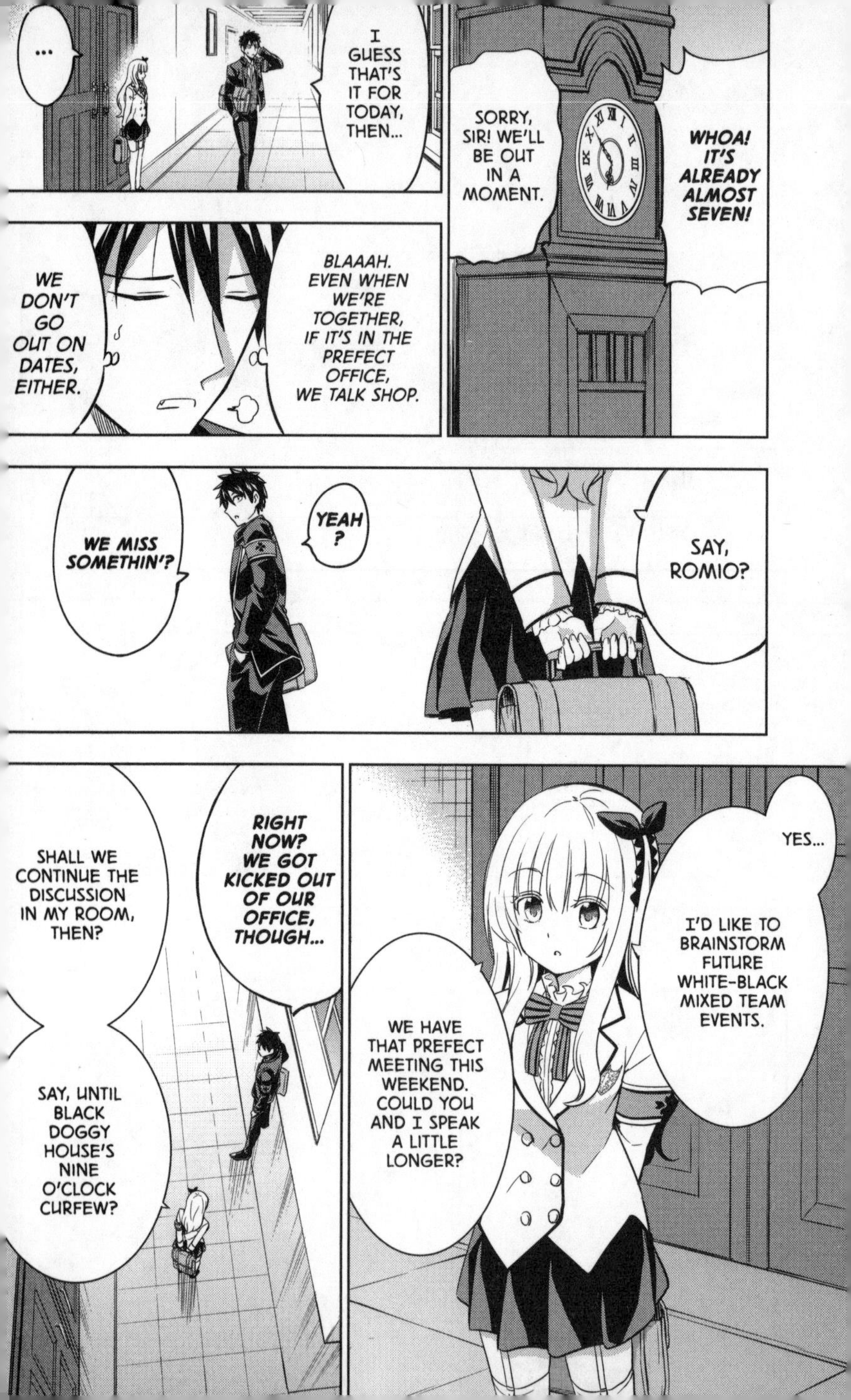
WHOA! IT'S ALREADY ALMOST SEVEN!
SORRY, SIR! WE'LL BE OUT IN A MOMENT.
I GUESS THAT'S IT FOR TODAY, THEN...
...
BLAAAH. EVEN WHEN WE'RE TOGETHER, IF IT'S IN THE PREFECT OFFICE, WE TALK SHOP.
WE DON'T GO OUT ON DATES, EITHER.
SAY, ROMIO?
YEAH?
WE MISS SOMETHIN'?
YES...
I'D LIKE TO BRAINSTORM FUTURE WHITE-BLACK MIXED TEAM EVENTS.
WE HAVE THAT PREFECT MEETING THIS WEEKEND. COULD YOU AND I SPEAK A LITTLE LONGER?
RIGHT NOW? WE GOT KICKED OUT OF OUR OFFICE, THOUGH...
SHALL WE CONTINUE THE DISCUSSION IN MY ROOM, THEN?
SAY, UNTIL BLACK DOGGY HOUSE'S NINE O'CLOCK CURFEW?

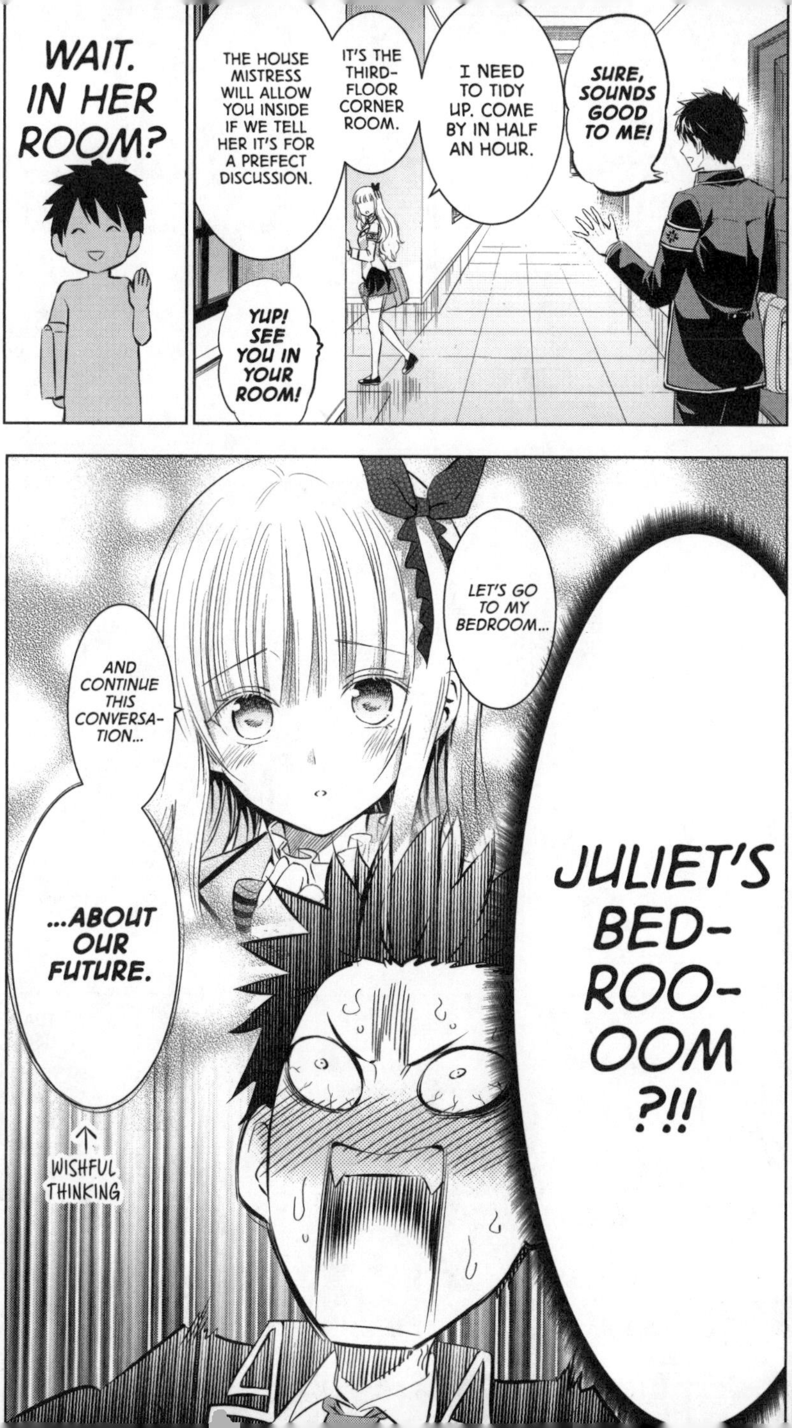
SURE, SOUNDS GOOD TO ME!
I NEED TO TIDY UP. COME BY IN HALF AN HOUR.
IT'S THE THIRD-FLOOR CORNER ROOM.
THE HOUSE MISTRESS WILL ALLOW YOU INSIDE IF WE TELL HER IT'S FOR A PREFECT DISCUSSION.
YUP! SEE YOU IN YOUR ROOM!
WAIT. IN HER ROOM?
LET'S GO TO MY BEDROOM...
AND CONTINUE THIS CONVERSATION...
...ABOUT OUR FUTURE.
WISHFUL THINKING
JULIET'S BED-ROOO-OOM?!!

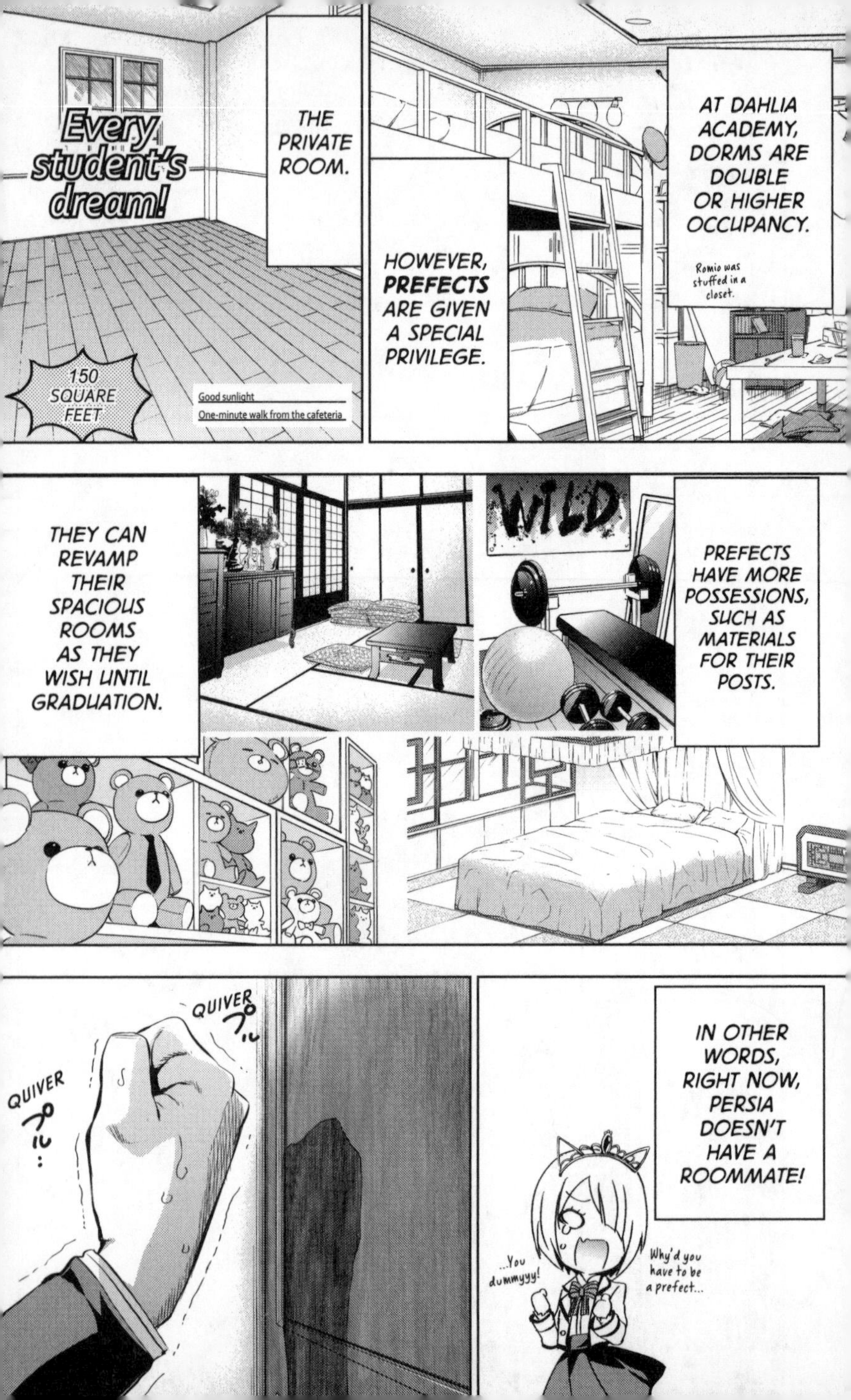
AT DAHLIA ACADEMY, DORMS ARE DOUBLE OR HIGHER OCCUPANCY.
Romio was stuffed in a closet.
HOWEVER, PREFECTS ARE GIVEN A SPECIAL PRIVILEGE.
THE PRIVATE ROOM.
Every student's dream!
150 SQUARE FEET
Good sunlight
One-minute walk from the cafeteria
PREFECTS HAVE MORE POSSESSIONS, SUCH AS MATERIALS FOR THEIR POSTS.
WILD
THEY CAN REVAMP THEIR SPACIOUS ROOMS AS THEY WISH UNTIL GRADUATION.
IN OTHER WORDS, RIGHT NOW, PERSIA DOESN'T HAVE A ROOMMATE!
Why'd you have to be a prefect...
...You dummyyy!
QUIVER
QUIVER

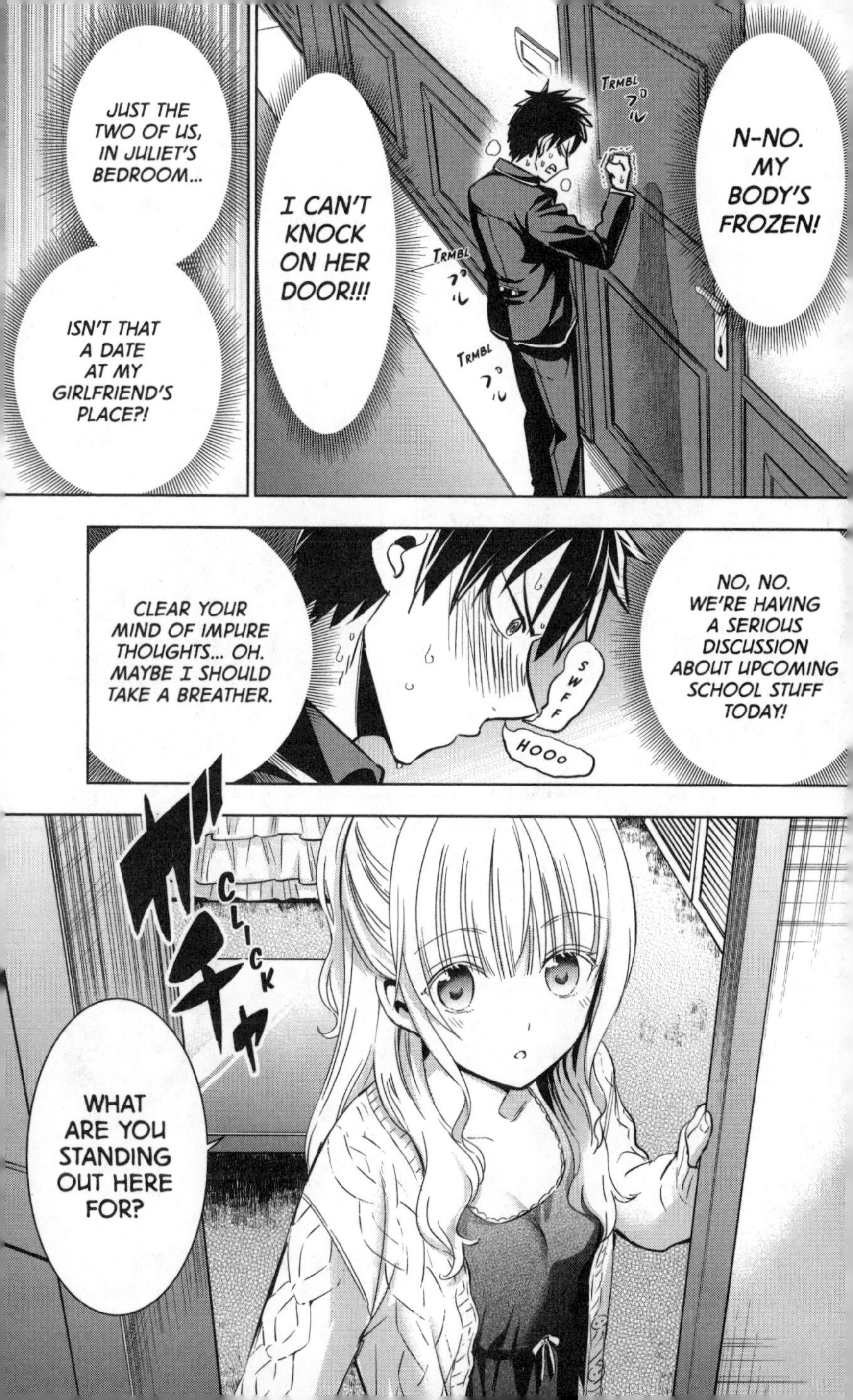
N-NO. MY BODY'S FROZEN!
TRMBL
I CAN'T KNOCK ON HER DOOR!!!
TRMBL
TRMBL
JUST THE TWO OF US, IN JULIET'S BEDROOM...
ISN'T THAT A DATE AT MY GIRLFRIEND'S PLACE?!
NO, NO. WE'RE HAVING A SERIOUS DISCUSSION ABOUT UPCOMING SCHOOL STUFF TODAY!
SWFF
HOOO
CLEAR YOUR MIND OF IMPURE THOUGHTS... OH. MAYBE I SHOULD TAKE A BREATHER.
CLICK
WHAT ARE YOU STANDING OUT HERE FOR?

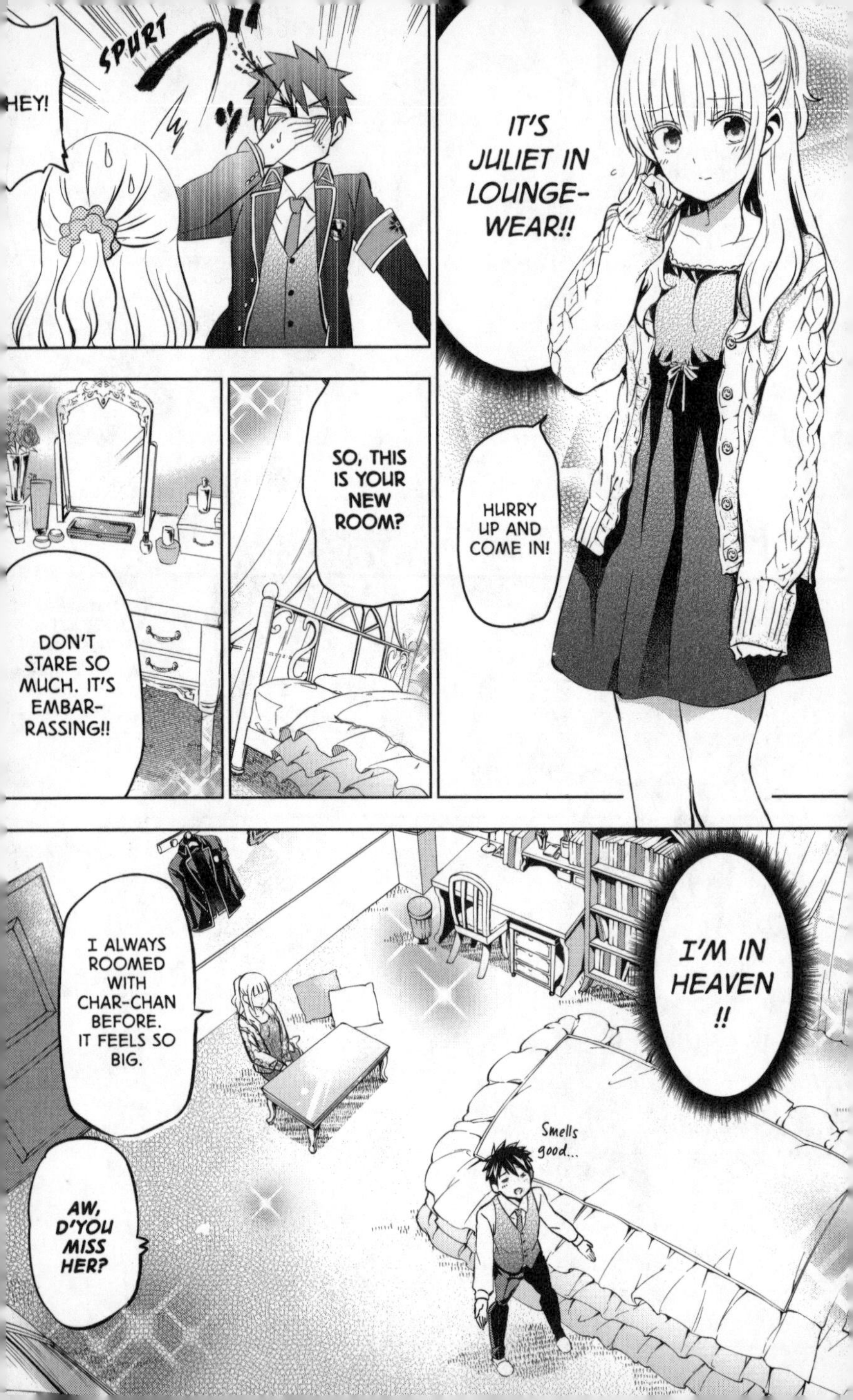
IT'S JULIET IN LOUNGE-WEAR!!
HURRY UP AND COME IN!
SPURT
HEY!
SO, THIS IS YOUR NEW ROOM?
DON'T STARE SO MUCH. IT'S EMBARRASSING!!
I'M IN HEAVEN !!
Smells good...
I ALWAYS ROOMED WITH CHAR-CHAN BEFORE. IT FEELS SO BIG.
AW, D'YOU MISS HER?

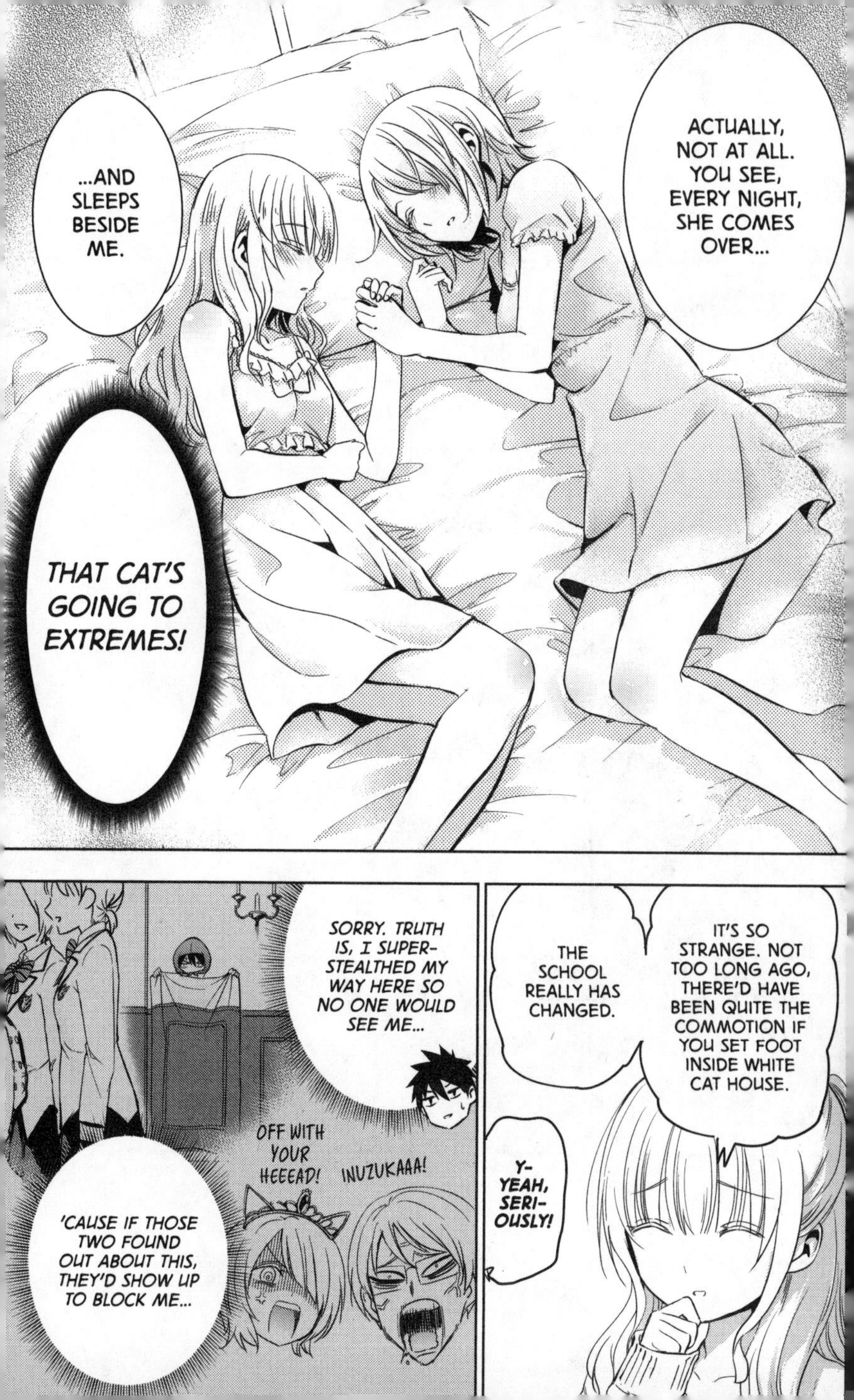
ACTUALLY, NOT AT ALL. YOU SEE, EVERY NIGHT, SHE COMES OVER...
...AND SLEEPS BESIDE ME.
THAT CAT'S GOING TO EXTREMES!
IT'S SO STRANGE. NOT TOO LONG AGO, THERE'D HAVE BEEN QUITE THE COMMOTION IF YOU SET FOOT INSIDE WHITE CAT HOUSE.
THE SCHOOL REALLY HAS CHANGED.
Y-YEAH, SERI-OUSLY!
SORRY. TRUTH IS, I SUPER-STEALTHED MY WAY HERE SO NO ONE WOULD SEE ME...
INUZUKAAA!
OFF WITH YOUR HEEEAD!
'CAUSE IF THOSE TWO FOUND OUT ABOUT THIS, THEY'D SHOW UP TO BLOCK ME...

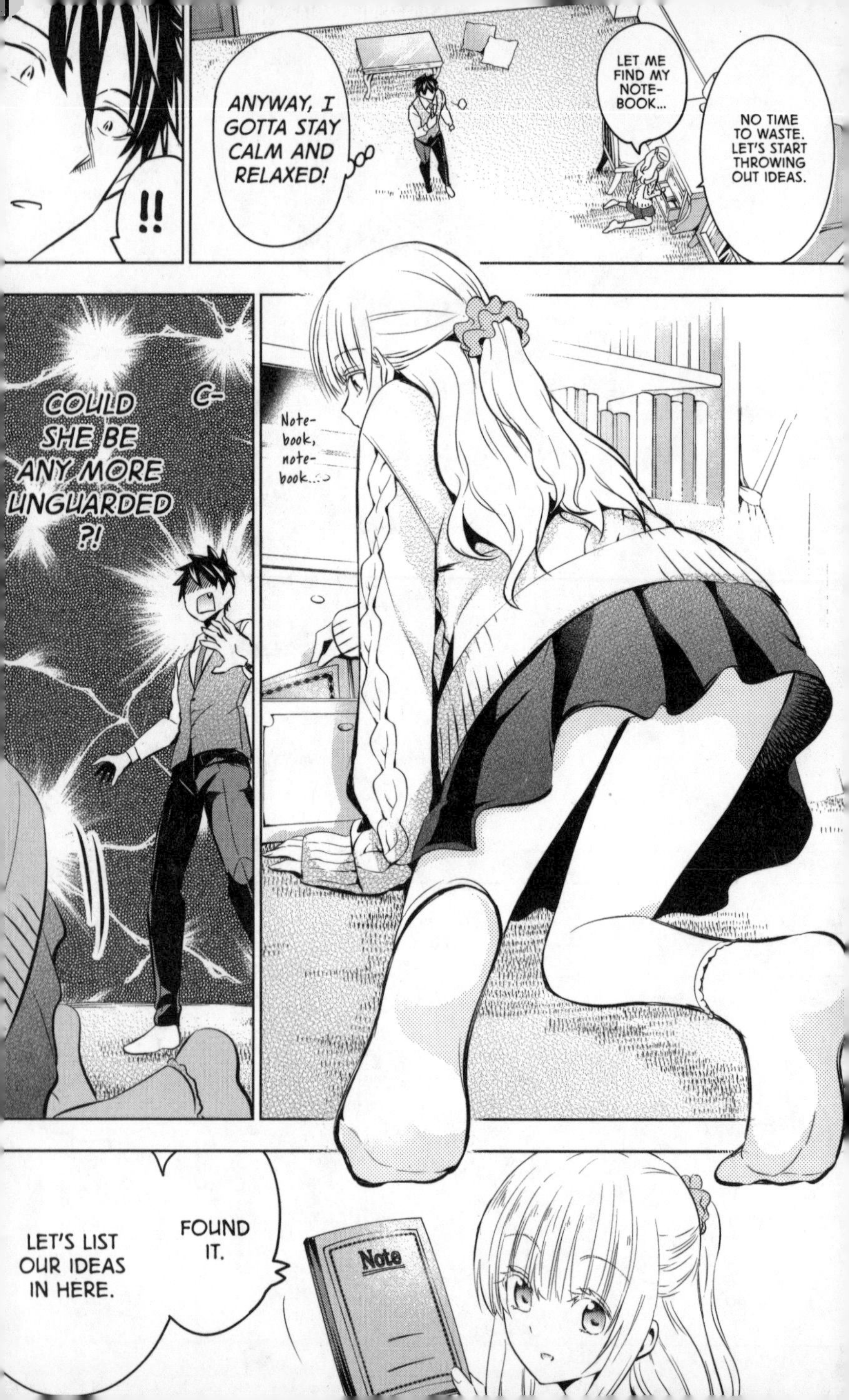
NO TIME TO WASTE. LET'S START THROWING OUT IDEAS.
LET ME FIND MY NOTE-BOOK...
ANYWAY, I GOTTA STAY CALM AND RELAXED!
!!
Note-book, note-book...
C-
COULD SHE BE ANY MORE UNGUARDED ?!
FOUND IT.
LET'S LIST OUR IDEAS IN HERE.
Note

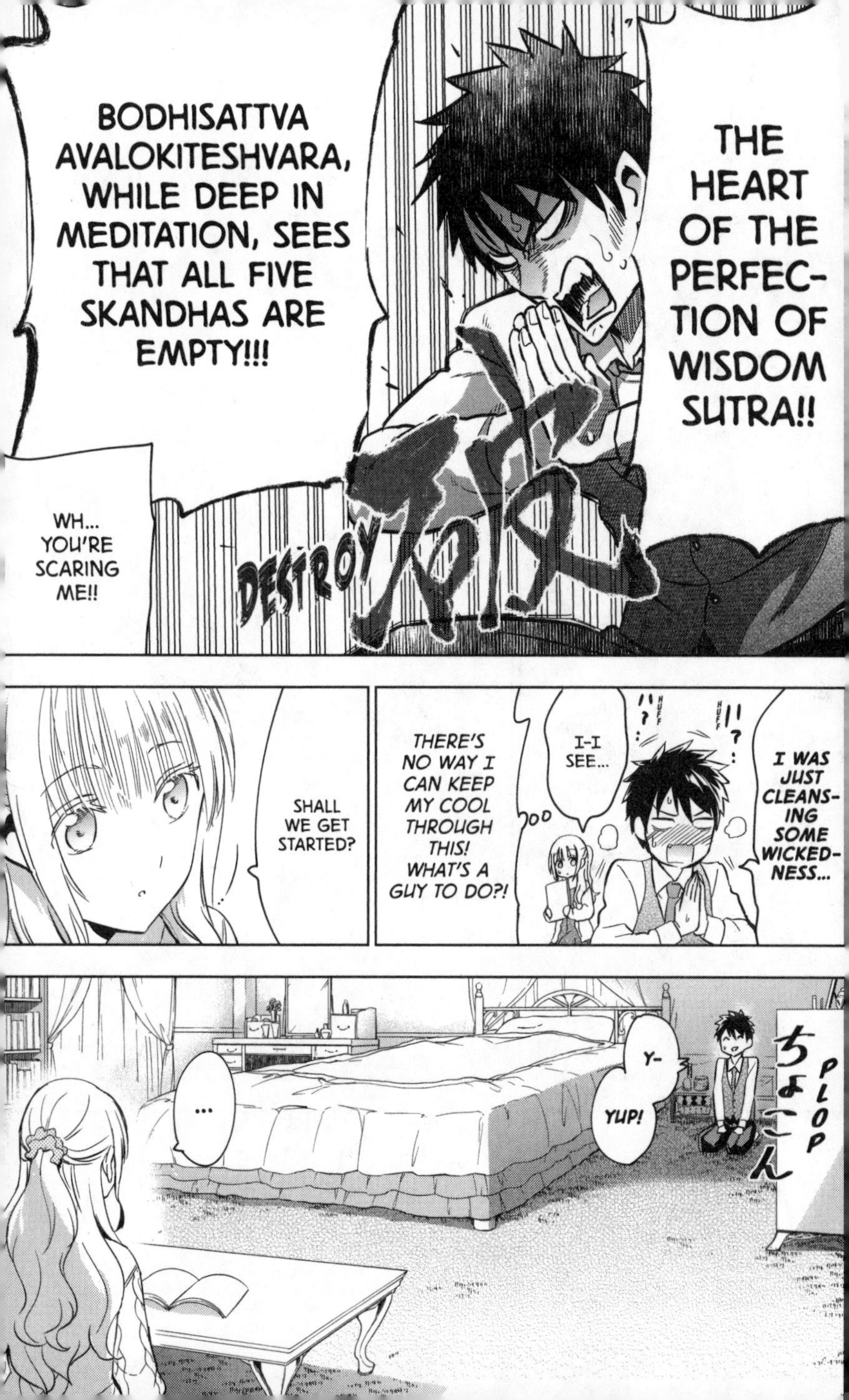
THE HEART OF THE PERFECTION OF WISDOM SUTRA!!
BODHISATTVA AVALOKITESHVARA, WHILE DEEP IN MEDITATION, SEES THAT ALL FIVE SKANDHAS ARE EMPTY!!!
DESTROY
WH... YOU'RE SCARING ME!!
I WAS JUST CLEANSING SOME WICKEDNESS...
HUFF
HUFF
I-I SEE...
THERE'S NO WAY I CAN KEEP MY COOL THROUGH THIS! WHAT'S A GUY TO DO?!
SHALL WE GET STARTED?
PLOP
Y-
YUP!
...

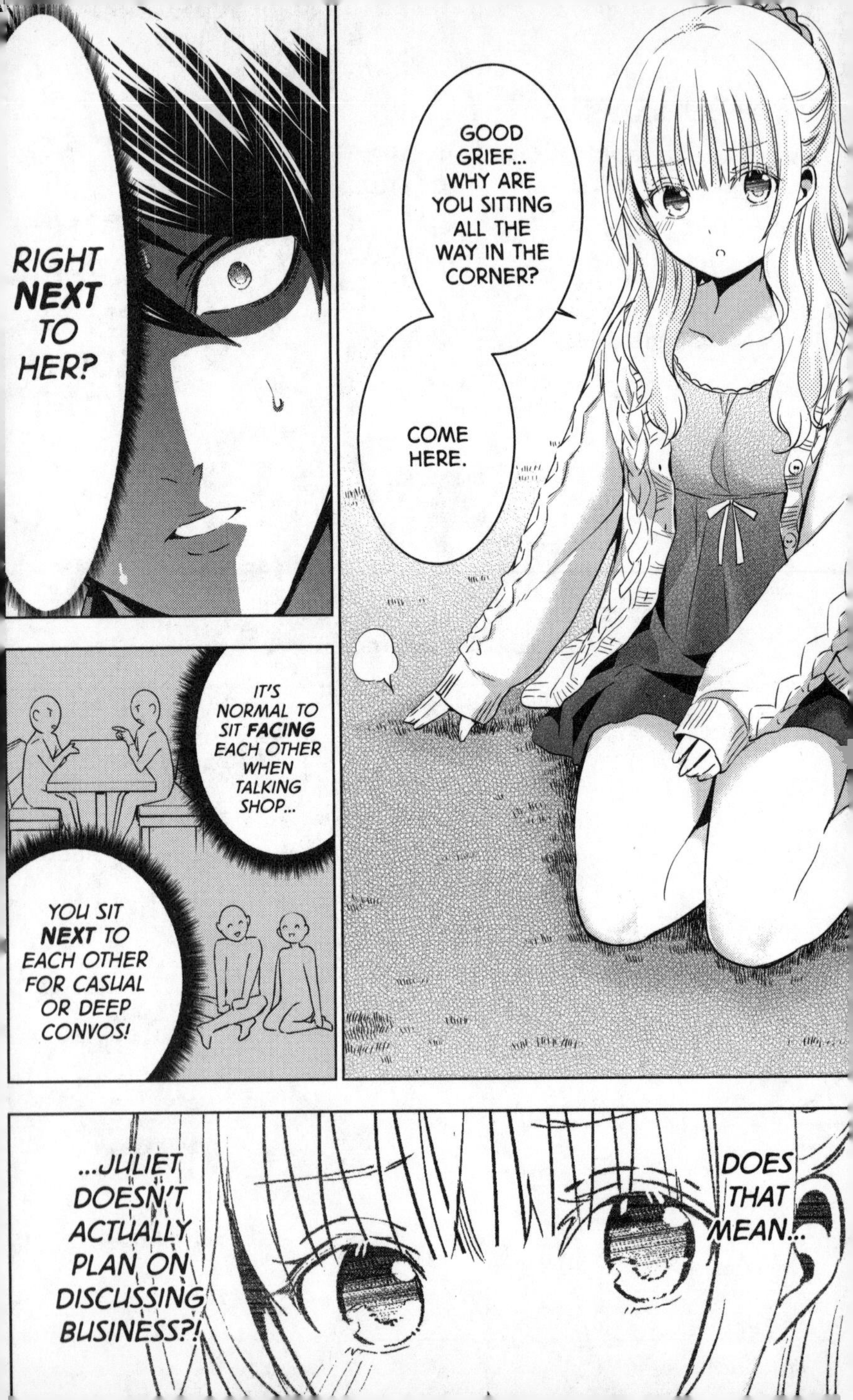
GOOD GRIEF... WHY ARE YOU SITTING ALL THE WAY IN THE CORNER?
COME HERE.
RIGHT NEXT TO HER?
IT'S NORMAL TO SIT FACING EACH OTHER WHEN TALKING SHOP...
YOU SIT NEXT TO EACH OTHER FOR CASUAL OR DEEP CONVOS!
DOES THAT MEAN...
...JULIET DOESN'T ACTUALLY PLAN ON DISCUSSING BUSINESS?!

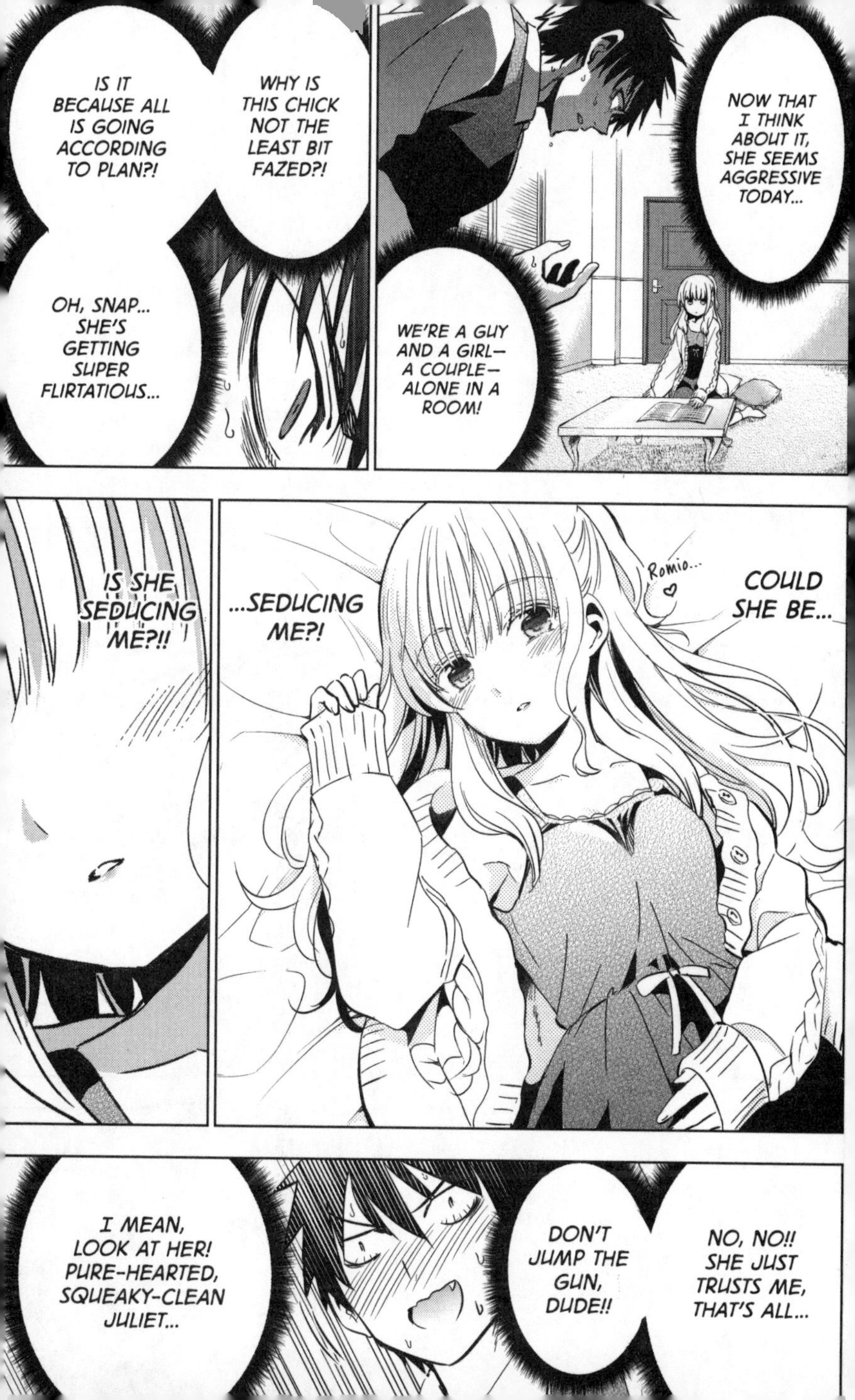
NOW THAT I THINK ABOUT IT, SHE SEEMS AGGRESSIVE TODAY...
WE'RE A GUY AND A GIRL—A COUPLE—ALONE IN A ROOM!
WHY IS THIS CHICK NOT THE LEAST BIT FAZED?!
IS IT BECAUSE ALL IS GOING ACCORDING TO PLAN?!
OH, SNAP... SHE'S GETTING SUPER FLIRTATIOUS...
Romio... ♡
COULD SHE BE...
...SEDUCING ME?!
IS SHE SEDUCING ME?!!
NO, NO!! SHE JUST TRUSTS ME, THAT'S ALL...
DON'T JUMP THE GUN, DUDE!!
I MEAN, LOOK AT HER! PURE-HEARTED, SQUEAKY-CLEAN JULIET...

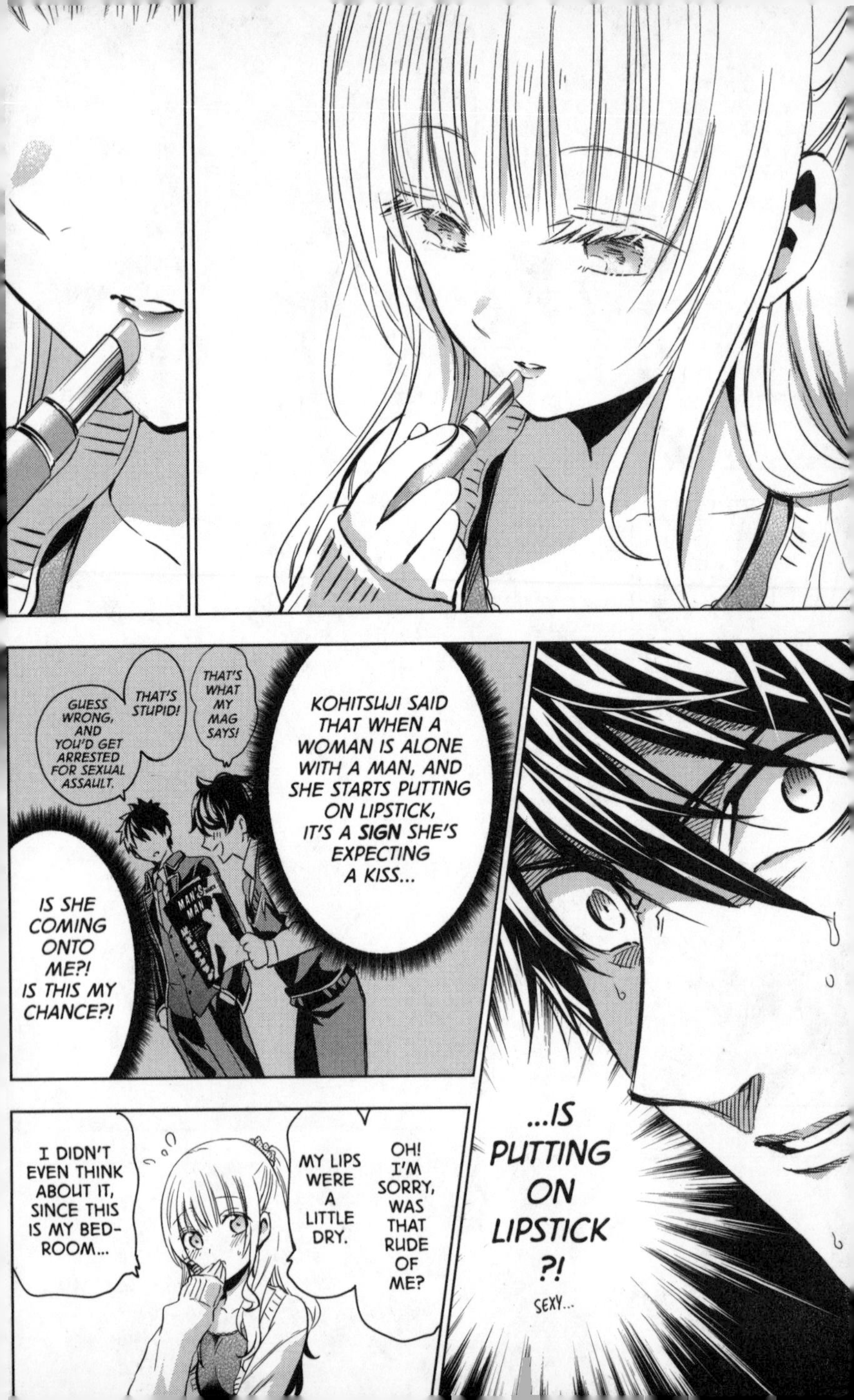

...IS PUTTING ON LIPSTICK ?!
SEXY...
KOHITSUJI SAID THAT WHEN A WOMAN IS ALONE WITH A MAN, AND SHE STARTS PUTTING ON LIPSTICK, IT'S A **SIGN** SHE'S EXPECTING A KISS...
THAT'S WHAT MY MAG SAYS!
THAT'S STUPID!
GUESS WRONG, AND YOU'D GET ARRESTED FOR SEXUAL ASSAULT.
MAN'S MAN
IS SHE COMING ONTO ME?! IS THIS MY CHANCE?!
OH! I'M SORRY, WAS THAT RUDE OF ME?
MY LIPS WERE A LITTLE DRY.
I DIDN'T EVEN THINK ABOUT IT, SINCE THIS IS MY BED-ROOM...

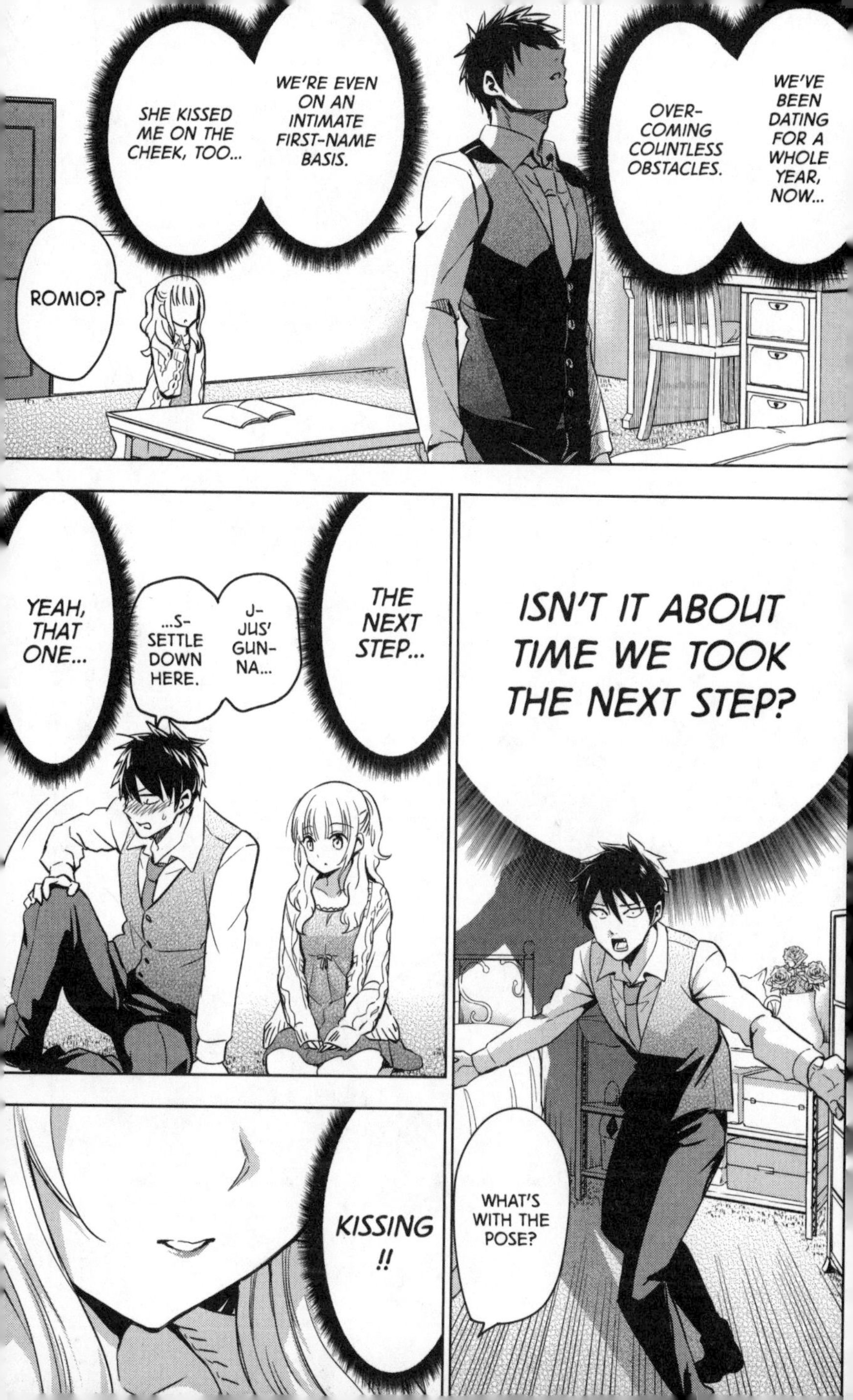
WE'VE BEEN DATING FOR A WHOLE YEAR, NOW...
OVER-COMING COUNTLESS OBSTACLES.
WE'RE EVEN ON AN INTIMATE FIRST-NAME BASIS.
SHE KISSED ME ON THE CHEEK, TOO...
ROMIO?
ISN'T IT ABOUT TIME WE TOOK THE NEXT STEP?
WHAT'S WITH THE POSE?
THE NEXT STEP...
J-JUS' GUN-NA...
...S-SETTLE DOWN HERE.
YEAH, THAT ONE...
KISSING !!

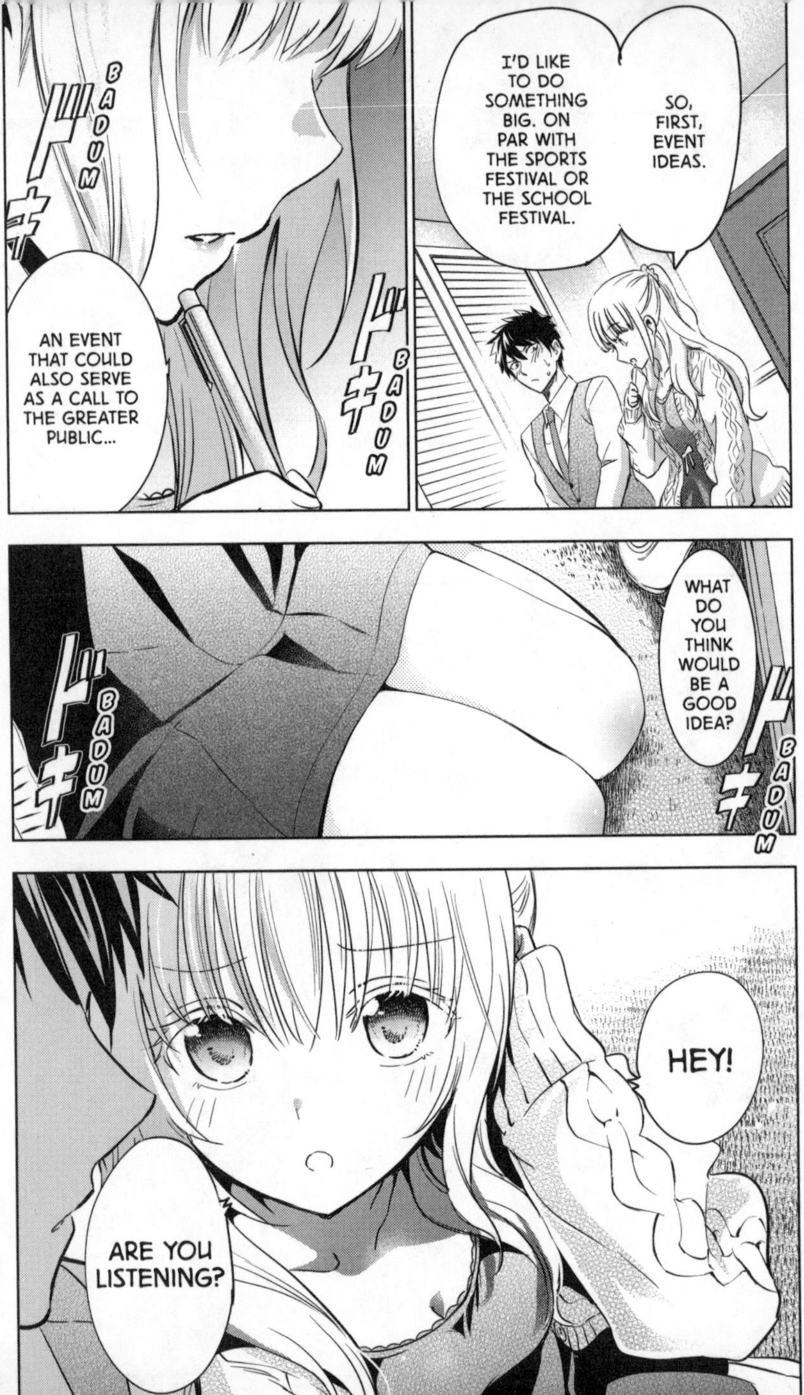
SO, FIRST, EVENT IDEAS.
I'D LIKE TO DO SOMETHING BIG. ON PAR WITH THE SPORTS FESTIVAL OR THE SCHOOL FESTIVAL.
ドキ BADUM
ドキ BADUM
AN EVENT THAT COULD ALSO SERVE AS A CALL TO THE GREATER PUBLIC...
WHAT DO YOU THINK WOULD BE A GOOD IDEA?
ドキ BADUM
ドキ BADUM
HEY!
ARE YOU LISTENING?

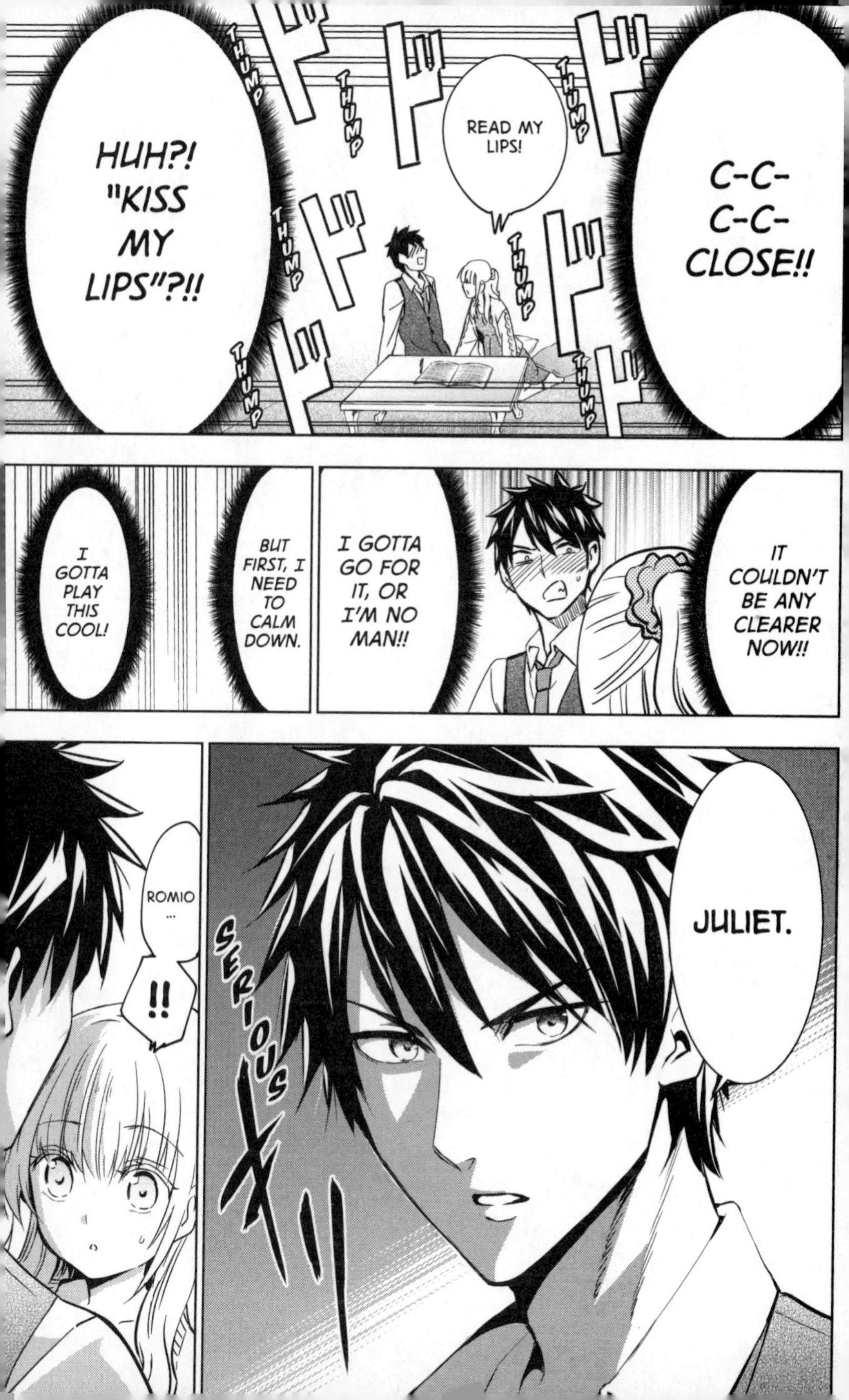
C-C-
C-C-
CLOSE!!
THUMP
THUMP
THUMP
READ MY LIPS!
THUMP
THUMP
HUH?! "KISS MY LIPS"?!!
THUMP
THUMP
IT COULDN'T BE ANY CLEARER NOW!!
I GOTTA GO FOR IT, OR I'M NO MAN!!
BUT FIRST, I NEED TO CALM DOWN.
I GOTTA PLAY THIS COOL!
JULIET.
SERIOUS
ROMIO ...
!!

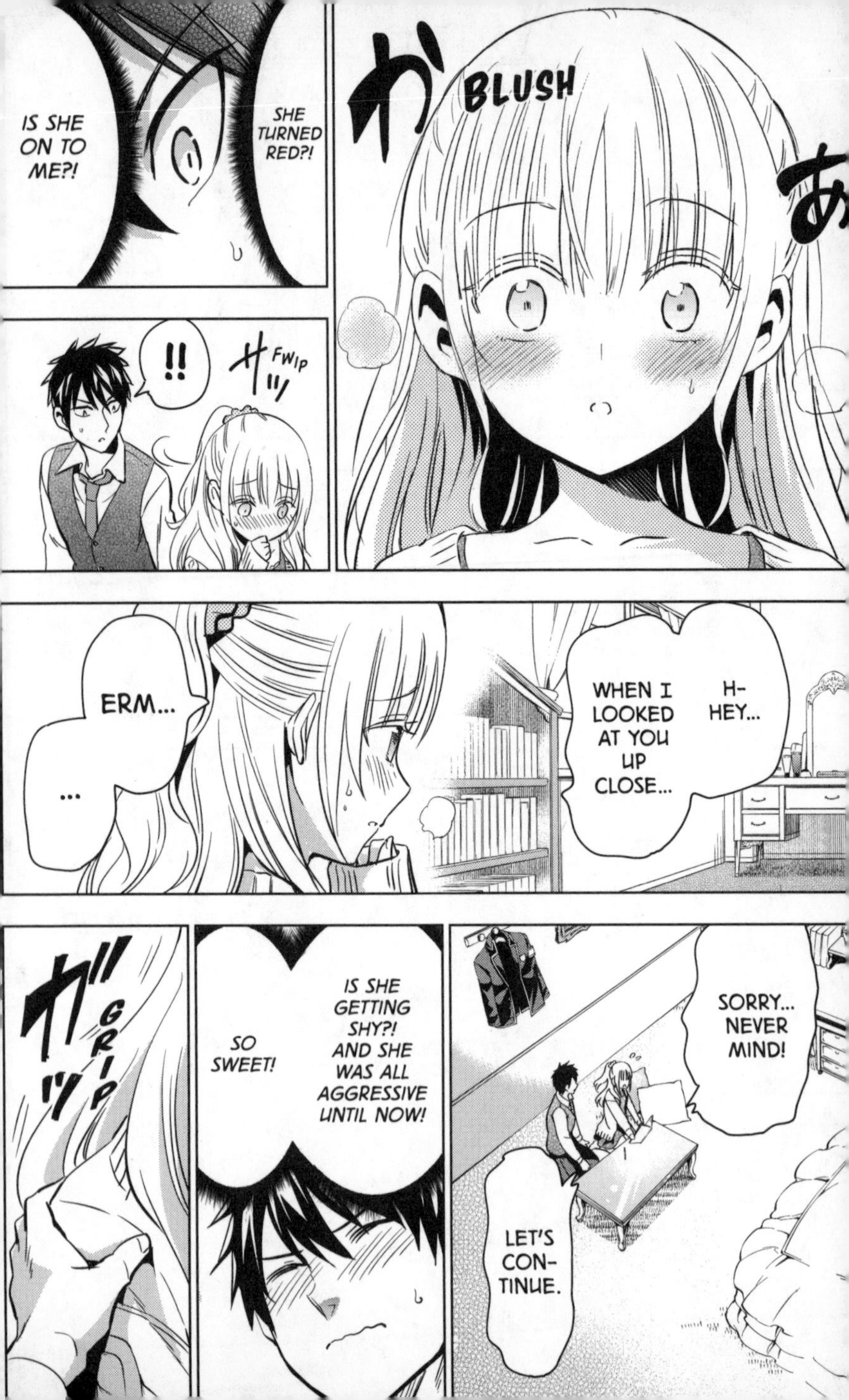
わ
BLUSH
あ
SHE TURNED RED?!
IS SHE ON TO ME?!
!!
サッ
FWIP
H-HEY...
WHEN I LOOKED AT YOU UP CLOSE...
ERM...
...
SORRY... NEVER MIND!
LET'S CON-TINUE.
IS SHE GETTING SHY?! AND SHE WAS ALL AGGRESSIVE UNTIL NOW!
SO SWEET!
ガッ
GRIP

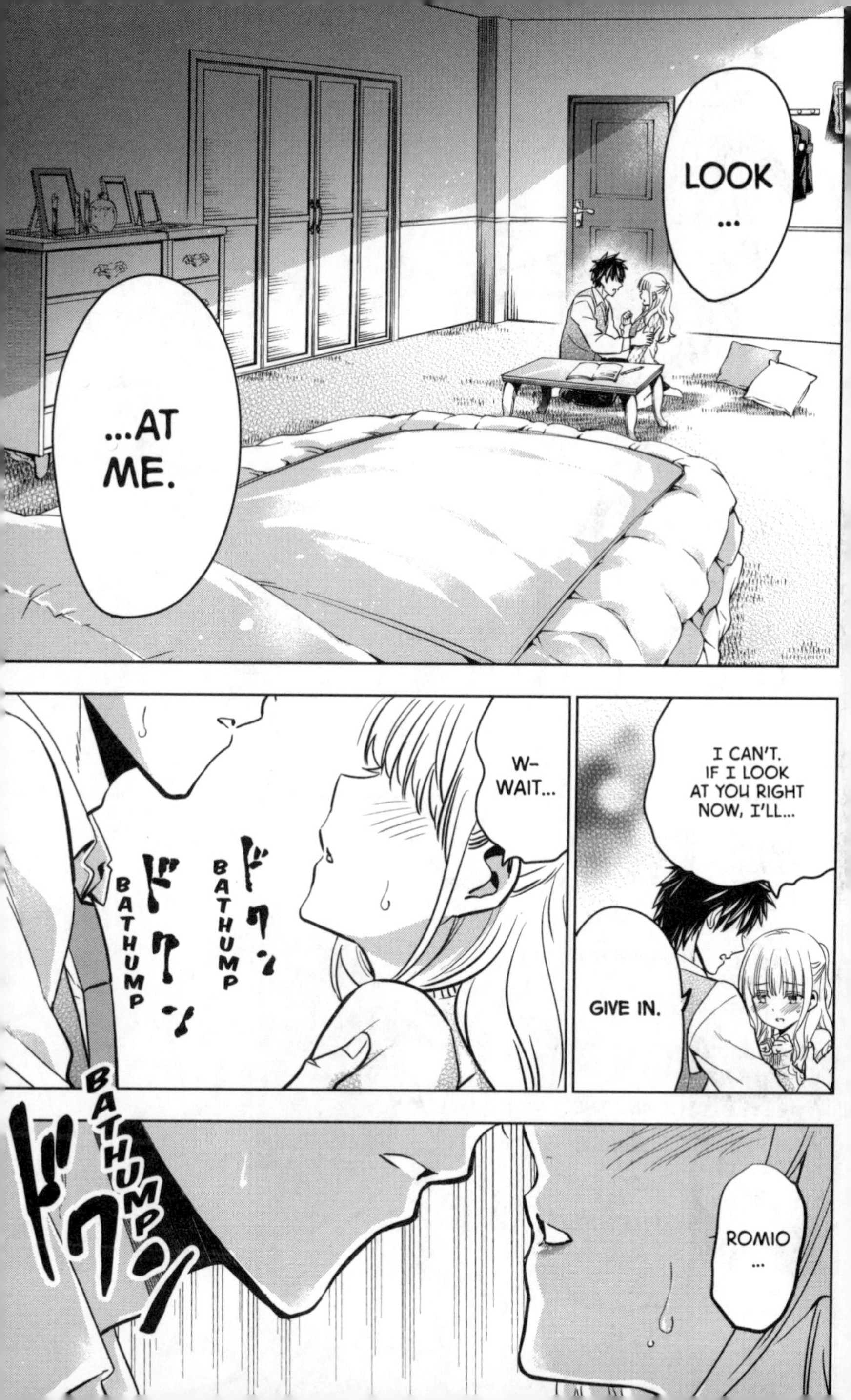
LOOK ...
...AT ME.
I CAN'T. IF I LOOK AT YOU RIGHT NOW, I'LL...
GIVE IN.
W-WAIT...
BATHUMP
BATHUMP
ROMIO ...
BATHUMP

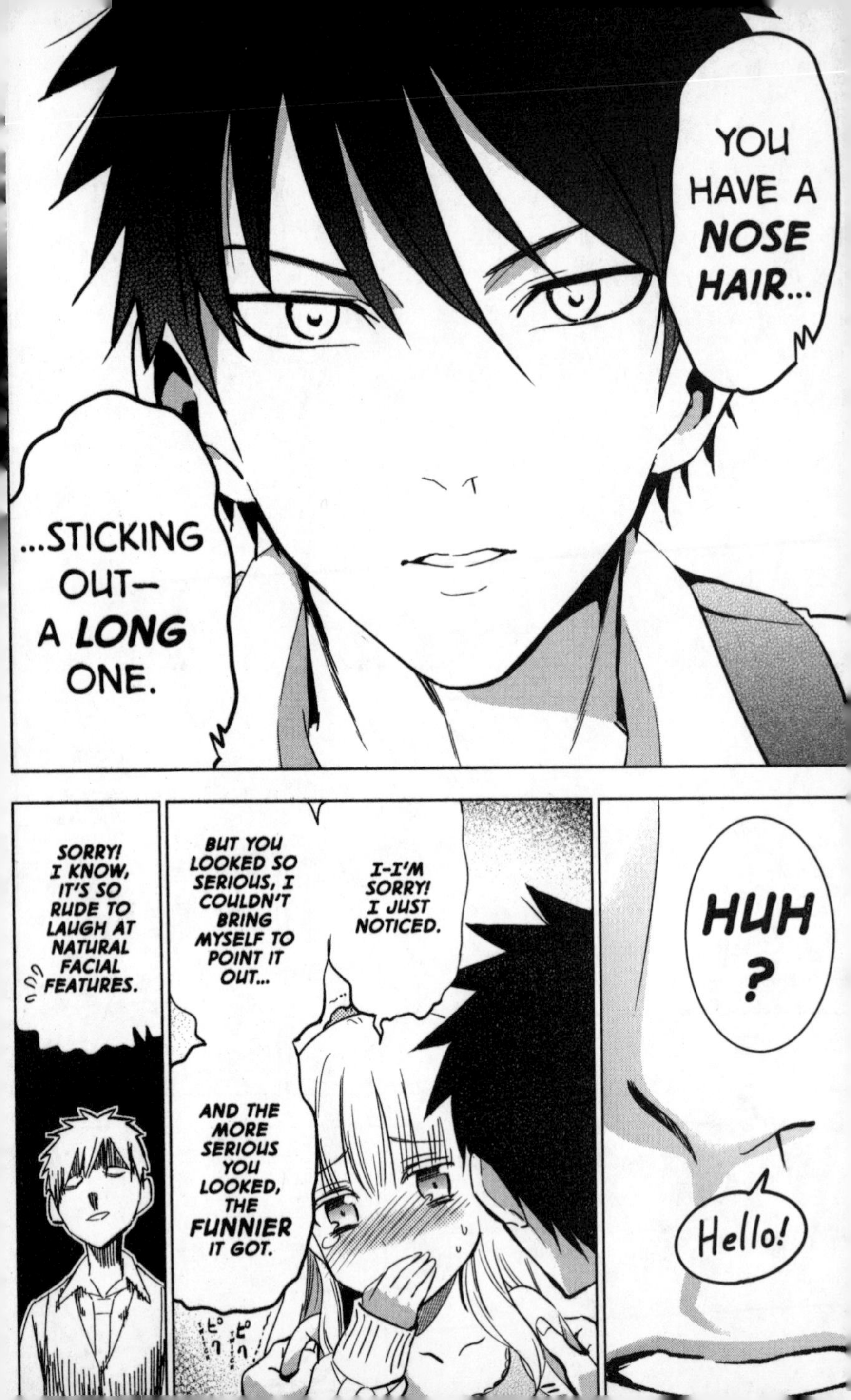
YOU HAVE A NOSE HAIR...
...STICKING OUT—A LONG ONE.
HUH?
Hello!
I-I'M SORRY! I JUST NOTICED.
BUT YOU LOOKED SO SERIOUS, I COULDN'T BRING MYSELF TO POINT IT OUT...
AND THE MORE SERIOUS YOU LOOKED, THE FUNNIER IT GOT.
SORRY! I KNOW, IT'S SO RUDE TO LAUGH AT NATURAL FACIAL FEATURES.

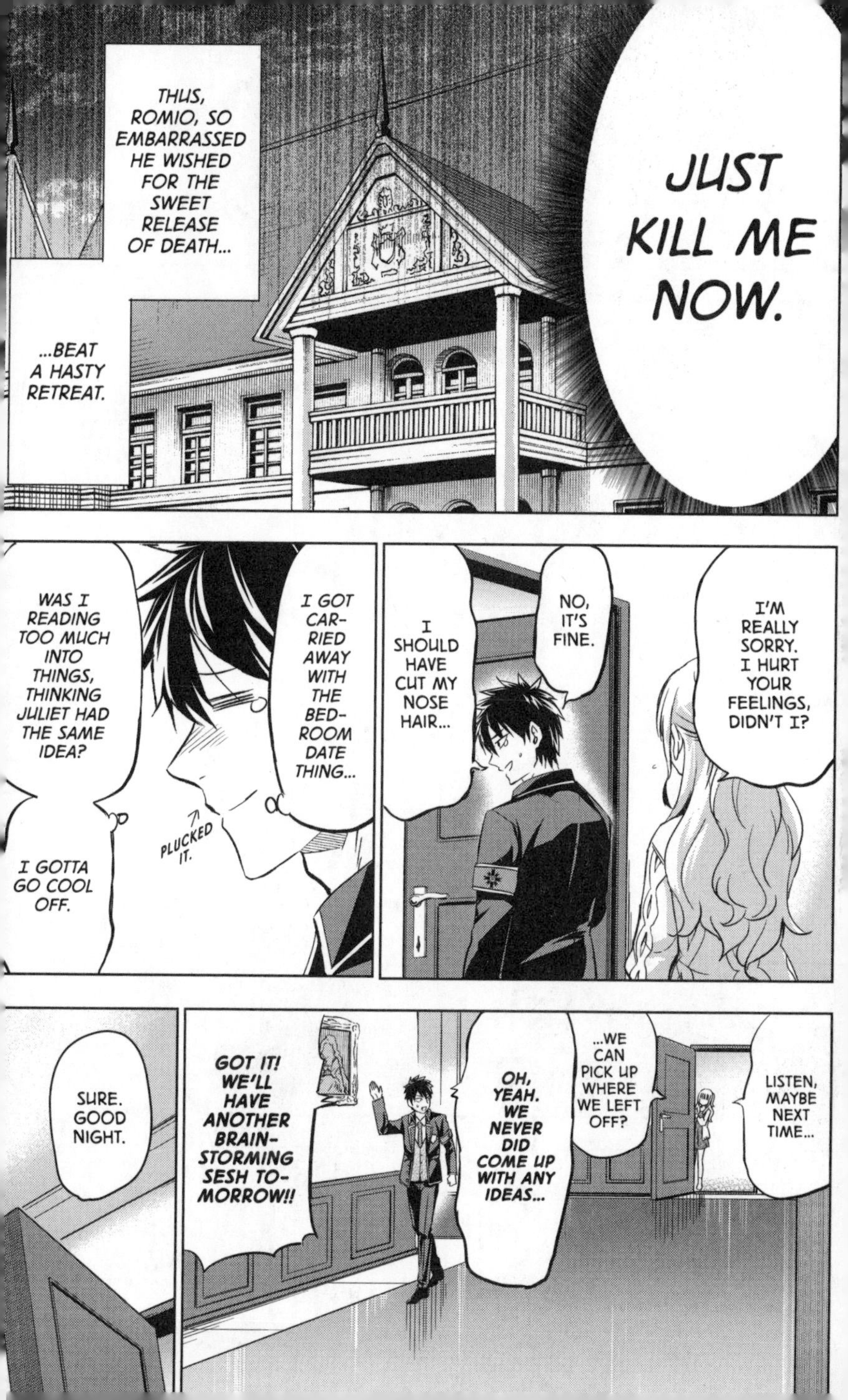
JUST KILL ME NOW.
THUS, ROMIO, SO EMBARRASSED HE WISHED FOR THE SWEET RELEASE OF DEATH...
...BEAT A HASTY RETREAT.
I'M REALLY SORRY. I HURT YOUR FEELINGS, DIDN'T I?
NO, IT'S FINE.
I SHOULD HAVE CUT MY NOSE HAIR...
I GOT CARRIED AWAY WITH THE BEDROOM DATE THING...
WAS I READING TOO MUCH INTO THINGS, THINKING JULIET HAD THE SAME IDEA?
PLUCKED IT.
I GOTTA GO COOL OFF.
LISTEN, MAYBE NEXT TIME...
...WE CAN PICK UP WHERE WE LEFT OFF?
OH, YEAH. WE NEVER DID COME UP WITH ANY IDEAS...
GOT IT! WE'LL HAVE ANOTHER BRAINSTORMING SESH TOMORROW!!
SURE. GOOD NIGHT.

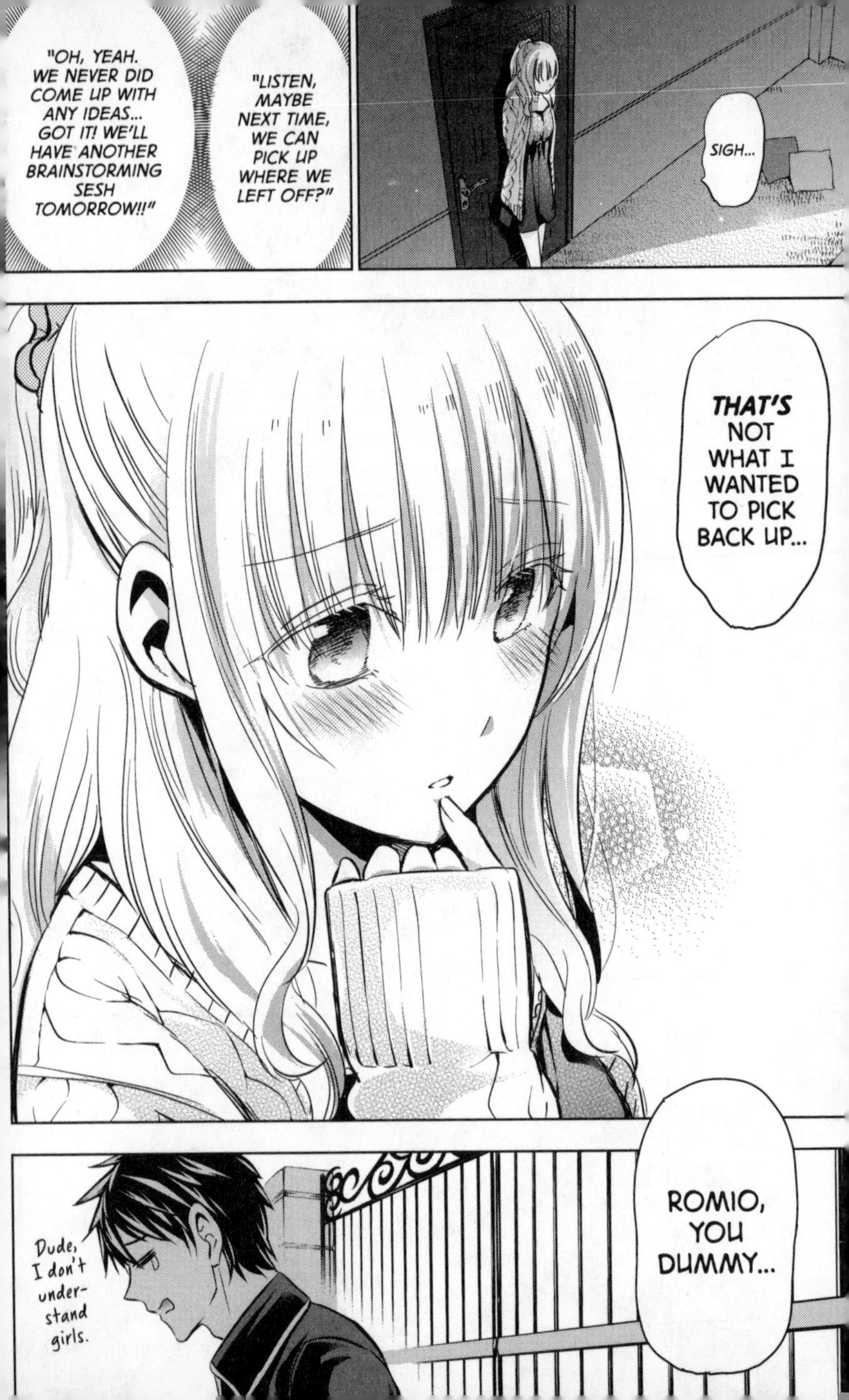
SIGH...
"LISTEN, MAYBE NEXT TIME, WE CAN PICK UP WHERE WE LEFT OFF?"
"OH, YEAH. WE NEVER DID COME UP WITH ANY IDEAS... GOT IT! WE'LL HAVE ANOTHER BRAINSTORMING SESH TOMORROW!!"
THAT'S NOT WHAT I WANTED TO PICK BACK UP...
ROMIO, YOU DUMMY...
Dude, I don't under-stand girls.

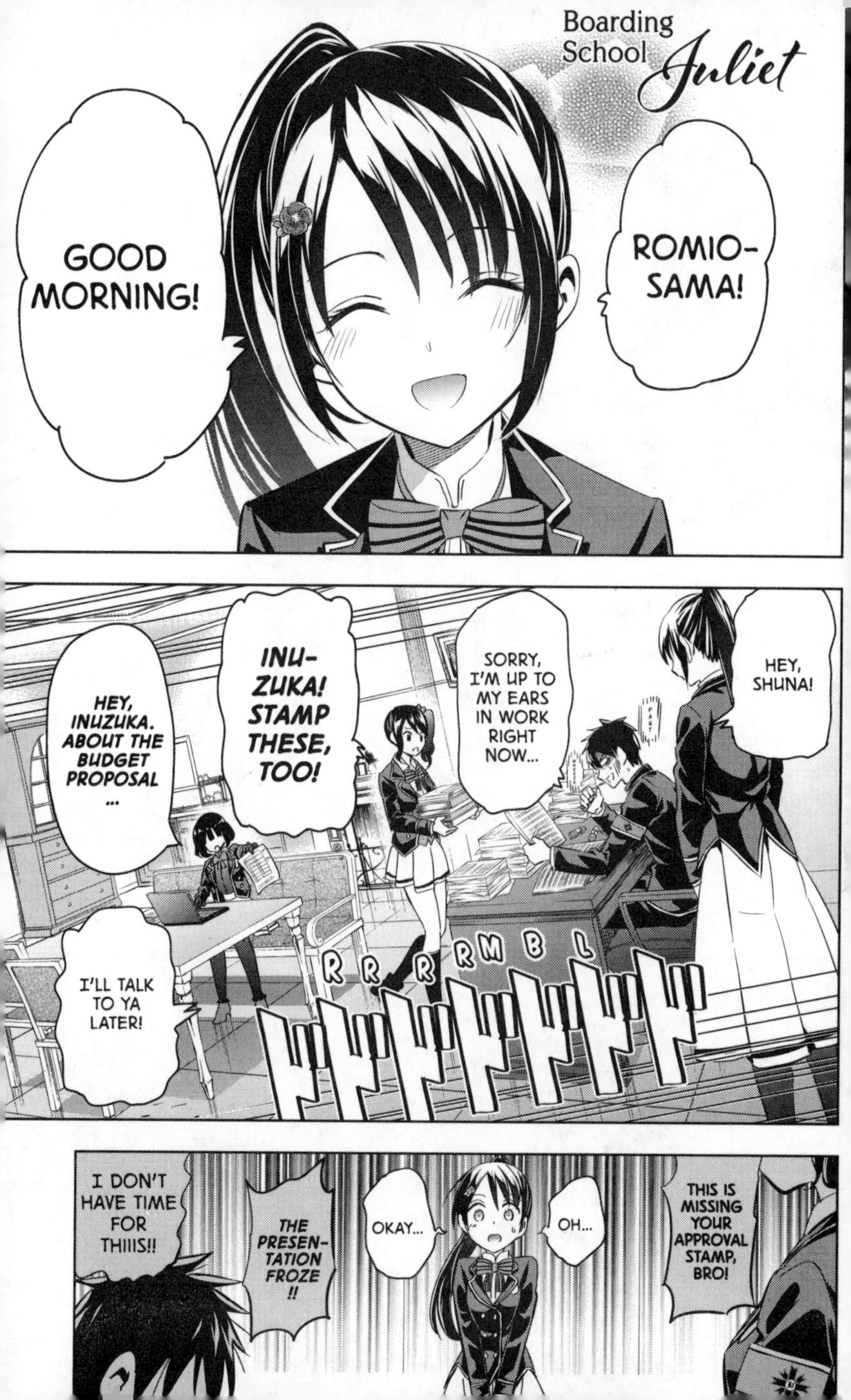
Boarding School Juliet
ROMIO-SAMA!
GOOD MORNING!
HEY, SHUNA!
SORRY, I'M UP TO MY EARS IN WORK RIGHT NOW...
PANT
INU-ZUKA! STAMP THESE, TOO!
HEY, INUZUKA. ABOUT THE BUDGET PROPOSAL ...
I'LL TALK TO YA LATER!
RRRRMBL
THIS IS MISSING YOUR APPROVAL STAMP, BRO!
OH...
OKAY...
THE PRESEN-TATION FROZE !!
I DON'T HAVE TIME FOR THIIIS!!

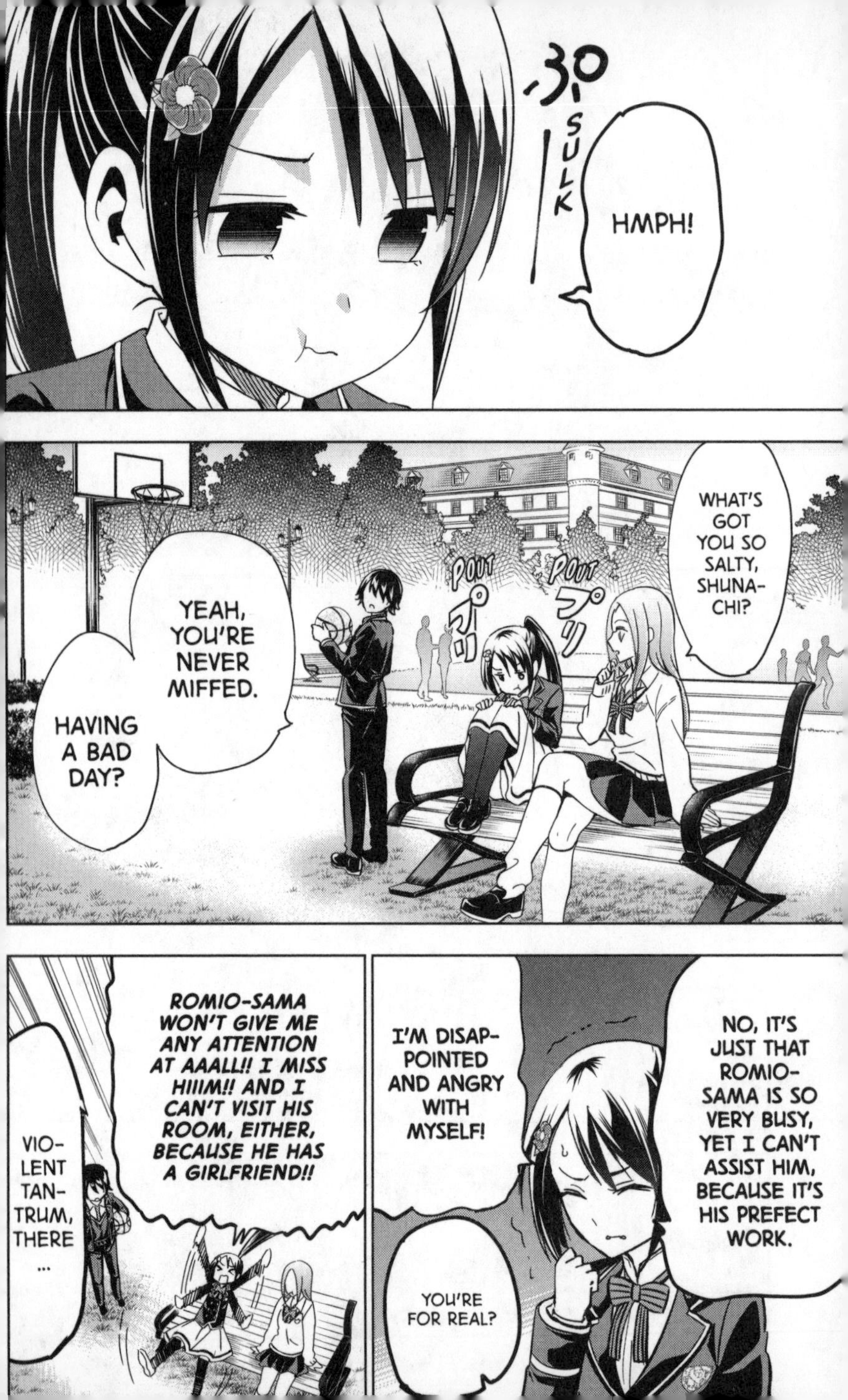
SULK
HMPH!
WHAT'S GOT YOU SO SALTY, SHUNA-CHI?
POUT
POUT
YEAH, YOU'RE NEVER MIFFED.
HAVING A BAD DAY?
NO, IT'S JUST THAT ROMIO-SAMA IS SO VERY BUSY, YET I CAN'T ASSIST HIM, BECAUSE IT'S HIS PREFECT WORK.
I'M DISAP-POINTED AND ANGRY WITH MYSELF!
YOU'RE FOR REAL?
ROMIO-SAMA WON'T GIVE ME ANY ATTENTION AT AAALL!! I MISS HIIIM!! AND I CAN'T VISIT HIS ROOM, EITHER, BECAUSE HE HAS A GIRLFRIEND!!
VIO-LENT TAN-TRUM, THERE ...

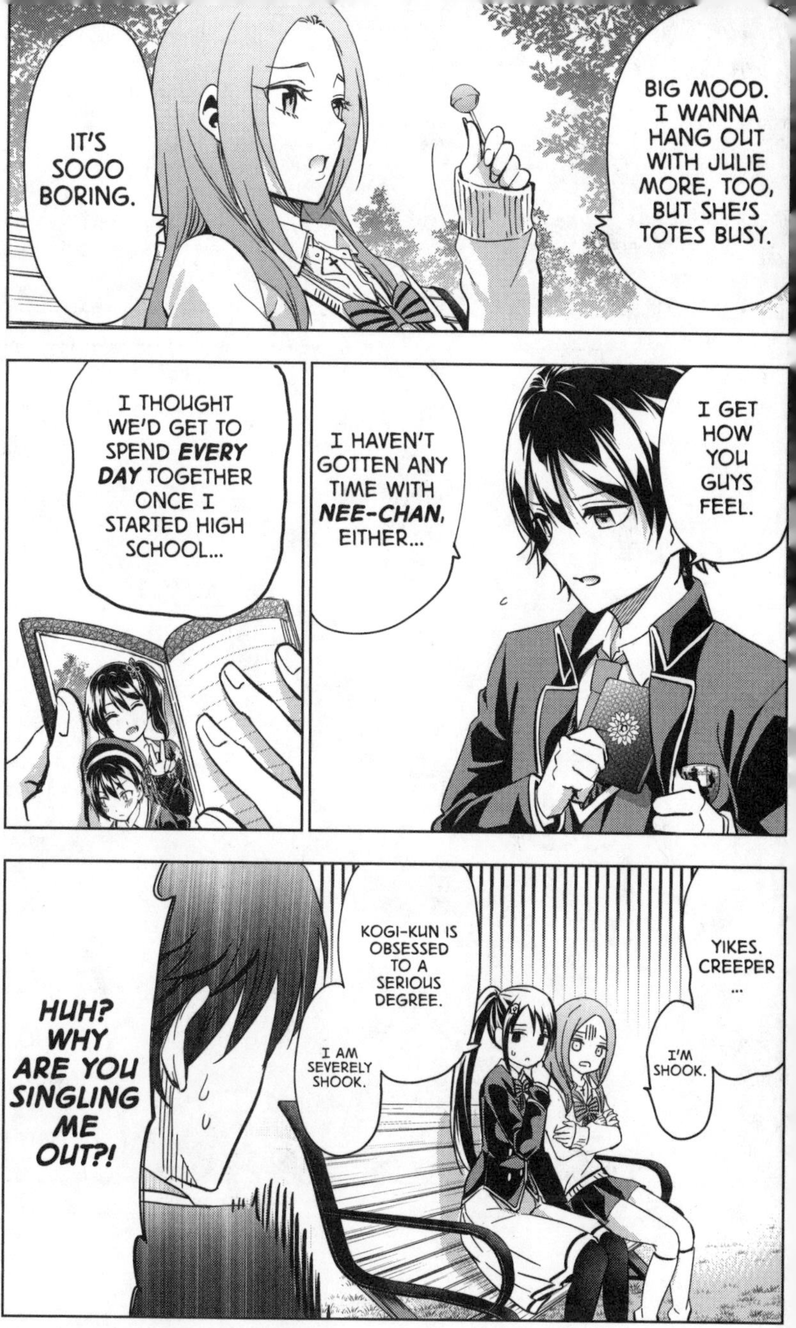
IT'S SOOO BORING.
BIG MOOD. I WANNA HANG OUT WITH JULIE MORE, TOO, BUT SHE'S TOTES BUSY.
I GET HOW YOU GUYS FEEL.
I HAVEN'T GOTTEN ANY TIME WITH NEE-CHAN, EITHER...
I THOUGHT WE'D GET TO SPEND EVERY DAY TOGETHER ONCE I STARTED HIGH SCHOOL...
YIKES. CREEPER...
KOGI-KUN IS OBSESSED TO A SERIOUS DEGREE.
I'M SHOOK.
I AM SEVERELY SHOOK.
HUH? WHY ARE YOU SINGLING ME OUT?!

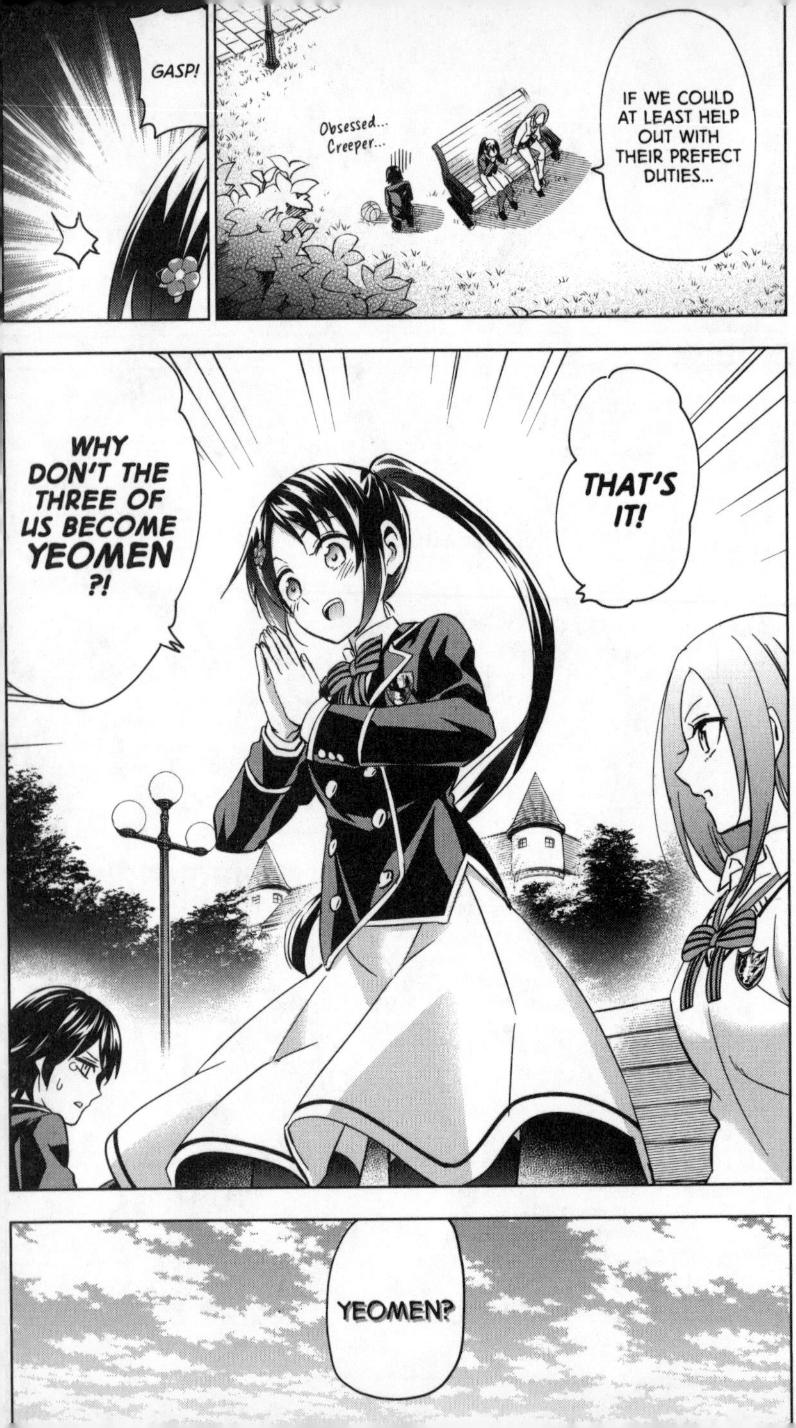
IF WE COULD AT LEAST HELP OUT WITH THEIR PREFECT DUTIES...
Obsessed... Creeper...
GASP!
THAT'S IT!
WHY DON'T THE THREE OF US BECOME YEOMEN ?!
YEOMEN?

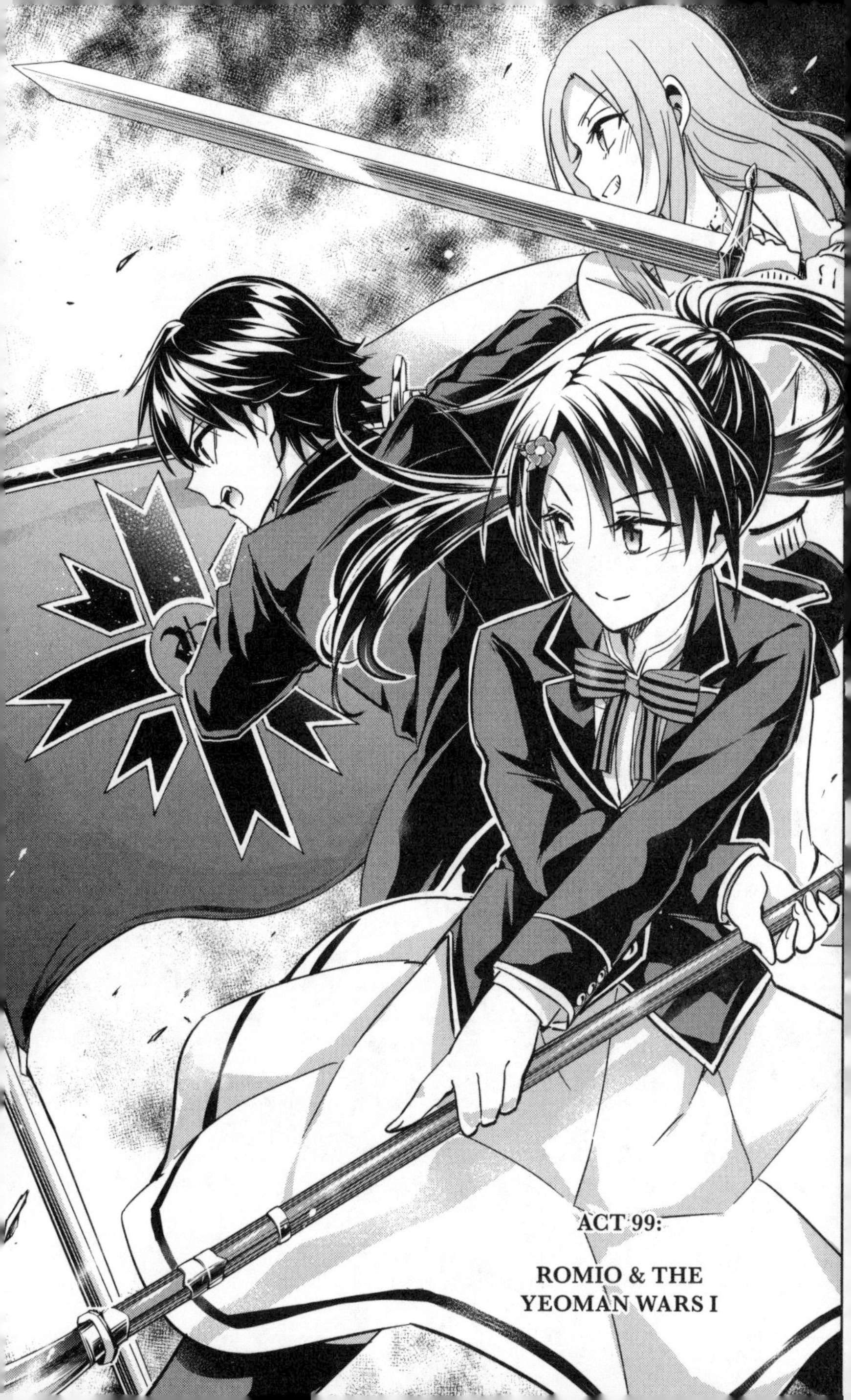

# ACT 99:

## ROMIO & THE YEOMAN WARS I

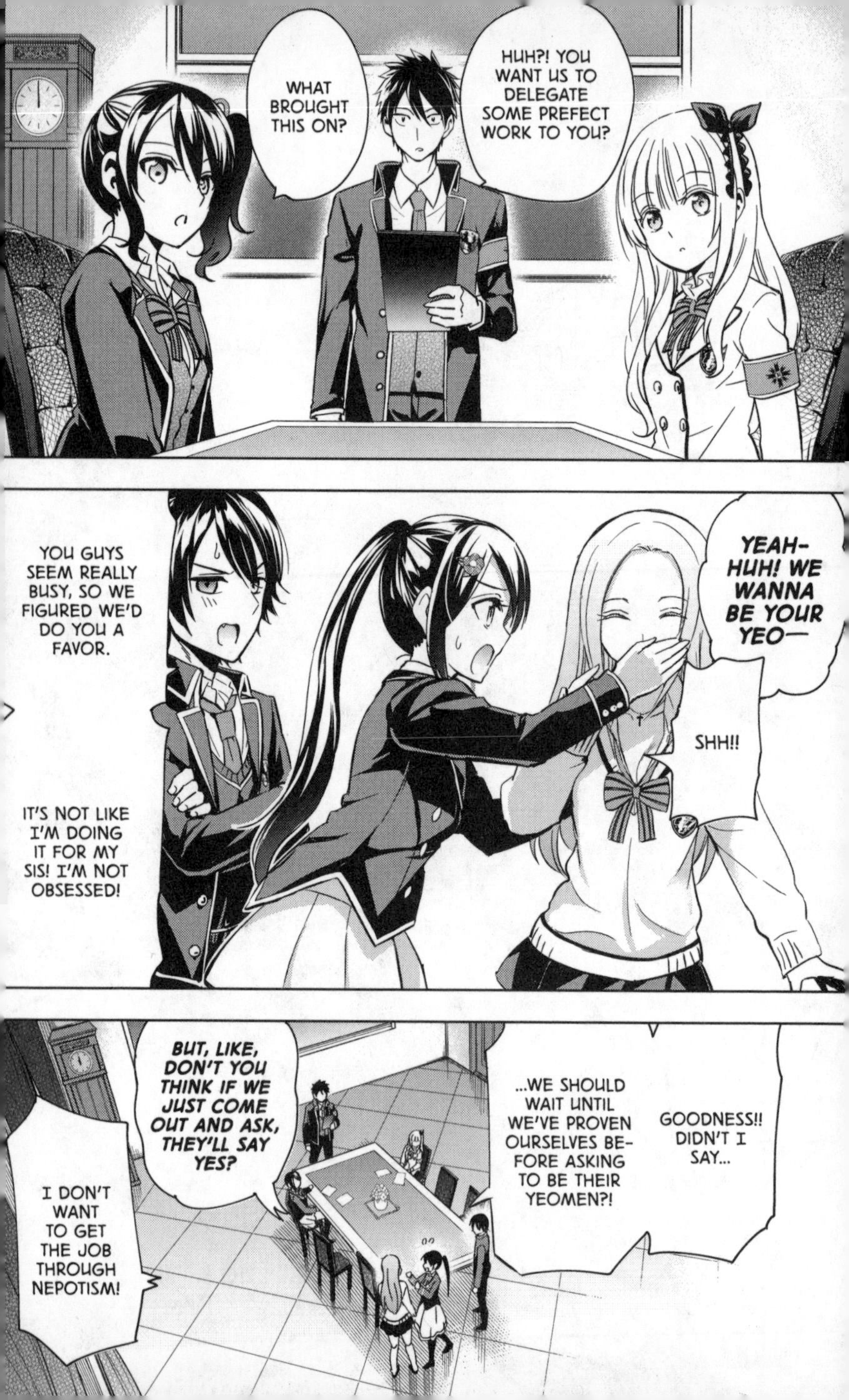
HUH?! YOU WANT US TO DELEGATE SOME PREFECT WORK TO YOU?
WHAT BROUGHT THIS ON?
YEAH-HUH! WE WANNA BE YOUR YEO—
SHH!!
YOU GUYS SEEM REALLY BUSY, SO WE FIGURED WE'D DO YOU A FAVOR.
IT'S NOT LIKE I'M DOING IT FOR MY SIS! I'M NOT OBSESSED!
GOODNESS!! DIDN'T I SAY...
...WE SHOULD WAIT UNTIL WE'VE PROVEN OURSELVES BEFORE ASKING TO BE THEIR YEOMEN?!
BUT, LIKE, DON'T YOU THINK IF WE JUST COME OUT AND ASK, THEY'LL SAY YES?
I DON'T WANT TO GET THE JOB THROUGH NEPOTISM!

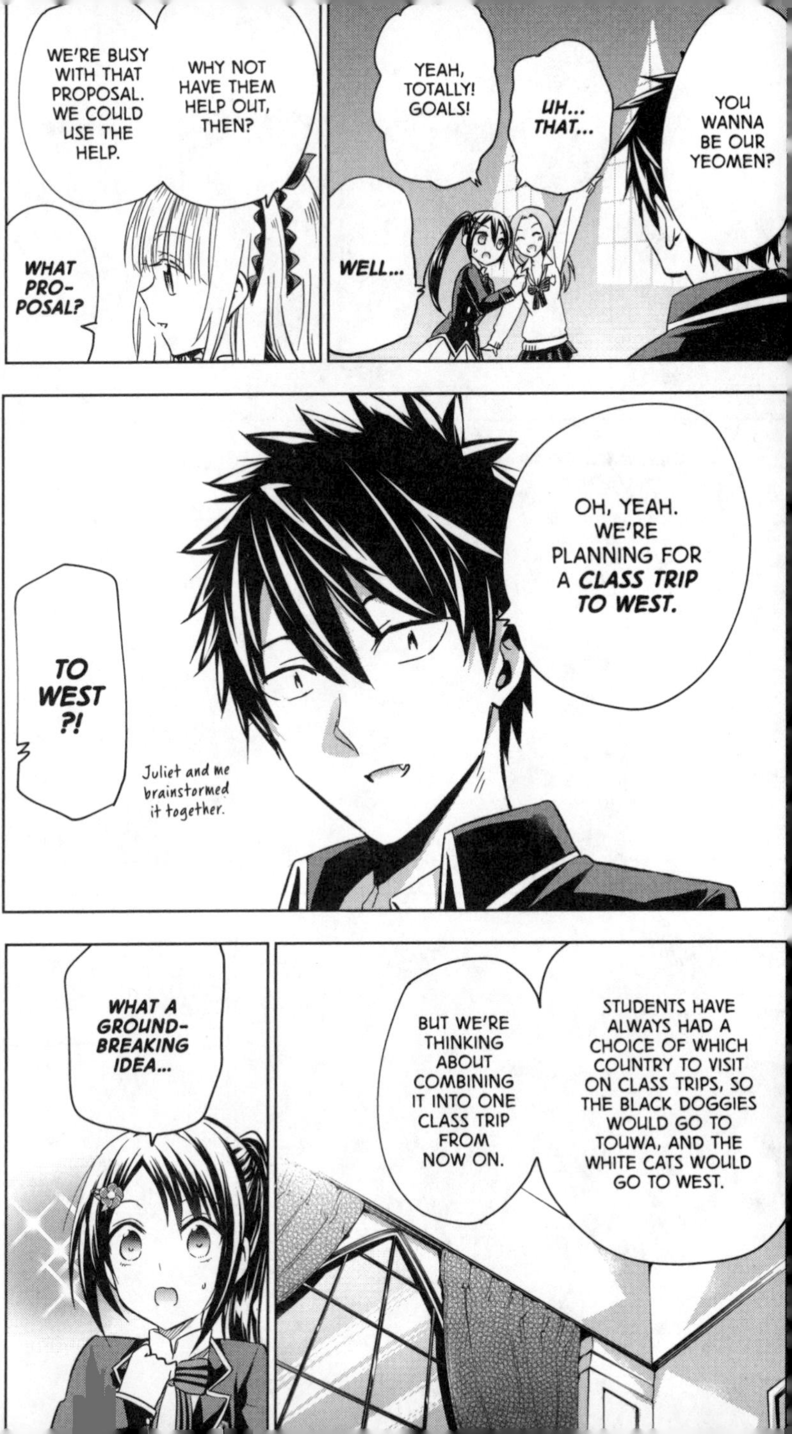
YOU WANNA BE OUR YEOMEN?
UH... THAT...
YEAH, TOTALLY! GOALS!
WELL...
WHY NOT HAVE THEM HELP OUT, THEN?
WE'RE BUSY WITH THAT PROPOSAL. WE COULD USE THE HELP.
WHAT PRO-POSAL?
OH, YEAH. WE'RE PLANNING FOR A CLASS TRIP TO WEST.
TO WEST ?!
Juliet and me brainstormed it together.
STUDENTS HAVE ALWAYS HAD A CHOICE OF WHICH COUNTRY TO VISIT ON CLASS TRIPS, SO THE BLACK DOGGIES WOULD GO TO TOUWA, AND THE WHITE CATS WOULD GO TO WEST.
BUT WE'RE THINKING ABOUT COMBINING IT INTO ONE CLASS TRIP FROM NOW ON.
WHAT A GROUND-BREAKING IDEA...

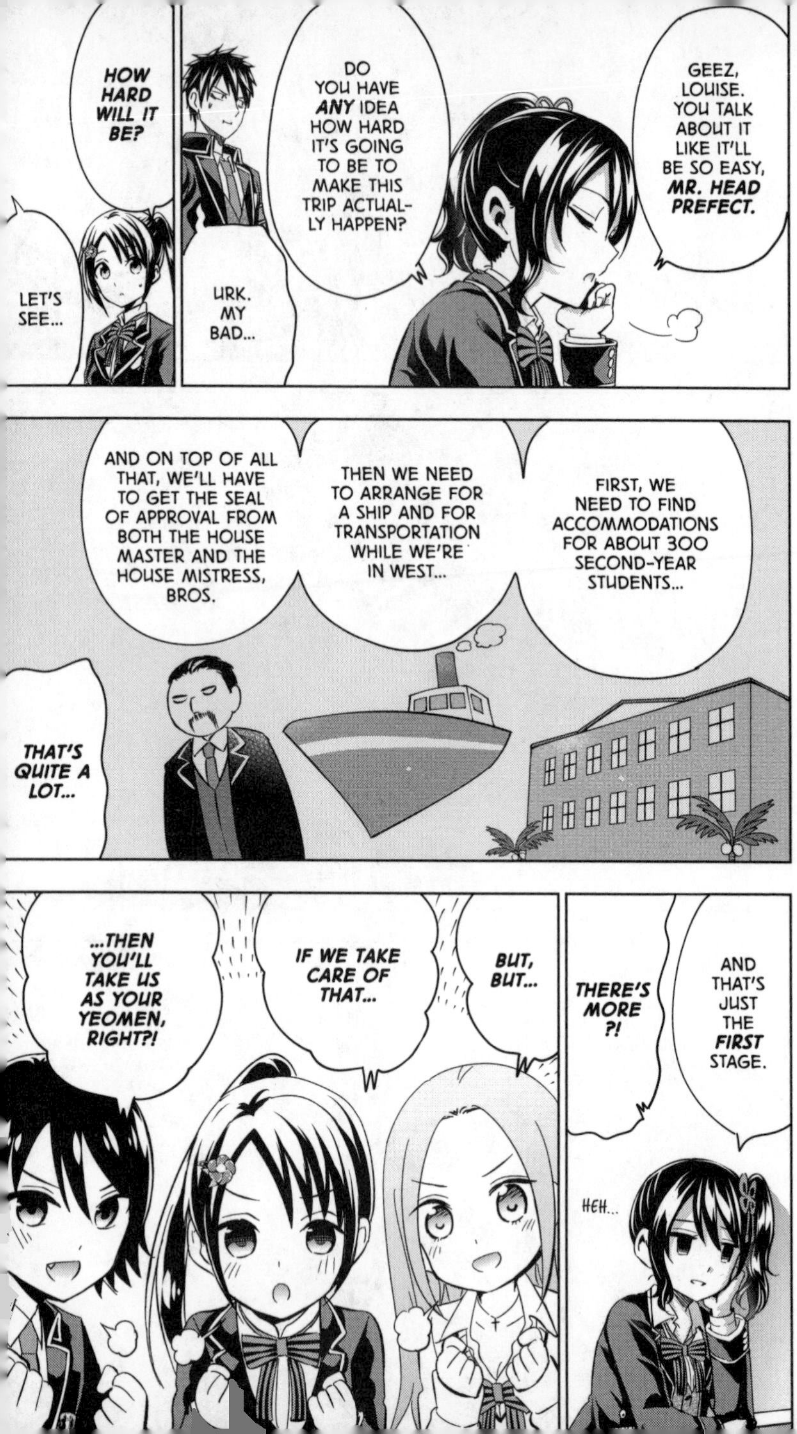
GEEZ, LOUISE. YOU TALK ABOUT IT LIKE IT'LL BE SO EASY, MR. HEAD PREFECT.
DO YOU HAVE ANY IDEA HOW HARD IT'S GOING TO BE TO MAKE THIS TRIP ACTUALLY HAPPEN?
URK. MY BAD...
HOW HARD WILL IT BE?
LET'S SEE...
FIRST, WE NEED TO FIND ACCOMMODATIONS FOR ABOUT 300 SECOND-YEAR STUDENTS...
THEN WE NEED TO ARRANGE FOR A SHIP AND FOR TRANSPORTATION WHILE WE'RE IN WEST...
AND ON TOP OF ALL THAT, WE'LL HAVE TO GET THE SEAL OF APPROVAL FROM BOTH THE HOUSE MASTER AND THE HOUSE MISTRESS, BROS.
THAT'S QUITE A LOT...
AND THAT'S JUST THE FIRST STAGE.
THERE'S MORE?!
HEH...
BUT, BUT...
IF WE TAKE CARE OF THAT...
...THEN YOU'LL TAKE US AS YOUR YEOMEN, RIGHT?!

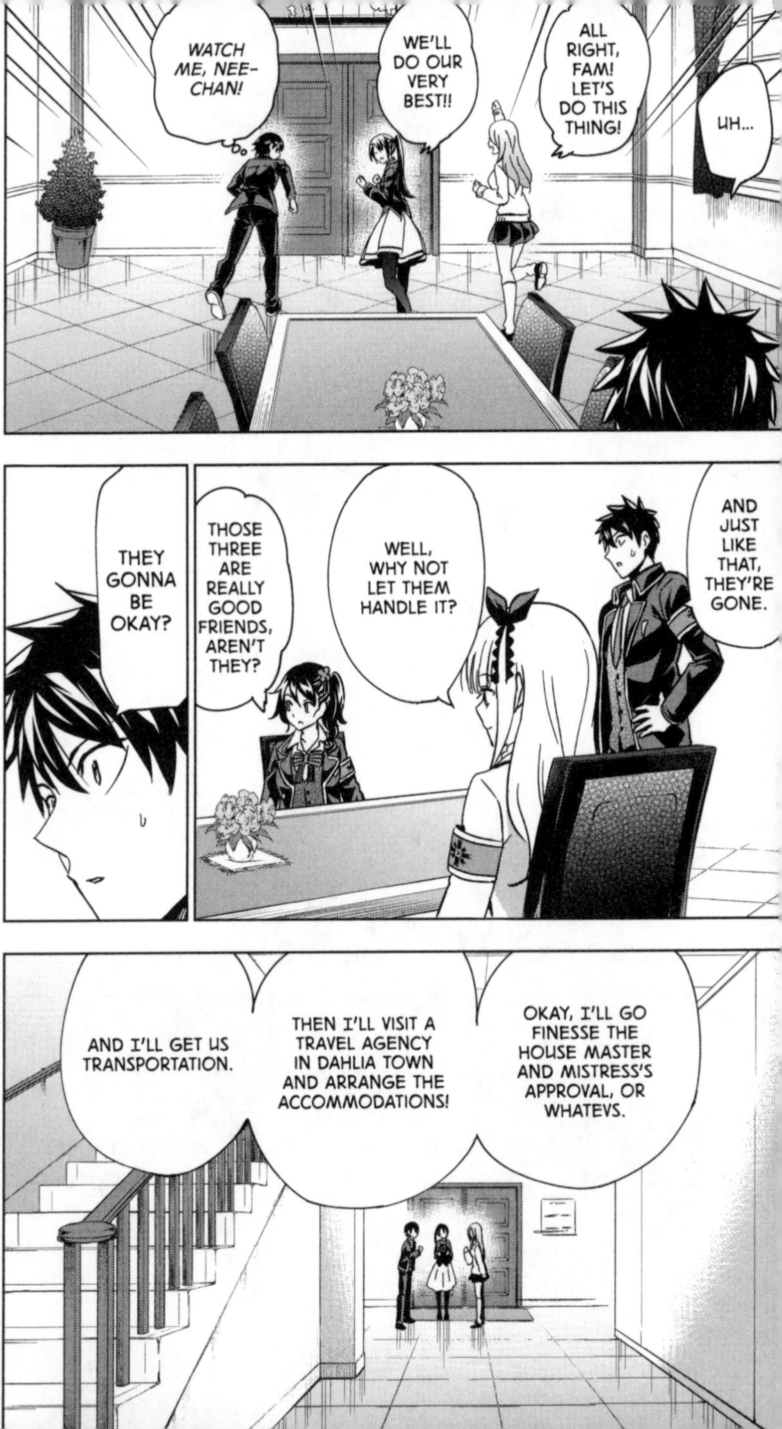
UH...
ALL RIGHT, FAM! LET'S DO THIS THING!
WE'LL DO OUR VERY BEST!!
WATCH ME, NEE-CHAN!
AND JUST LIKE THAT, THEY'RE GONE.
WELL, WHY NOT LET THEM HANDLE IT?
THOSE THREE ARE REALLY GOOD FRIENDS, AREN'T THEY?
THEY GONNA BE OKAY?
OKAY, I'LL GO FINESSE THE HOUSE MASTER AND MISTRESS'S APPROVAL, OR WHATEVS.
THEN I'LL VISIT A TRAVEL AGENCY IN DAHLIA TOWN AND ARRANGE THE ACCOMMODATIONS!
AND I'LL GET US TRANSPORTATION.

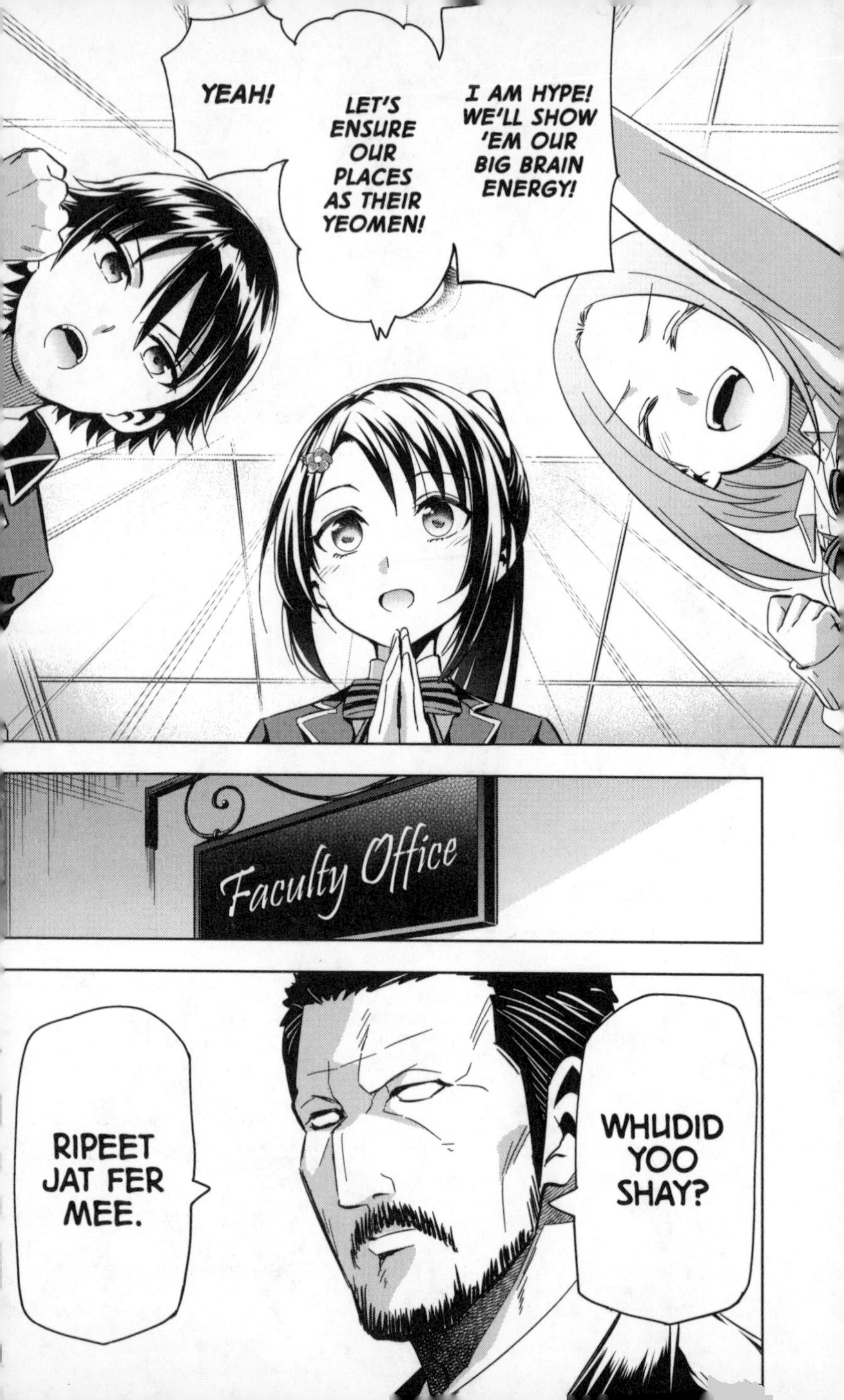
I AM HYPE! WE'LL SHOW 'EM OUR BIG BRAIN ENERGY!
LET'S ENSURE OUR PLACES AS THEIR YEOMEN!
YEAH!
Faculty Office
WHUDID YOO SHAY?
RIPEET JAT FER MEE.

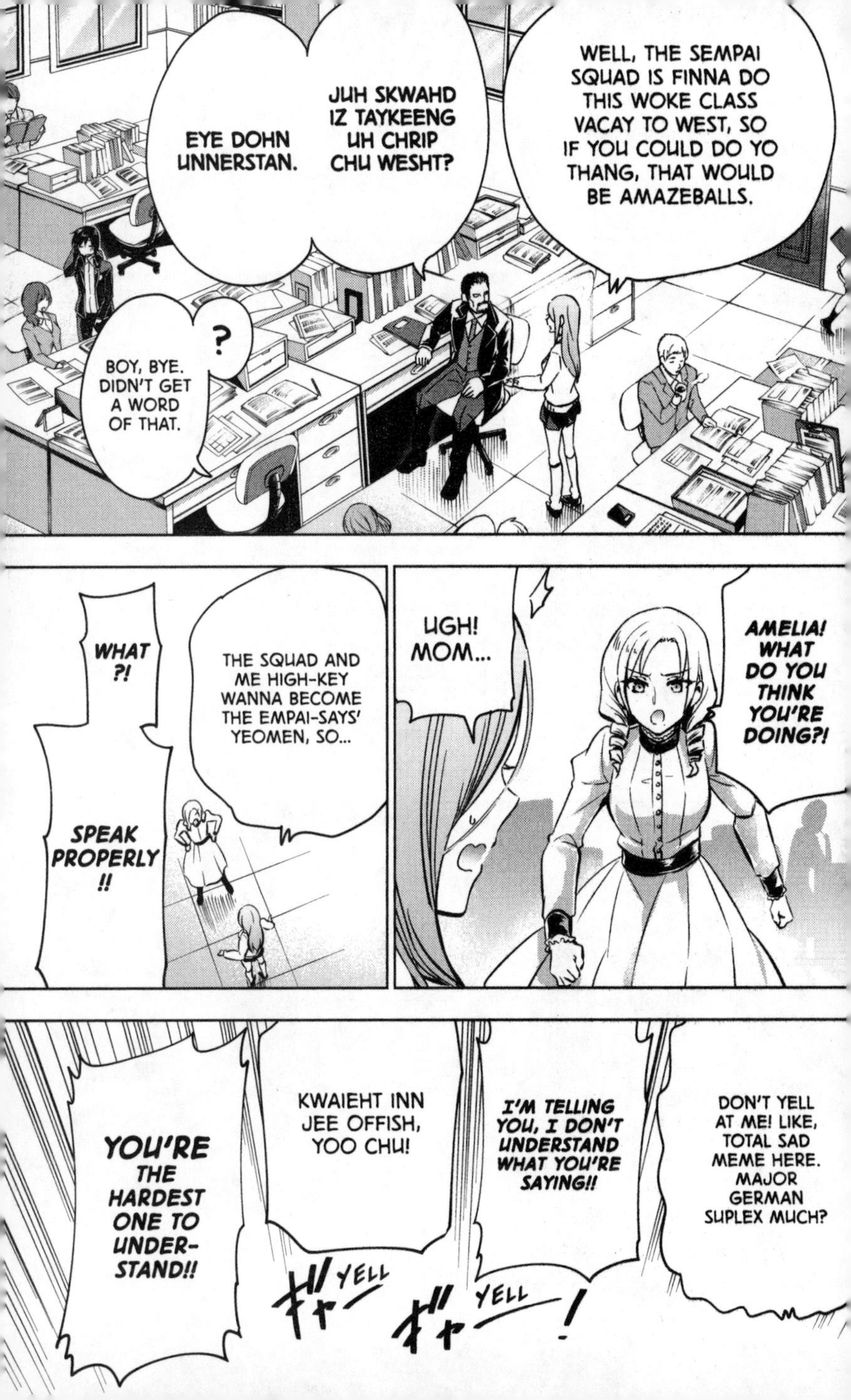
WELL, THE SEMPAI SQUAD IS FINNA DO THIS WOKE CLASS VACAY TO WEST, SO IF YOU COULD DO YO THANG, THAT WOULD BE AMAZEBALLS.
JUH SKWAHD IZ TAYKEENG UH CHRIP CHU WESHT?
EYE DOHN UNNERSTAN.
?
BOY, BYE. DIDN'T GET A WORD OF THAT.
AMELIA! WHAT DO YOU THINK YOU'RE DOING?!
UGH! MOM...
THE SQUAD AND ME HIGH-KEY WANNA BECOME THE EMPAI-SAYS' YEOMEN, SO...
WHAT?!
SPEAK PROPERLY!!
DON'T YELL AT ME! LIKE, TOTAL SAD MEME HERE. MAJOR GERMAN SUPLEX MUCH?
I'M TELLING YOU, I DON'T UNDERSTAND WHAT YOU'RE SAYING!!
KWAIEHT INN JEE OFFISH, YOO CHU!
YOU'RE THE HARDEST ONE TO UNDER-STAND!!
YELL
YELL
!

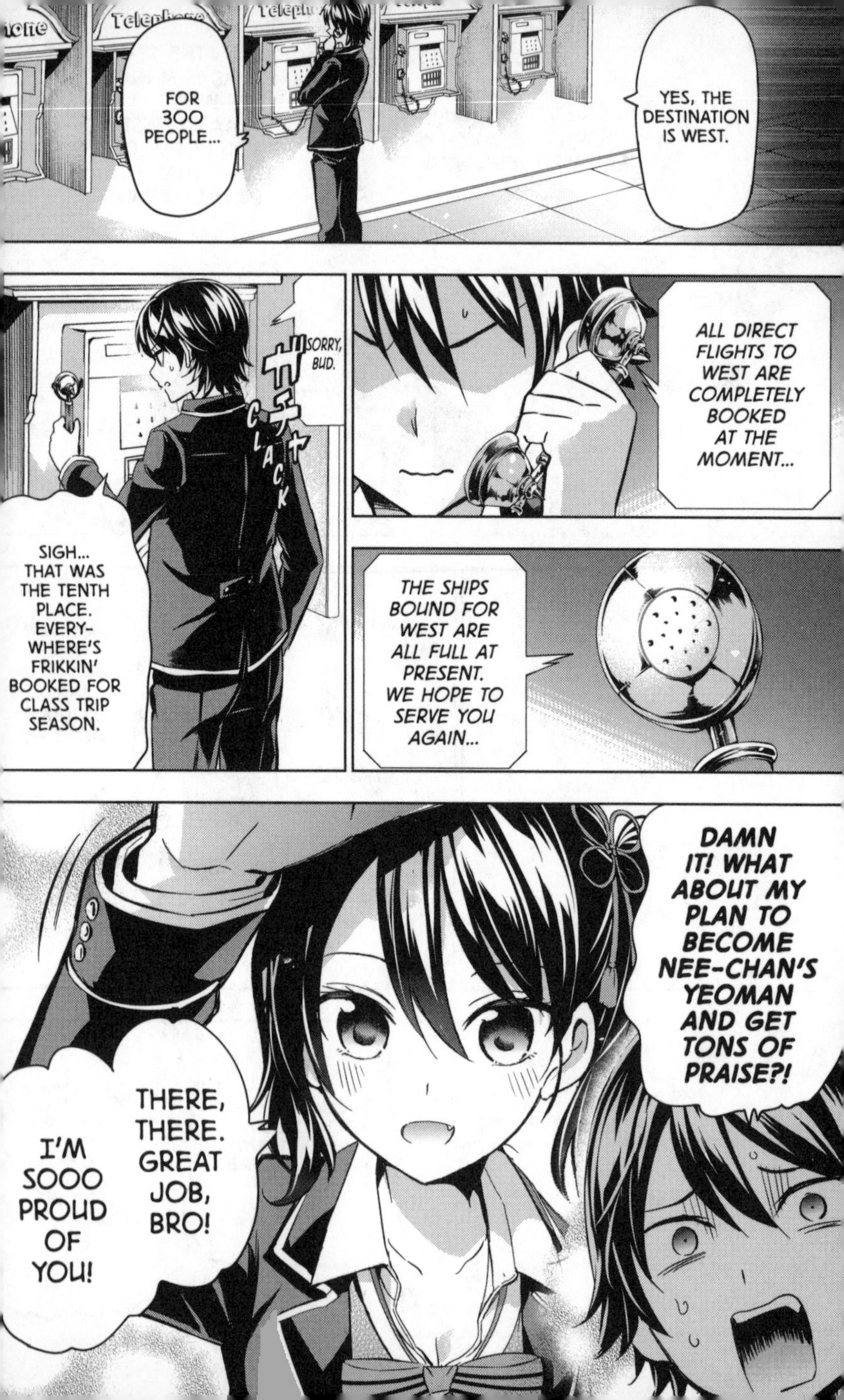
YES, THE DESTINATION IS WEST.
FOR 300 PEOPLE...
ALL DIRECT FLIGHTS TO WEST ARE COMPLETELY BOOKED AT THE MOMENT...
THE SHIPS BOUND FOR WEST ARE ALL FULL AT PRESENT. WE HOPE TO SERVE YOU AGAIN...
SORRY, BUD.
ガチャ
CLACK
SIGH... THAT WAS THE TENTH PLACE. EVERY-WHERE'S FRIKKIN' BOOKED FOR CLASS TRIP SEASON.
DAMN IT! WHAT ABOUT MY PLAN TO BECOME NEE-CHAN'S YEOMAN AND GET TONS OF PRAISE?!
THERE, THERE. GREAT JOB, BRO!
I'M SOOO PROUD OF YOU!

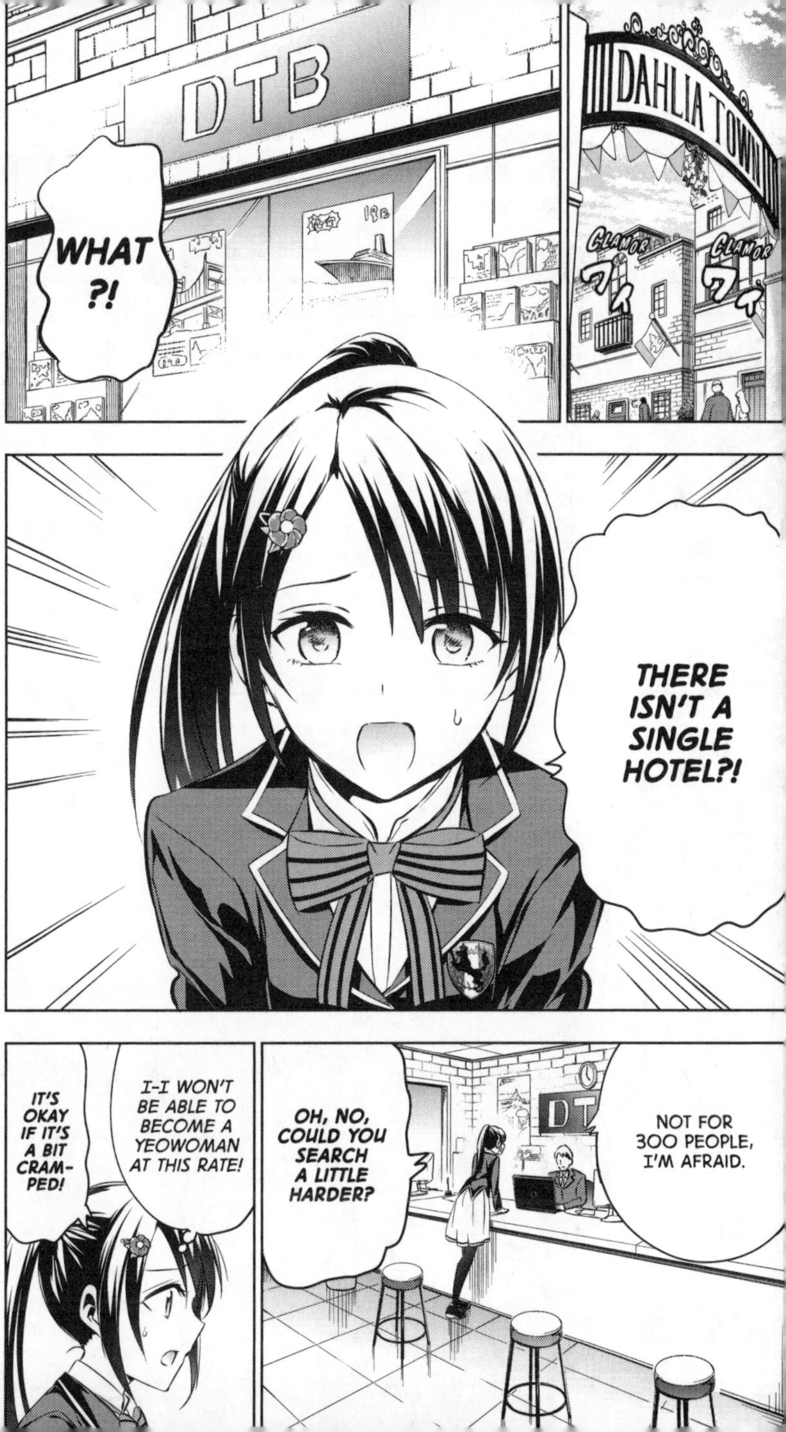
DAHLIA TOWN
CLAMOR ワイ
CLAMOR ワイ
DTB
WHAT?!
THERE ISN'T A SINGLE HOTEL?!
NOT FOR 300 PEOPLE, I'M AFRAID.
DT
OH, NO, COULD YOU SEARCH A LITTLE HARDER?
I-I WON'T BE ABLE TO BECOME A YEOWOMAN AT THIS RATE!
IT'S OKAY IF IT'S A BIT CRAM-PED!

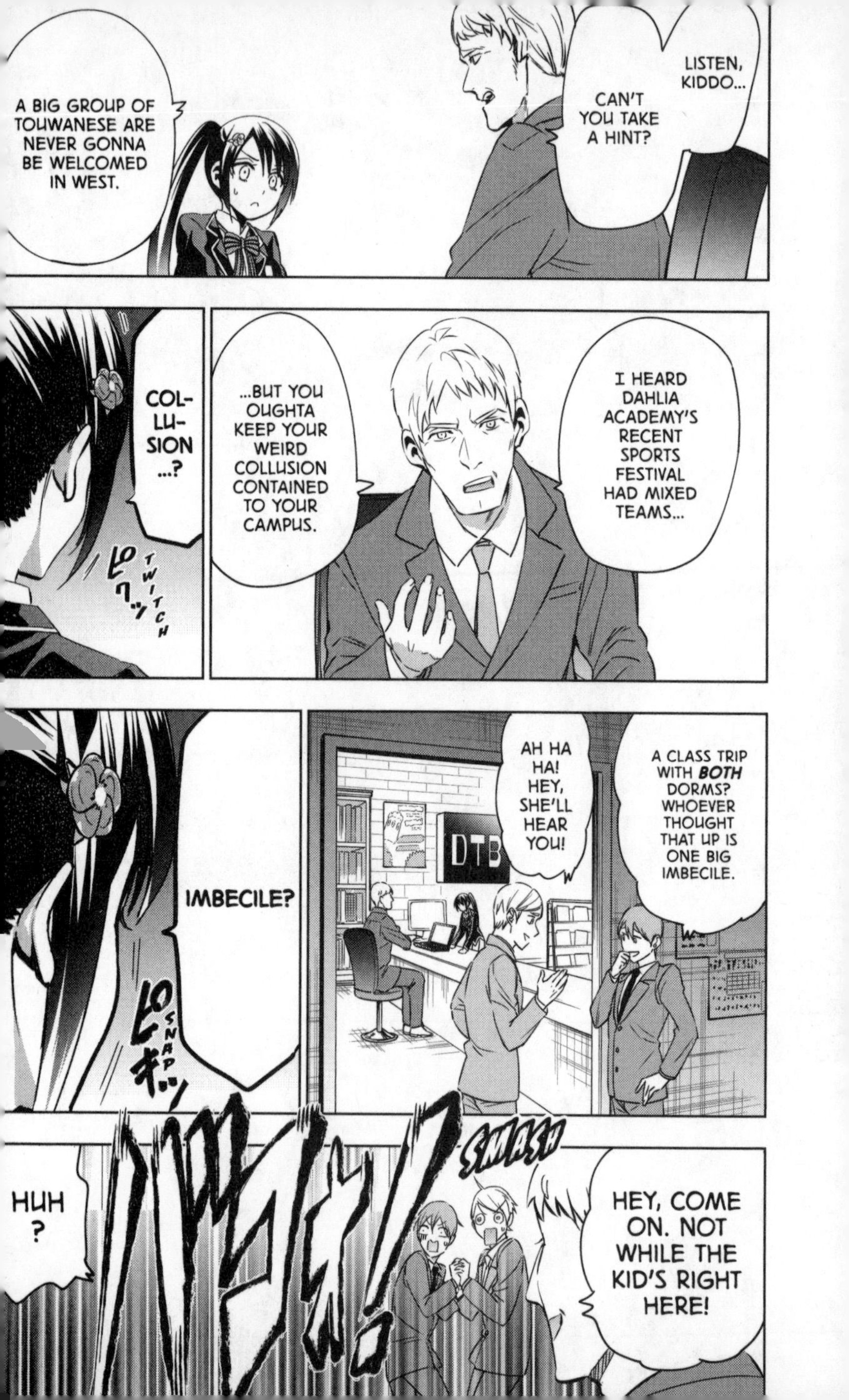
LISTEN, KIDDO... CAN'T YOU TAKE A HINT?
A BIG GROUP OF TOUWANESE ARE NEVER GONNA BE WELCOMED IN WEST.
I HEARD DAHLIA ACADEMY'S RECENT SPORTS FESTIVAL HAD MIXED TEAMS...
...BUT YOU OUGHTA KEEP YOUR WEIRD COLLUSION CONTAINED TO YOUR CAMPUS.
COL-LU-SION ...?
TWITCH
A CLASS TRIP WITH BOTH DORMS? WHOEVER THOUGHT THAT UP IS ONE BIG IMBECILE.
AH HA HA! HEY, SHE'LL HEAR YOU!
DTB
IMBECILE?
SNAP
SMASH
HEY, COME ON. NOT WHILE THE KID'S RIGHT HERE!
HUH ?

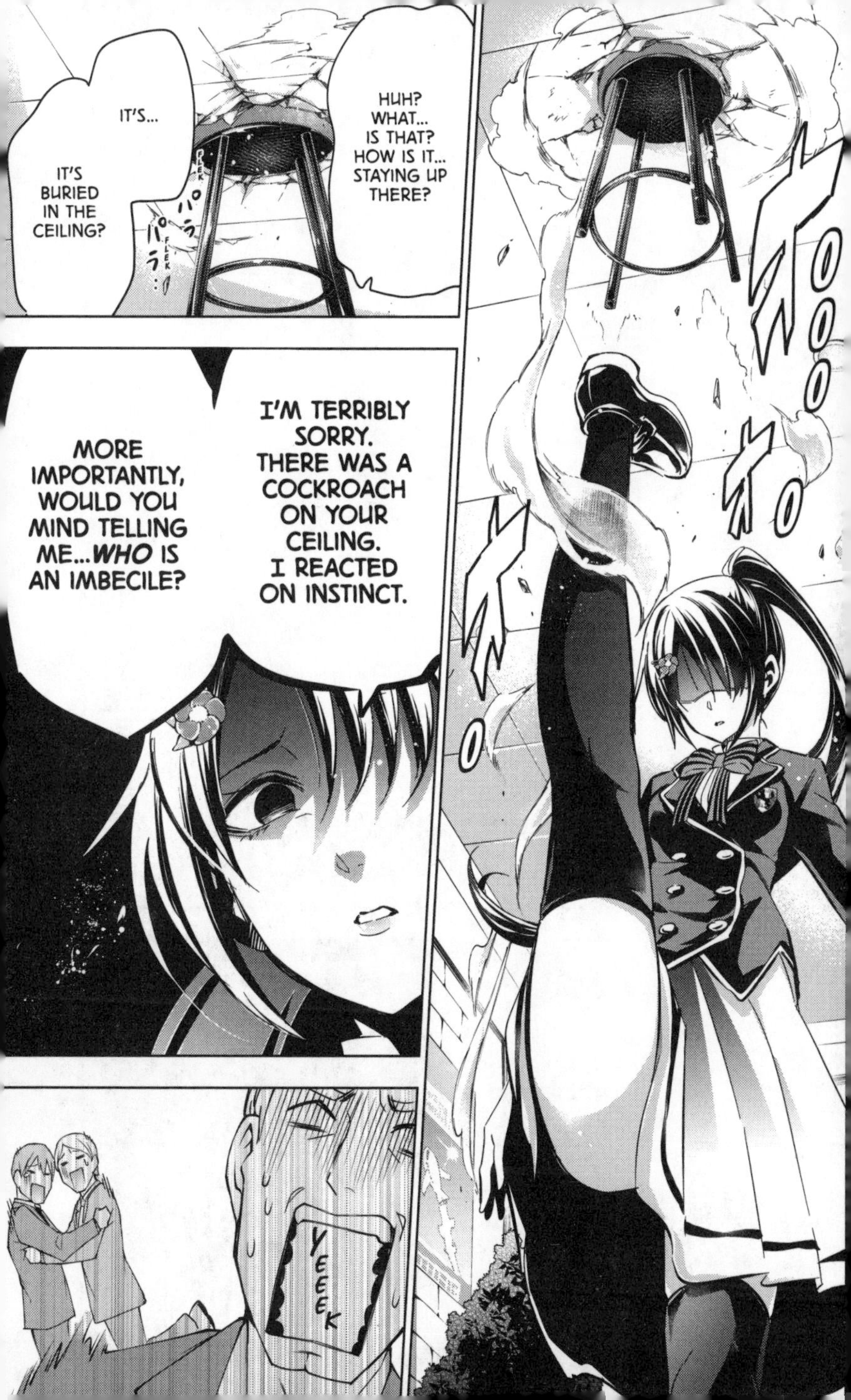
HUH? WHAT... IS THAT? HOW IS IT... STAYING UP THERE?
IT'S...
IT'S BURIED IN THE CEILING?
FLEK
FLEK
I'M TERRIBLY SORRY. THERE WAS A COCKROACH ON YOUR CEILING. I REACTED ON INSTINCT.
MORE IMPORTANTLY, WOULD YOU MIND TELLING ME...*WHO* IS AN IMBECILE?
YEEEK

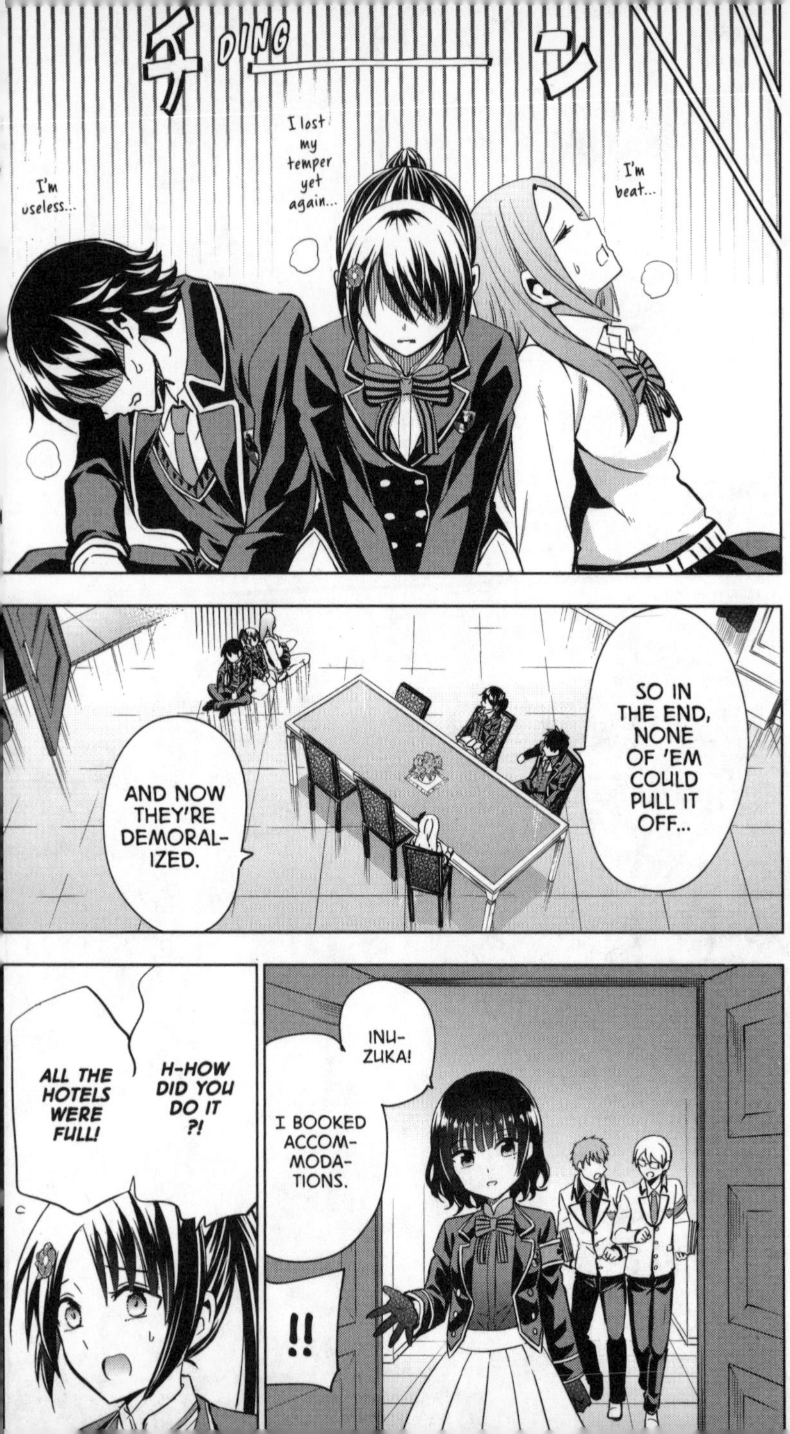
チ DING ーン
I'm beat...
I lost my temper yet again...
I'm useless...
SO IN THE END, NONE OF 'EM COULD PULL IT OFF...
AND NOW THEY'RE DEMORAL-IZED.
INU-ZUKA!
I BOOKED ACCOM-MODA-TIONS.
!!
H-HOW DID YOU DO IT ?!
ALL THE HOTELS WERE FULL!

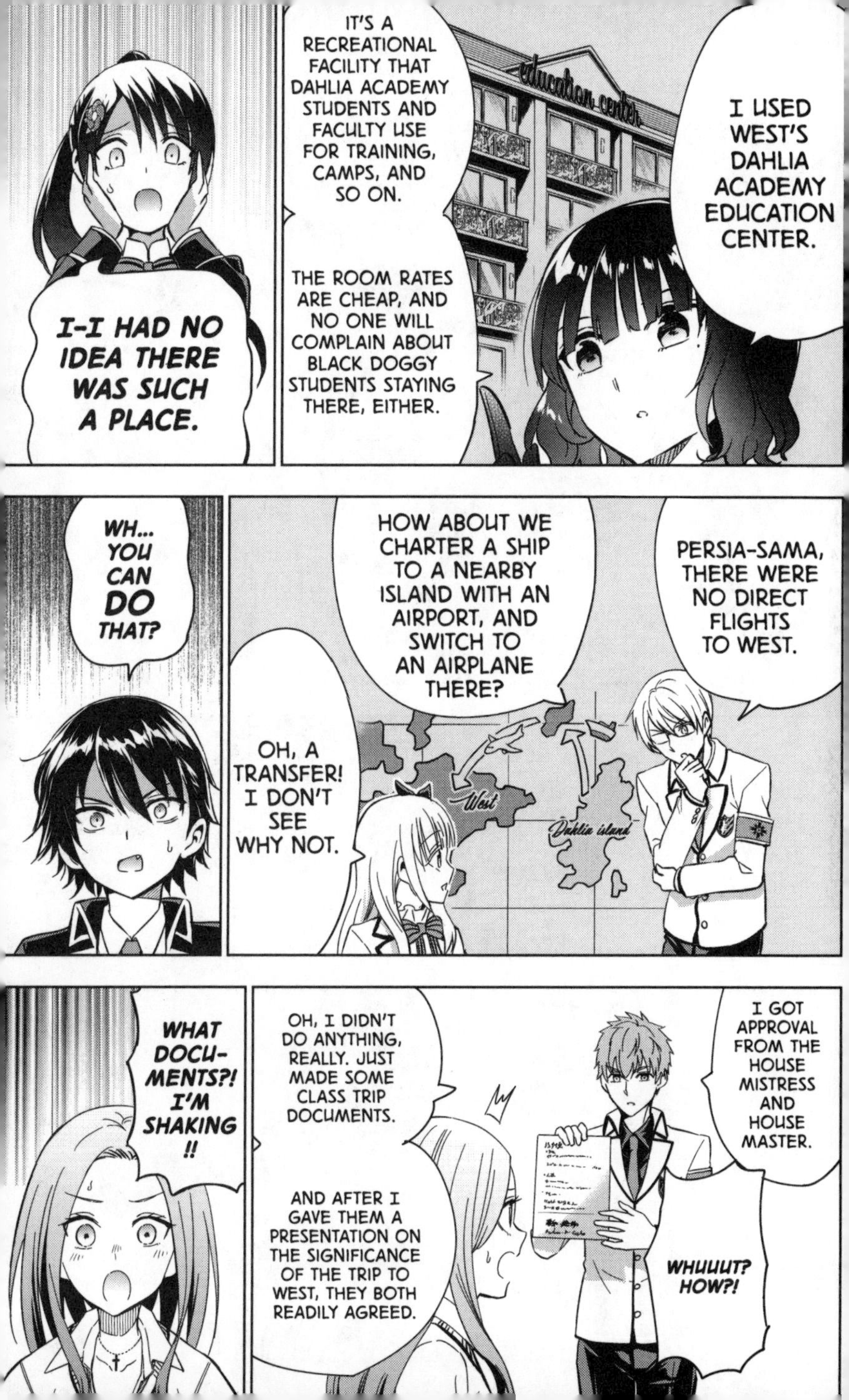
I USED WEST'S DAHLIA ACADEMY EDUCATION CENTER.
education center
IT'S A RECREATIONAL FACILITY THAT DAHLIA ACADEMY STUDENTS AND FACULTY USE FOR TRAINING, CAMPS, AND SO ON.
THE ROOM RATES ARE CHEAP, AND NO ONE WILL COMPLAIN ABOUT BLACK DOGGY STUDENTS STAYING THERE, EITHER.
I-I HAD NO IDEA THERE WAS SUCH A PLACE.
PERSIA-SAMA, THERE WERE NO DIRECT FLIGHTS TO WEST.
HOW ABOUT WE CHARTER A SHIP TO A NEARBY ISLAND WITH AN AIRPORT, AND SWITCH TO AN AIRPLANE THERE?
West
Dahlia island
OH, A TRANSFER! I DON'T SEE WHY NOT.
WH... YOU CAN DO THAT?
I GOT APPROVAL FROM THE HOUSE MISTRESS AND HOUSE MASTER.
OH, I DIDN'T DO ANYTHING, REALLY. JUST MADE SOME CLASS TRIP DOCUMENTS.
AND AFTER I GAVE THEM A PRESENTATION ON THE SIGNIFICANCE OF THE TRIP TO WEST, THEY BOTH READILY AGREED.
WHUUUT? HOW?!
WHAT DOCUMENTS?! I'M SHAKING!!

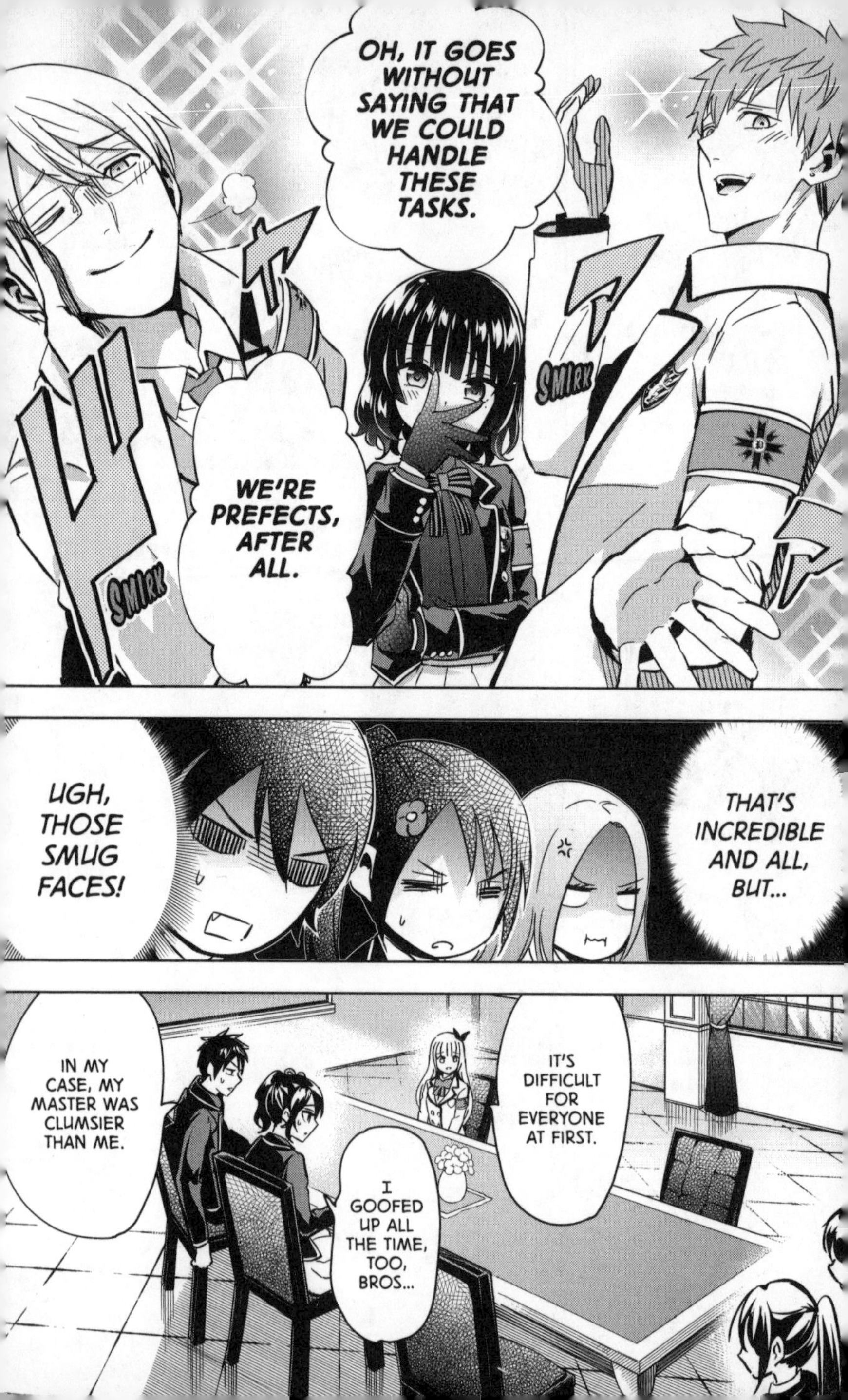
OH, IT GOES WITHOUT SAYING THAT WE COULD HANDLE THESE TASKS.
SMIRK
WE'RE PREFECTS, AFTER ALL.
SMIRK
THAT'S INCREDIBLE AND ALL, BUT...
UGH, THOSE SMUG FACES!
IT'S DIFFICULT FOR EVERYONE AT FIRST.
I GOOFED UP ALL THE TIME, TOO, BROS...
IN MY CASE, MY MASTER WAS CLUMSIER THAN ME.

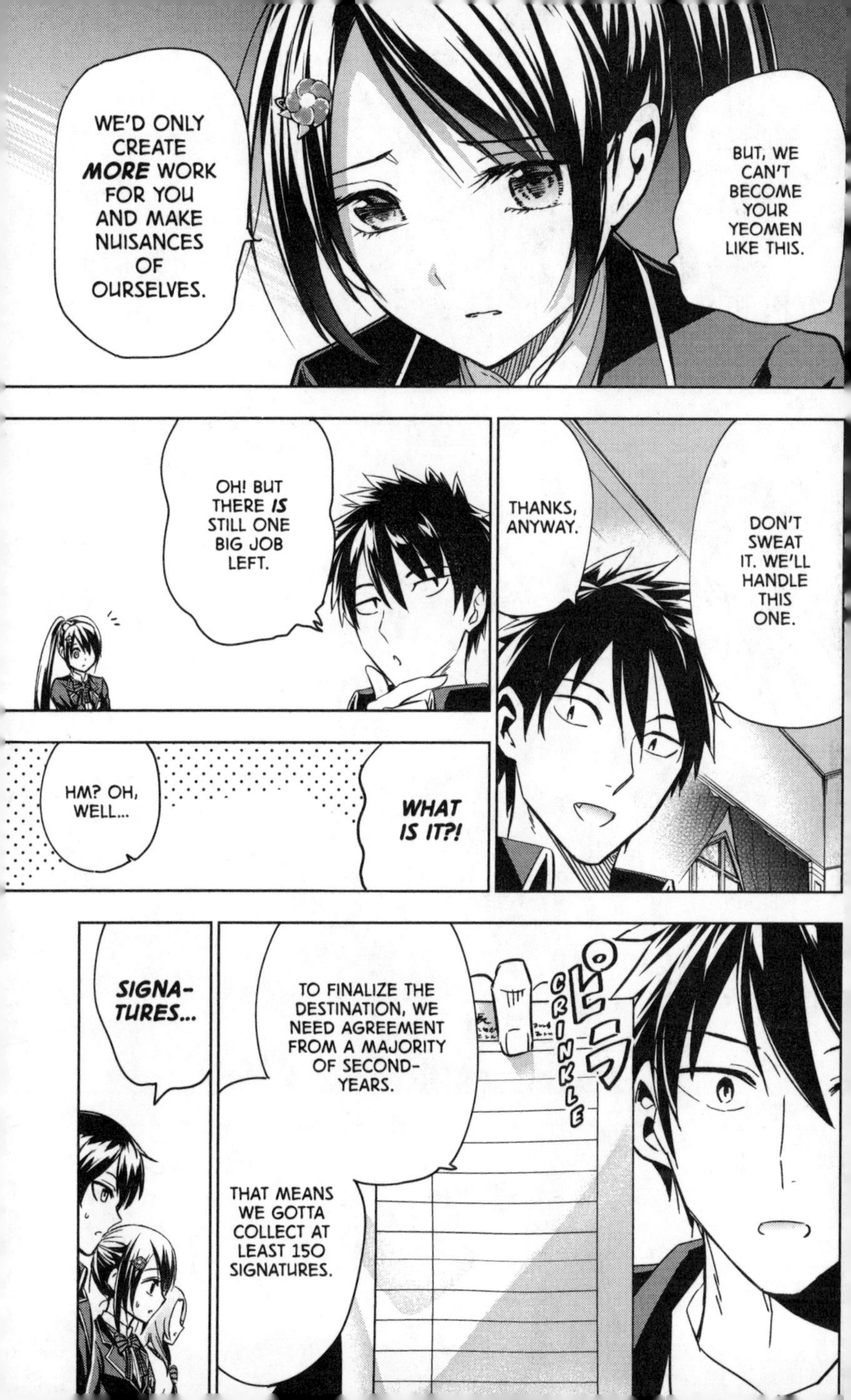
BUT, WE CAN'T BECOME YOUR YEOMEN LIKE THIS.
WE'D ONLY CREATE *MORE* WORK FOR YOU AND MAKE NUISANCES OF OURSELVES.
DON'T SWEAT IT. WE'LL HANDLE THIS ONE.
THANKS, ANYWAY.
OH! BUT THERE *IS* STILL ONE BIG JOB LEFT.
*WHAT IS IT?!*
HM? OH, WELL...
ピラ
CRINKLE
TO FINALIZE THE DESTINATION, WE NEED AGREEMENT FROM A MAJORITY OF SECOND-YEARS.
THAT MEANS WE GOTTA COLLECT AT LEAST 150 SIGNATURES.
*SIGNA-TURES...*

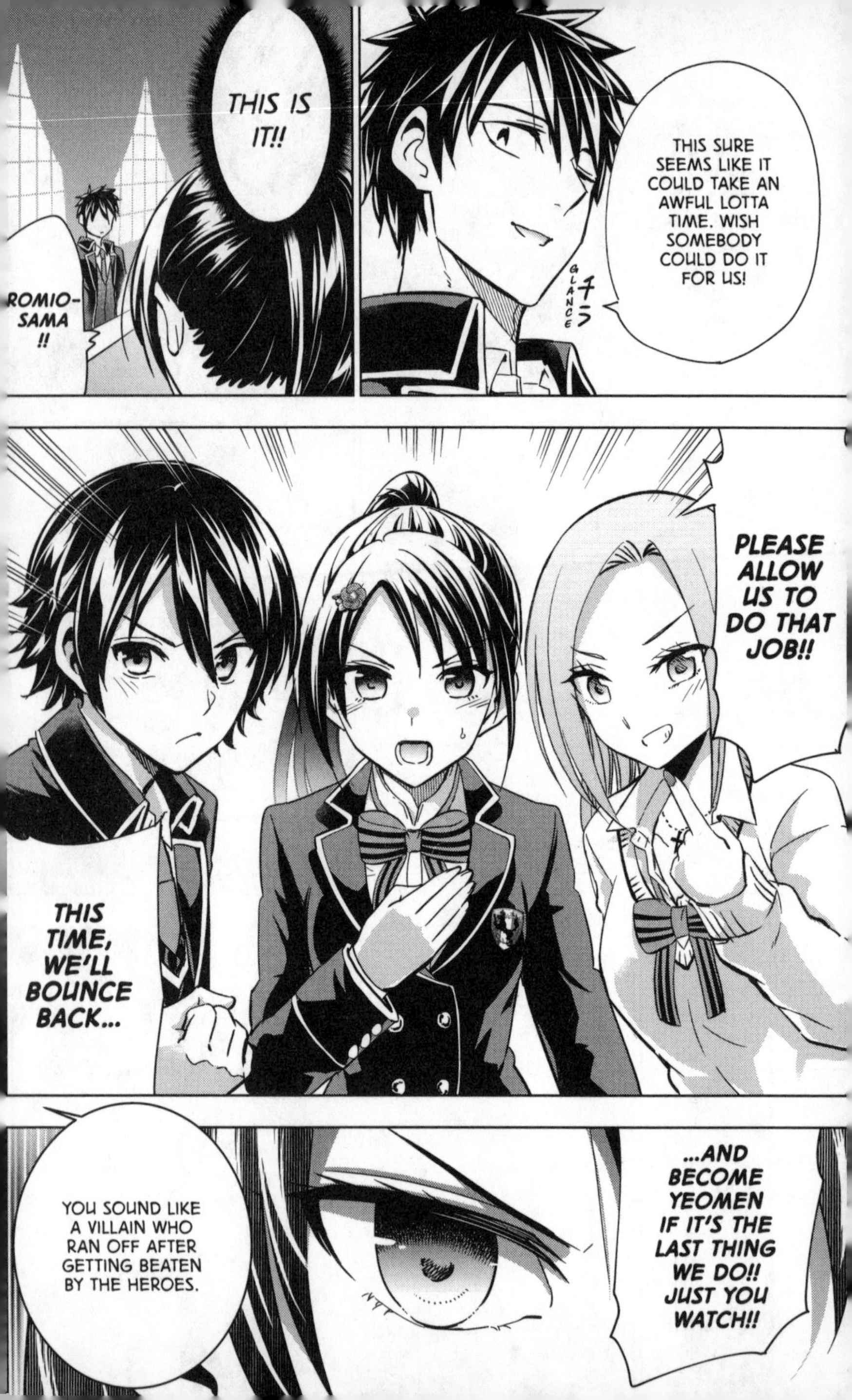
THIS SURE SEEMS LIKE IT COULD TAKE AN AWFUL LOTTA TIME. WISH SOMEBODY COULD DO IT FOR US!
チラ
GLANCE
THIS IS IT!!
ROMIO-SAMA !!
PLEASE ALLOW US TO DO THAT JOB!!
THIS TIME, WE'LL BOUNCE BACK...
...AND BECOME YEOMEN IF IT'S THE LAST THING WE DO!! JUST YOU WATCH!!
YOU SOUND LIKE A VILLAIN WHO RAN OFF AFTER GETTING BEATEN BY THE HEROES.

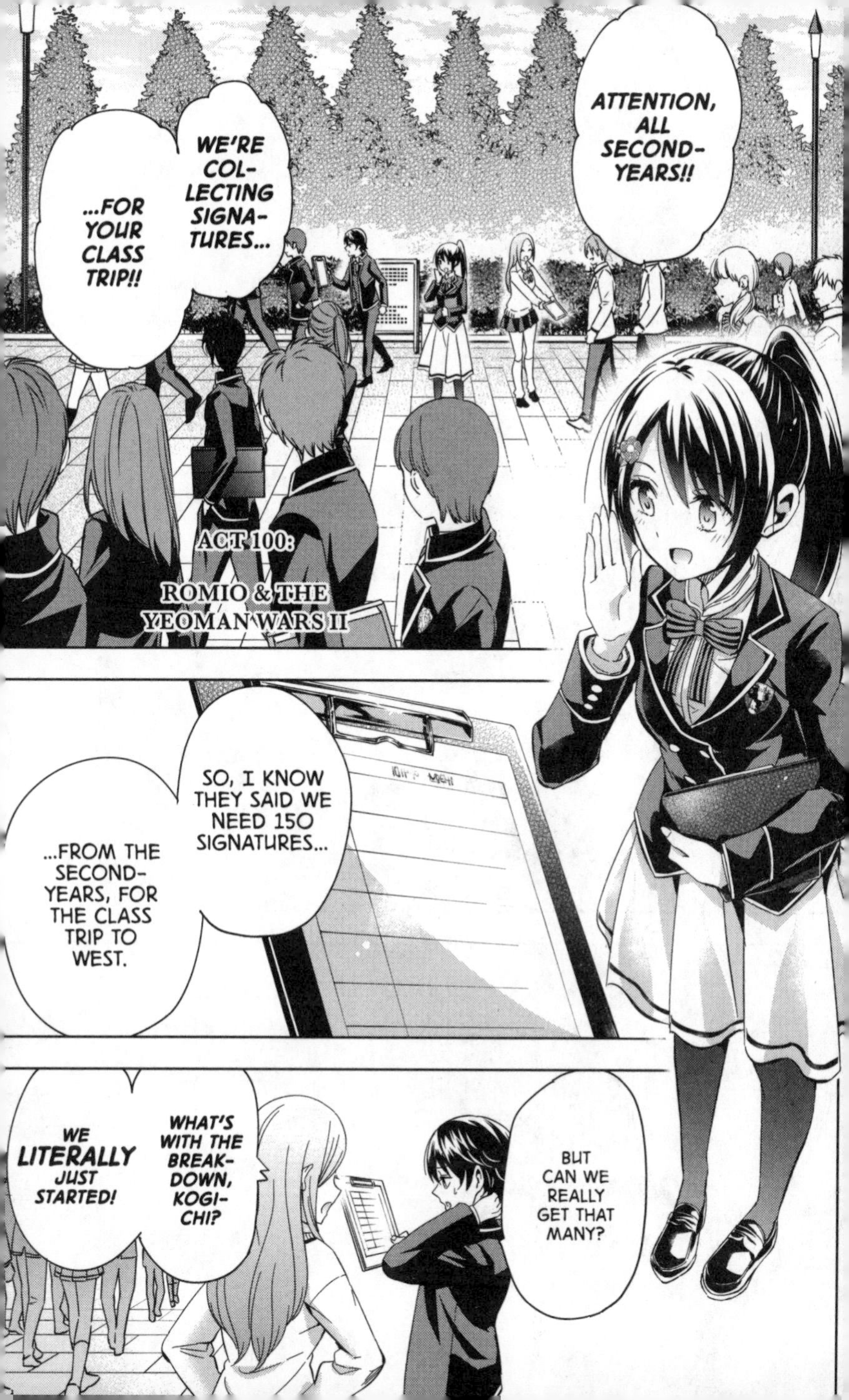
ATTENTION, ALL SECOND-YEARS!!
WE'RE COLLECTING SIGNATURES...
...FOR YOUR CLASS TRIP!!
ACT 100:
ROMIO & THE YEOMAN WARS II
SO, I KNOW THEY SAID WE NEED 150 SIGNATURES...
...FROM THE SECOND-YEARS, FOR THE CLASS TRIP TO WEST.
BUT CAN WE REALLY GET THAT MANY?
WHAT'S WITH THE BREAKDOWN, KOGI-CHI?
WE **LITERALLY** JUST STARTED!

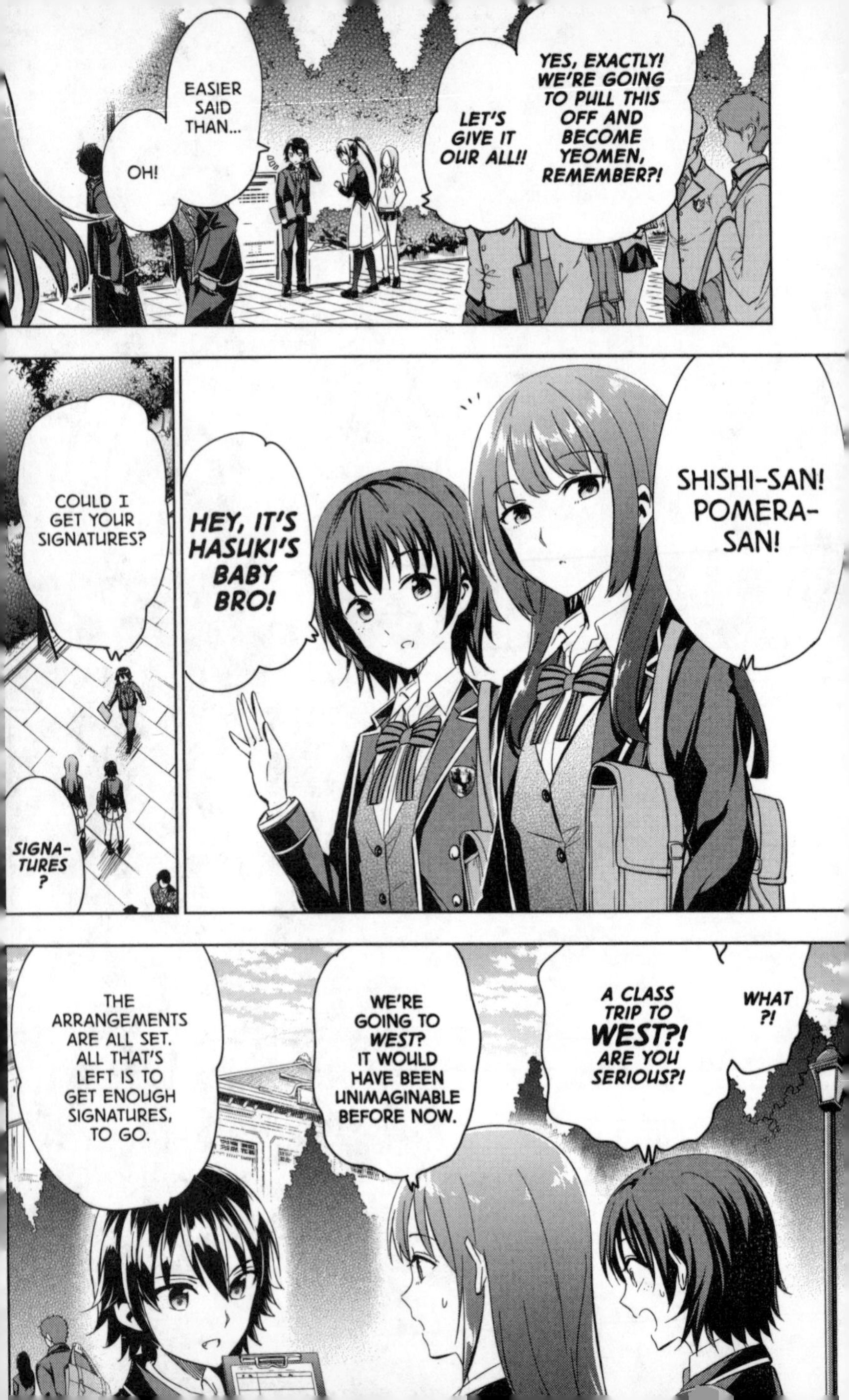
YES, EXACTLY! WE'RE GOING TO PULL THIS OFF AND BECOME YEOMEN, REMEMBER?!
LET'S GIVE IT OUR ALL!!
EASIER SAID THAN...
OH!
SHISHI-SAN! POMERA-SAN!
HEY, IT'S HASUKI'S BABY BRO!
COULD I GET YOUR SIGNATURES?
SIGNATURES?
WHAT?!
A CLASS TRIP TO WEST?! ARE YOU SERIOUS?!
WE'RE GOING TO WEST? IT WOULD HAVE BEEN UNIMAGINABLE BEFORE NOW.
THE ARRANGEMENTS ARE ALL SET. ALL THAT'S LEFT IS TO GET ENOUGH SIGNATURES, TO GO.

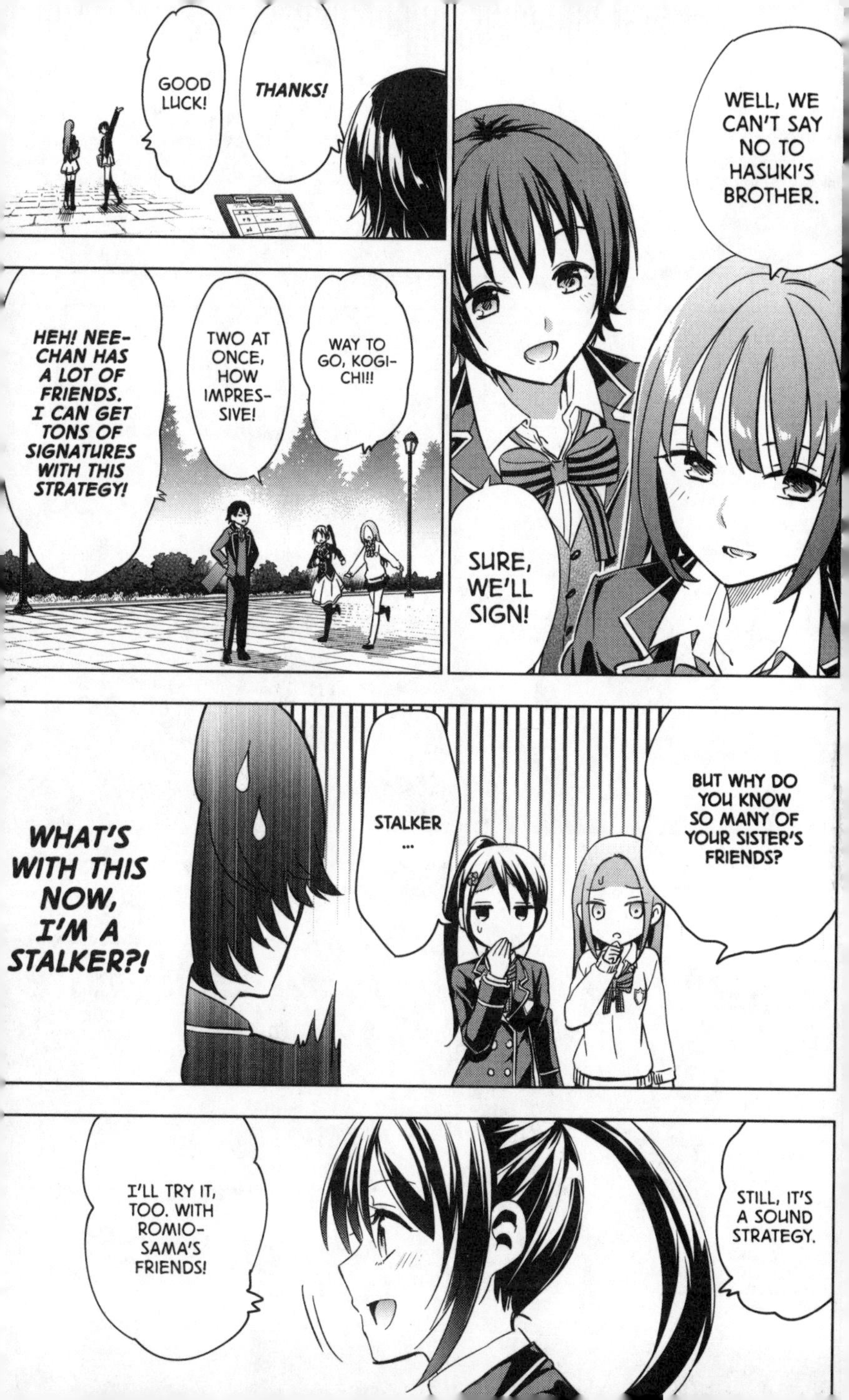
WELL, WE CAN'T SAY NO TO HASUKI'S BROTHER.
SURE, WE'LL SIGN!
THANKS!
GOOD LUCK!
WAY TO GO, KOGI-CHI!!
TWO AT ONCE, HOW IMPRESSIVE!
HEH! NEE-CHAN HAS A LOT OF FRIENDS. I CAN GET TONS OF SIGNATURES WITH THIS STRATEGY!
BUT WHY DO YOU KNOW SO MANY OF YOUR SISTER'S FRIENDS?
STALKER ...
WHAT'S WITH THIS NOW, I'M A STALKER?!
STILL, IT'S A SOUND STRATEGY.
I'LL TRY IT, TOO. WITH ROMIO-SAMA'S FRIENDS!

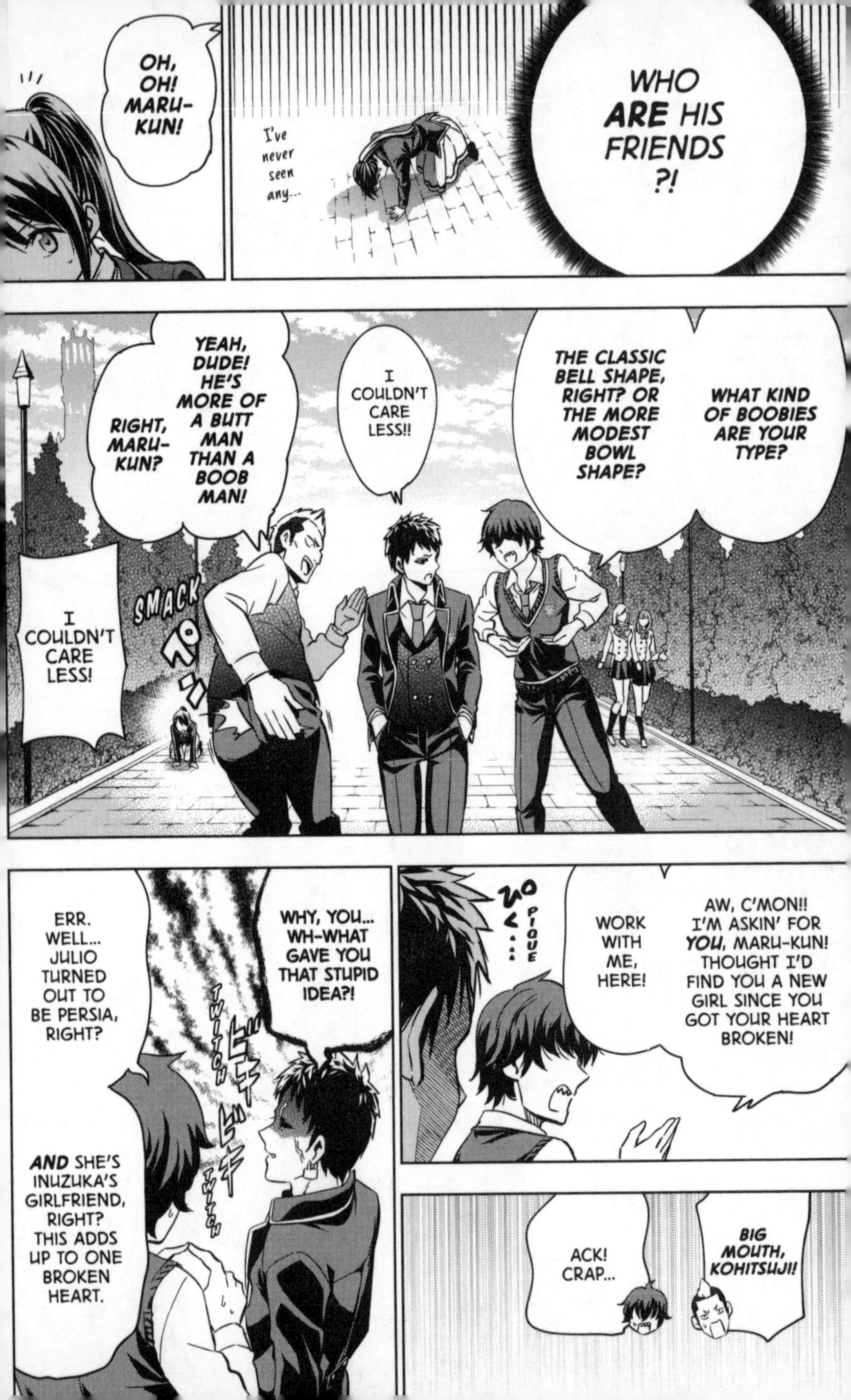
WHO ARE HIS FRIENDS ?!
I've never seen any...
OH, OH! MARU-KUN!
WHAT KIND OF BOOBIES ARE YOUR TYPE?
THE CLASSIC BELL SHAPE, RIGHT? OR THE MORE MODEST BOWL SHAPE?
I COULDN'T CARE LESS!!
YEAH, DUDE! HE'S MORE OF A BUTT MAN THAN A BOOB MAN!
RIGHT, MARU-KUN?
SMACK
I COULDN'T CARE LESS!
AW, C'MON!! I'M ASKIN' FOR YOU, MARU-KUN! THOUGHT I'D FIND YOU A NEW GIRL SINCE YOU GOT YOUR HEART BROKEN!
WORK WITH ME, HERE!
PIQUE
BIG MOUTH, KOHITSUJI!
ACK! CRAP...
WHY, YOU... WH-WHAT GAVE YOU THAT STUPID IDEA?!
TWITCH
TWITCH
ERR. WELL... JULIO TURNED OUT TO BE PERSIA, RIGHT?
AND SHE'S INUZUKA'S GIRLFRIEND, RIGHT? THIS ADDS UP TO ONE BROKEN HEART.

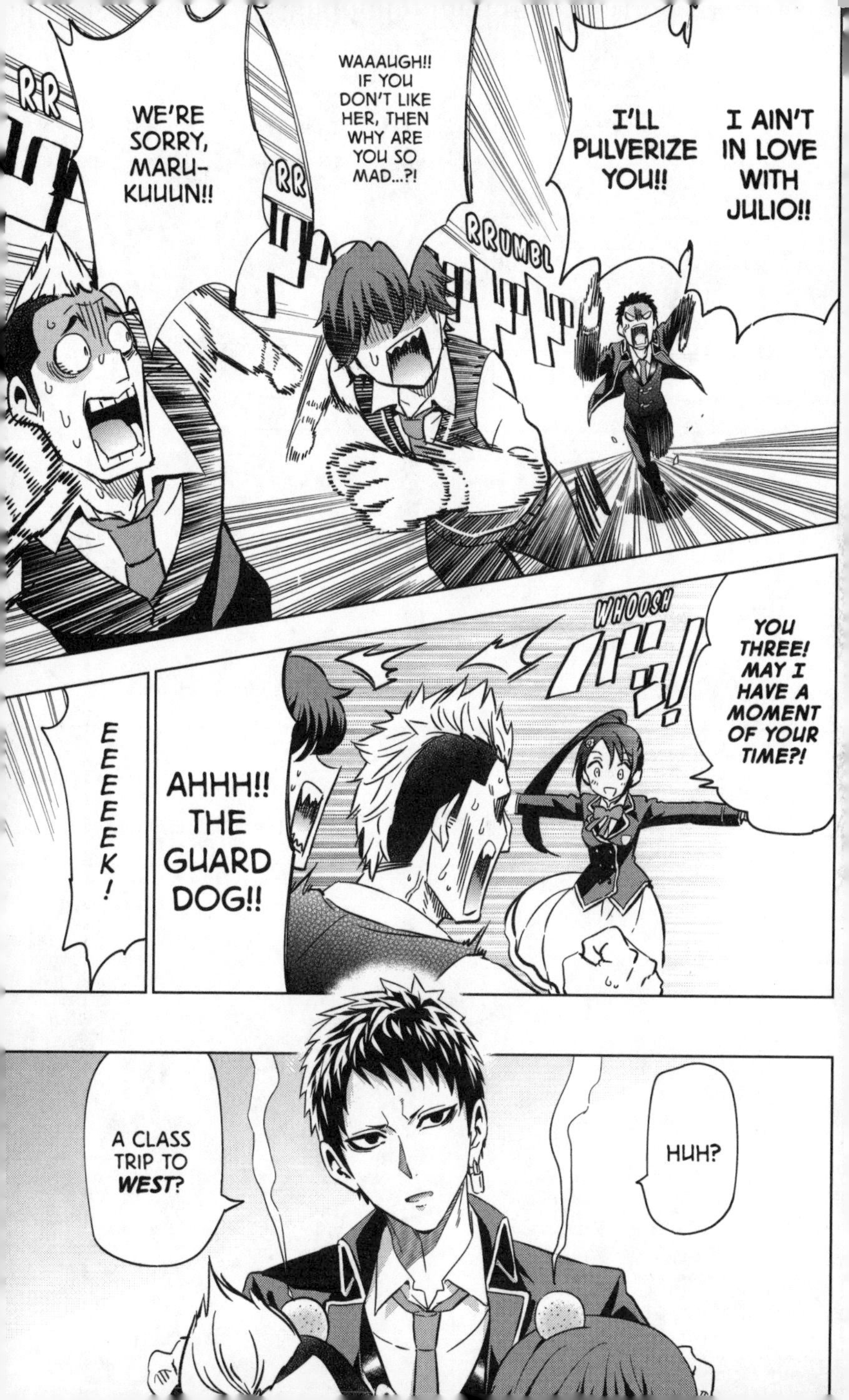
I AIN'T IN LOVE WITH JULIO!!
I'LL PULVERIZE YOU!!
RRUMBL
WAAAUGH!! IF YOU DON'T LIKE HER, THEN WHY ARE YOU SO MAD...?!
RR
WE'RE SORRY, MARU-KUUUN!!
RR
WHOOSH
YOU THREE! MAY I HAVE A MOMENT OF YOUR TIME?!
AHHH!! THE GUARD DOG!!
EEEEEK!
HUH?
A CLASS TRIP TO *WEST*?

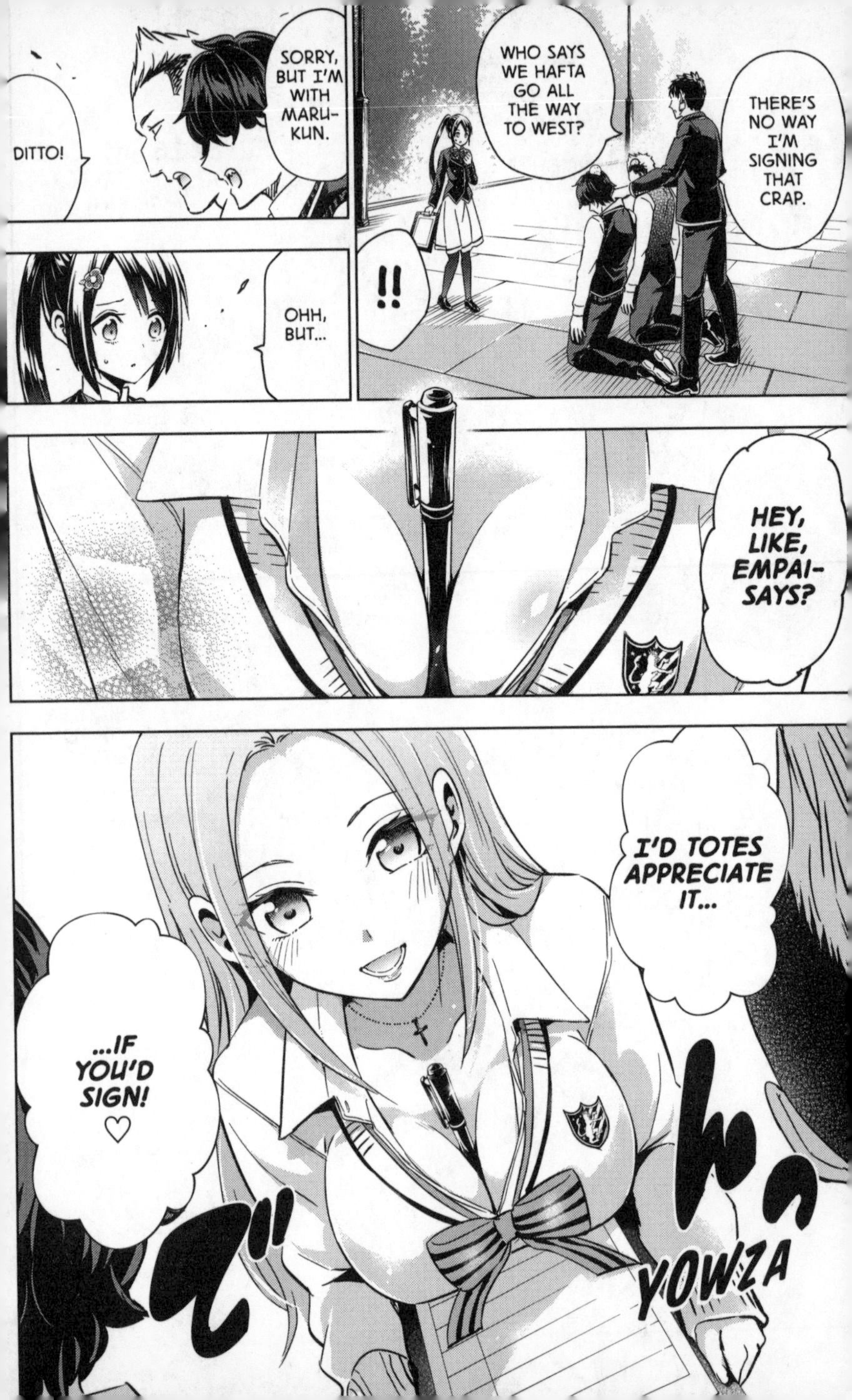
THERE'S NO WAY I'M SIGNING THAT CRAP.
WHO SAYS WE HAFTA GO ALL THE WAY TO WEST?
!!
SORRY, BUT I'M WITH MARU-KUN.
DITTO!
OHH, BUT...
HEY, LIKE, EMPAI-SAYS?
I'D TOTES APPRECIATE IT...
...IF YOU'D SIGN! ♡
YOWZA

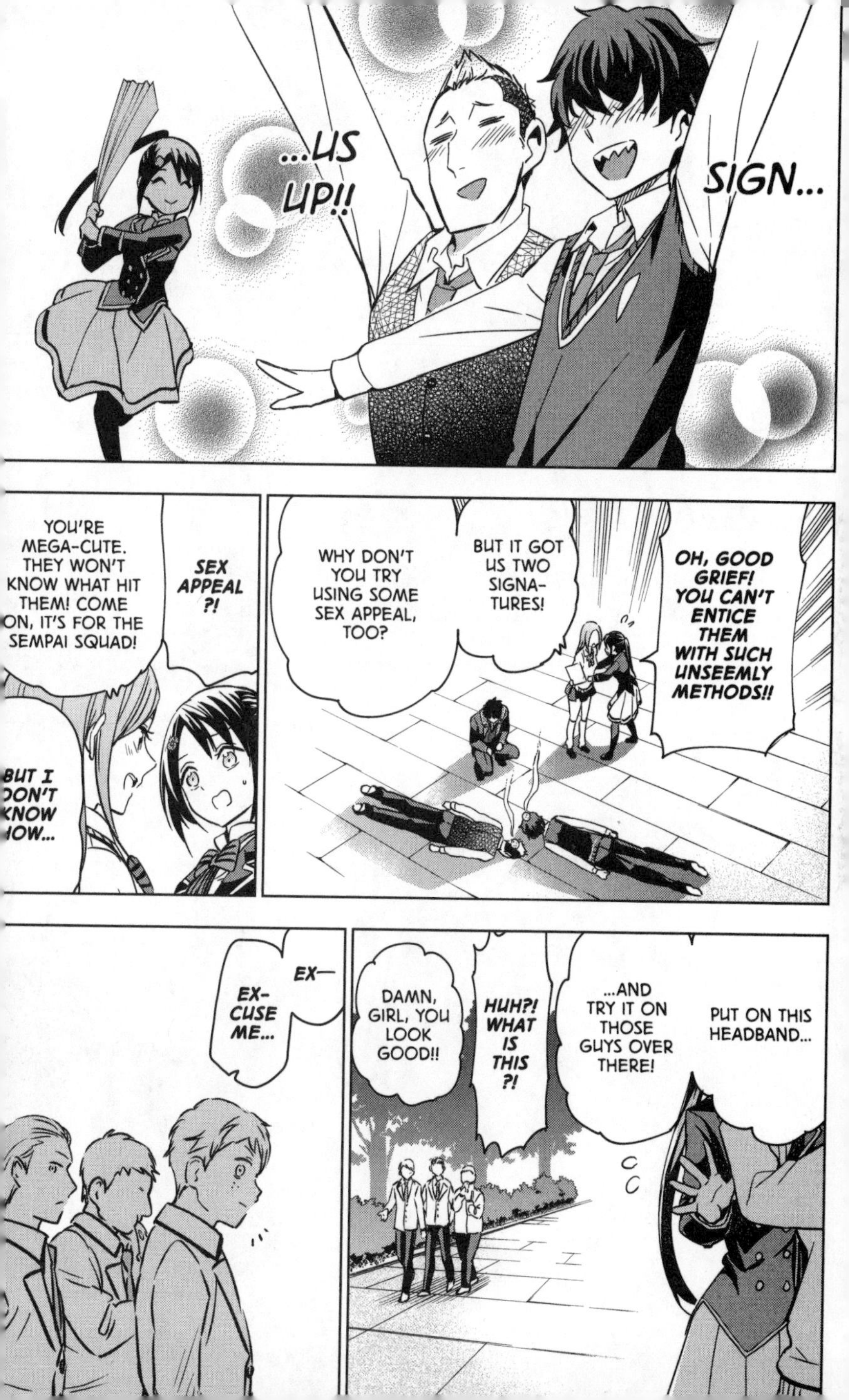

SIGN...
...US UP!!
OH, GOOD GRIEF! YOU CAN'T ENTICE THEM WITH SUCH UNSEEMLY METHODS!!
BUT IT GOT US TWO SIGNA-TURES!
WHY DON'T YOU TRY USING SOME SEX APPEAL, TOO?
SEX APPEAL?!
YOU'RE MEGA-CUTE. THEY WON'T KNOW WHAT HIT THEM! COME ON, IT'S FOR THE SEMPAI SQUAD!
BUT I DON'T KNOW HOW...
PUT ON THIS HEADBAND...
...AND TRY IT ON THOSE GUYS OVER THERE!
HUH?! WHAT IS THIS?!
DAMN, GIRL, YOU LOOK GOOD!!
EX—
EX-CUSE ME...

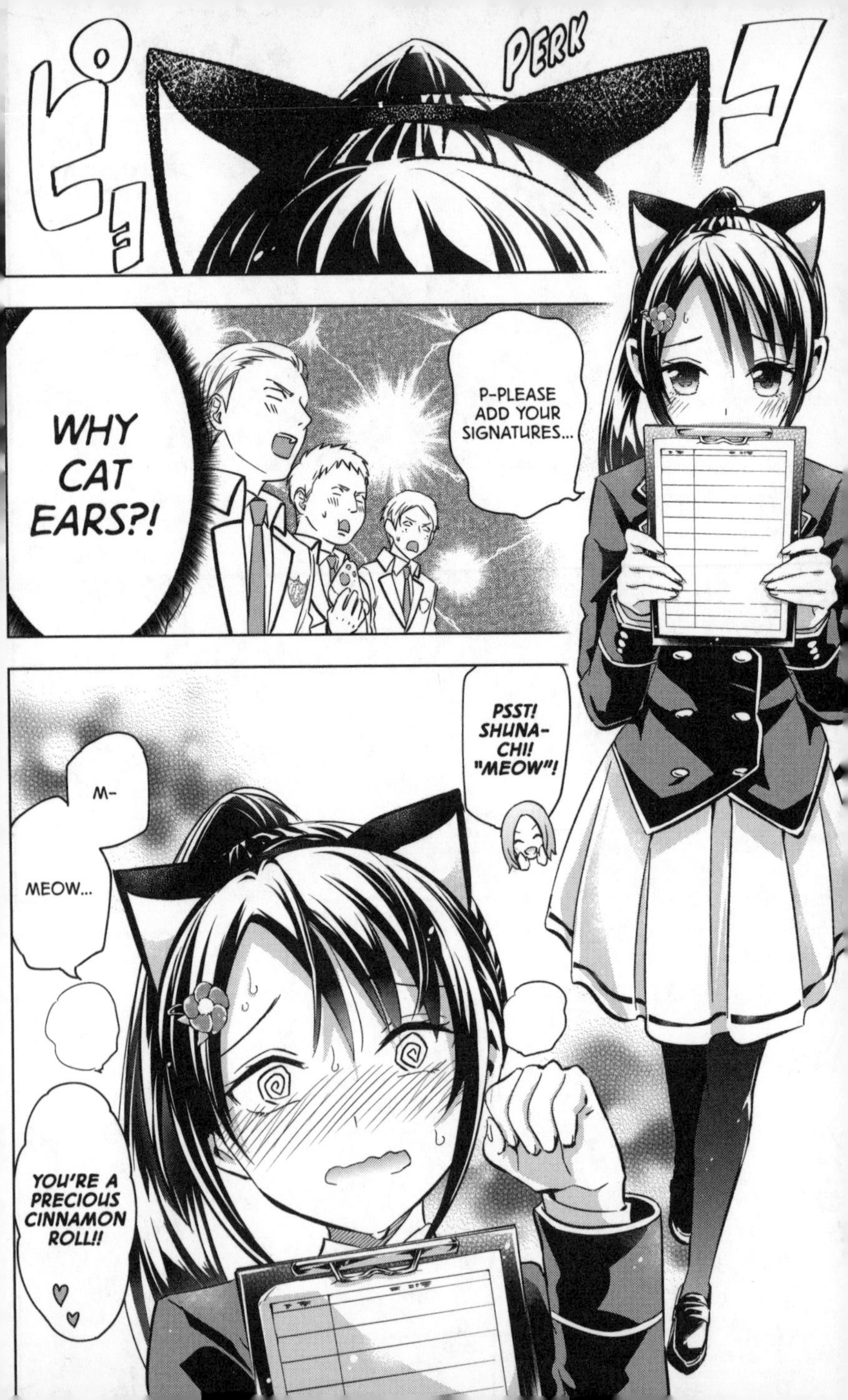
PERK
P-PLEASE ADD YOUR SIGNATURES...
WHY CAT EARS?!
PSST! SHUNA-CHI! "MEOW"!
M-
MEOW...
YOU'RE A PRECIOUS CINNAMON ROLL!! ♥ ♥

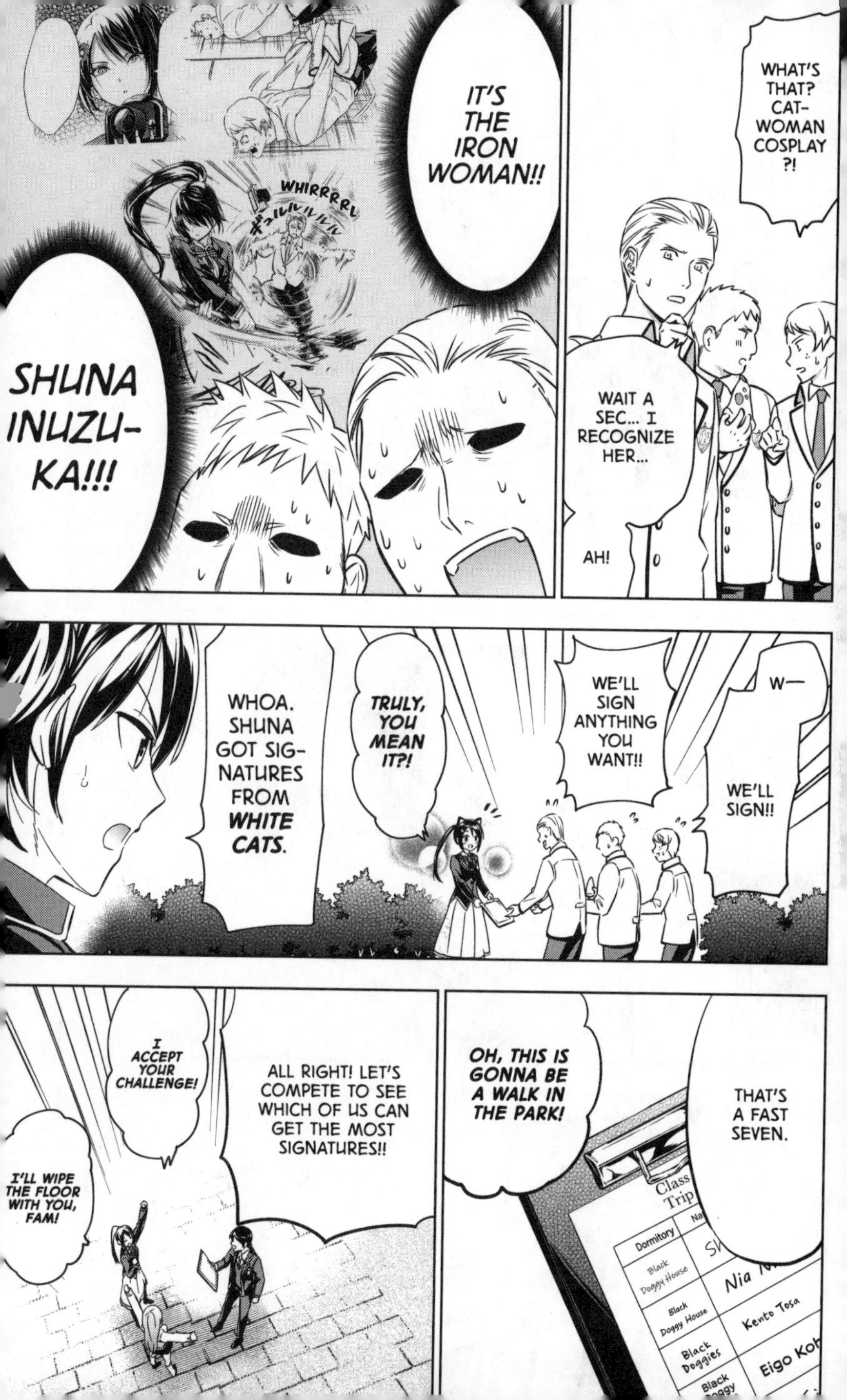
WHAT'S THAT? CAT-WOMAN COSPLAY?!
WAIT A SEC... I RECOGNIZE HER...
AH!
IT'S THE IRON WOMAN!!
WHIRRRRL
SHUNA INUZUKA!!!
W—
WE'LL SIGN!!
WE'LL SIGN ANYTHING YOU WANT!!
TRULY, YOU MEAN IT?!
WHOA. SHUNA GOT SIGNATURES FROM WHITE CATS.
THAT'S A FAST SEVEN.
OH, THIS IS GONNA BE A WALK IN THE PARK!
Class Trip
Dormitory
Black Doggy House
Nia
Black Doggy House
Kento Tosa
Black Doggies
ALL RIGHT! LET'S COMPETE TO SEE WHICH OF US CAN GET THE MOST SIGNATURES!!
I ACCEPT YOUR CHALLENGE!
I'LL WIPE THE FLOOR WITH YOU, FAM!

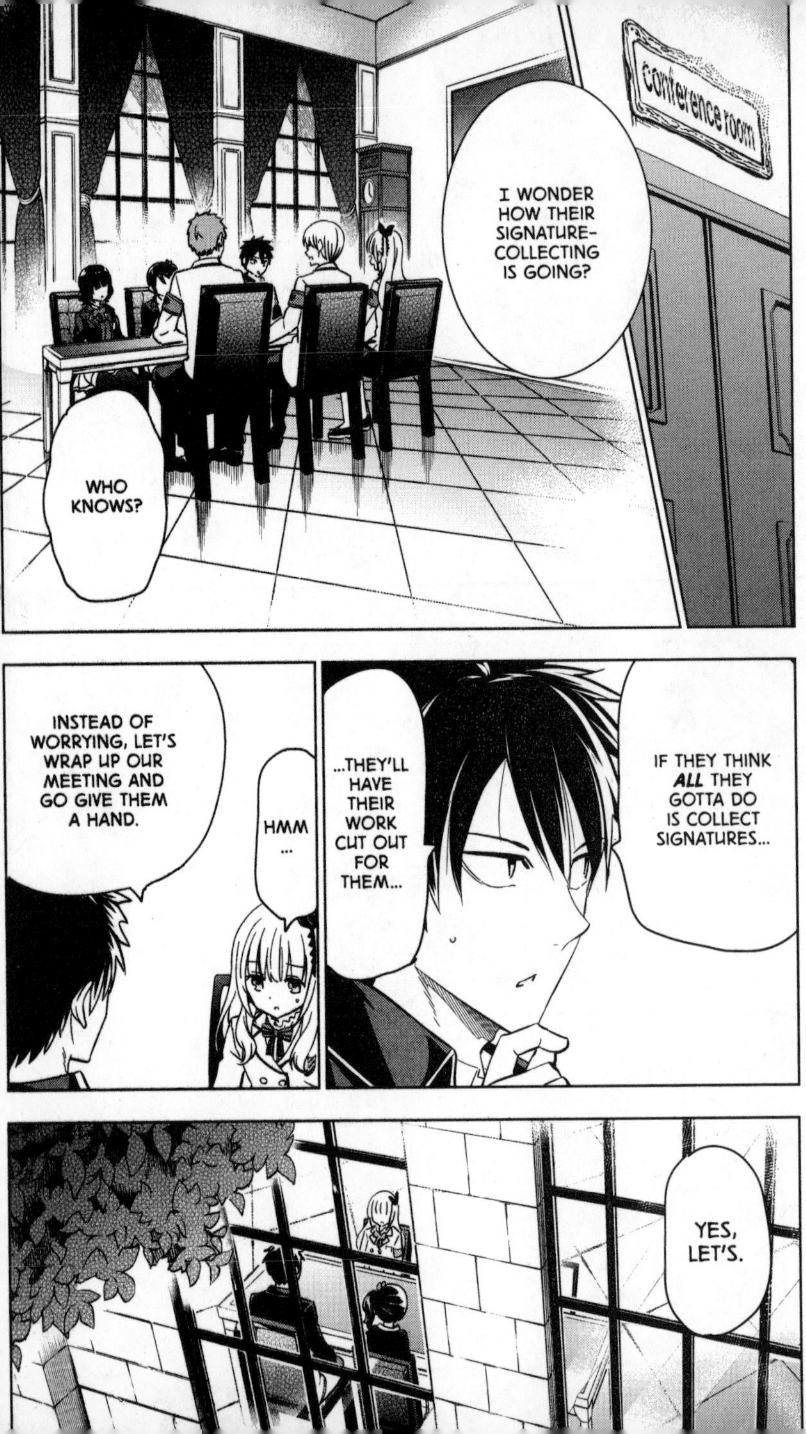
Conference room
I WONDER HOW THEIR SIGNATURE-COLLECTING IS GOING?
WHO KNOWS?
IF THEY THINK *ALL* THEY GOTTA DO IS COLLECT SIGNATURES...
...THEY'LL HAVE THEIR WORK CUT OUT FOR THEM...
HMM ...
INSTEAD OF WORRYING, LET'S WRAP UP OUR MEETING AND GO GIVE THEM A HAND.
YES, LET'S.

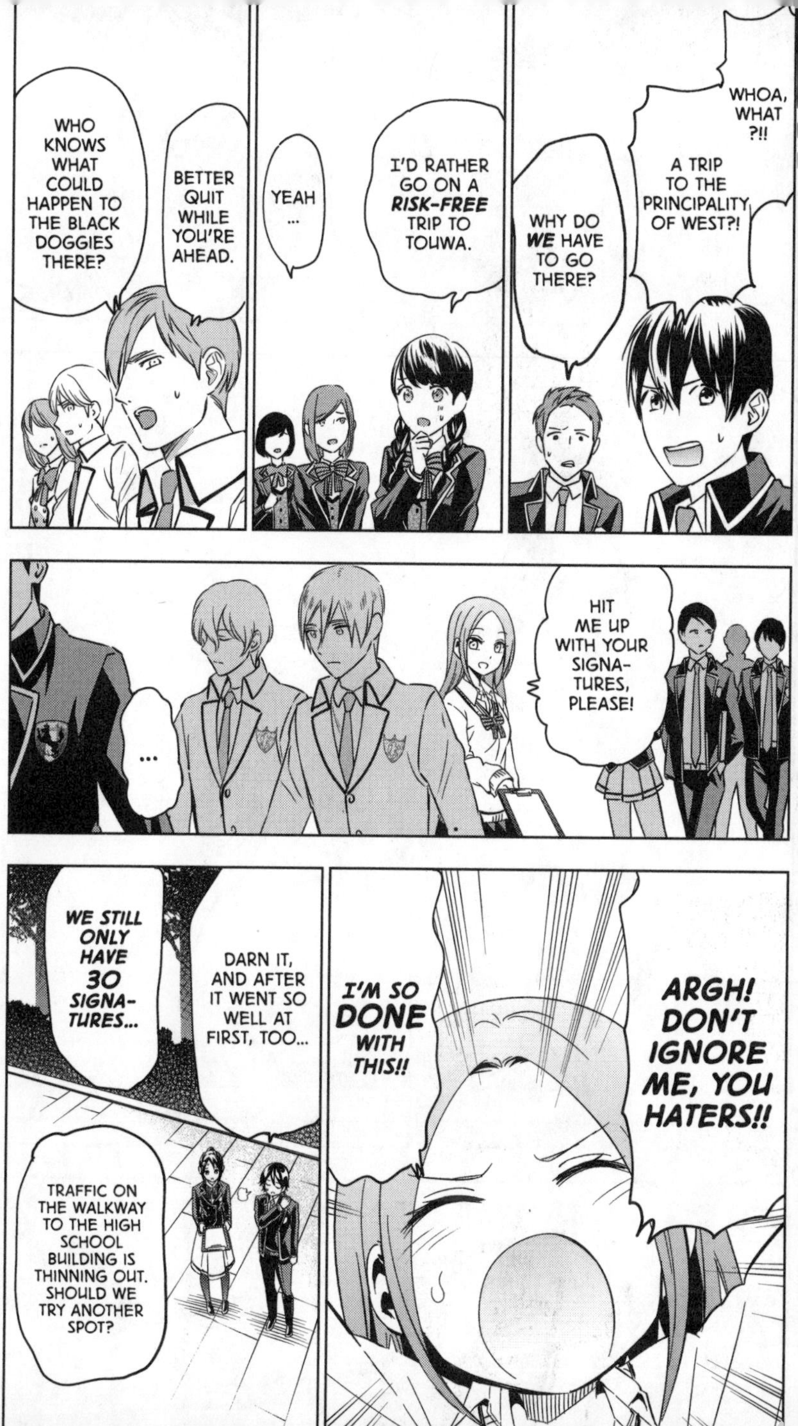
WHOA, WHAT ?!!
A TRIP TO THE PRINCIPALITY OF WEST?!
WHY DO WE HAVE TO GO THERE?
I'D RATHER GO ON A RISK-FREE TRIP TO TOUWA.
YEAH ...
BETTER QUIT WHILE YOU'RE AHEAD.
WHO KNOWS WHAT COULD HAPPEN TO THE BLACK DOGGIES THERE?
HIT ME UP WITH YOUR SIGNATURES, PLEASE!
...
ARGH! DON'T IGNORE ME, YOU HATERS!!
I'M SO DONE WITH THIS!!
DARN IT, AND AFTER IT WENT SO WELL AT FIRST, TOO...
WE STILL ONLY HAVE 30 SIGNATURES...
TRAFFIC ON THE WALKWAY TO THE HIGH SCHOOL BUILDING IS THINNING OUT. SHOULD WE TRY ANOTHER SPOT?

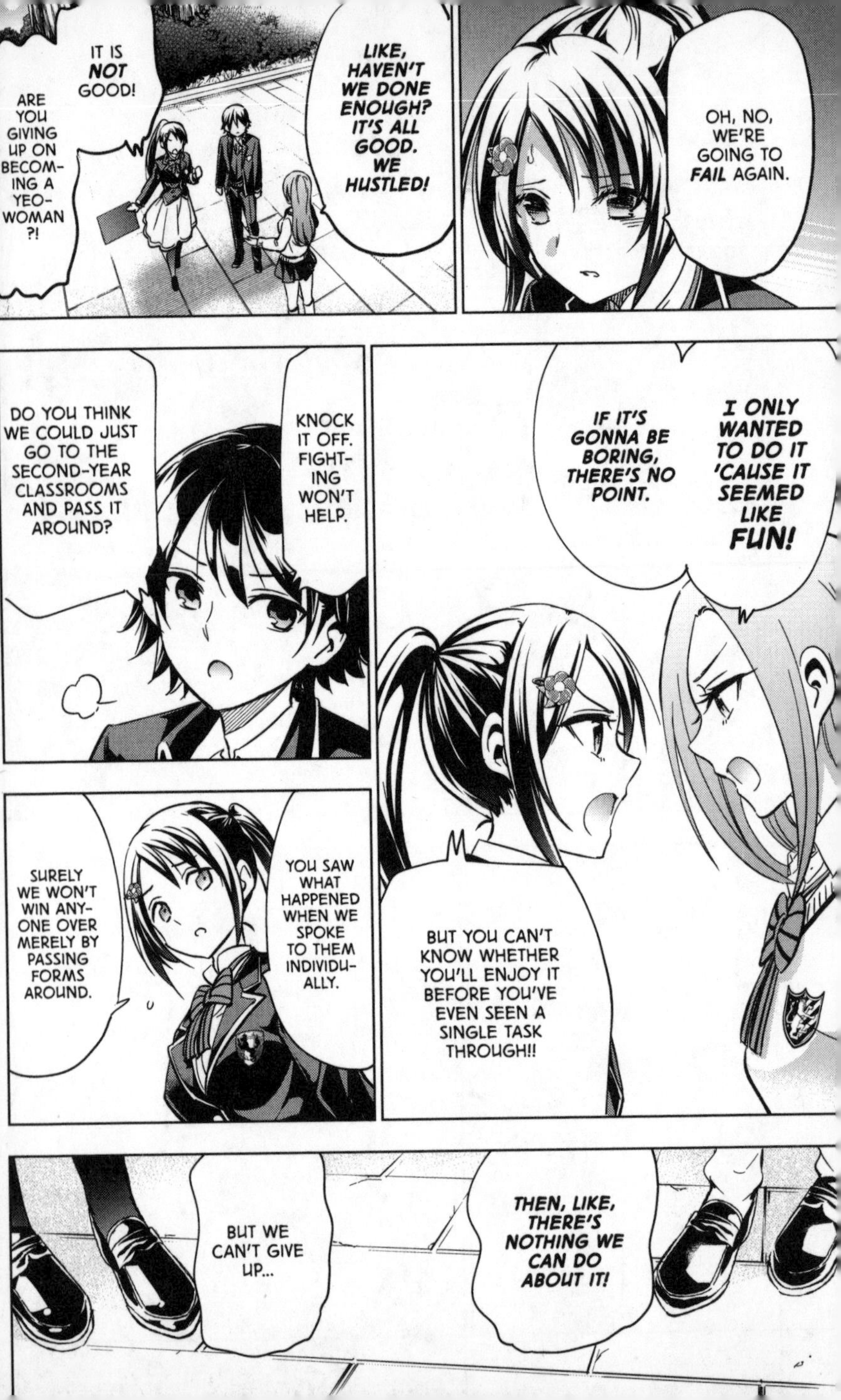
OH, NO, WE'RE GOING TO FAIL AGAIN.
LIKE, HAVEN'T WE DONE ENOUGH? IT'S ALL GOOD. WE HUSTLED!
IT IS NOT GOOD!
ARE YOU GIVING UP ON BECOMING A YEO-WOMAN?!
I ONLY WANTED TO DO IT 'CAUSE IT SEEMED LIKE FUN!
IF IT'S GONNA BE BORING, THERE'S NO POINT.
BUT YOU CAN'T KNOW WHETHER YOU'LL ENJOY IT BEFORE YOU'VE EVEN SEEN A SINGLE TASK THROUGH!!
KNOCK IT OFF. FIGHTING WON'T HELP.
DO YOU THINK WE COULD JUST GO TO THE SECOND-YEAR CLASSROOMS AND PASS IT AROUND?
YOU SAW WHAT HAPPENED WHEN WE SPOKE TO THEM INDIVIDUALLY.
SURELY WE WON'T WIN ANYONE OVER MERELY BY PASSING FORMS AROUND.
THEN, LIKE, THERE'S NOTHING WE CAN DO ABOUT IT!
BUT WE CAN'T GIVE UP...

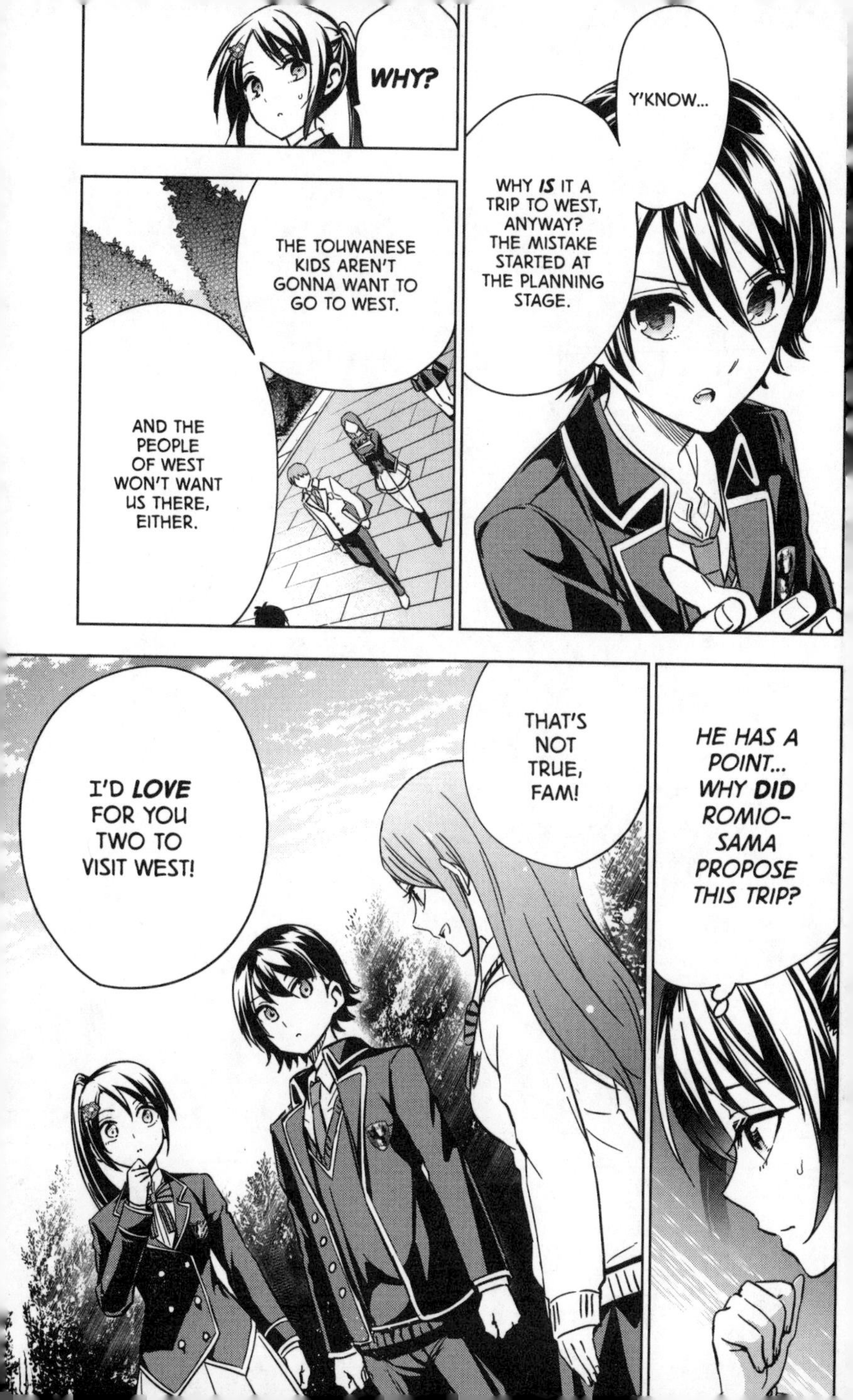
Y'KNOW...
WHY **IS** IT A TRIP TO WEST, ANYWAY? THE MISTAKE STARTED AT THE PLANNING STAGE.
WHY?
THE TOUWANESE KIDS AREN'T GONNA WANT TO GO TO WEST.
AND THE PEOPLE OF WEST WON'T WANT US THERE, EITHER.
HE HAS A POINT... WHY **DID** ROMIO-SAMA PROPOSE THIS TRIP?
THAT'S NOT TRUE, FAM!
I'D **LOVE** FOR YOU TWO TO VISIT WEST!

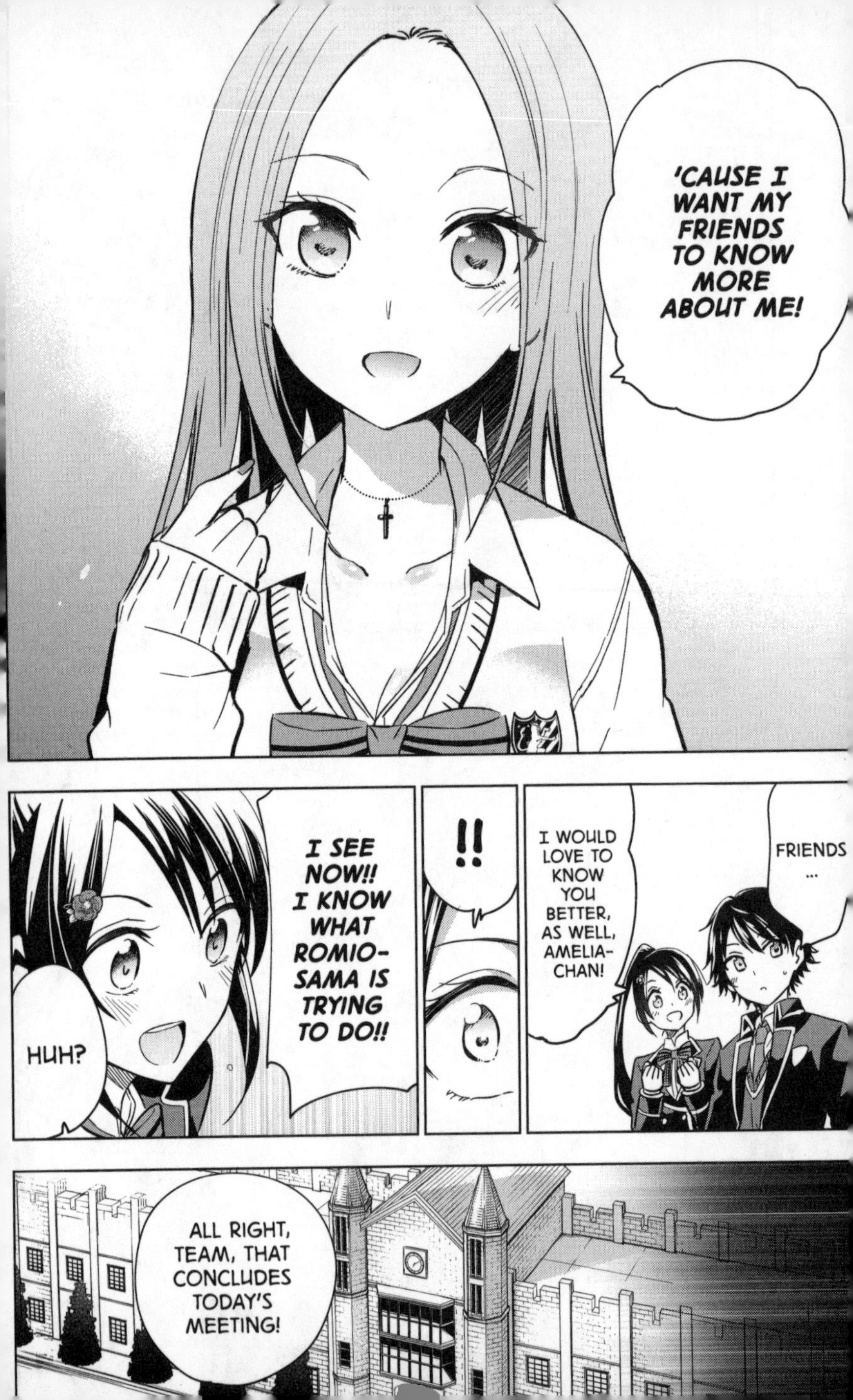
'CAUSE I WANT MY FRIENDS TO KNOW MORE ABOUT ME!
FRIENDS ...
I WOULD LOVE TO KNOW YOU BETTER, AS WELL, AMELIA-CHAN!
!!
I SEE NOW!! I KNOW WHAT ROMIO-SAMA IS TRYING TO DO!!
HUH?
ALL RIGHT, TEAM, THAT CONCLUDES TODAY'S MEETING!

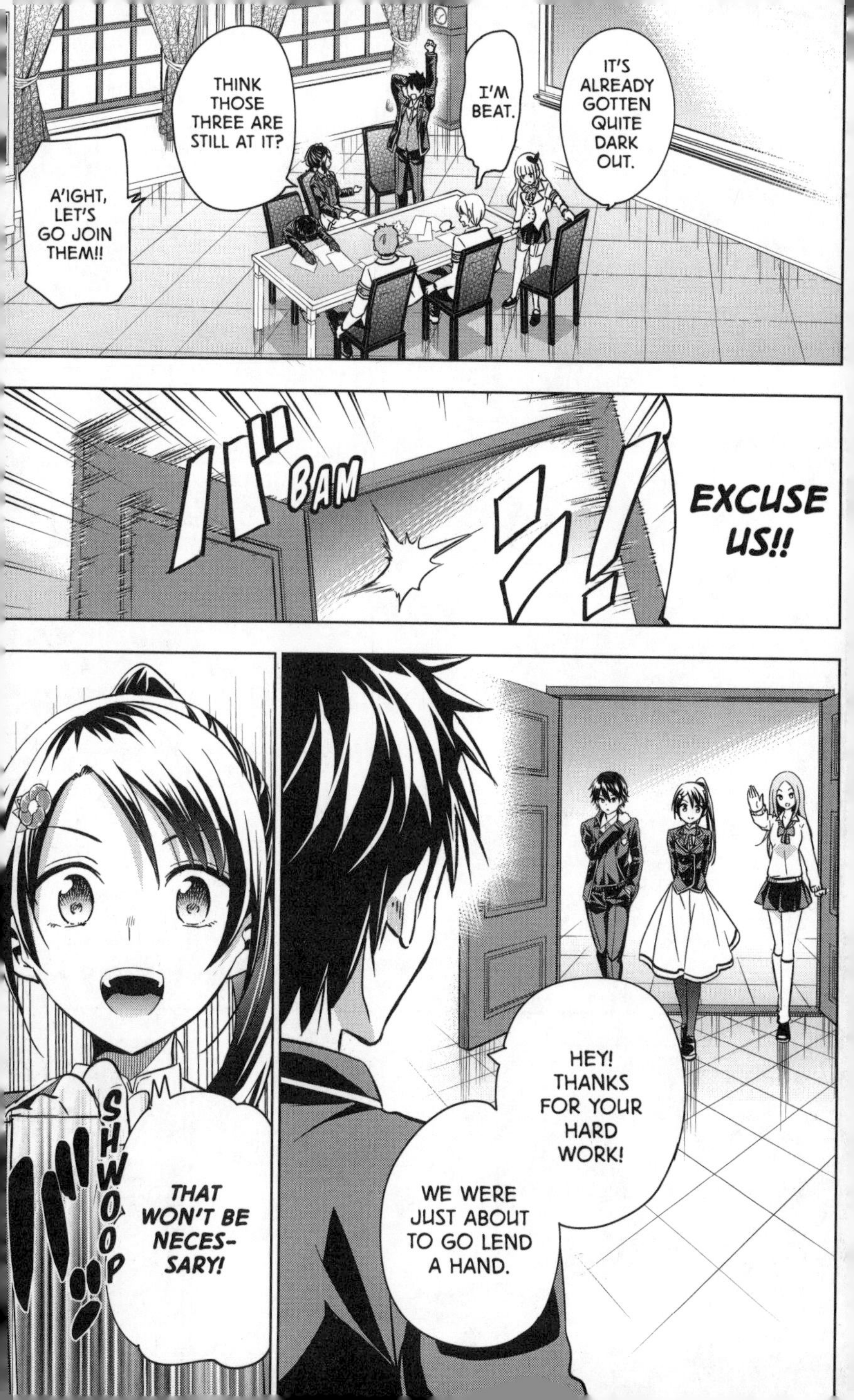
IT'S ALREADY GOTTEN QUITE DARK OUT.
I'M BEAT.
THINK THOSE THREE ARE STILL AT IT?
A'IGHT, LET'S GO JOIN THEM!!
EXCUSE US!!
BAM
HEY! THANKS FOR YOUR HARD WORK!
WE WERE JUST ABOUT TO GO LEND A HAND.
SHWOOP
THAT WON'T BE NECES-SARY!

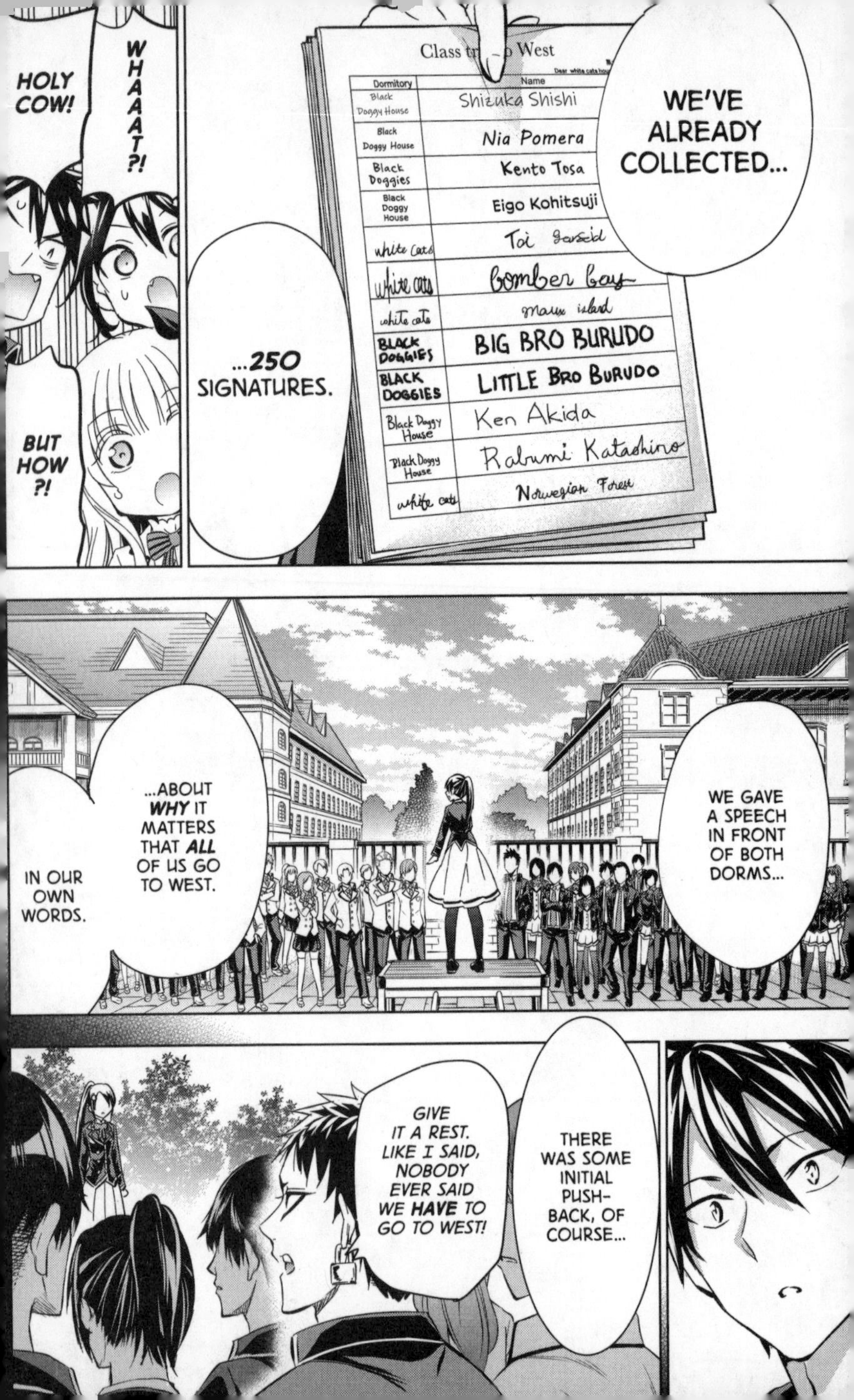
WE'VE ALREADY COLLECTED...
...250 SIGNATURES.
Class tr o West
Dormitory
Name
Black Doggy House
Shizuka Shishi
Black Doggy House
Nia Pomera
Black Doggies
Kento Tosa
Black Doggy House
Eigo Kohitsuji
white cats
Toi
white cats
Bomber Bay
white cats
Manx island
BLACK DOGGIES
BIG BRO BURUDO
BLACK DOGGIES
LITTLE BRO BURUDO
Black Doggy House
Ken Akida
Black Doggy House
Rabumi Katashiro
white cats
Norwegian Forest
WHAAAAT?!
HOLY COW!
BUT HOW ?!
WE GAVE A SPEECH IN FRONT OF BOTH DORMS...
...ABOUT WHY IT MATTERS THAT ALL OF US GO TO WEST.
IN OUR OWN WORDS.
THERE WAS SOME INITIAL PUSH-BACK, OF COURSE...
GIVE IT A REST. LIKE I SAID, NOBODY EVER SAID WE HAVE TO GO TO WEST!

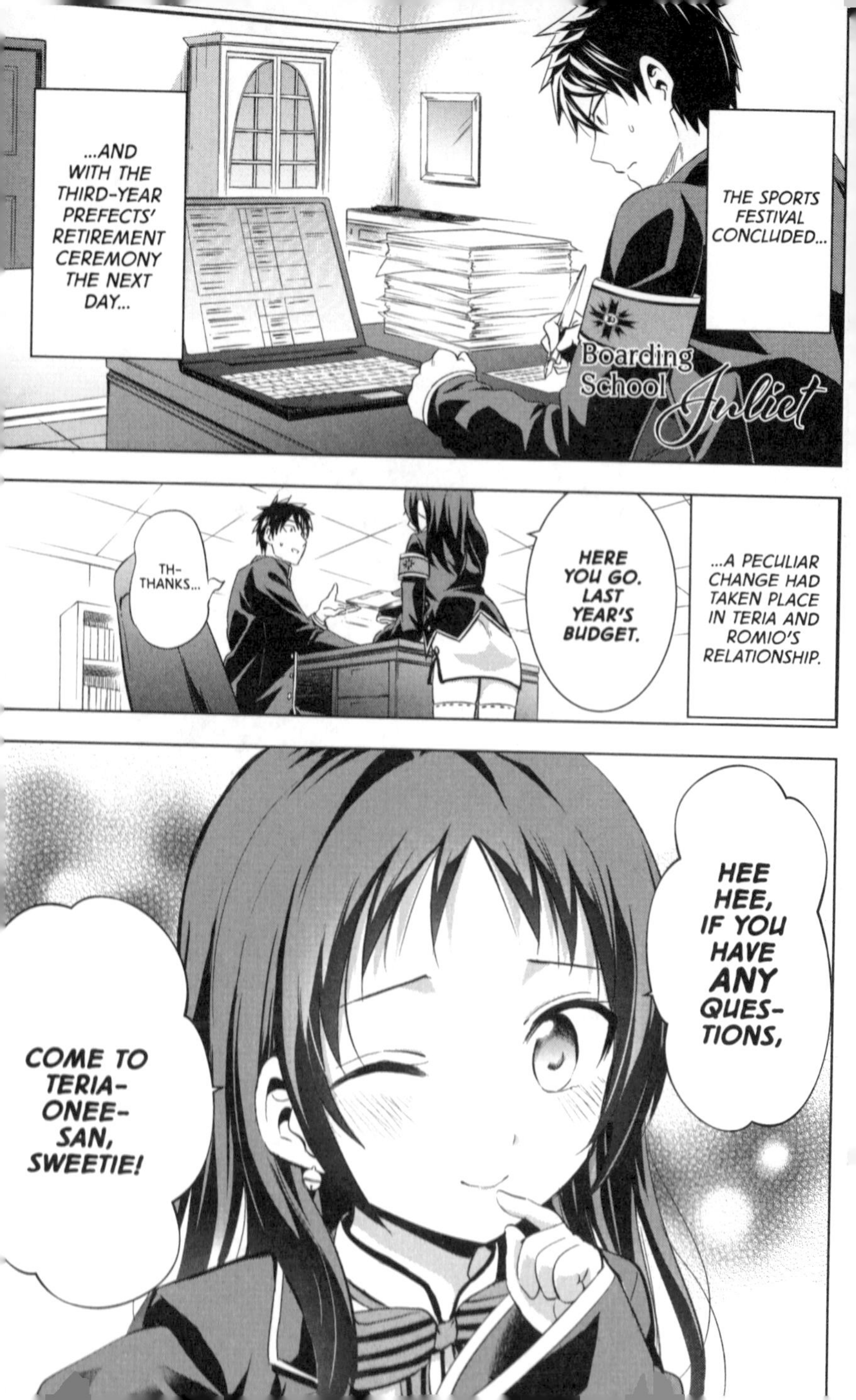
THE SPORTS FESTIVAL CONCLUDED...
Boarding School Juliet
...AND WITH THE THIRD-YEAR PREFECTS' RETIREMENT CEREMONY THE NEXT DAY...
...A PECULIAR CHANGE HAD TAKEN PLACE IN TERIA AND ROMIO'S RELATIONSHIP.
HERE YOU GO. LAST YEAR'S BUDGET.
TH-THANKS...
HEE HEE, IF YOU HAVE ANY QUES-TIONS,
COME TO TERIA-ONEE-SAN, SWEETIE!

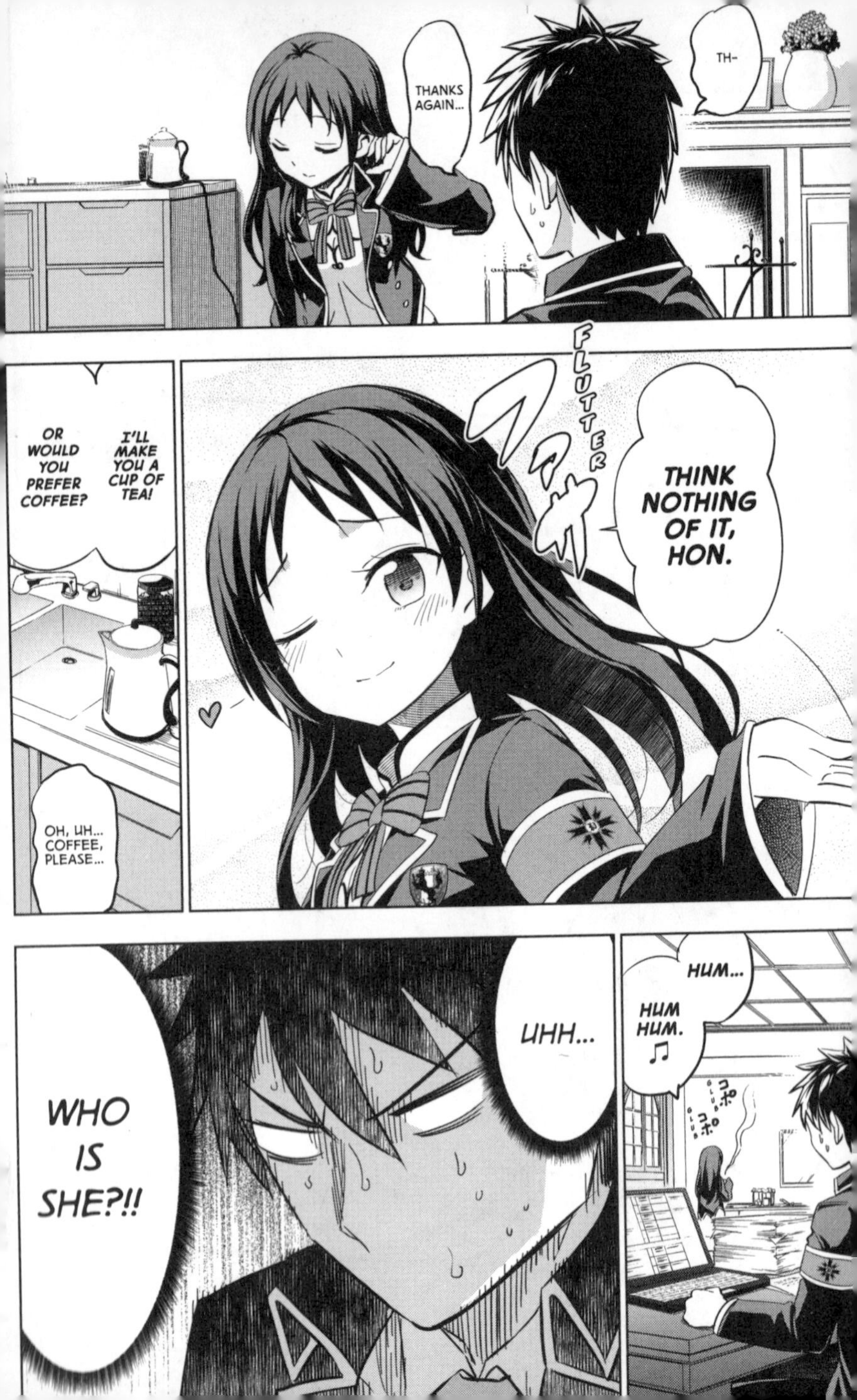
TH-
THANKS AGAIN...
FLUTTER
THINK NOTHING OF IT, HON.
I'LL MAKE YOU A CUP OF TEA!
OR WOULD YOU PREFER COFFEE?
OH, UH... COFFEE, PLEASE...
HUM... HUM HUM. ♫
UHH...
WHO IS SHE?!!

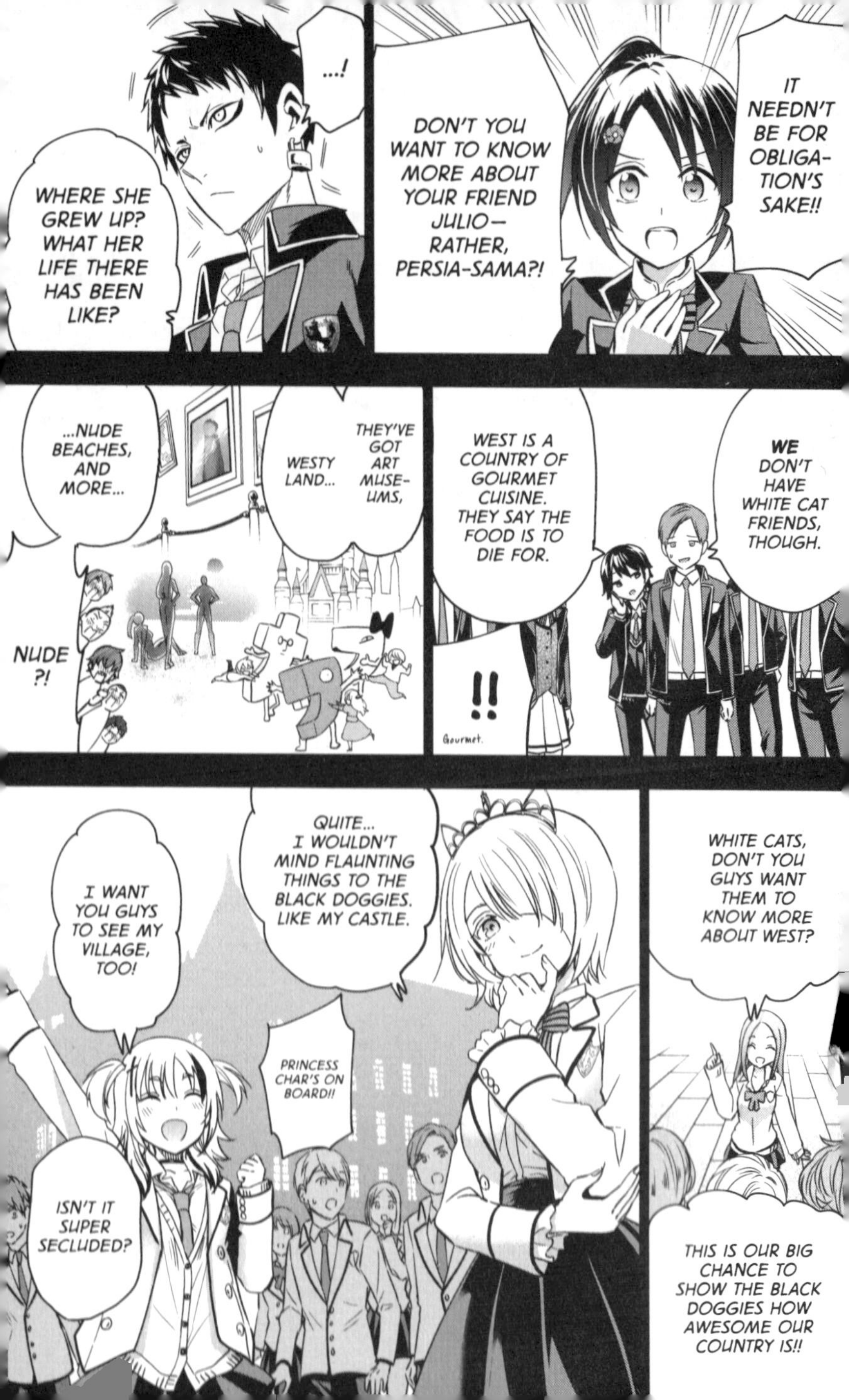
IT NEEDN'T BE FOR OBLIGATION'S SAKE!!
DON'T YOU WANT TO KNOW MORE ABOUT YOUR FRIEND JULIO—RATHER, PERSIA-SAMA?!
...!
WHERE SHE GREW UP? WHAT HER LIFE THERE HAS BEEN LIKE?
**WE** DON'T HAVE WHITE CAT FRIENDS, THOUGH.
WEST IS A COUNTRY OF GOURMET CUISINE. THEY SAY THE FOOD IS TO DIE FOR.
!!
Gourmet.
WESTY LAND... THEY'VE GOT ART MUSEUMS,
...NUDE BEACHES, AND MORE...
NUDE?!
WHITE CATS, DON'T YOU GUYS WANT THEM TO KNOW MORE ABOUT WEST?
THIS IS OUR BIG CHANCE TO SHOW THE BLACK DOGGIES HOW AWESOME OUR COUNTRY IS!!
QUITE... I WOULDN'T MIND FLAUNTING THINGS TO THE BLACK DOGGIES. LIKE MY CASTLE.
PRINCESS CHAR'S ON BOARD!!
I WANT YOU GUYS TO SEE MY VILLAGE, TOO!
ISN'T IT SUPER SECLUDED?

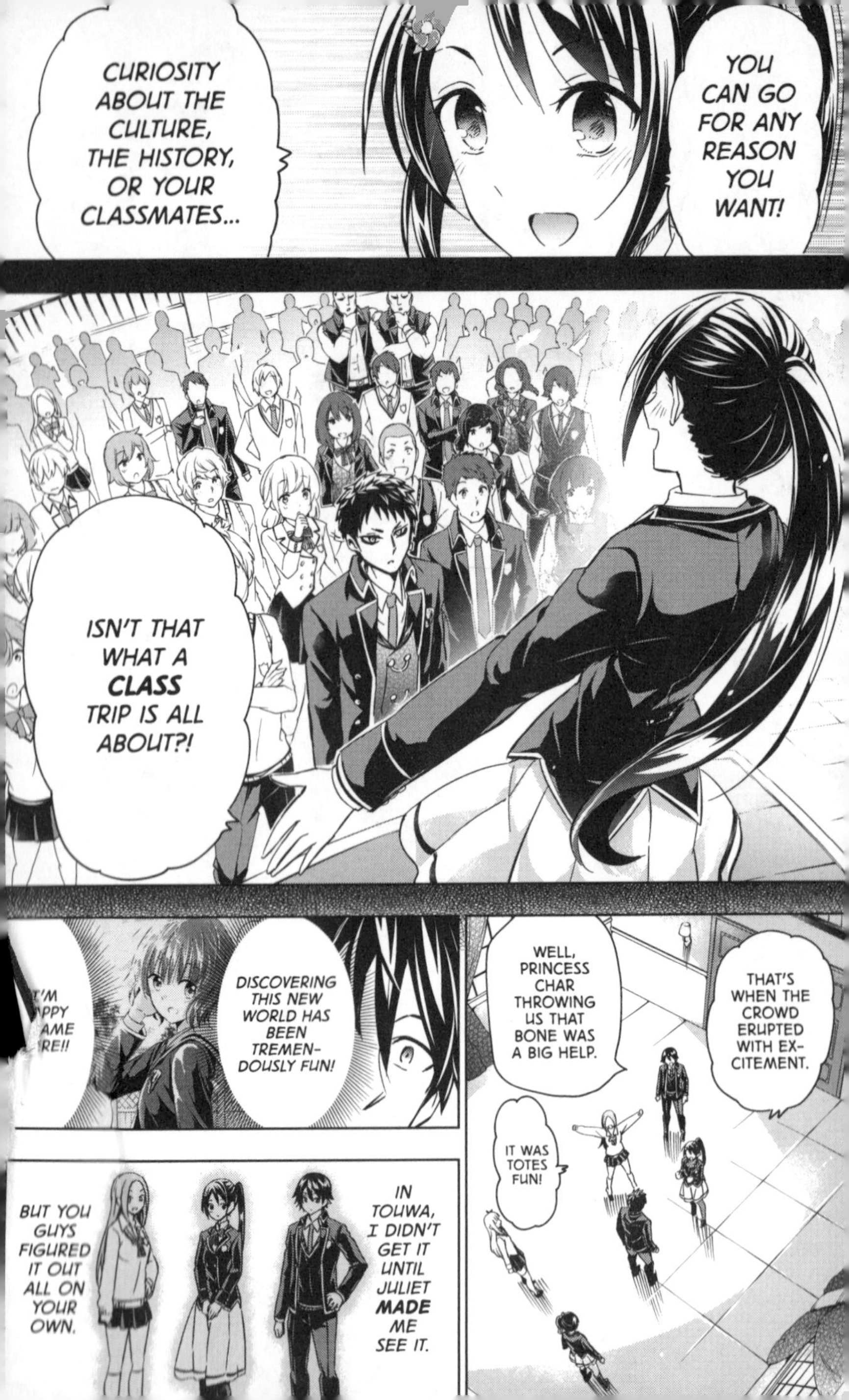
YOU CAN GO FOR ANY REASON YOU WANT!
CURIOSITY ABOUT THE CULTURE, THE HISTORY, OR YOUR CLASSMATES...
ISN'T THAT WHAT A CLASS TRIP IS ALL ABOUT?!
THAT'S WHEN THE CROWD ERUPTED WITH EXCITEMENT.
WELL, PRINCESS CHAR THROWING US THAT BONE WAS A BIG HELP.
IT WAS TOTES FUN!
DISCOVERING THIS NEW WORLD HAS BEEN TREMENDOUSLY FUN!
IN TOUWA, I DIDN'T GET IT UNTIL JULIET MADE ME SEE IT.
BUT YOU GUYS FIGURED IT OUT ALL ON YOUR OWN.

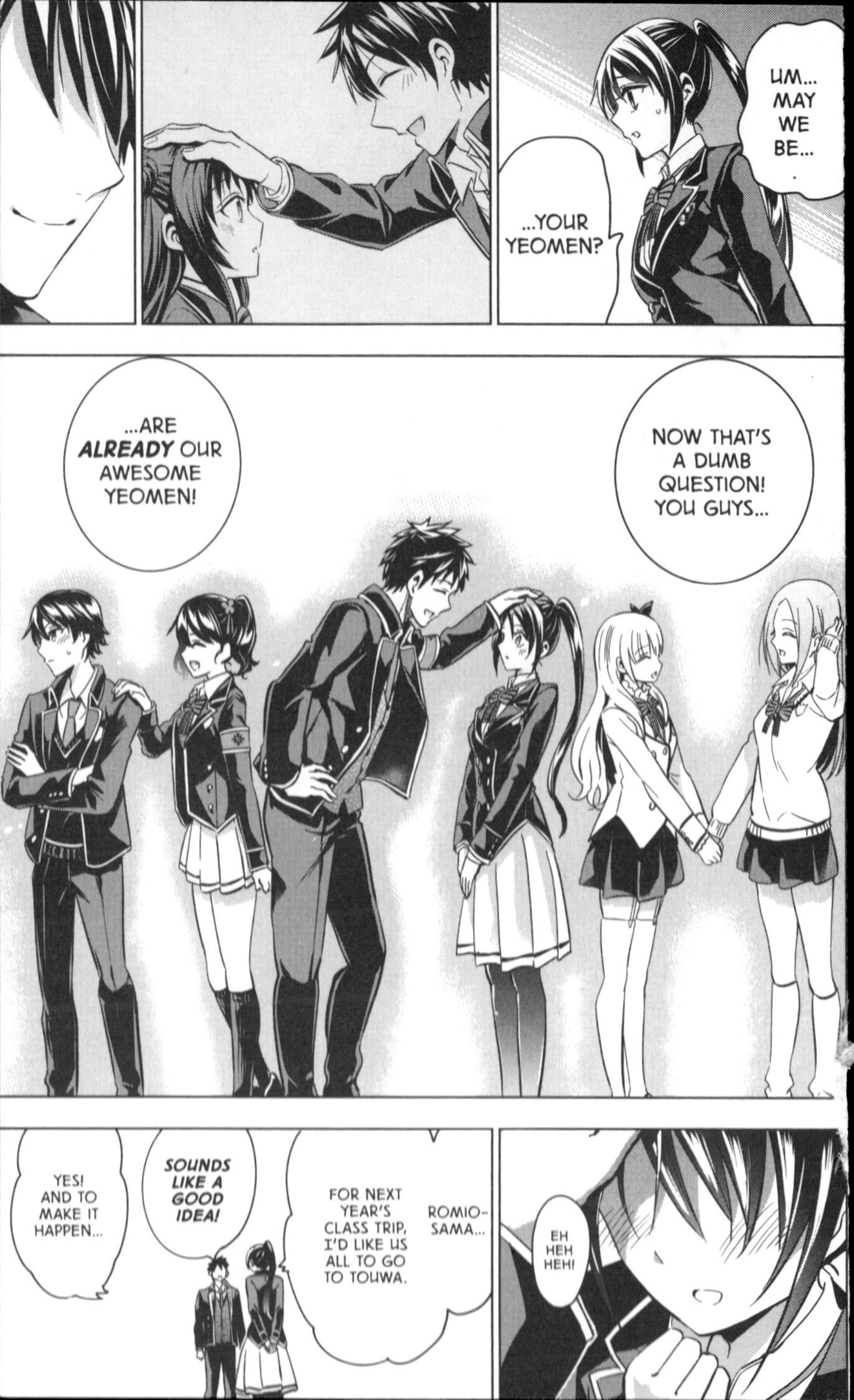
UM... MAY WE BE...
...YOUR YEOMEN?
NOW THAT'S A DUMB QUESTION! YOU GUYS...
...ARE *ALREADY* OUR AWESOME YEOMEN!
EH HEH HEH!
ROMIO-SAMA...
FOR NEXT YEAR'S CLASS TRIP, I'D LIKE US ALL TO GO TO TOUWA.
*SOUNDS LIKE A GOOD IDEA!*
YES! AND TO MAKE IT HAPPEN...

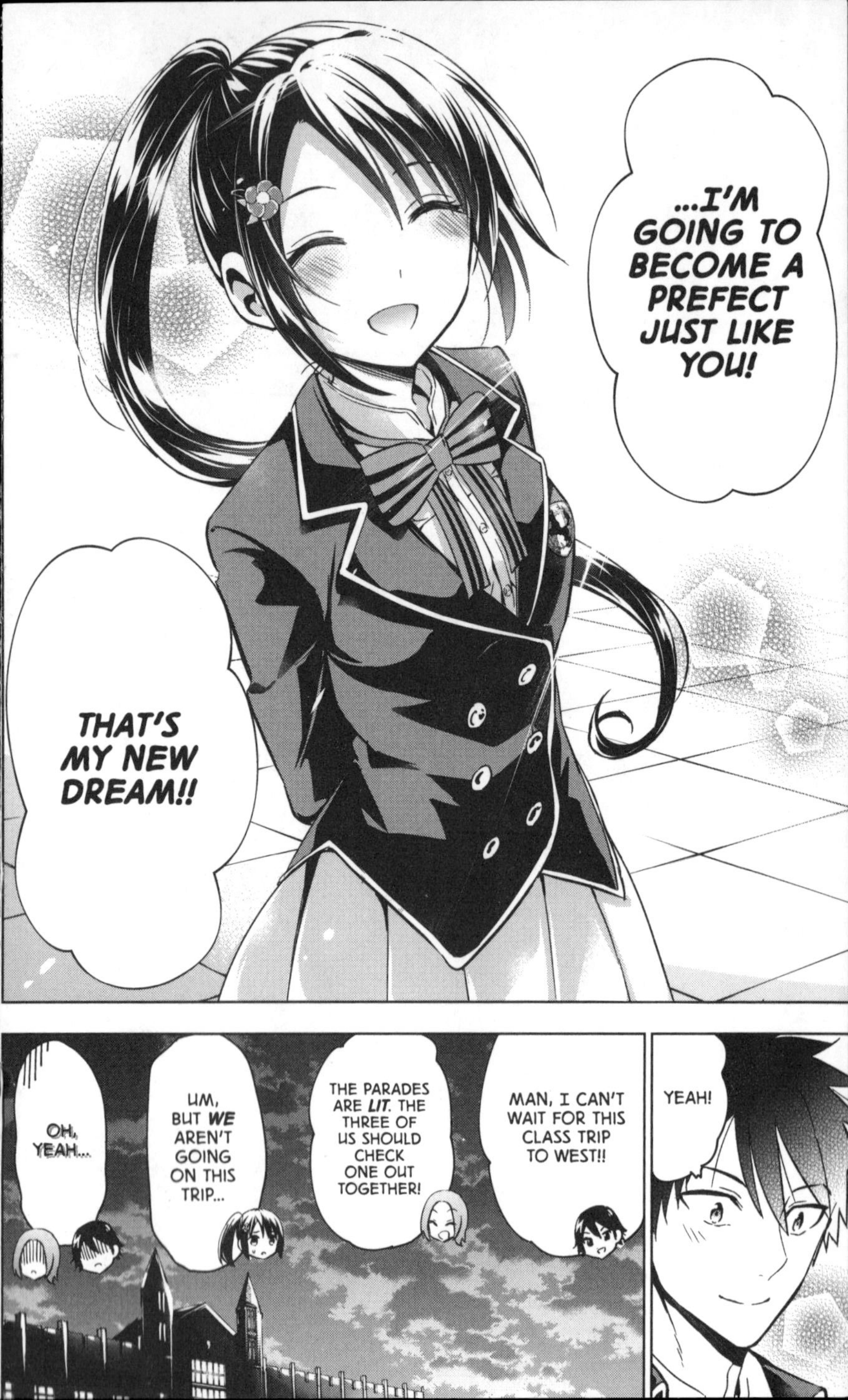
...I'M GOING TO BECOME A PREFECT JUST LIKE YOU!
THAT'S MY NEW DREAM!!
YEAH!
MAN, I CAN'T WAIT FOR THIS CLASS TRIP TO WEST!!
THE PARADES ARE *LIT*. THE THREE OF US SHOULD CHECK ONE OUT TOGETHER!
UM, BUT *WE* AREN'T GOING ON THIS TRIP...
OH, YEAH...

Boarding
School *Juliet*

To LOVE, or not to LOVE

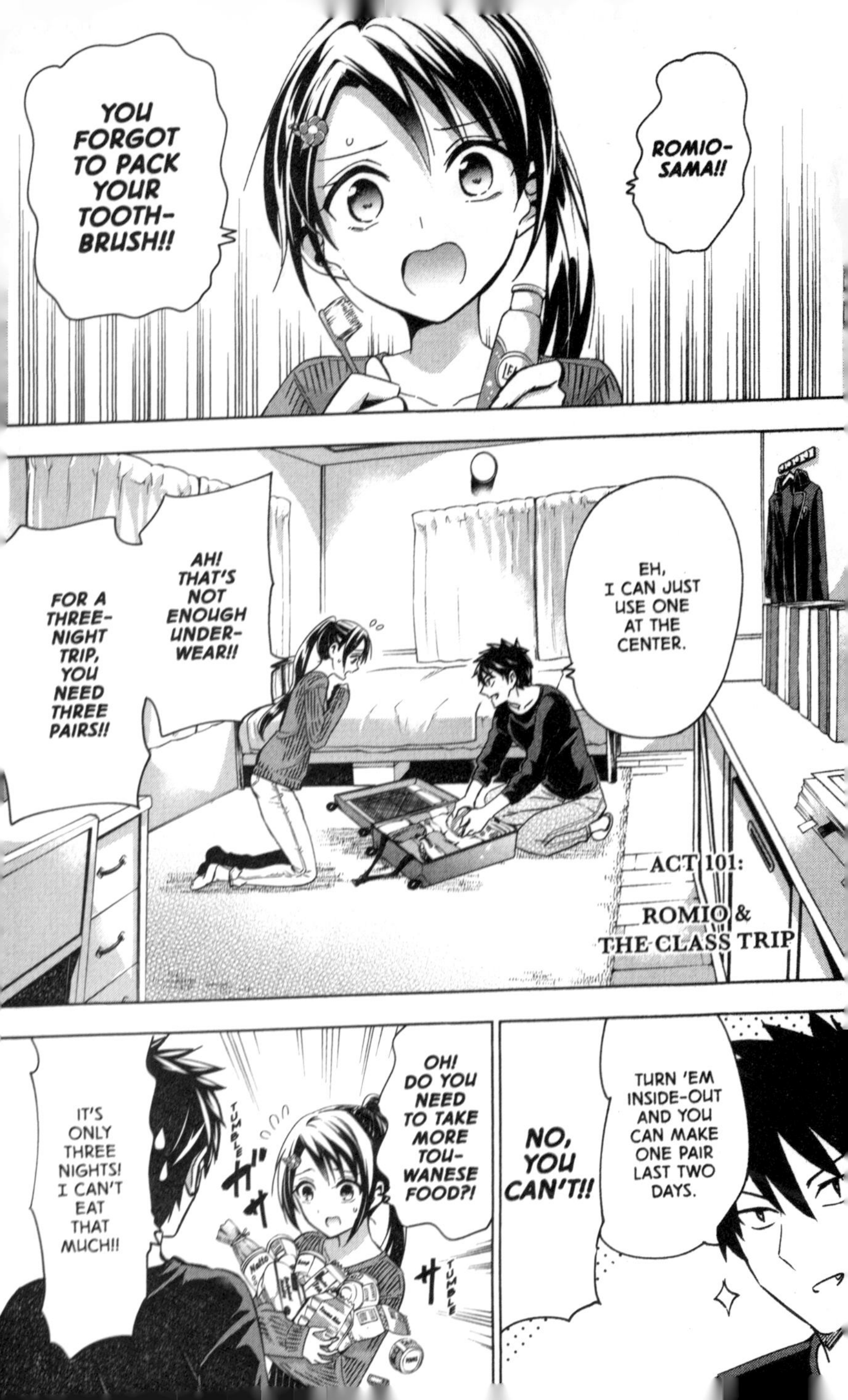
ROMIO-SAMA!!
YOU FORGOT TO PACK YOUR TOOTH-BRUSH!!
EH, I CAN JUST USE ONE AT THE CENTER.
AH! THAT'S NOT ENOUGH UNDER-WEAR!!
FOR A THREE-NIGHT TRIP, YOU NEED THREE PAIRS!!
ACT 101:
ROMIO & THE CLASS TRIP
TURN 'EM INSIDE-OUT AND YOU CAN MAKE ONE PAIR LAST TWO DAYS.
NO, YOU CAN'T!!
OH! DO YOU NEED TO TAKE MORE TOU-WANESE FOOD?!
TUMBLE
TUMBLE
IT'S ONLY THREE NIGHTS! I CAN'T EAT THAT MUCH!!

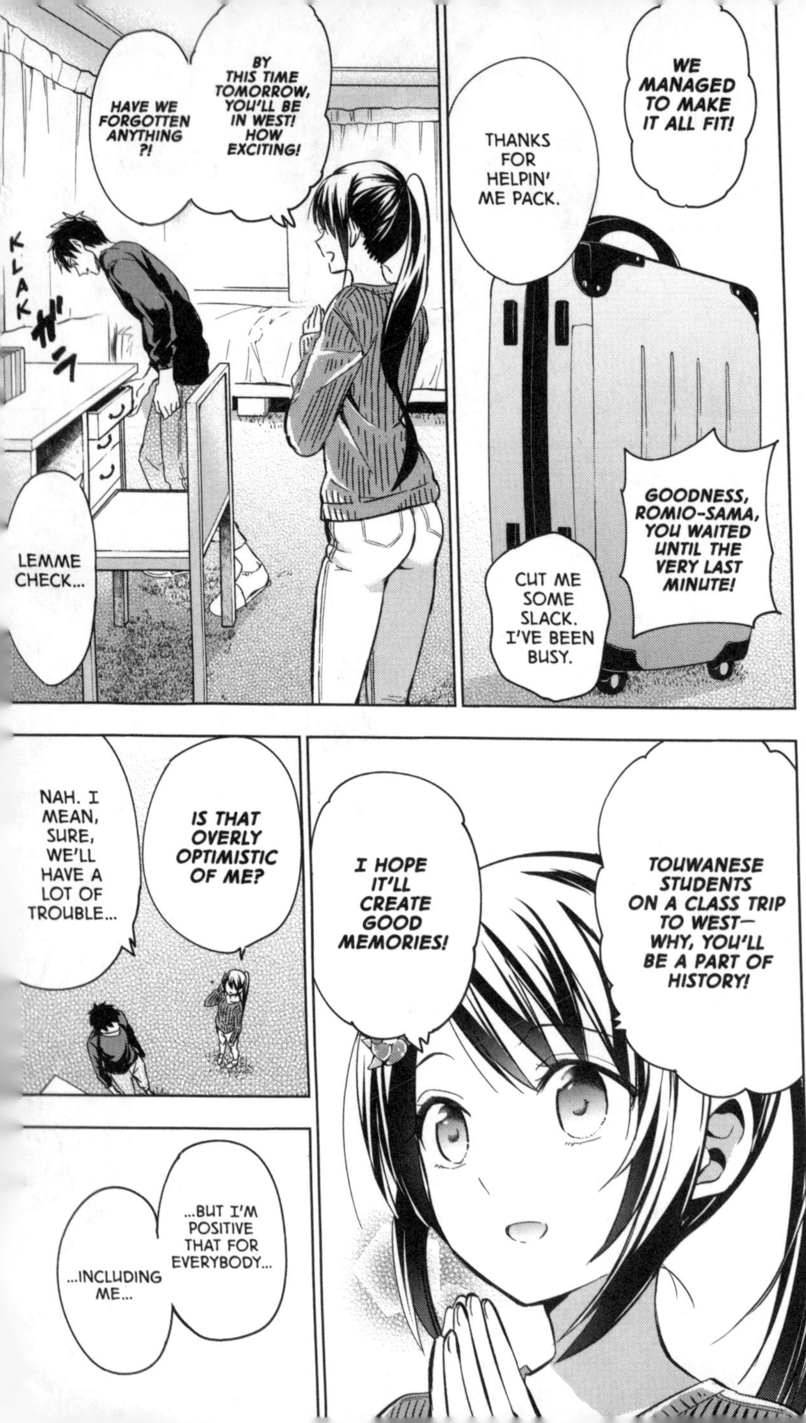
WE MANAGED TO MAKE IT ALL FIT!
THANKS FOR HELPIN' ME PACK.
GOODNESS, ROMIO-SAMA, YOU WAITED UNTIL THE VERY LAST MINUTE!
CUT ME SOME SLACK. I'VE BEEN BUSY.
BY THIS TIME TOMORROW, YOU'LL BE IN WEST! HOW EXCITING!
HAVE WE FORGOTTEN ANYTHING?!
KLAK
LEMME CHECK...
TOUWANESE STUDENTS ON A CLASS TRIP TO WEST— WHY, YOU'LL BE A PART OF HISTORY!
I HOPE IT'LL CREATE GOOD MEMORIES!
IS THAT OVERLY OPTIMISTIC OF ME?
NAH. I MEAN, SURE, WE'LL HAVE A LOT OF TROUBLE...
...BUT I'M POSITIVE THAT FOR EVERYBODY...
...INCLUDING ME...

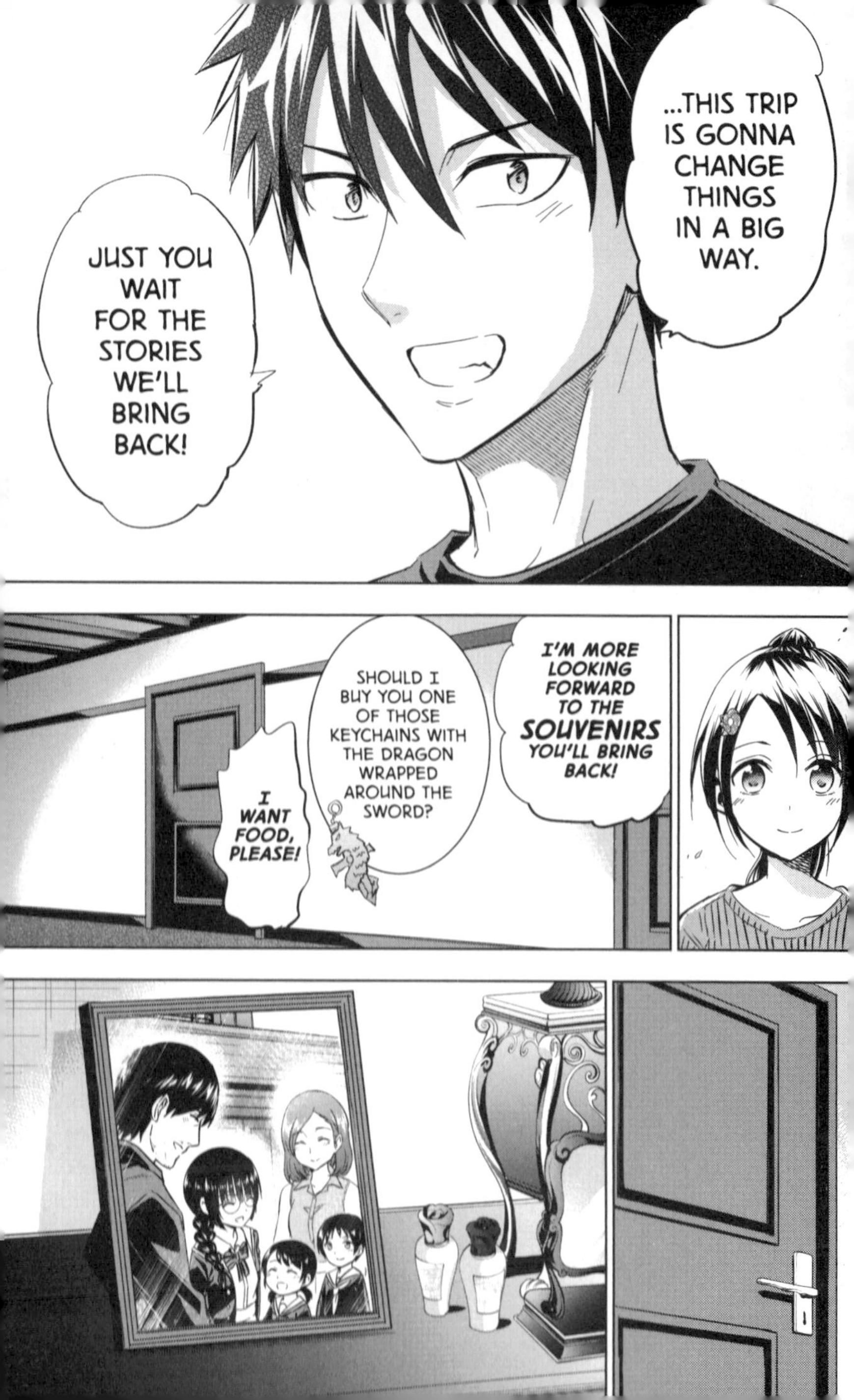
...THIS TRIP IS GONNA CHANGE THINGS IN A BIG WAY.
JUST YOU WAIT FOR THE STORIES WE'LL BRING BACK!
I'M MORE LOOKING FORWARD TO THE SOUVENIRS YOU'LL BRING BACK!
SHOULD I BUY YOU ONE OF THOSE KEYCHAINS WITH THE DRAGON WRAPPED AROUND THE SWORD?
I WANT FOOD, PLEASE!

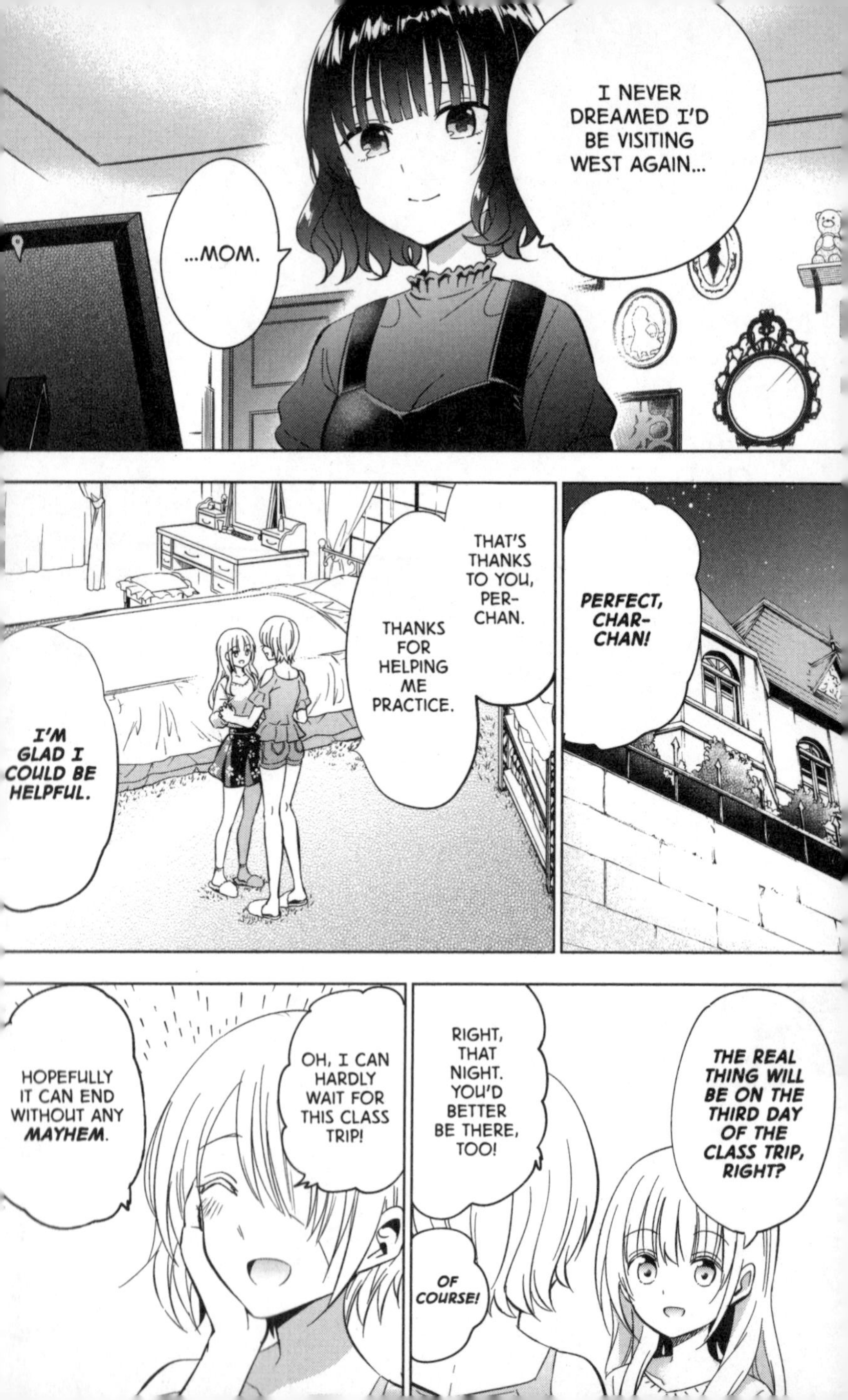
I NEVER DREAMED I'D BE VISITING WEST AGAIN...
...MOM.
***PERFECT, CHAR-CHAN!***
THAT'S THANKS TO YOU, PER-CHAN.
THANKS FOR HELPING ME PRACTICE.
***I'M GLAD I COULD BE HELPFUL.***
***THE REAL THING WILL BE ON THE THIRD DAY OF THE CLASS TRIP, RIGHT?***
RIGHT, THAT NIGHT. YOU'D BETTER BE THERE, TOO!
***OF COURSE!***
OH, I CAN HARDLY WAIT FOR THIS CLASS TRIP!
HOPEFULLY IT CAN END WITHOUT ANY *MAYHEM*.

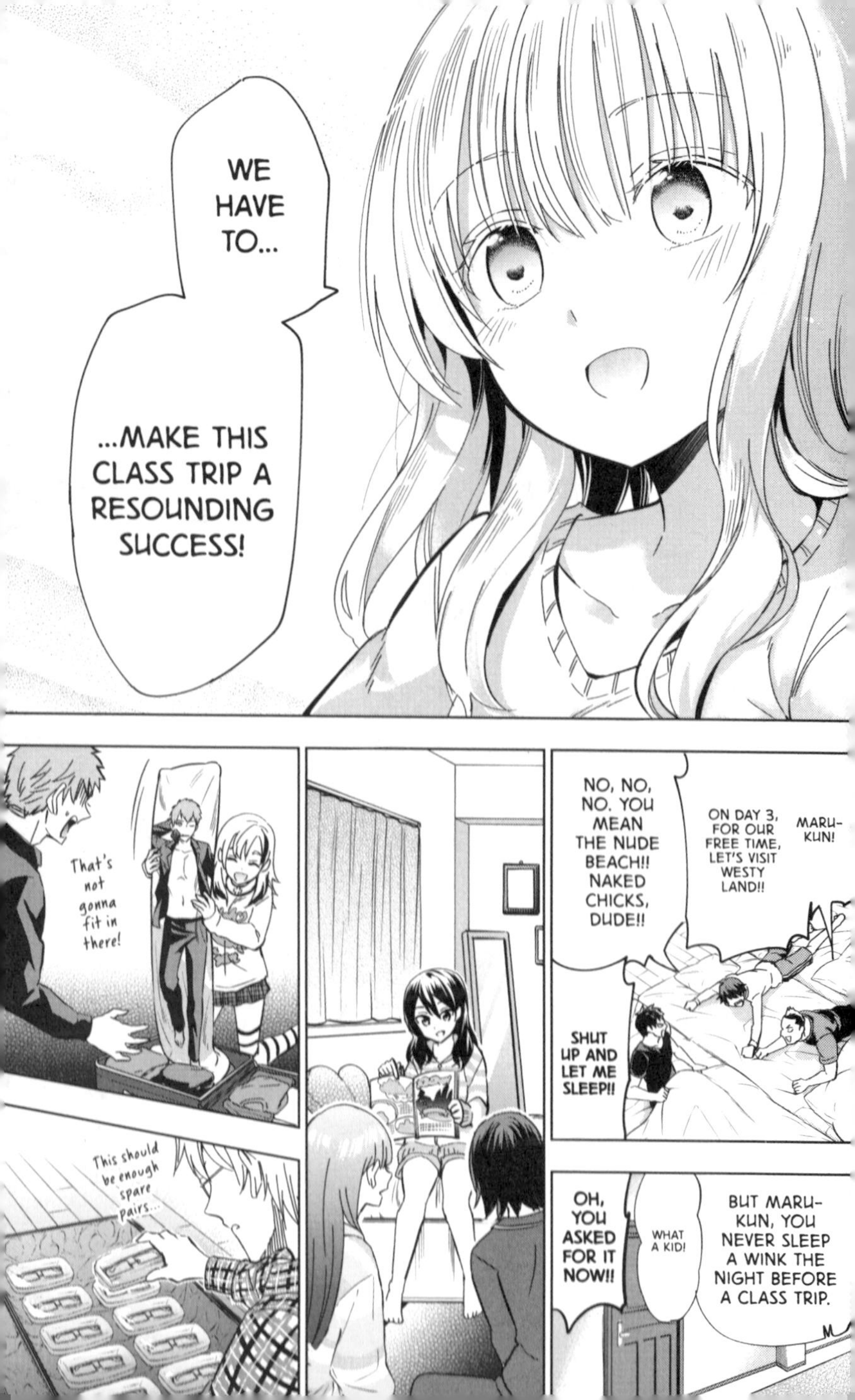
WE HAVE TO...
...MAKE THIS CLASS TRIP A RESOUNDING SUCCESS!
MARU-KUN!
ON DAY 3, FOR OUR FREE TIME, LET'S VISIT WESTY LAND!!
NO, NO, NO. YOU MEAN THE NUDE BEACH!! NAKED CHICKS, DUDE!!
SHUT UP AND LET ME SLEEP!!
BUT MARU-KUN, YOU NEVER SLEEP A WINK THE NIGHT BEFORE A CLASS TRIP.
WHAT A KID!
OH, YOU ASKED FOR IT NOW!!
That's not gonna fit in there!
This should be enough spare pairs...

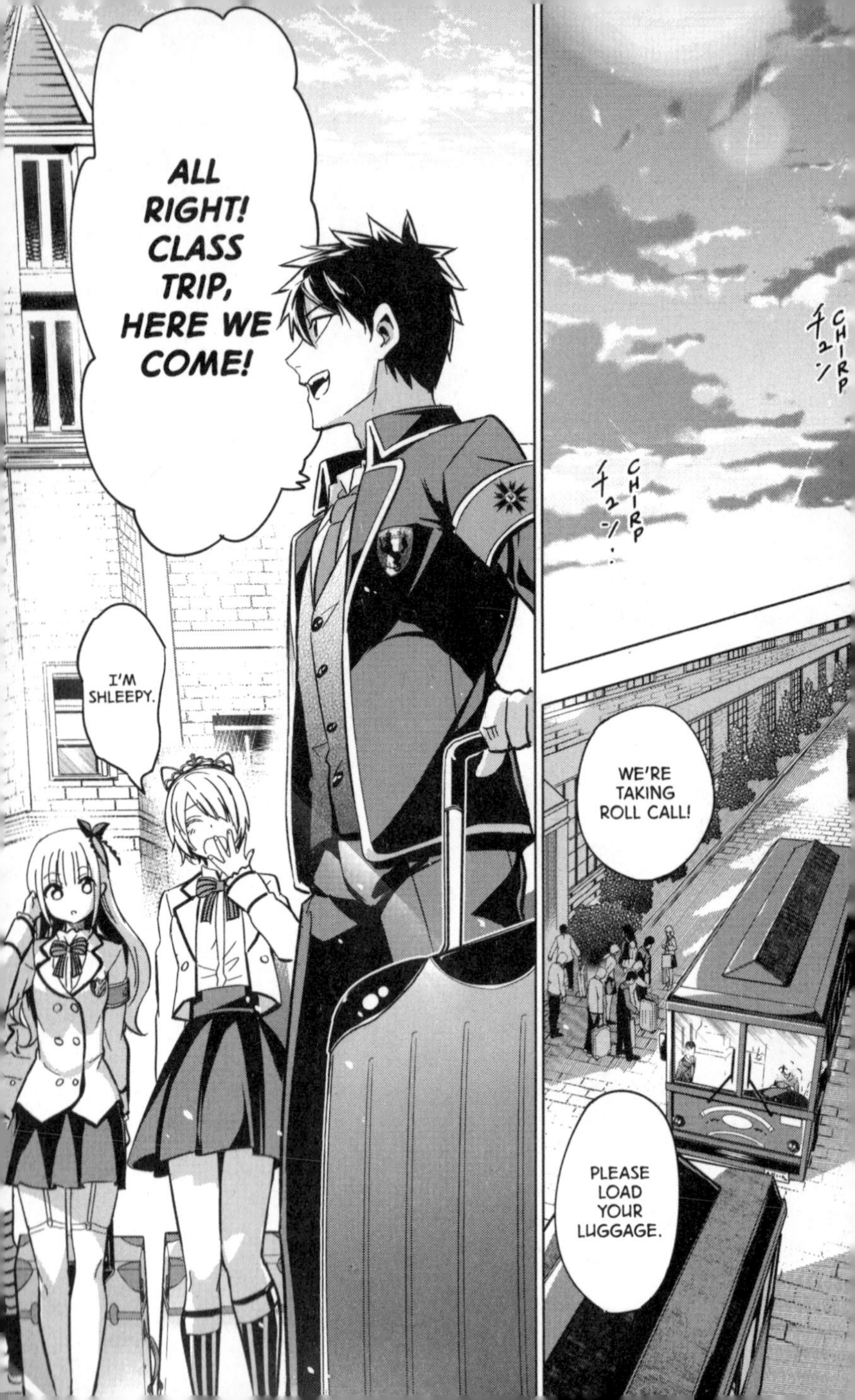

チュン
CHIRP
チュン…
CHIRP
WE'RE TAKING ROLL CALL!
PLEASE LOAD YOUR LUGGAGE.
ALL RIGHT! CLASS TRIP, HERE WE COME!
I'M SHLEEPY.

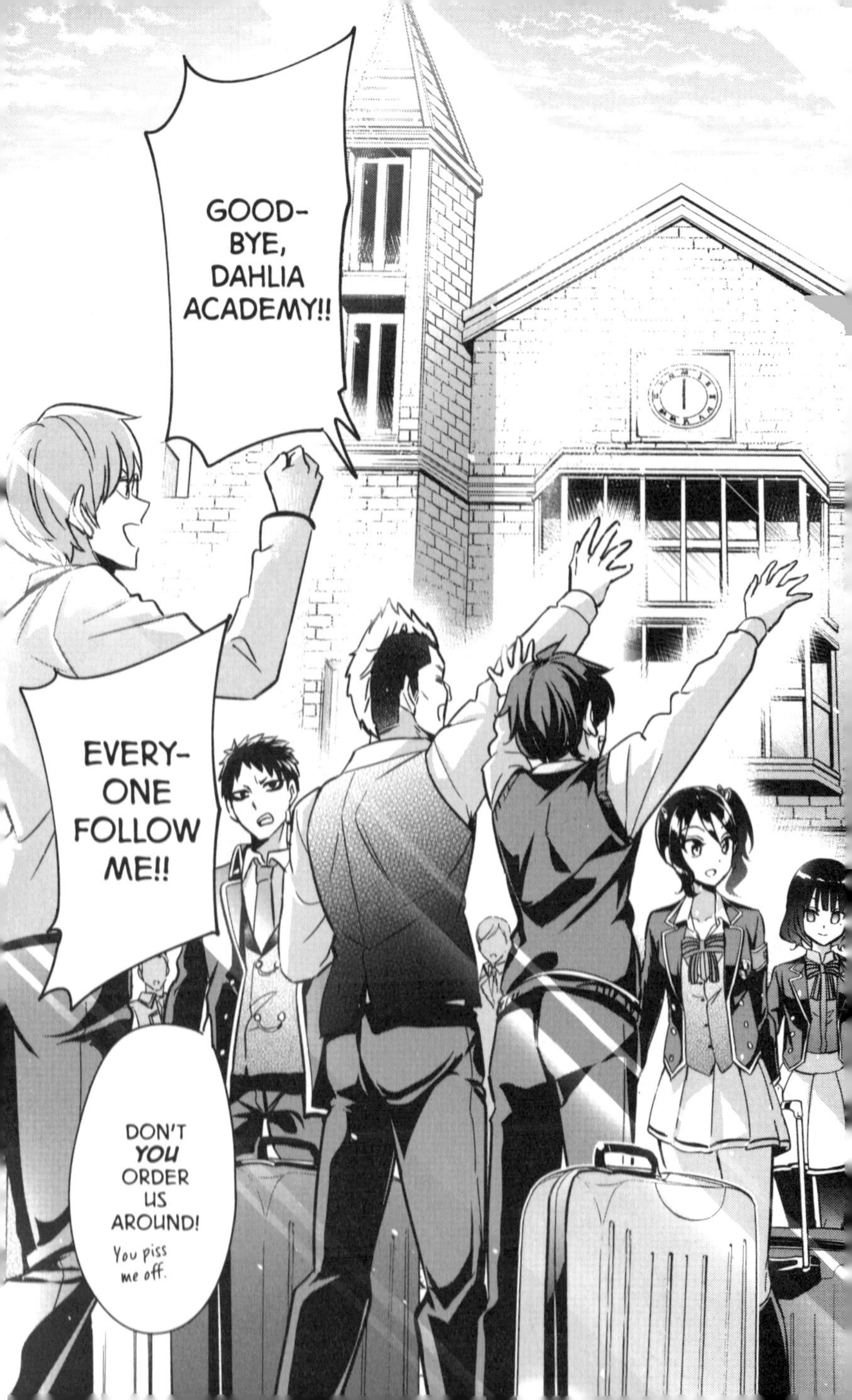
GOOD-BYE, DAHLIA ACADEMY!!
EVERY-ONE FOLLOW ME!!
DON'T YOU ORDER US AROUND!
You piss me off.

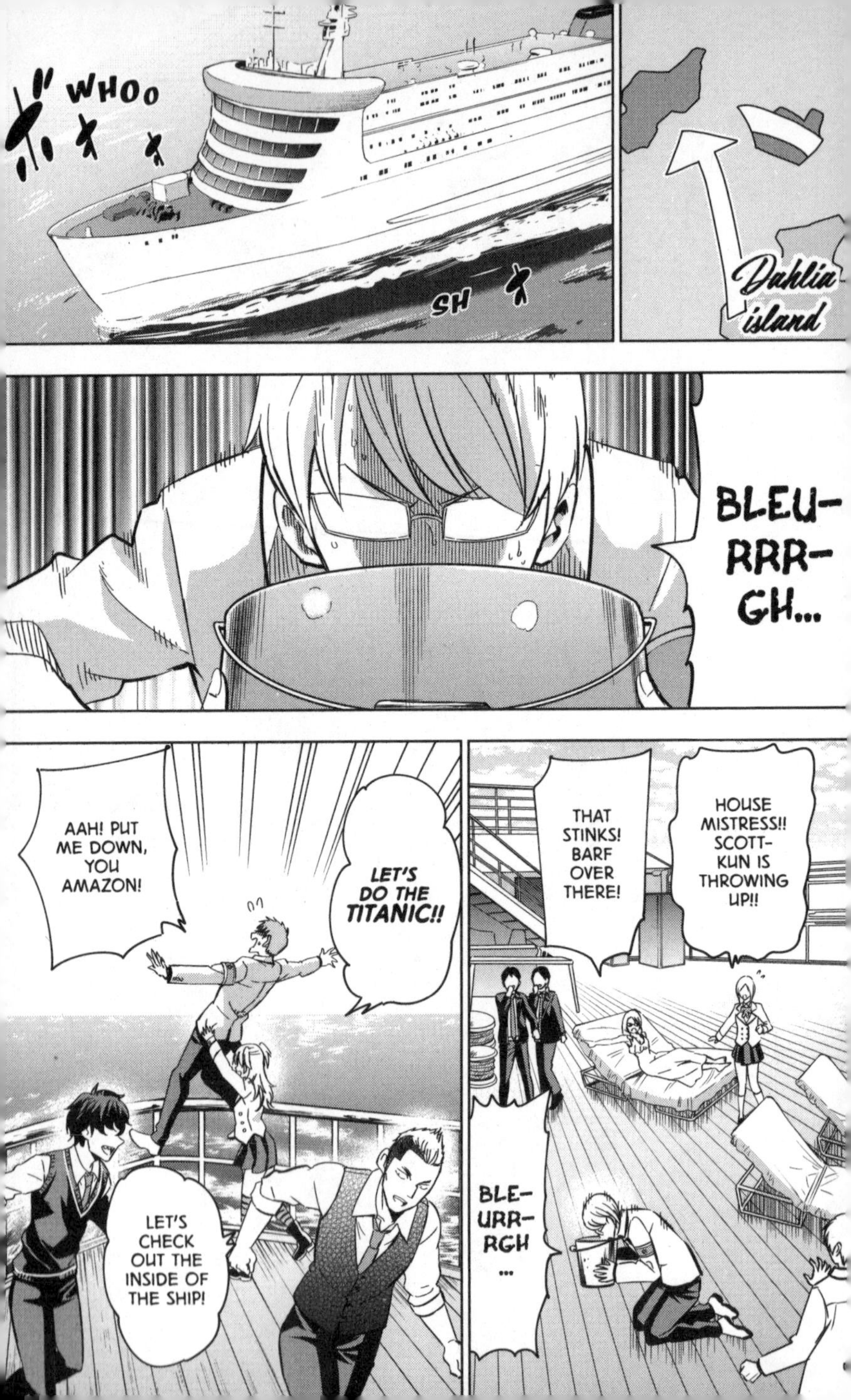
Dahlia island
WHOO
SH
BLEU-RRR-GH...
HOUSE MISTRESS!! SCOTT-KUN IS THROWING UP!!
THAT STINKS! BARF OVER THERE!
BLE-URR-RGH ...
LET'S DO THE TITANIC!!
AAH! PUT ME DOWN, YOU AMAZON!
LET'S CHECK OUT THE INSIDE OF THE SHIP!

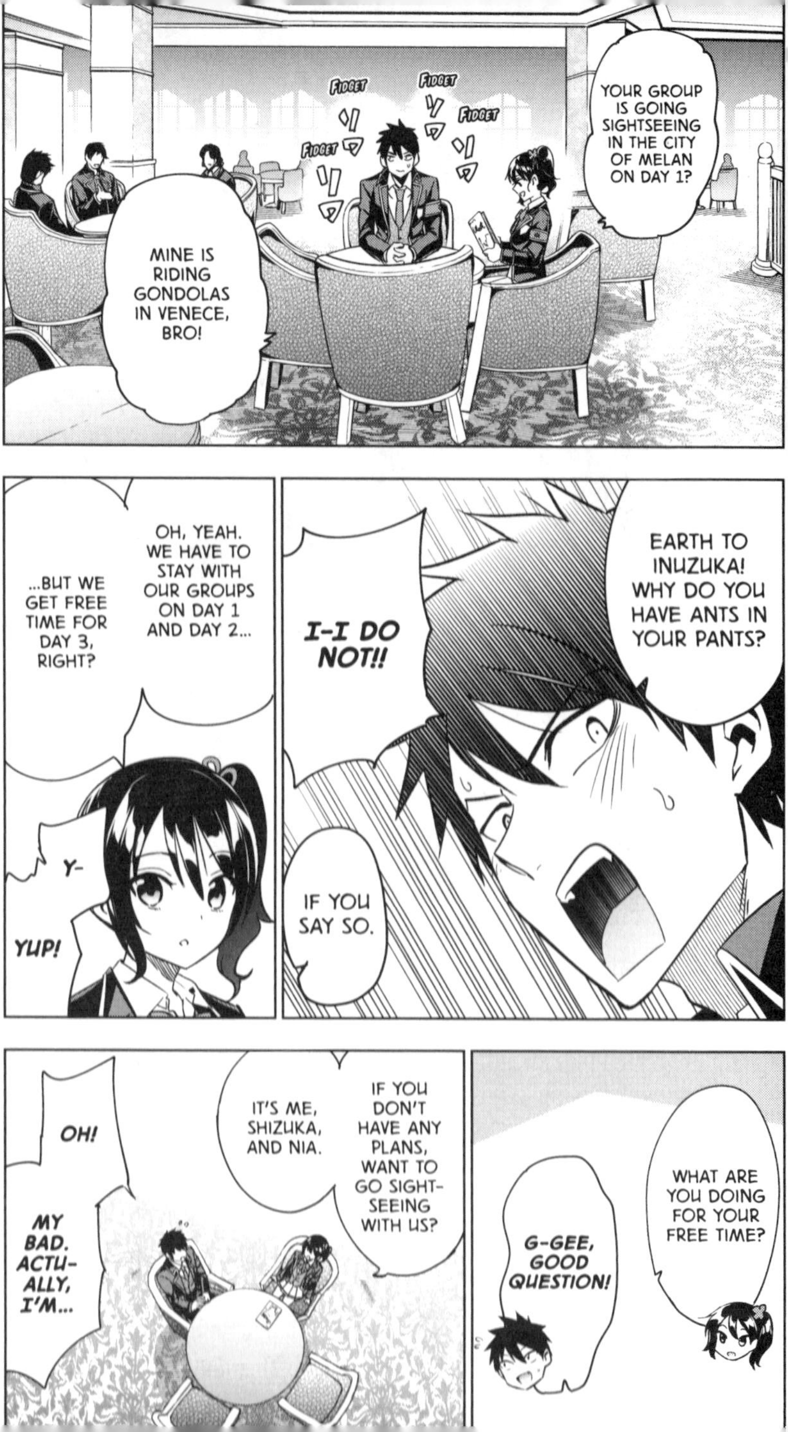
YOUR GROUP IS GOING SIGHTSEEING IN THE CITY OF MELAN ON DAY 1?
FIDGET
FIDGET
FIDGET
FIDGET
MINE IS RIDING GONDOLAS IN VENECE, BRO!
EARTH TO INUZUKA! WHY DO YOU HAVE ANTS IN YOUR PANTS?
I-I DO NOT!!
IF YOU SAY SO.
OH, YEAH. WE HAVE TO STAY WITH OUR GROUPS ON DAY 1 AND DAY 2...
...BUT WE GET FREE TIME FOR DAY 3, RIGHT?
Y-
YUP!
WHAT ARE YOU DOING FOR YOUR FREE TIME?
G-GEE, GOOD QUESTION!
IF YOU DON'T HAVE ANY PLANS, WANT TO GO SIGHT-SEEING WITH US?
IT'S ME, SHIZUKA, AND NIA.
OH!
MY BAD. ACTU-ALLY, I'M...

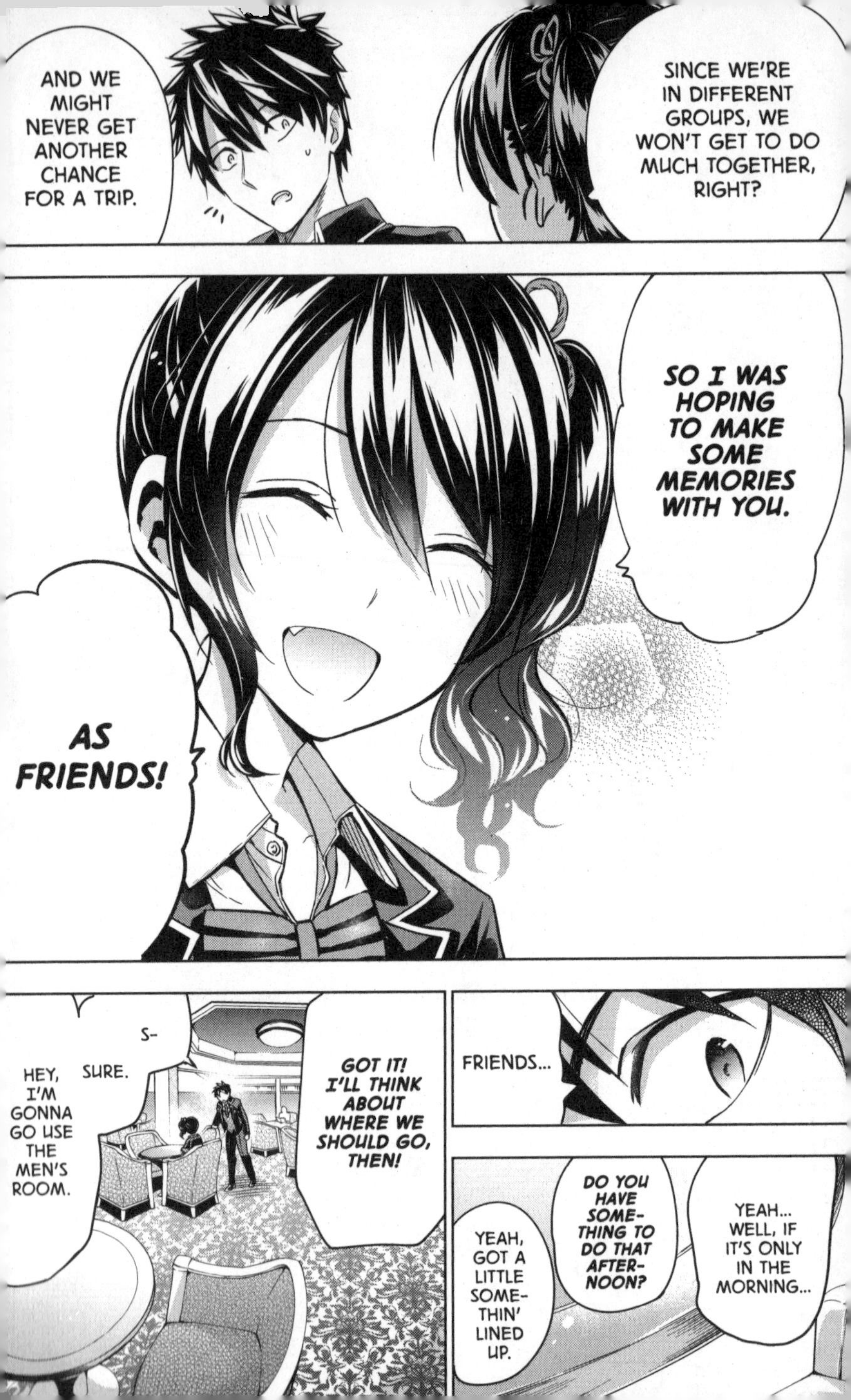
SINCE WE'RE IN DIFFERENT GROUPS, WE WON'T GET TO DO MUCH TOGETHER, RIGHT?
AND WE MIGHT NEVER GET ANOTHER CHANCE FOR A TRIP.
SO I WAS HOPING TO MAKE SOME MEMORIES WITH YOU.
AS FRIENDS!
FRIENDS...
YEAH... WELL, IF IT'S ONLY IN THE MORNING...
DO YOU HAVE SOME-THING TO DO THAT AFTER-NOON?
YEAH, GOT A LITTLE SOME-THIN' LINED UP.
GOT IT! I'LL THINK ABOUT WHERE WE SHOULD GO, THEN!
S- SURE.
HEY, I'M GONNA GO USE THE MEN'S ROOM.

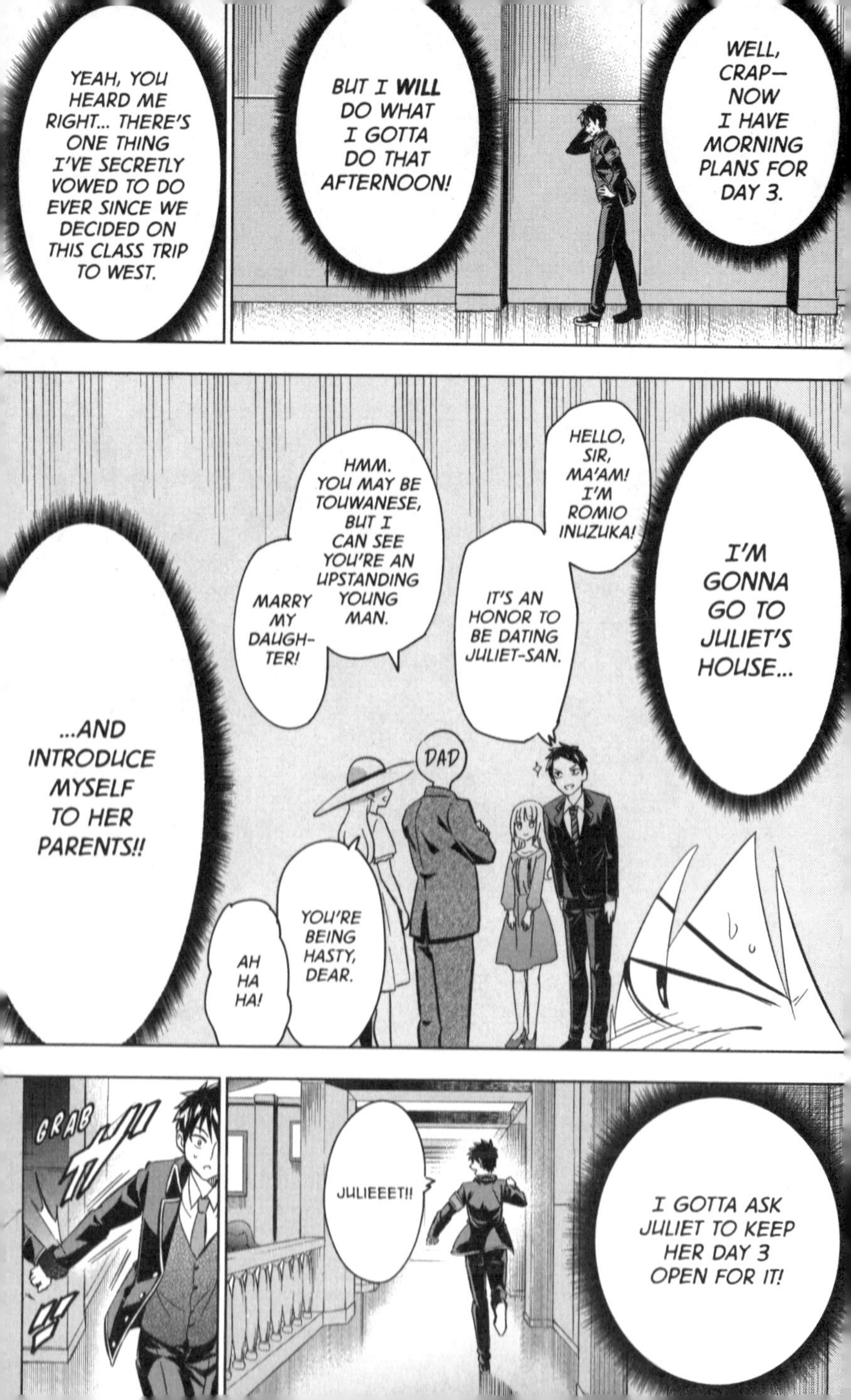
WELL, CRAP— NOW I HAVE MORNING PLANS FOR DAY 3.
BUT I **WILL** DO WHAT I GOTTA DO THAT AFTERNOON!
YEAH, YOU HEARD ME RIGHT... THERE'S ONE THING I'VE SECRETLY VOWED TO DO EVER SINCE WE DECIDED ON THIS CLASS TRIP TO WEST.
I'M GONNA GO TO JULIET'S HOUSE...
HELLO, SIR, MA'AM! I'M ROMIO INUZUKA!
IT'S AN HONOR TO BE DATING JULIET-SAN.
HMM. YOU MAY BE TOUWANESE, BUT I CAN SEE YOU'RE AN UPSTANDING YOUNG MAN.
MARRY MY DAUGH-TER!
DAD
YOU'RE BEING HASTY, DEAR.
AH HA HA!
...AND INTRODUCE MYSELF TO HER PARENTS!!
I GOTTA ASK JULIET TO KEEP HER DAY 3 OPEN FOR IT!
JULIEEET!!
GRAB

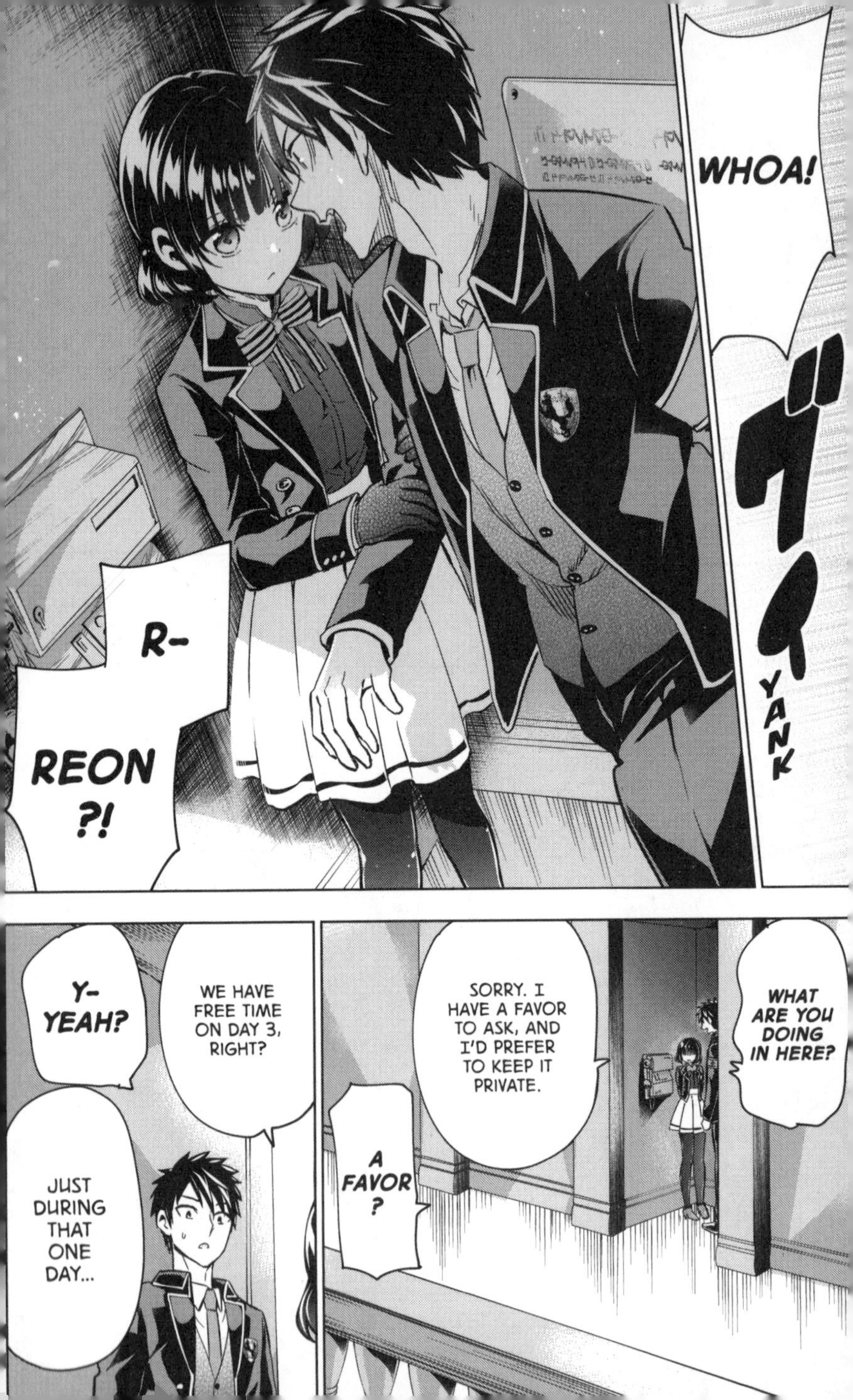
WHOA!
YANK
R- REON?!
WHAT ARE YOU DOING IN HERE?
SORRY. I HAVE A FAVOR TO ASK, AND I'D PREFER TO KEEP IT PRIVATE.
A FAVOR?
WE HAVE FREE TIME ON DAY 3, RIGHT?
Y- YEAH?
JUST DURING THAT ONE DAY...

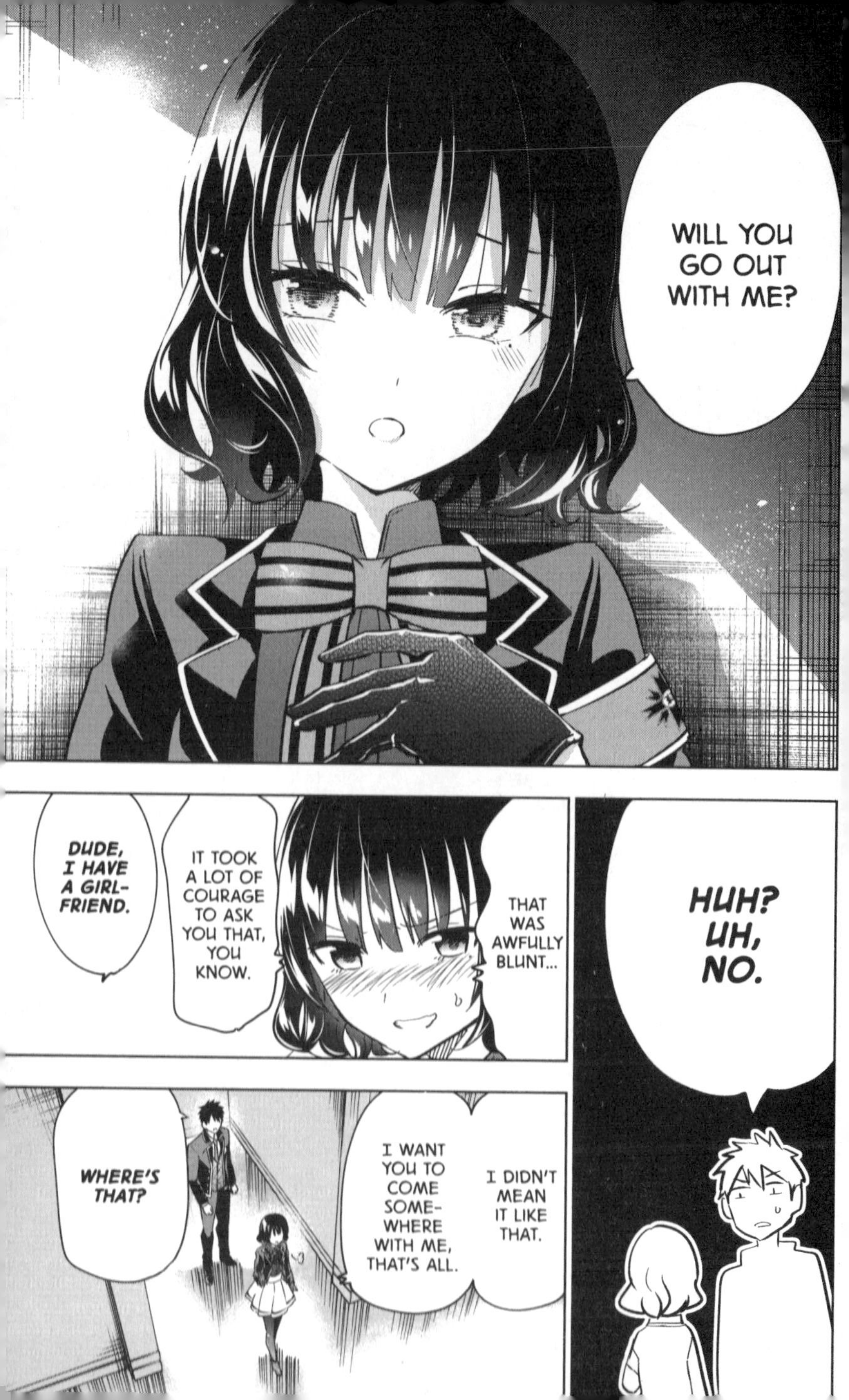
WILL YOU GO OUT WITH ME?
HUH? UH, NO.
THAT WAS AWFULLY BLUNT...
IT TOOK A LOT OF COURAGE TO ASK YOU THAT, YOU KNOW.
DUDE, I HAVE A GIRL-FRIEND.
I DIDN'T MEAN IT LIKE THAT.
I WANT YOU TO COME SOME-WHERE WITH ME, THAT'S ALL.
WHERE'S THAT?

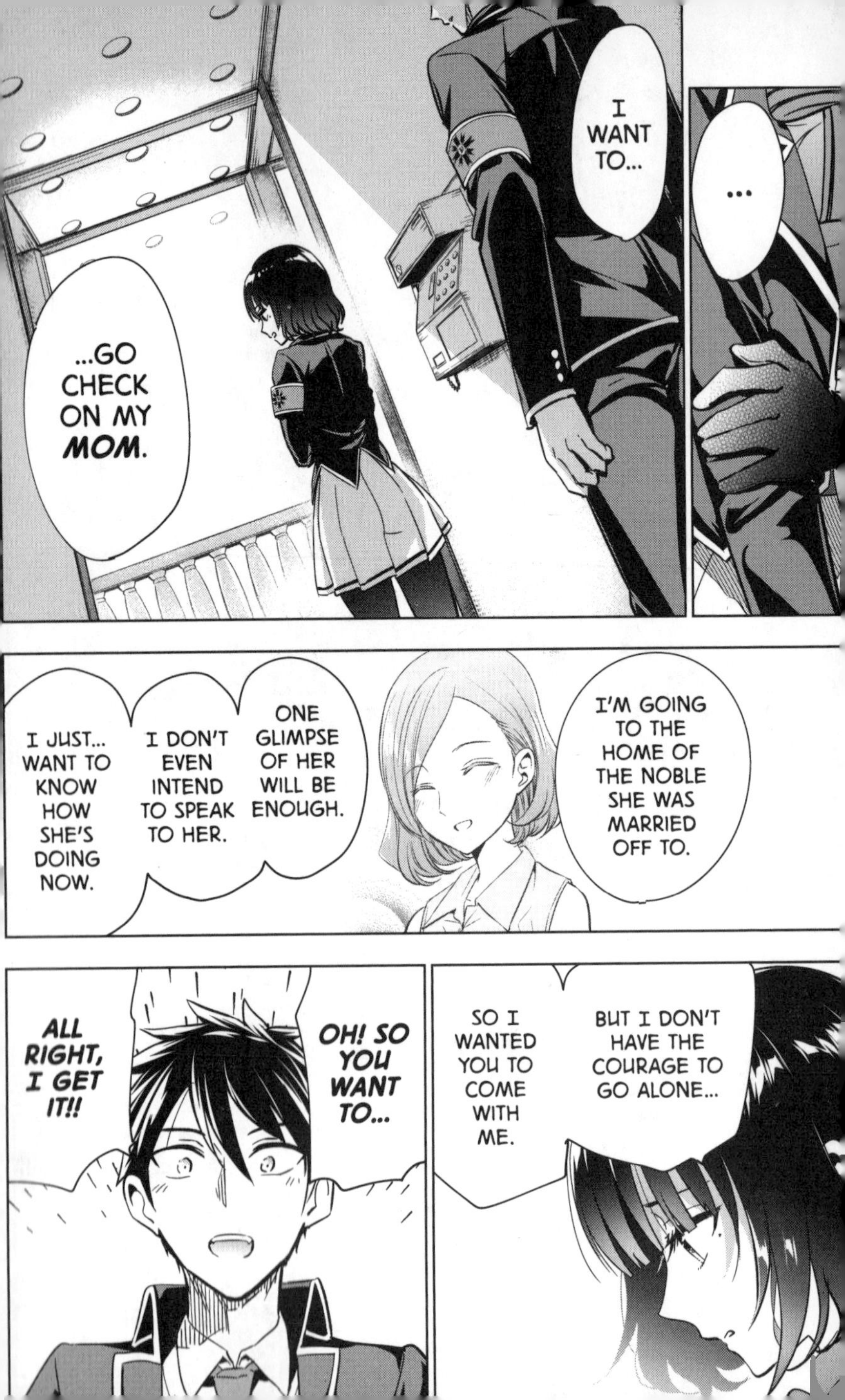
...
I WANT TO...
...GO CHECK ON MY *MOM*.
I'M GOING TO THE HOME OF THE NOBLE SHE WAS MARRIED OFF TO.
ONE GLIMPSE OF HER WILL BE ENOUGH.
I DON'T EVEN INTEND TO SPEAK TO HER.
I JUST... WANT TO KNOW HOW SHE'S DOING NOW.
BUT I DON'T HAVE THE COURAGE TO GO ALONE...
SO I WANTED YOU TO COME WITH ME.
OH! SO YOU WANT TO...
ALL RIGHT, I GET IT!!

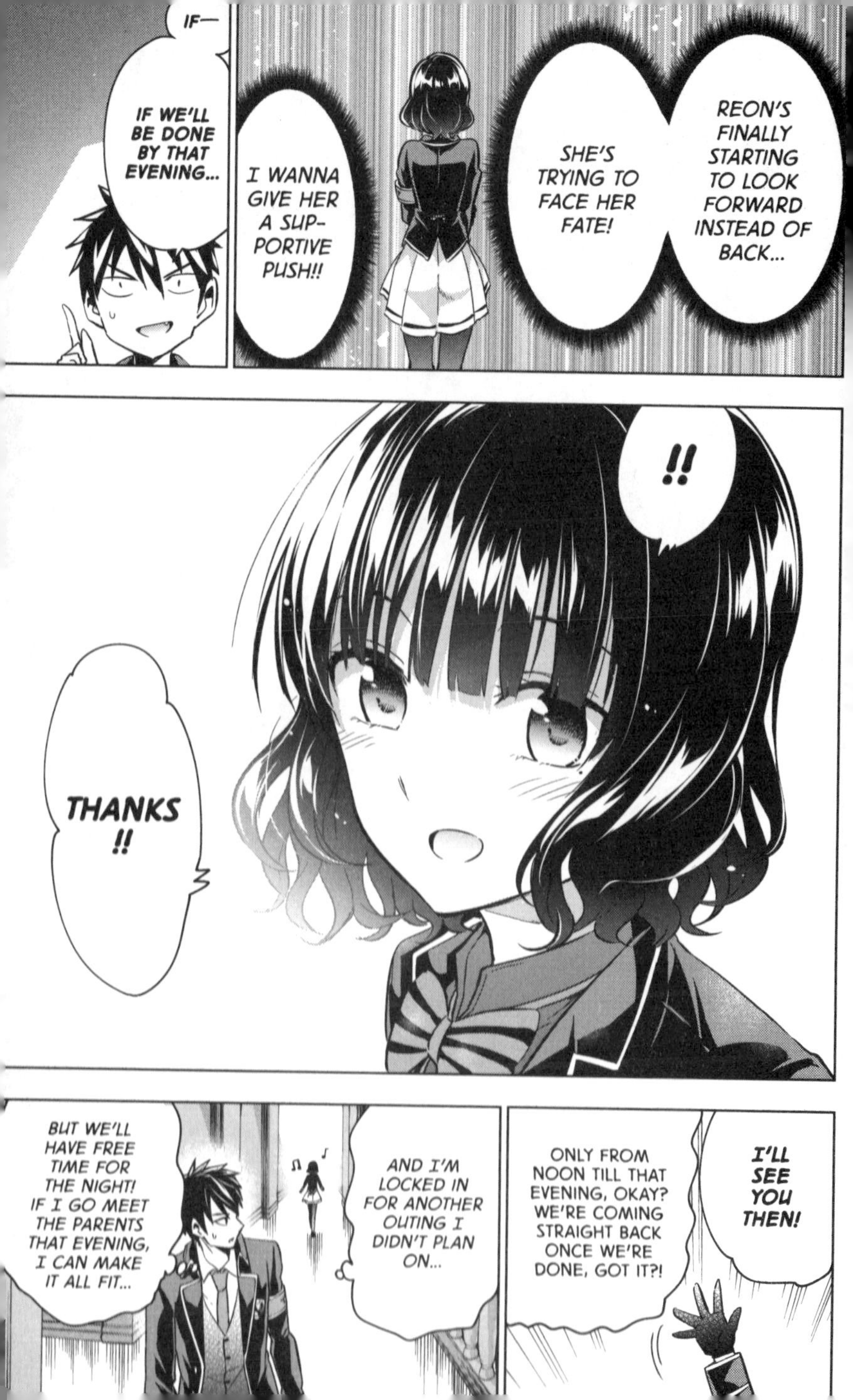
REON'S FINALLY STARTING TO LOOK FORWARD INSTEAD OF BACK...
SHE'S TRYING TO FACE HER FATE!
I WANNA GIVE HER A SUP-PORTIVE PUSH!!
IF—
IF WE'LL BE DONE BY THAT EVENING...
!!
THANKS !!
I'LL SEE YOU THEN!
ONLY FROM NOON TILL THAT EVENING, OKAY? WE'RE COMING STRAIGHT BACK ONCE WE'RE DONE, GOT IT?!
AND I'M LOCKED IN FOR ANOTHER OUTING I DIDN'T PLAN ON...
BUT WE'LL HAVE FREE TIME FOR THE NIGHT! IF I GO MEET THE PARENTS THAT EVENING, I CAN MAKE IT ALL FIT...

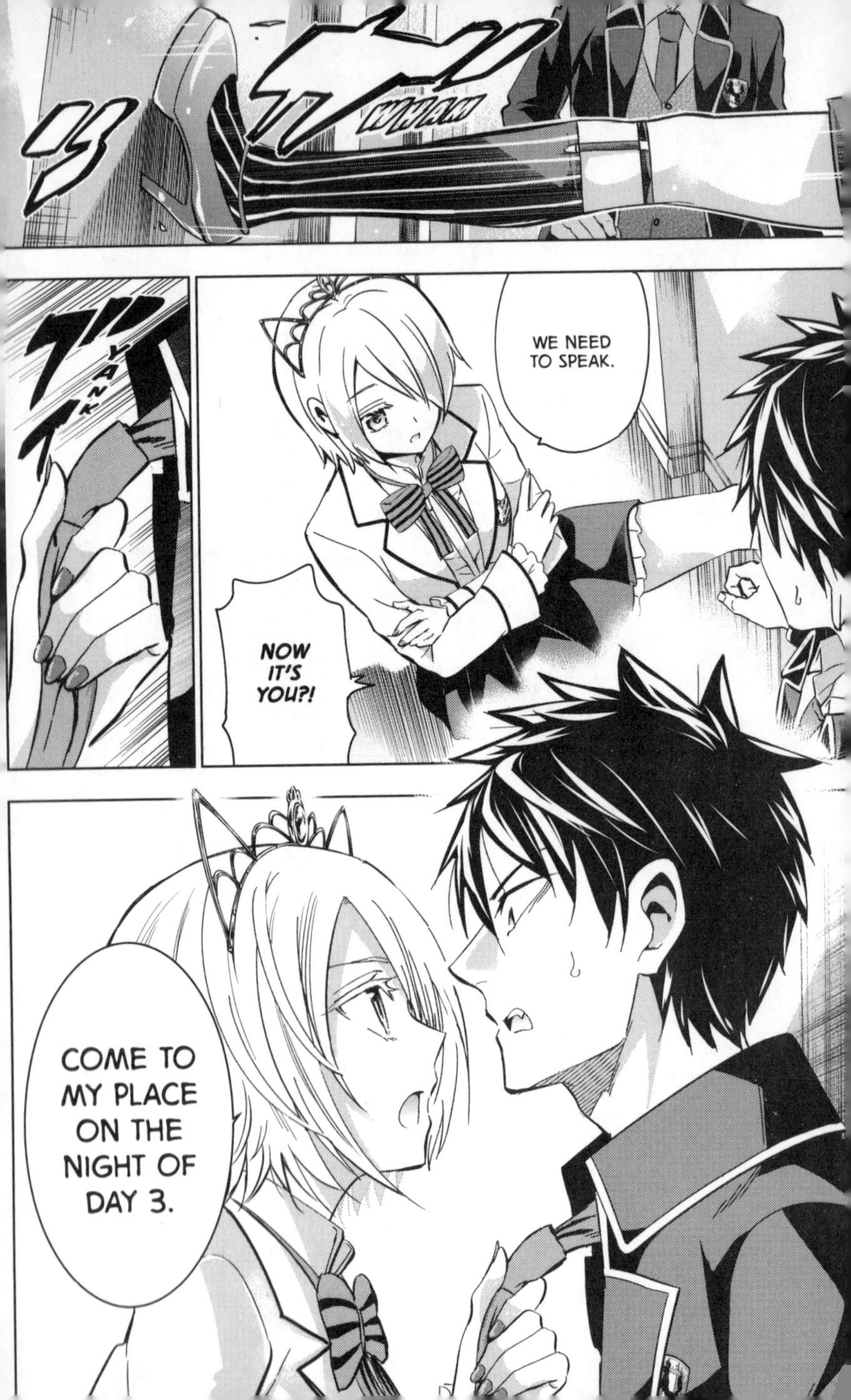
WHAM
WE NEED TO SPEAK.
NOW IT'S YOU?!
YANK
COME TO MY PLACE ON THE NIGHT OF DAY 3.

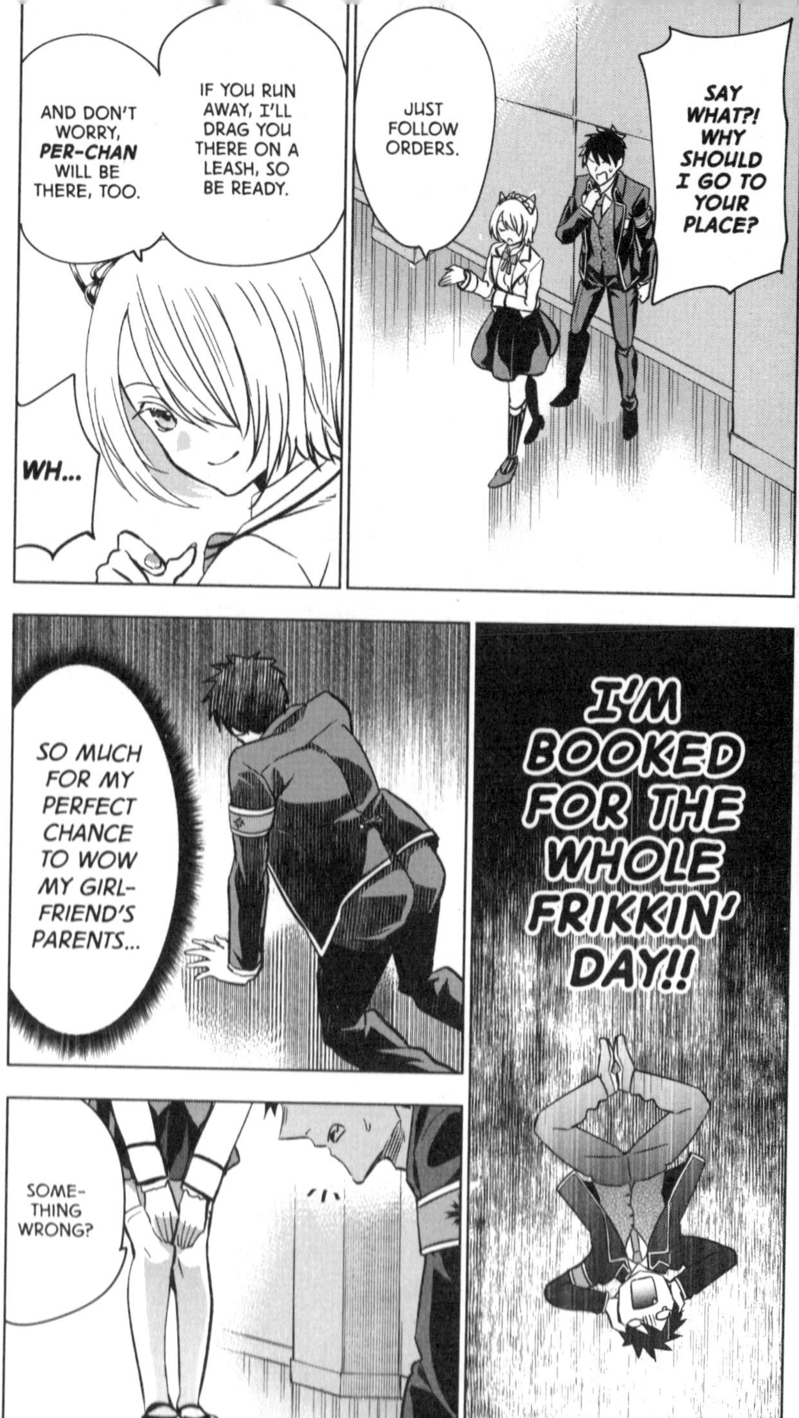
SAY WHAT?! WHY SHOULD I GO TO YOUR PLACE?
JUST FOLLOW ORDERS.
IF YOU RUN AWAY, I'LL DRAG YOU THERE ON A LEASH, SO BE READY.
AND DON'T WORRY, PER-CHAN WILL BE THERE, TOO.
WH...
I'M BOOKED FOR THE WHOLE FRIKKIN' DAY!!
SO MUCH FOR MY PERFECT CHANCE TO WOW MY GIRL-FRIEND'S PARENTS...
SOME-THING WRONG?

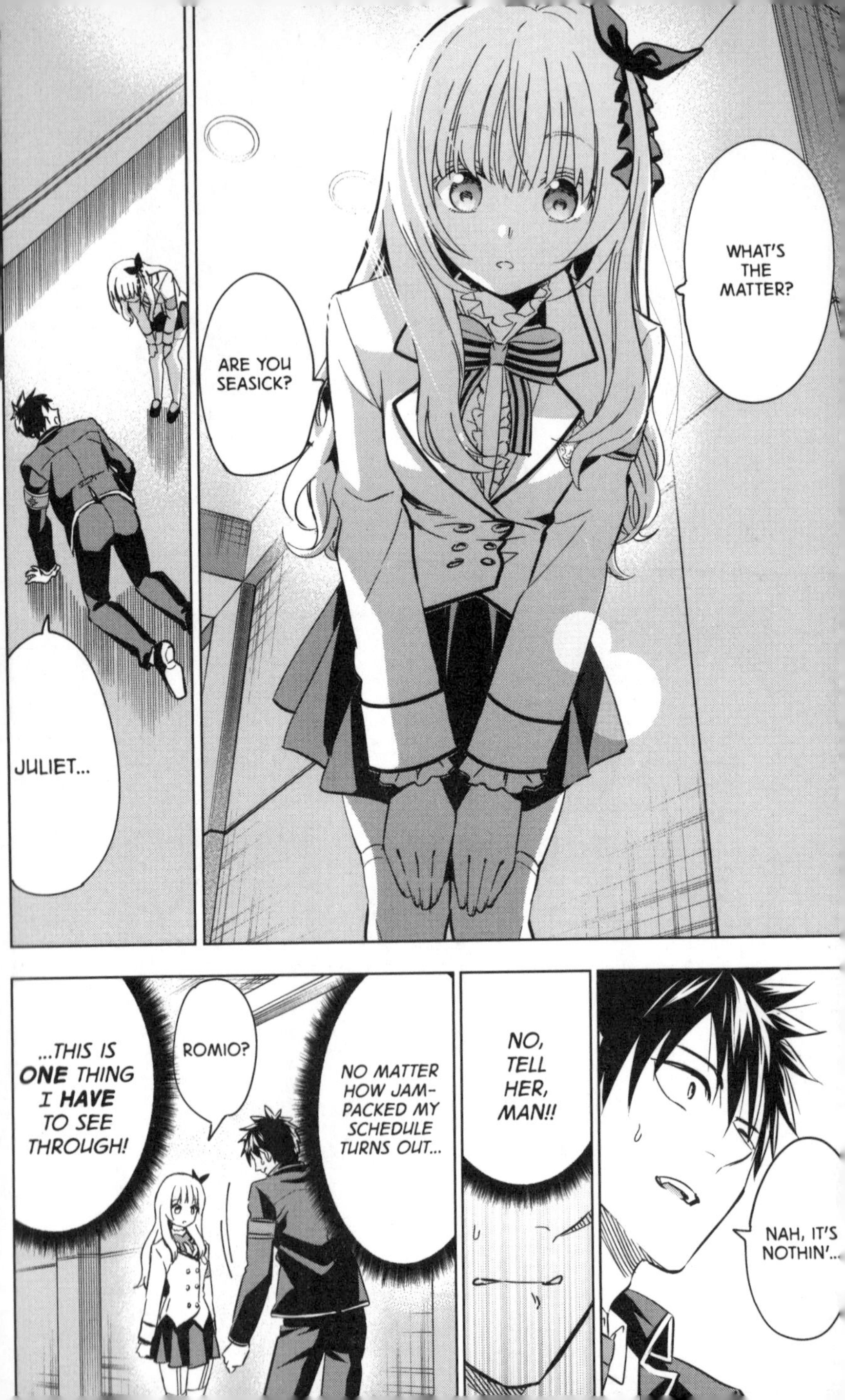
WHAT'S THE MATTER?
ARE YOU SEASICK?
JULIET...
NAH, IT'S NOTHIN'...
NO, TELL HER, MAN!!
NO MATTER HOW JAM-PACKED MY SCHEDULE TURNS OUT...
ROMIO?
...THIS IS ONE THING I HAVE TO SEE THROUGH!

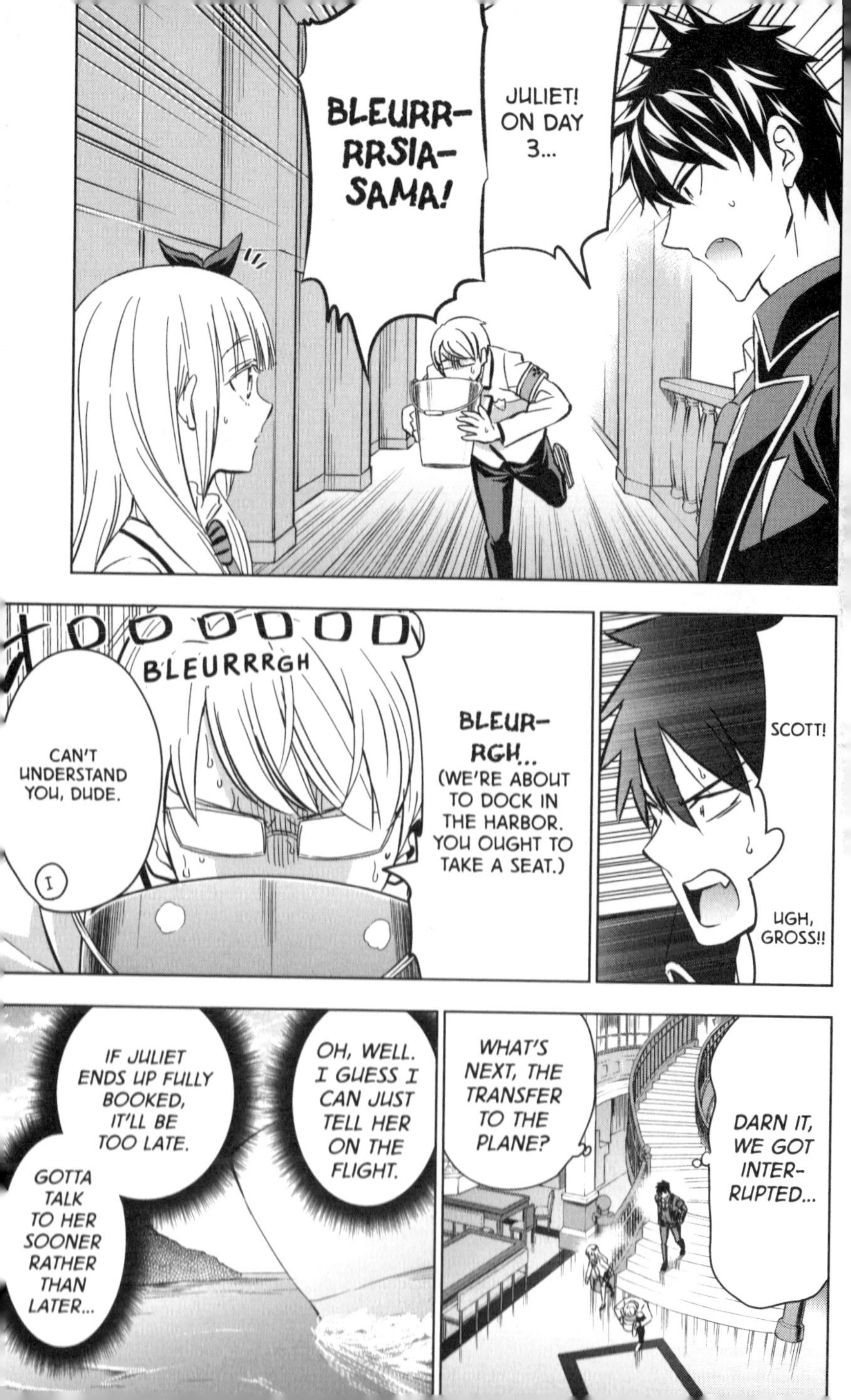
JULIET! ON DAY 3...
BLEURRR-RRSIA-SAMA!
SCOTT!
UGH, GROSS!!
BLEUR-RGH... (WE'RE ABOUT TO DOCK IN THE HARBOR. YOU OUGHT TO TAKE A SEAT.)
BLEURRRGH
CAN'T UNDERSTAND YOU, DUDE.
DARN IT, WE GOT INTER-RUPTED...
WHAT'S NEXT, THE TRANSFER TO THE PLANE?
OH, WELL. I GUESS I CAN JUST TELL HER ON THE FLIGHT.
IF JULIET ENDS UP FULLY BOOKED, IT'LL BE TOO LATE.
GOTTA TALK TO HER SOONER RATHER THAN LATER...

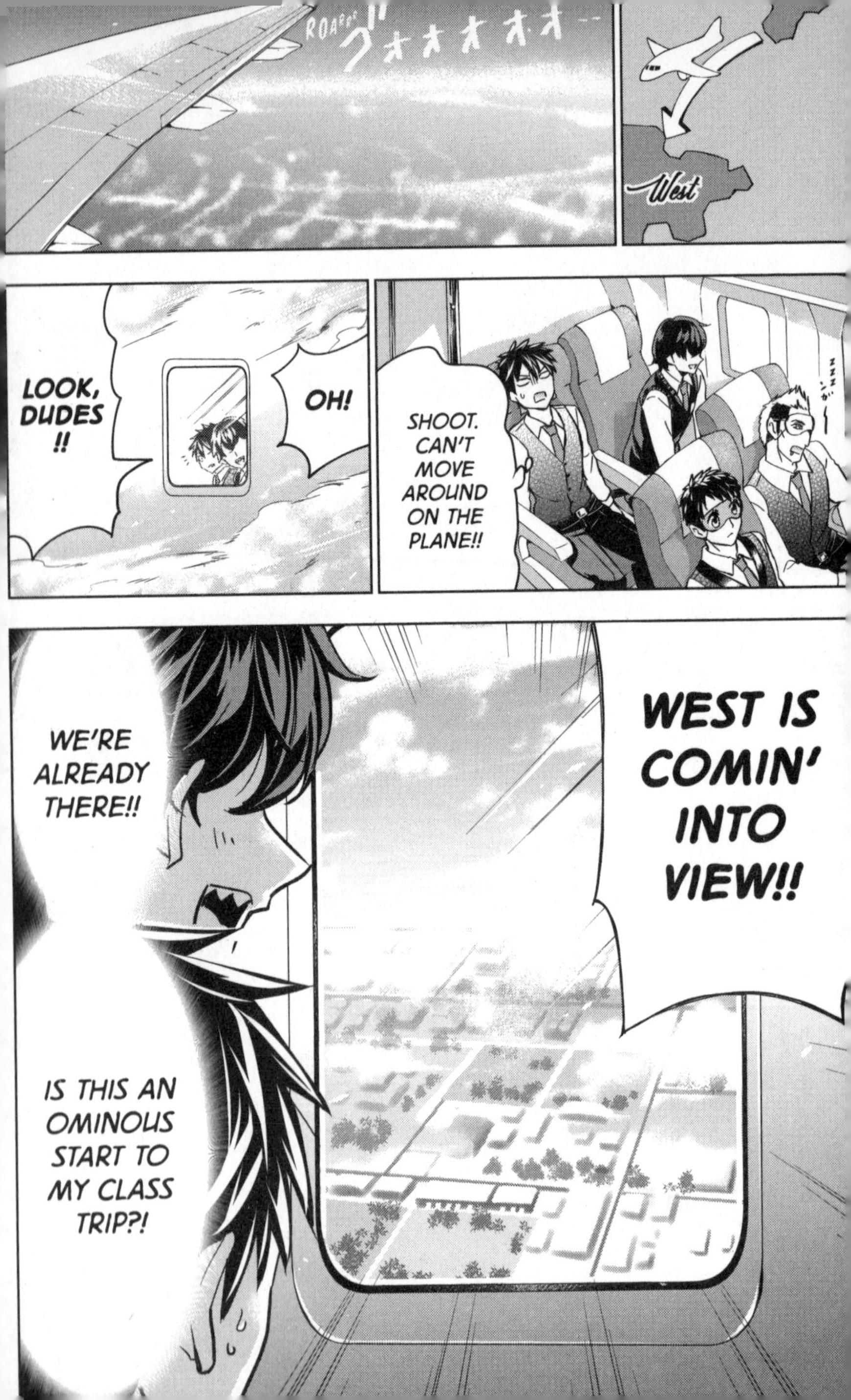
West
SHOOT. CAN'T MOVE AROUND ON THE PLANE!!
OH!
LOOK, DUDES!!
WEST IS COMIN' INTO VIEW!!
WE'RE ALREADY THERE!!
IS THIS AN OMINOUS START TO MY CLASS TRIP?!

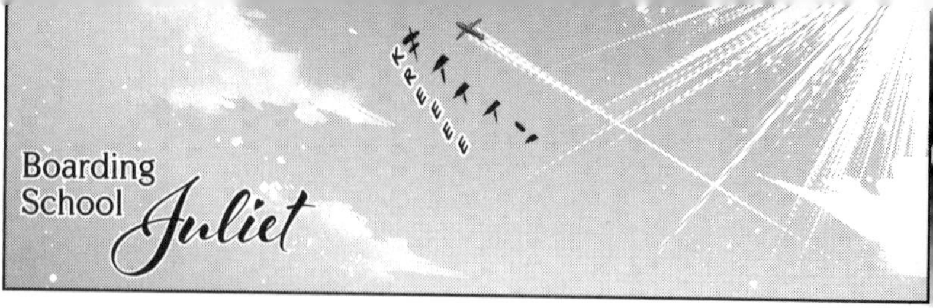
KREEEEE
Boarding School Juliet

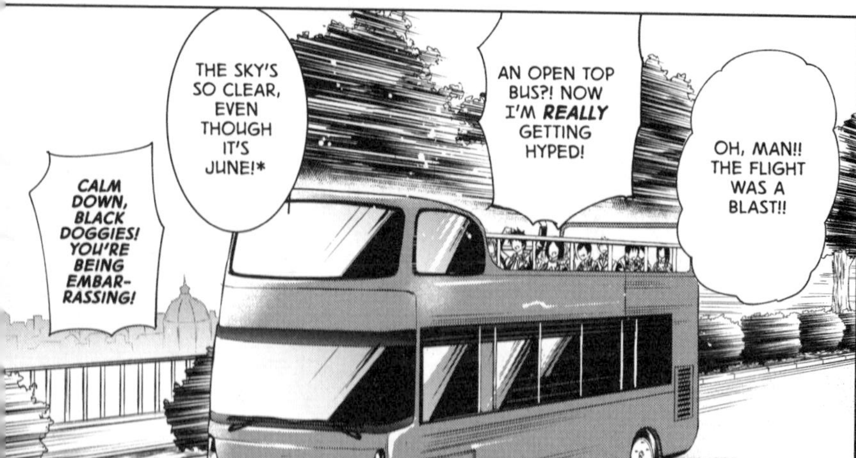
OH, MAN!! THE FLIGHT WAS A BLAST!!
AN OPEN TOP BUS?! NOW I'M REALLY GETTING HYPED!
THE SKY'S SO CLEAR, EVEN THOUGH IT'S JUNE!*
CALM DOWN, BLACK DOGGIES! YOU'RE BEING EMBARRASSING!
VROOM

*Translator's note: June is the rainy season in Japan (and thus, in Touwa).

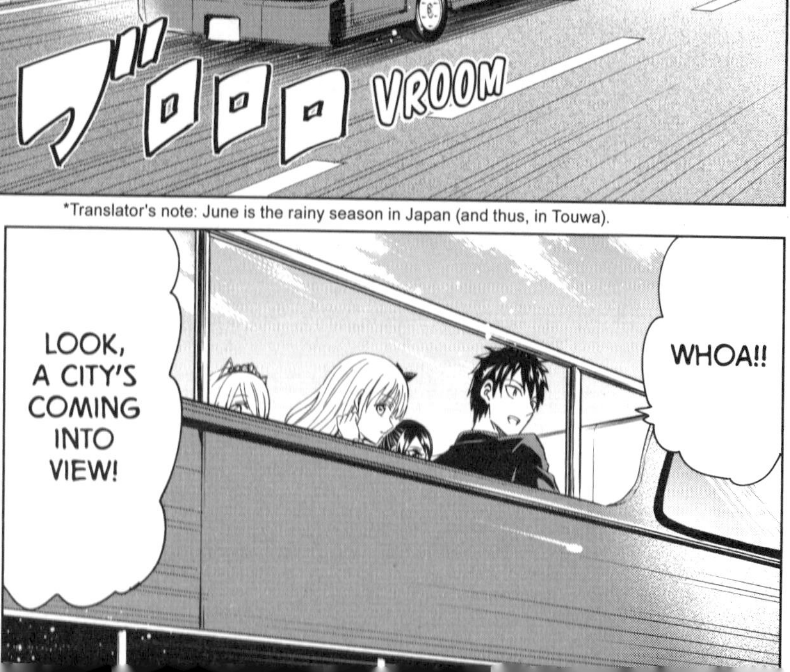
WHOA!!
LOOK, A CITY'S COMING INTO VIEW!

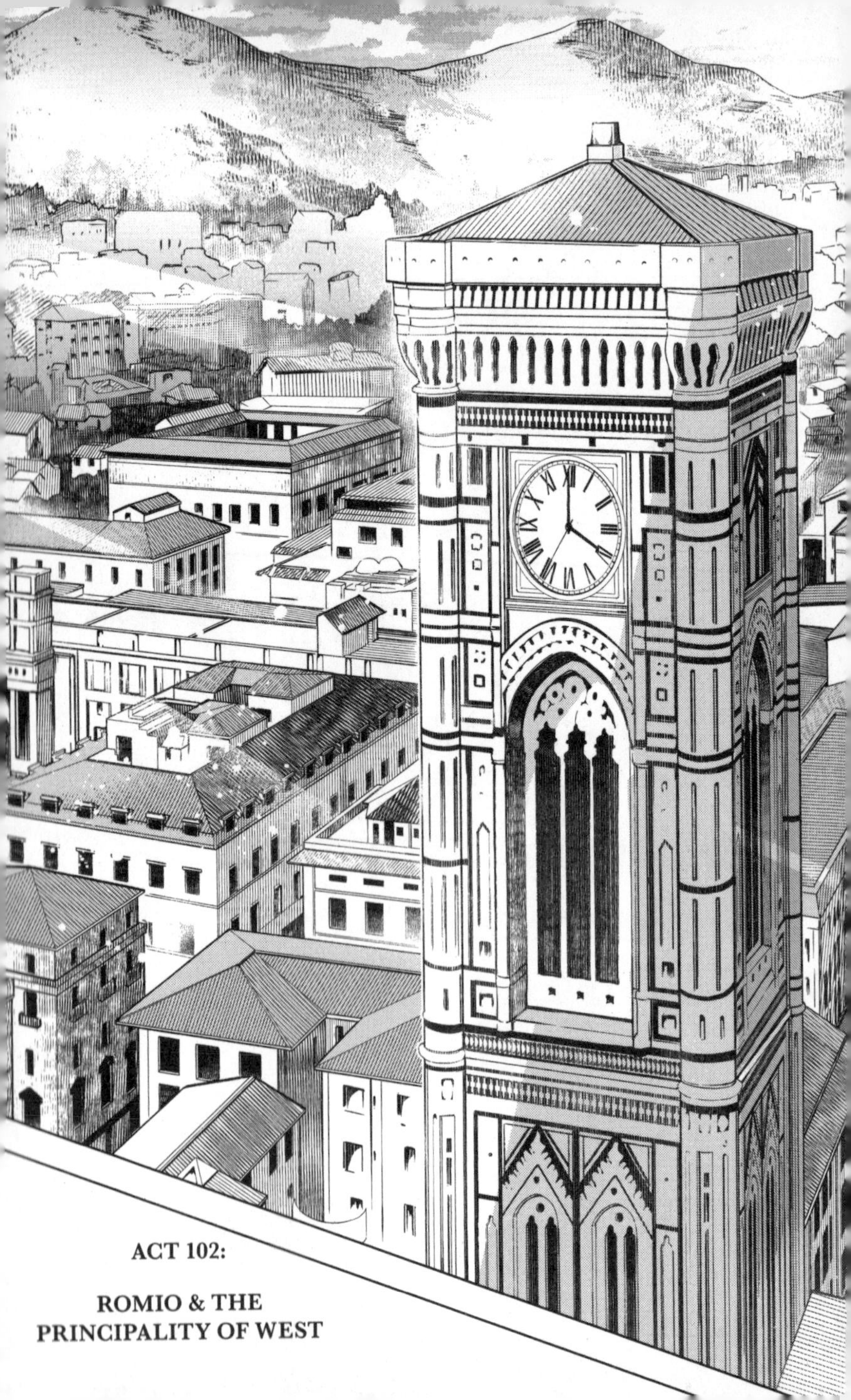
ACT 102:
ROMIO & THE PRINCIPALITY OF WEST

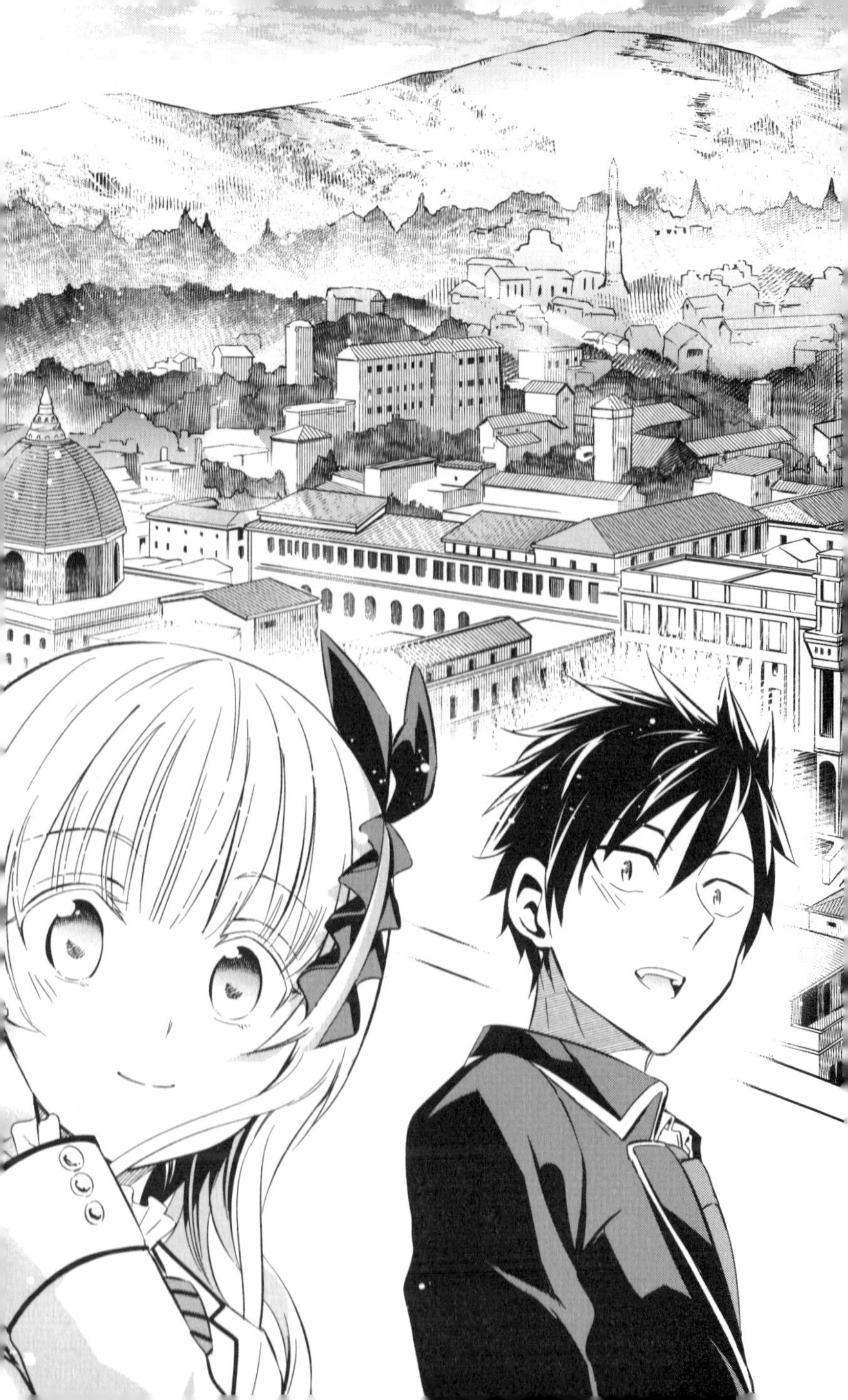

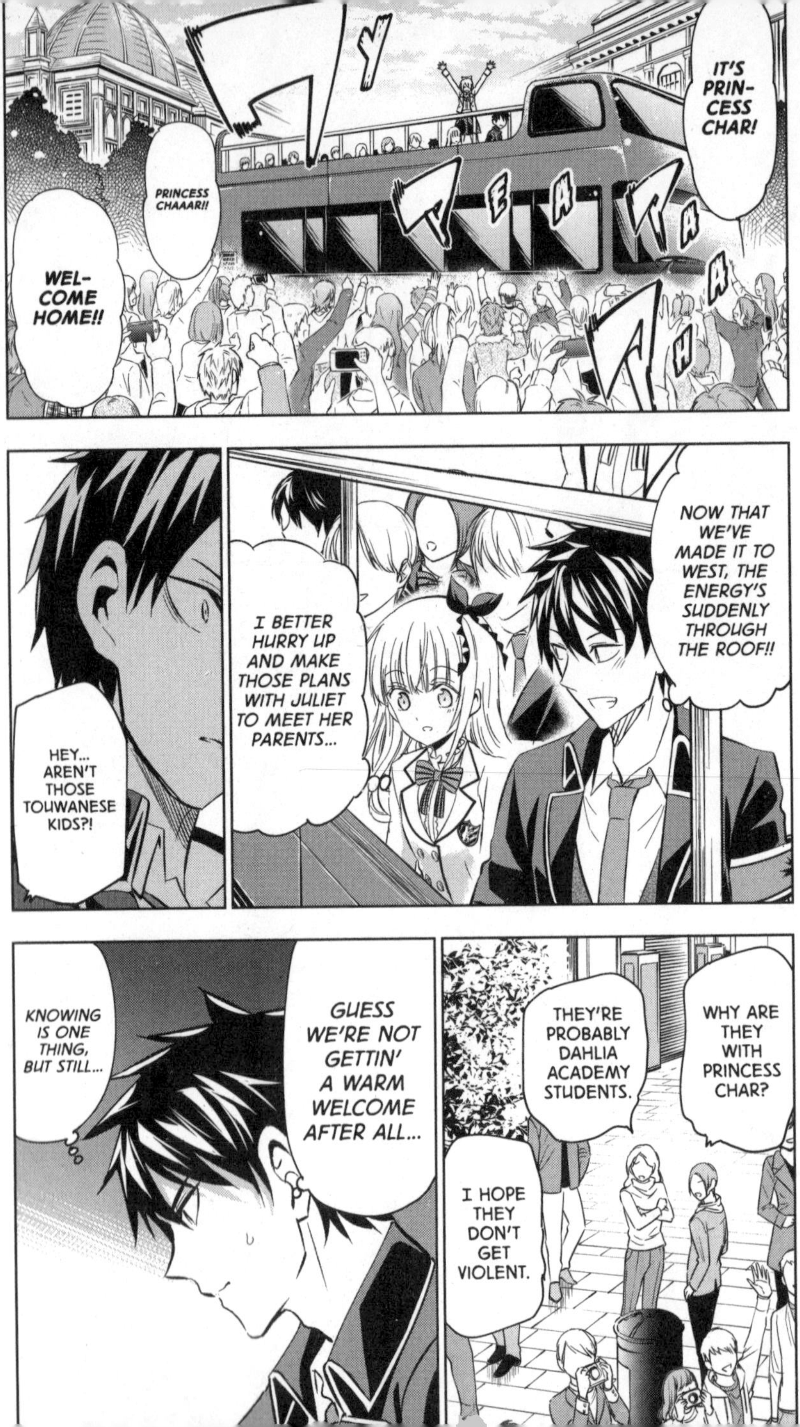
IT'S PRIN-CESS CHAR!
PRINCESS CHAAAR!!
WEL-COME HOME!!
NOW THAT WE'VE MADE IT TO WEST, THE ENERGY'S SUDDENLY THROUGH THE ROOF!!
I BETTER HURRY UP AND MAKE THOSE PLANS WITH JULIET TO MEET HER PARENTS...
HEY... AREN'T THOSE TOUWANESE KIDS?!
WHY ARE THEY WITH PRINCESS CHAR?
THEY'RE PROBABLY DAHLIA ACADEMY STUDENTS.
I HOPE THEY DON'T GET VIOLENT.
GUESS WE'RE NOT GETTIN' A WARM WELCOME AFTER ALL...
KNOWING IS ONE THING, BUT STILL...

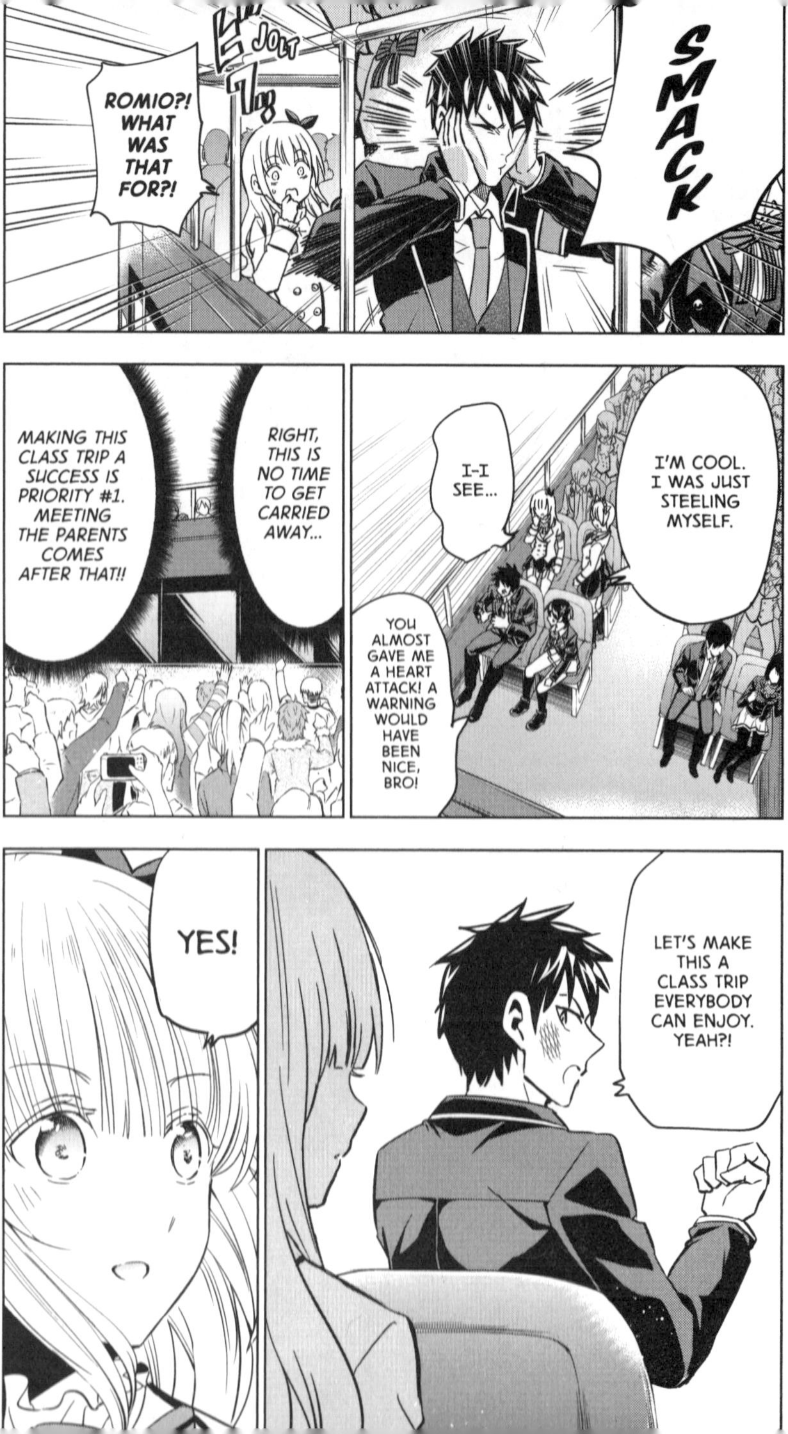
SMACK
JOLT
ROMIO?! WHAT WAS THAT FOR?!
I'M COOL. I WAS JUST STEELING MYSELF.
I-I SEE...
YOU ALMOST GAVE ME A HEART ATTACK! A WARNING WOULD HAVE BEEN NICE, BRO!
RIGHT, THIS IS NO TIME TO GET CARRIED AWAY...
MAKING THIS CLASS TRIP A SUCCESS IS PRIORITY #1. MEETING THE PARENTS COMES AFTER THAT!!
LET'S MAKE THIS A CLASS TRIP EVERYBODY CAN ENJOY. YEAH?!
YES!

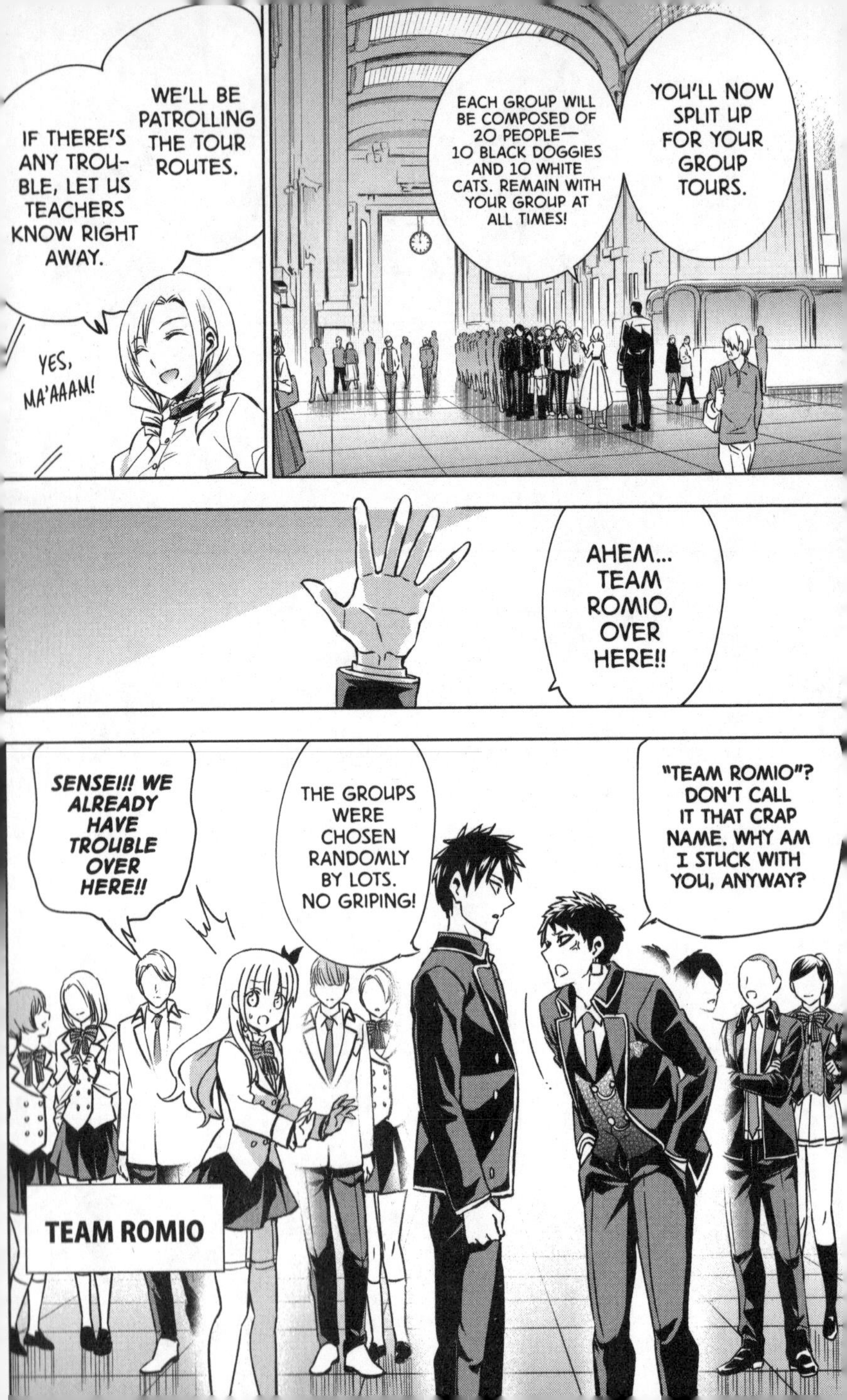
YOU'LL NOW SPLIT UP FOR YOUR GROUP TOURS.
EACH GROUP WILL BE COMPOSED OF 20 PEOPLE— 10 BLACK DOGGIES AND 10 WHITE CATS. REMAIN WITH YOUR GROUP AT ALL TIMES!
WE'LL BE PATROLLING THE TOUR ROUTES.
IF THERE'S ANY TROU-BLE, LET US TEACHERS KNOW RIGHT AWAY.
YES, MA'AAAM!
AHEM... TEAM ROMIO, OVER HERE!!
"TEAM ROMIO"? DON'T CALL IT THAT CRAP NAME. WHY AM I STUCK WITH YOU, ANYWAY?
THE GROUPS WERE CHOSEN RANDOMLY BY LOTS. NO GRIPING!
SENSEI!!! WE ALREADY HAVE TROUBLE OVER HERE!!
TEAM ROMIO

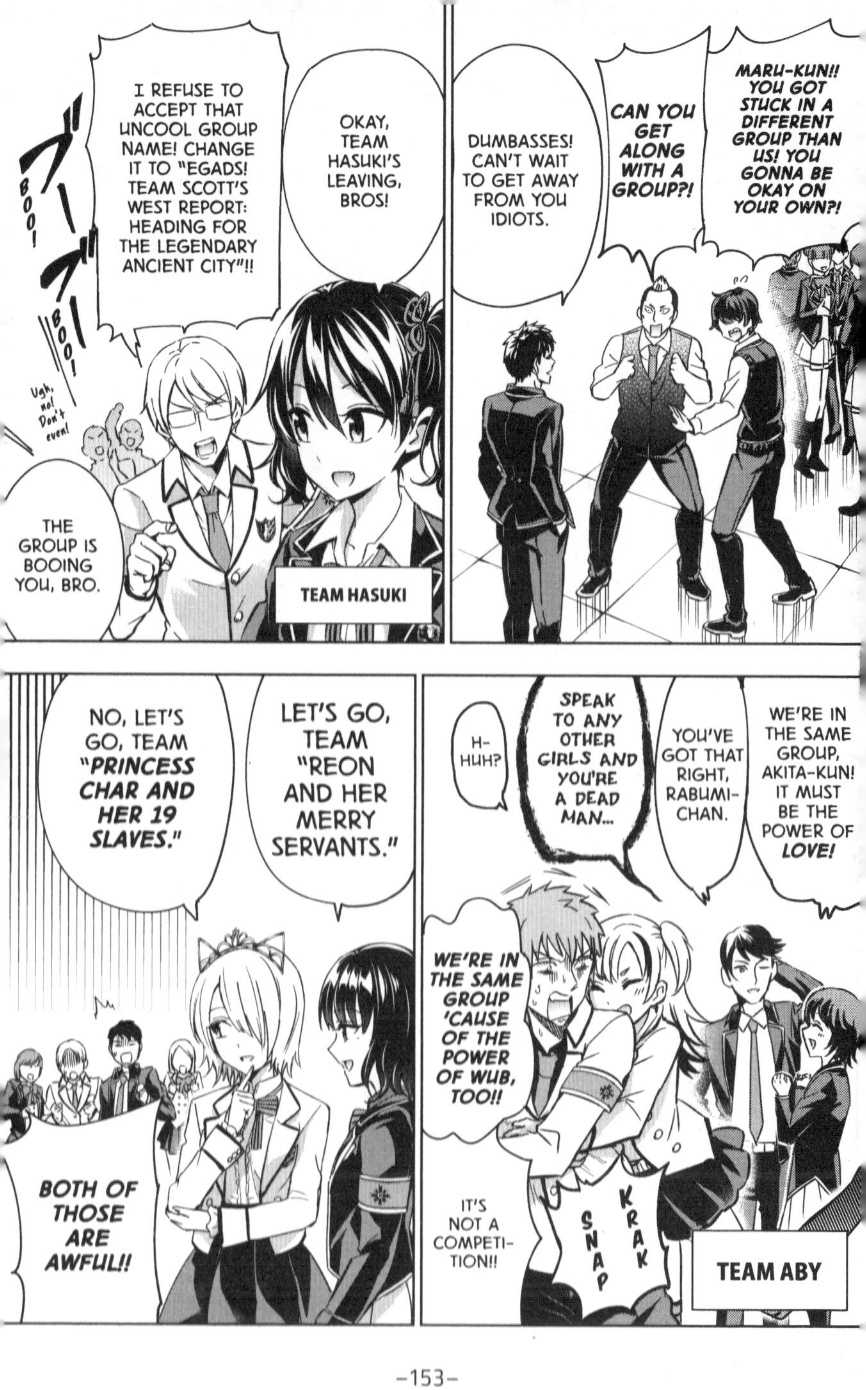
MARU-KUN!! YOU GOT STUCK IN A DIFFERENT GROUP THAN US! YOU GONNA BE OKAY ON YOUR OWN?!
CAN YOU GET ALONG WITH A GROUP?!
DUMBASSES! CAN'T WAIT TO GET AWAY FROM YOU IDIOTS.
OKAY, TEAM HASUKI'S LEAVING, BROS!
I REFUSE TO ACCEPT THAT UNCOOL GROUP NAME! CHANGE IT TO "EGADS! TEAM SCOTT'S WEST REPORT: HEADING FOR THE LEGENDARY ANCIENT CITY"!!
BOO! BOO!
Ugh, no! Don't even!
THE GROUP IS BOOING YOU, BRO.
TEAM HASUKI
WE'RE IN THE SAME GROUP, AKITA-KUN! IT MUST BE THE POWER OF LOVE!
YOU'VE GOT THAT RIGHT, RABUMI-CHAN.
SPEAK TO ANY OTHER GIRLS AND YOU'RE A DEAD MAN...
H-HUH?
WE'RE IN THE SAME GROUP 'CAUSE OF THE POWER OF WUB, TOO!!
KRAK
SNAP
IT'S NOT A COMPETITION!!
TEAM ABY
LET'S GO, TEAM "REON AND HER MERRY SERVANTS."
NO, LET'S GO, TEAM "PRINCESS CHAR AND HER 19 SLAVES."
BOTH OF THOSE ARE AWFUL!!

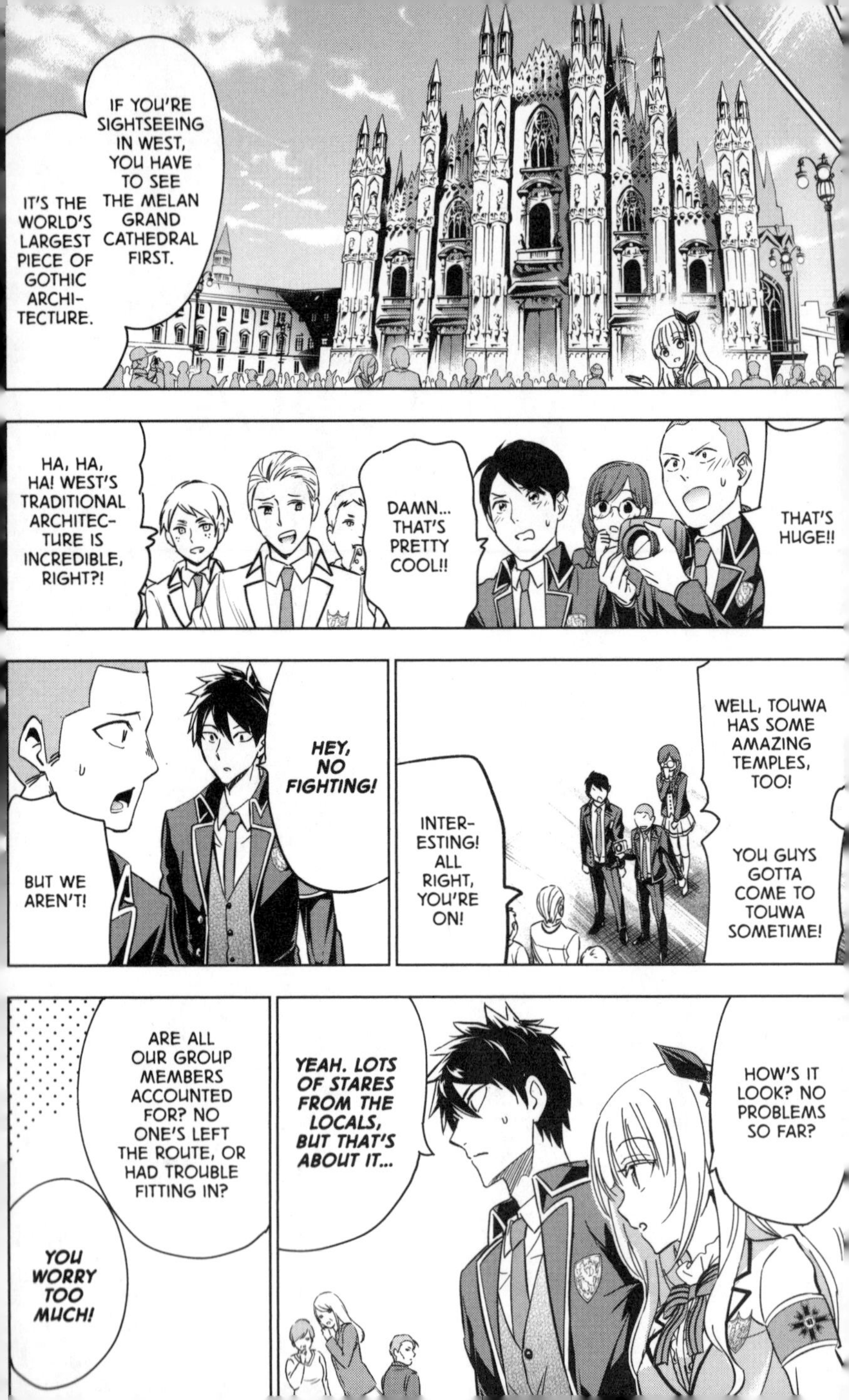
IF YOU'RE SIGHTSEEING IN WEST, YOU HAVE TO SEE THE MELAN GRAND CATHEDRAL FIRST.
IT'S THE WORLD'S LARGEST PIECE OF GOTHIC ARCHI-TECTURE.
THAT'S HUGE!!
DAMN... THAT'S PRETTY COOL!!
HA, HA, HA! WEST'S TRADITIONAL ARCHITEC-TURE IS INCREDIBLE, RIGHT?!
WELL, TOUWA HAS SOME AMAZING TEMPLES, TOO!
YOU GUYS GOTTA COME TO TOUWA SOMETIME!
INTER-ESTING! ALL RIGHT, YOU'RE ON!
HEY, NO FIGHTING!
BUT WE AREN'T!
HOW'S IT LOOK? NO PROBLEMS SO FAR?
YEAH. LOTS OF STARES FROM THE LOCALS, BUT THAT'S ABOUT IT...
ARE ALL OUR GROUP MEMBERS ACCOUNTED FOR? NO ONE'S LEFT THE ROUTE, OR HAD TROUBLE FITTING IN?
YOU WORRY TOO MUCH!

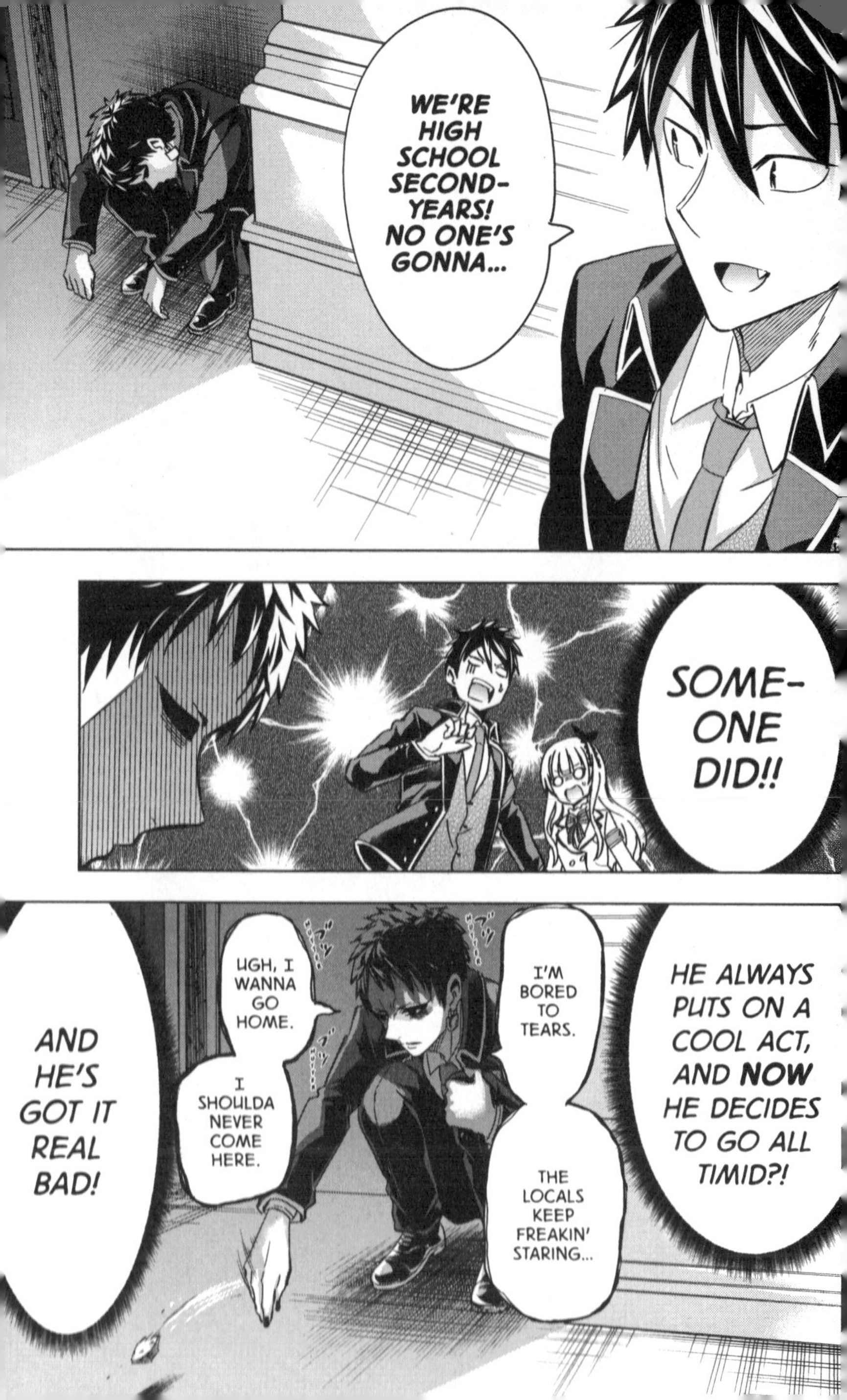
WE'RE HIGH SCHOOL SECOND-YEARS! NO ONE'S GONNA...
SOME-ONE DID!!
HE ALWAYS PUTS ON A COOL ACT, AND **NOW** HE DECIDES TO GO ALL TIMID?!
I'M BORED TO TEARS.
THE LOCALS KEEP FREAKIN' STARING...
UGH, I WANNA GO HOME.
I SHOULDA NEVER COME HERE.
AND HE'S GOT IT REAL BAD!

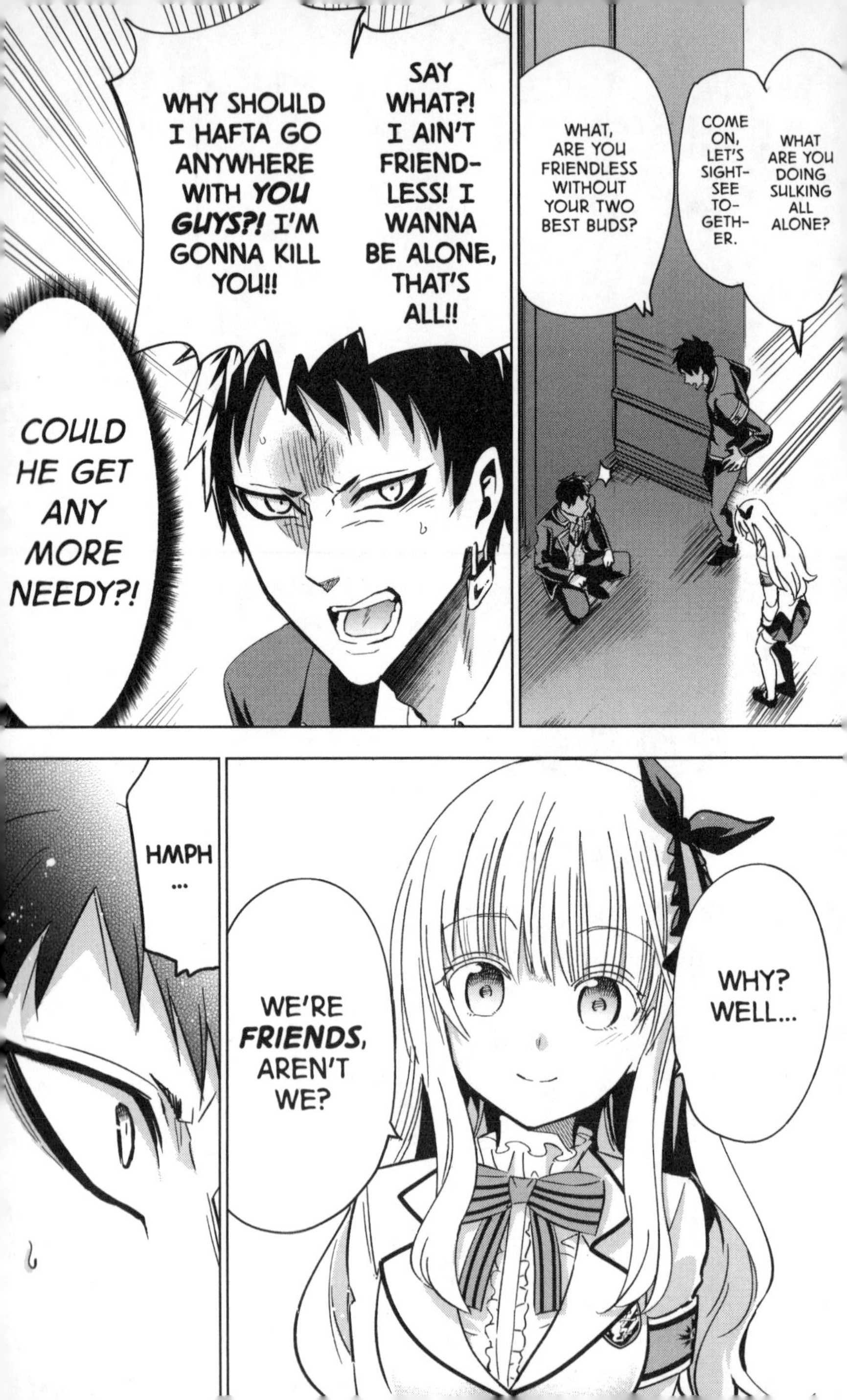
WHAT ARE YOU DOING SULKING ALL ALONE?
COME ON, LET'S SIGHT-SEE TO-GETH-ER.
WHAT, ARE YOU FRIENDLESS WITHOUT YOUR TWO BEST BUDS?
SAY WHAT?! I AIN'T FRIEND-LESS! I WANNA BE ALONE, THAT'S ALL!!
WHY SHOULD I HAFTA GO ANYWHERE WITH *YOU GUYS?!* I'M GONNA KILL YOU!!
COULD HE GET ANY MORE NEEDY?!
WHY? WELL...
WE'RE *FRIENDS*, AREN'T WE?
HMPH...

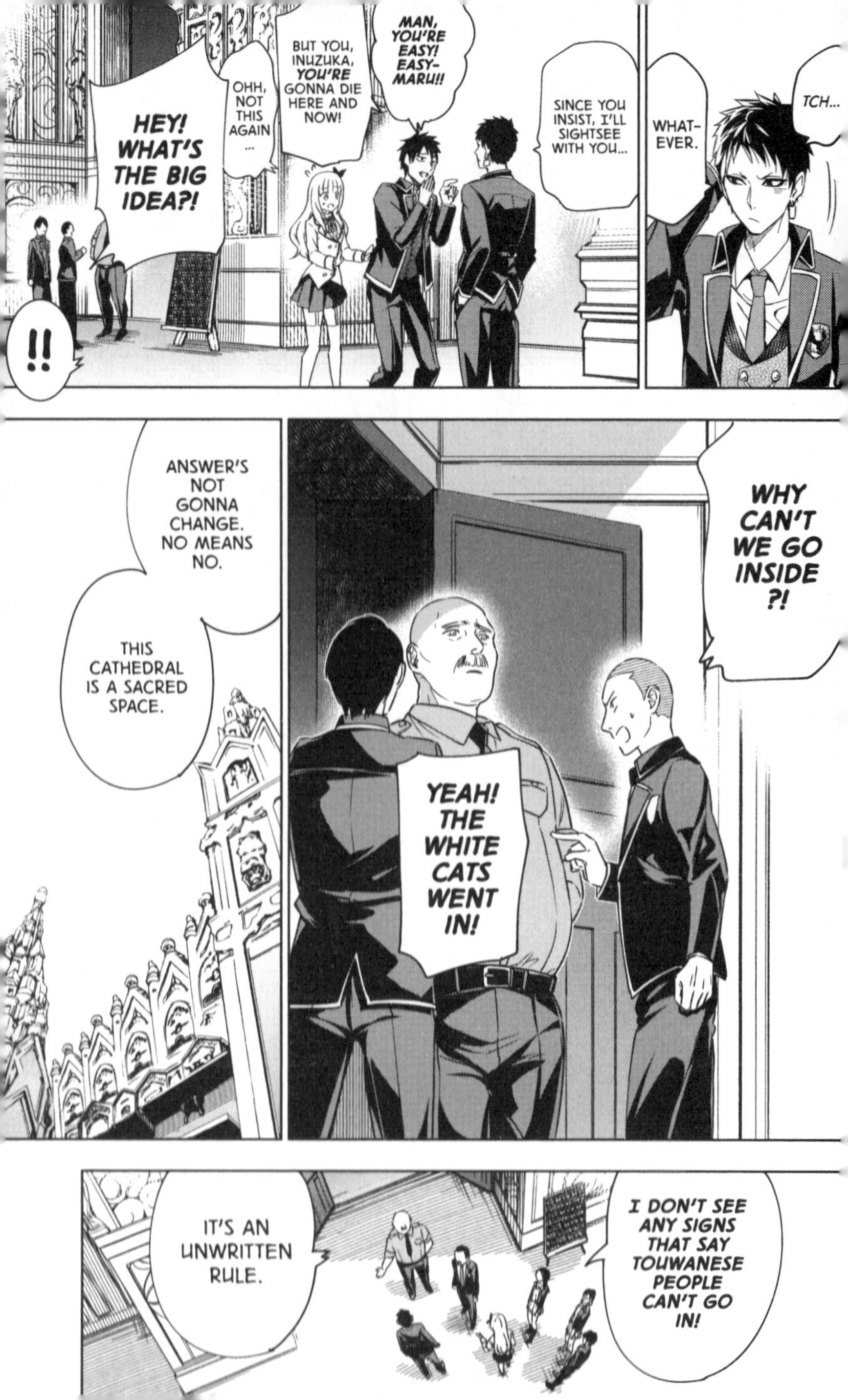
TCH...
WHAT-EVER.
SINCE YOU INSIST, I'LL SIGHTSEE WITH YOU...
MAN, YOU'RE EASY! EASY-MARU!!
BUT YOU, INUZUKA, YOU'RE GONNA DIE HERE AND NOW!
OHH, NOT THIS AGAIN ...
HEY! WHAT'S THE BIG IDEA?!
!!
WHY CAN'T WE GO INSIDE ?!
YEAH! THE WHITE CATS WENT IN!
ANSWER'S NOT GONNA CHANGE. NO MEANS NO.
THIS CATHEDRAL IS A SACRED SPACE.
I DON'T SEE ANY SIGNS THAT SAY TOUWANESE PEOPLE CAN'T GO IN!
IT'S AN UNWRITTEN RULE.

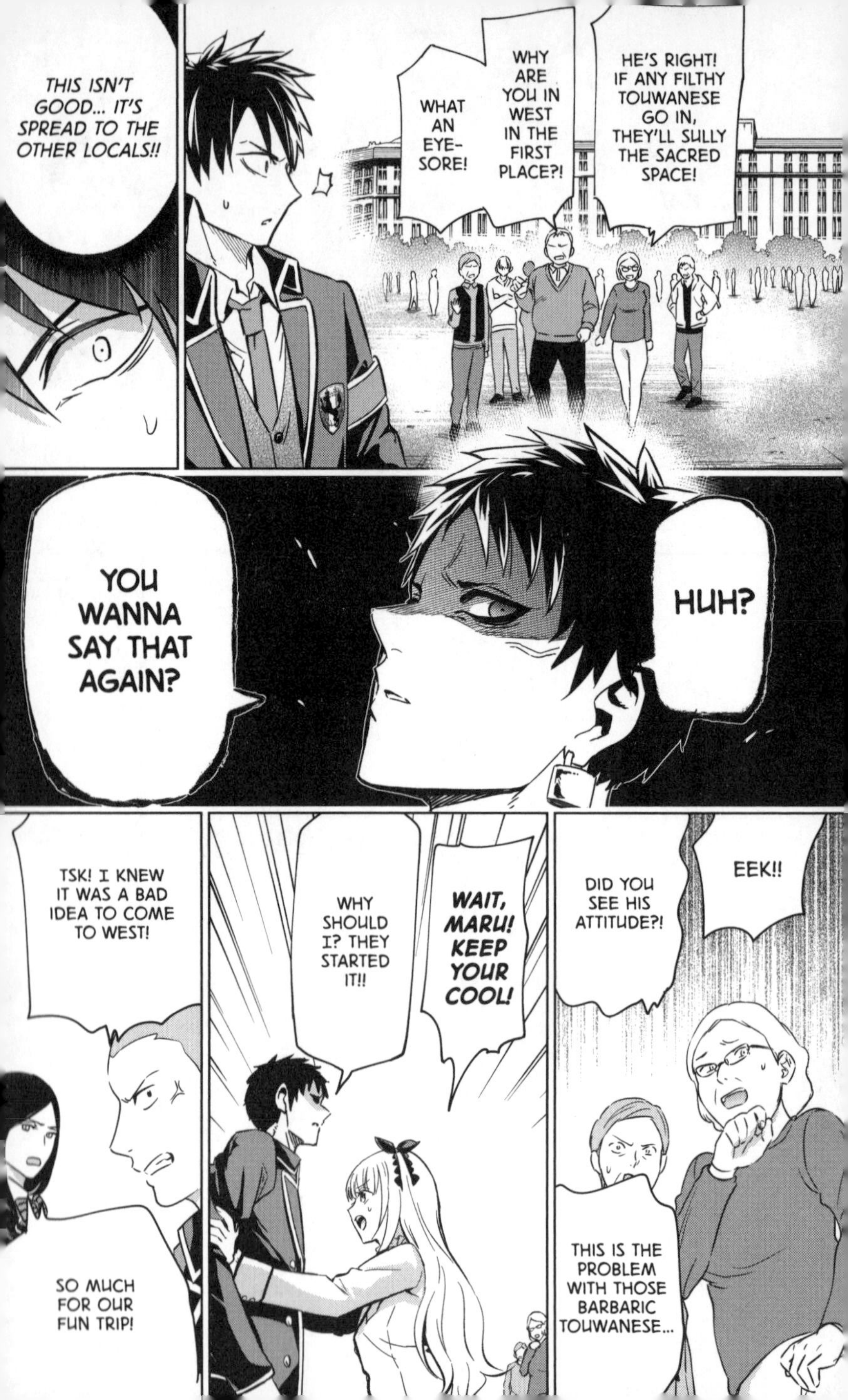
HE'S RIGHT! IF ANY FILTHY TOUWANESE GO IN, THEY'LL SULLY THE SACRED SPACE!
WHY ARE YOU IN WEST IN THE FIRST PLACE?!
WHAT AN EYE-SORE!
THIS ISN'T GOOD... IT'S SPREAD TO THE OTHER LOCALS!!
HUH?
YOU WANNA SAY THAT AGAIN?
EEK!!
DID YOU SEE HIS ATTITUDE?!
THIS IS THE PROBLEM WITH THOSE BARBARIC TOUWANESE...
WAIT, MARU! KEEP YOUR COOL!
WHY SHOULD I? THEY STARTED IT!!
TSK! I KNEW IT WAS A BAD IDEA TO COME TO WEST!
SO MUCH FOR OUR FUN TRIP!

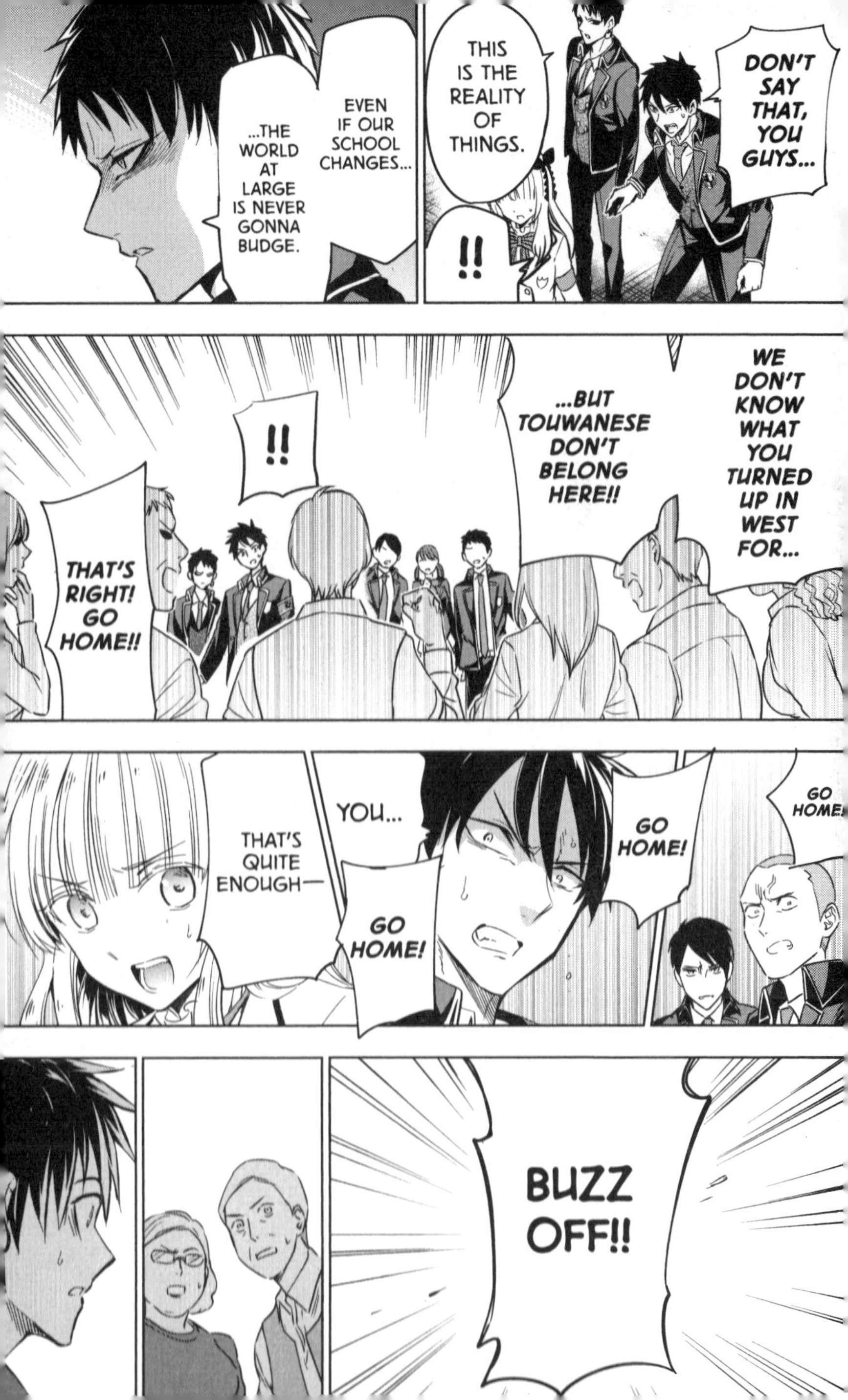
DON'T SAY THAT, YOU GUYS...
THIS IS THE REALITY OF THINGS.
!!
EVEN IF OUR SCHOOL CHANGES...
...THE WORLD AT LARGE IS NEVER GONNA BUDGE.
WE DON'T KNOW WHAT YOU TURNED UP IN WEST FOR...
...BUT TOUWANESE DON'T BELONG HERE!!
!!
THAT'S RIGHT! GO HOME!!
GO HOME
GO HOME!
YOU...
GO HOME!
THAT'S QUITE ENOUGH—
BUZZ OFF!!

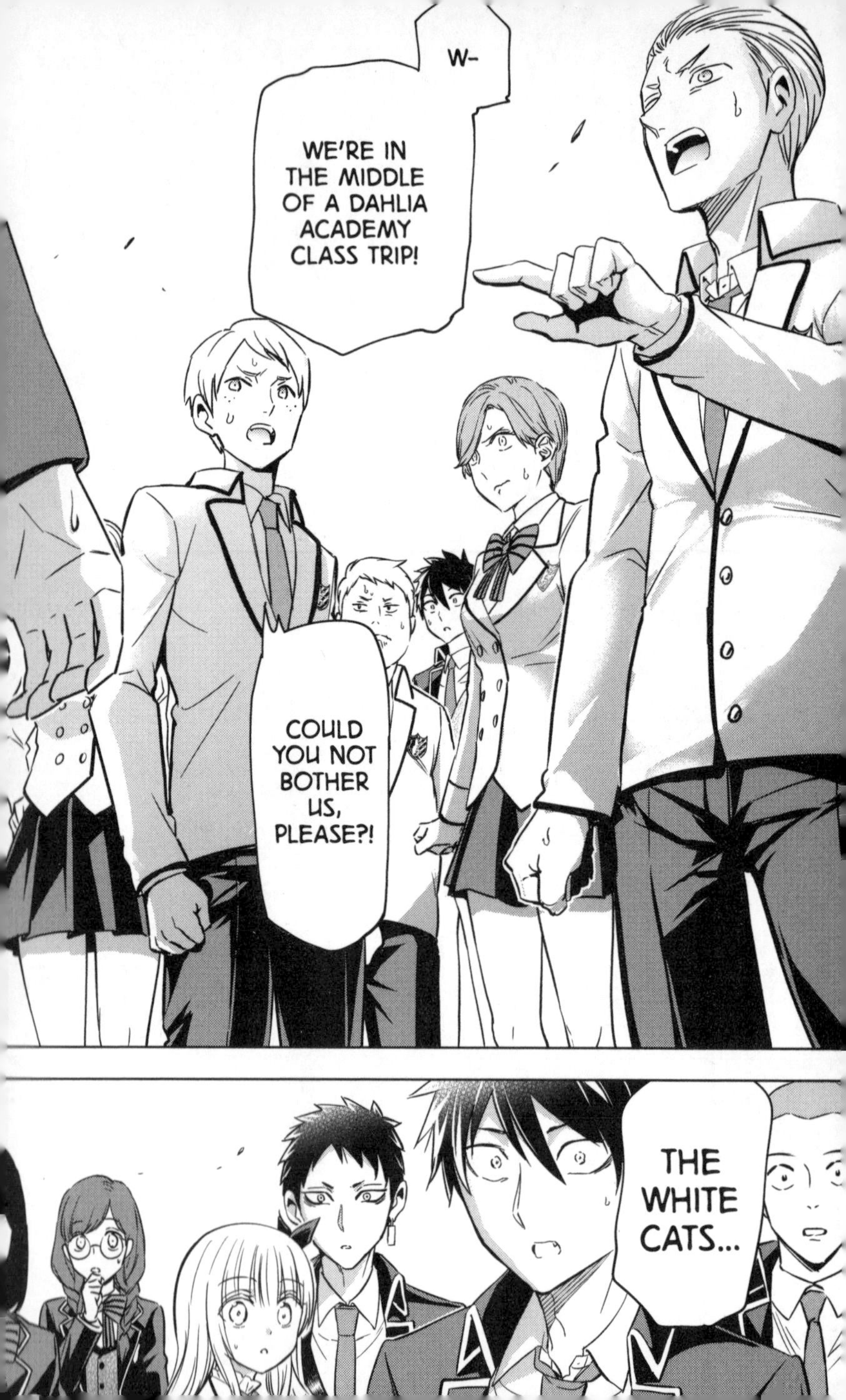
W-
WE'RE IN THE MIDDLE OF A DAHLIA ACADEMY CLASS TRIP!
COULD YOU NOT BOTHER US, PLEASE?!
THE WHITE CATS...

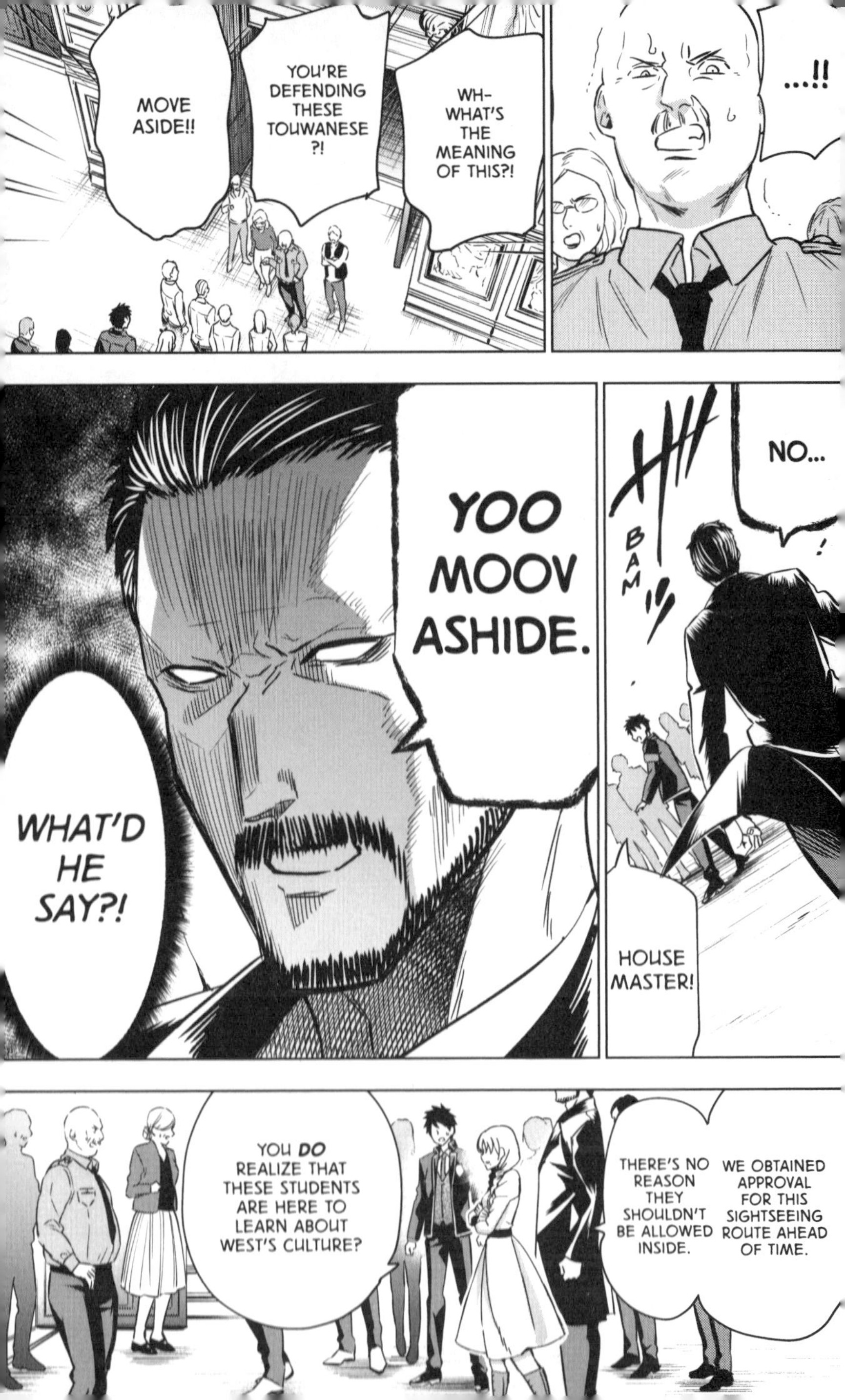
...!!
WH- WHAT'S THE MEANING OF THIS?!
YOU'RE DEFENDING THESE TOUWANESE ?!
MOVE ASIDE!!
NO...
BAM
HOUSE MASTER!
YOO MOOV ASHIDE.
WHAT'D HE SAY?!
WE OBTAINED APPROVAL FOR THIS SIGHTSEEING ROUTE AHEAD OF TIME.
THERE'S NO REASON THEY SHOULDN'T BE ALLOWED INSIDE.
YOU DO REALIZE THAT THESE STUDENTS ARE HERE TO LEARN ABOUT WEST'S CULTURE?

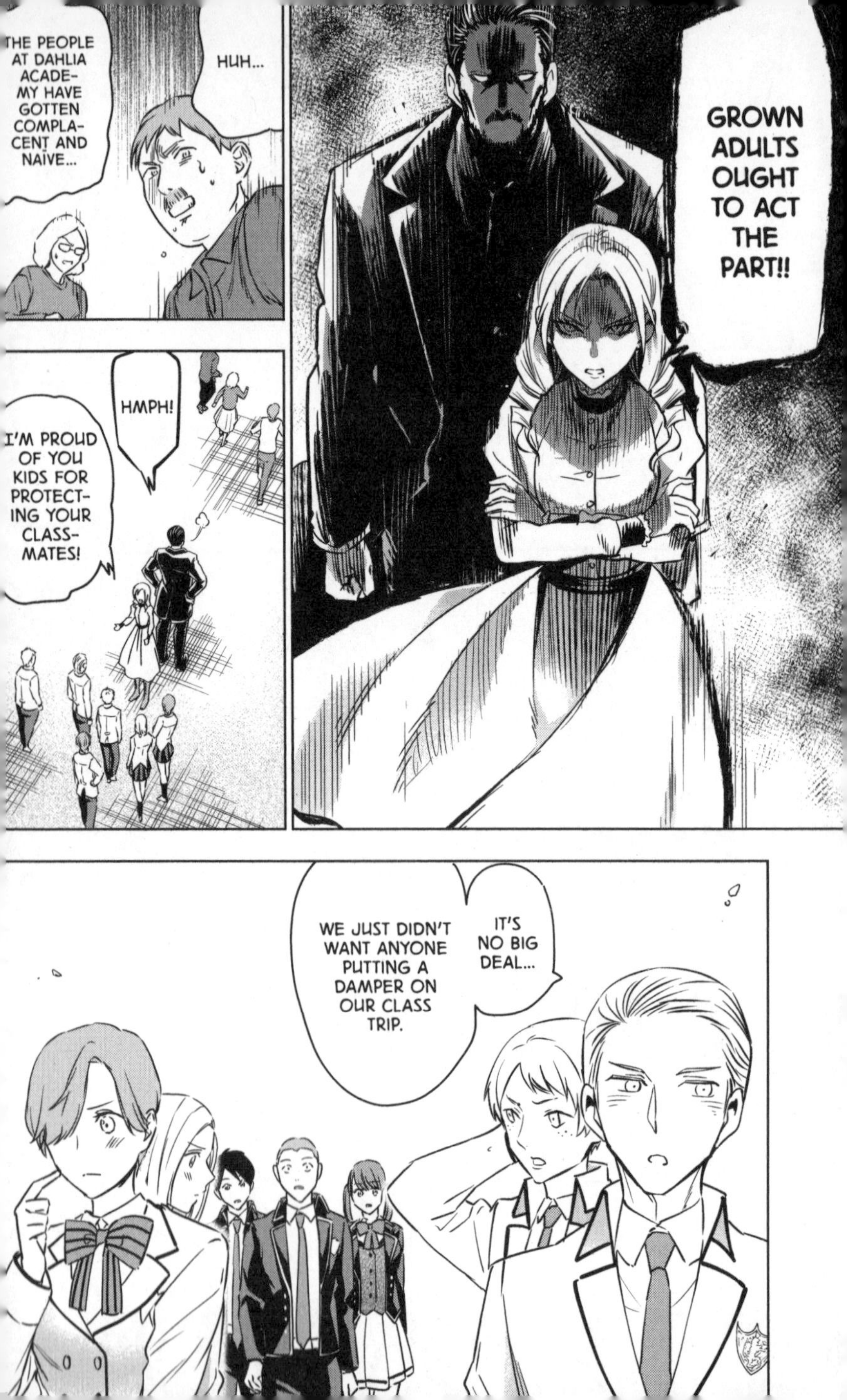
GROWN ADULTS OUGHT TO ACT THE PART!!
HUH...
THE PEOPLE AT DAHLIA ACADE-MY HAVE GOTTEN COMPLA-CENT AND NAÏVE...
HMPH!
I'M PROUD OF YOU KIDS FOR PROTECT-ING YOUR CLASS-MATES!
IT'S NO BIG DEAL...
WE JUST DIDN'T WANT ANYONE PUTTING A DAMPER ON OUR CLASS TRIP.

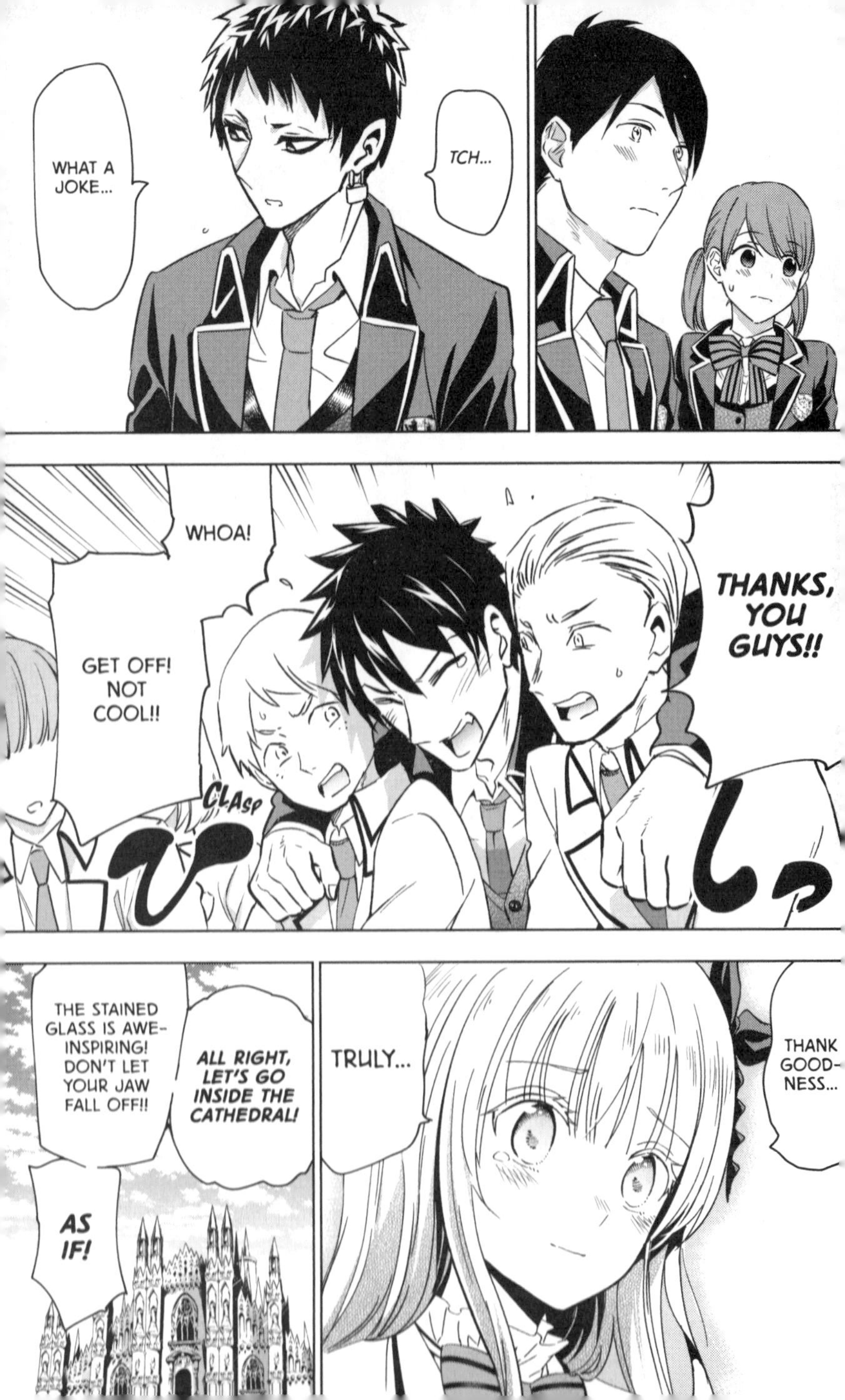
TCH...
WHAT A JOKE...
THANKS, YOU GUYS!!
WHOA!
GET OFF! NOT COOL!!
CLASP
THANK GOODNESS...
TRULY...
ALL RIGHT, LET'S GO INSIDE THE CATHEDRAL!
THE STAINED GLASS IS AWE-INSPIRING! DON'T LET YOUR JAW FALL OFF!!
AS IF!

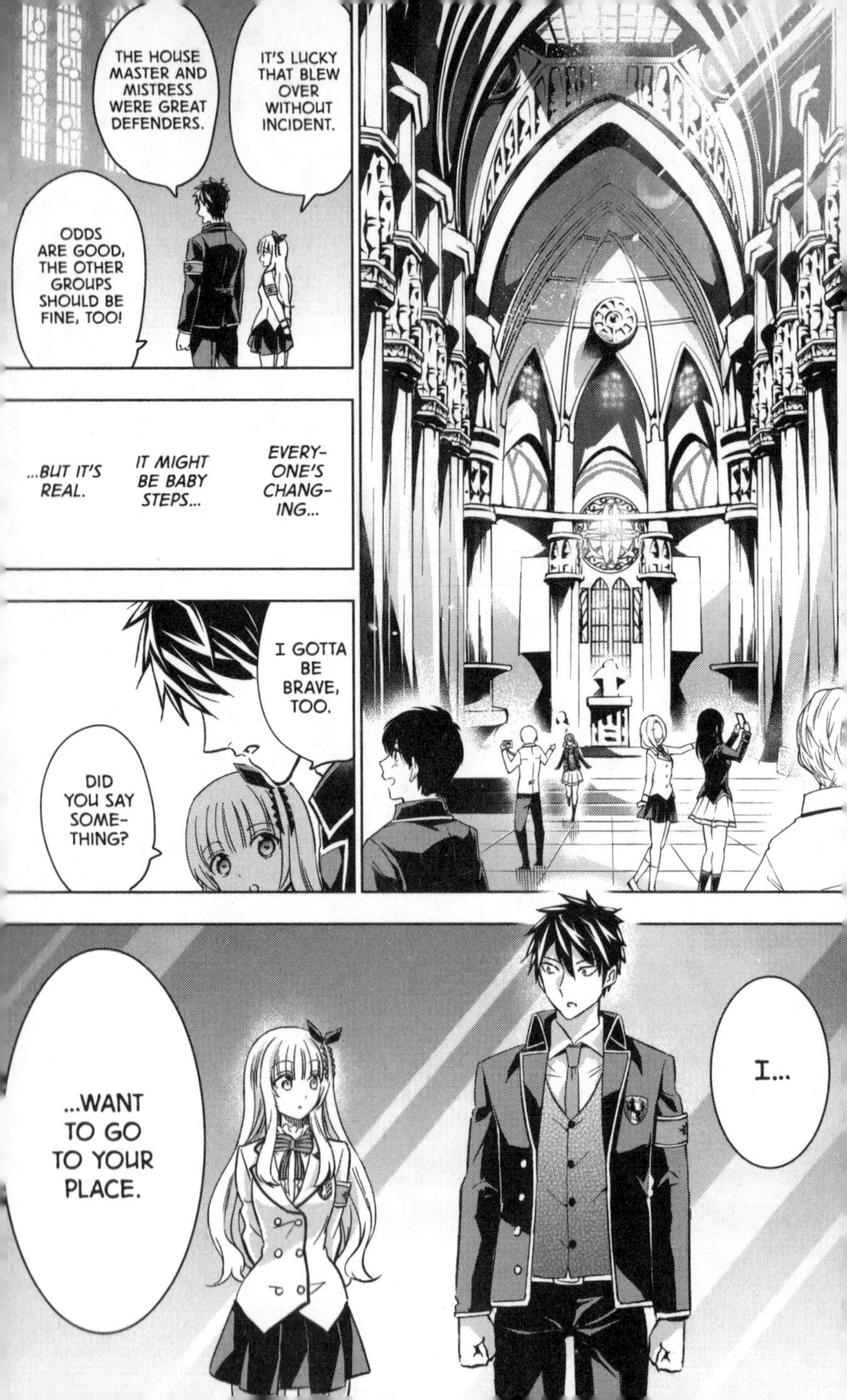
IT'S LUCKY THAT BLEW OVER WITHOUT INCIDENT.
THE HOUSE MASTER AND MISTRESS WERE GREAT DEFENDERS.
ODDS ARE GOOD, THE OTHER GROUPS SHOULD BE FINE, TOO!
EVERY-ONE'S CHANG-ING...
IT MIGHT BE BABY STEPS...
...BUT IT'S REAL.
I GOTTA BE BRAVE, TOO.
DID YOU SAY SOME-THING?
I...
...WANT TO GO TO YOUR PLACE.

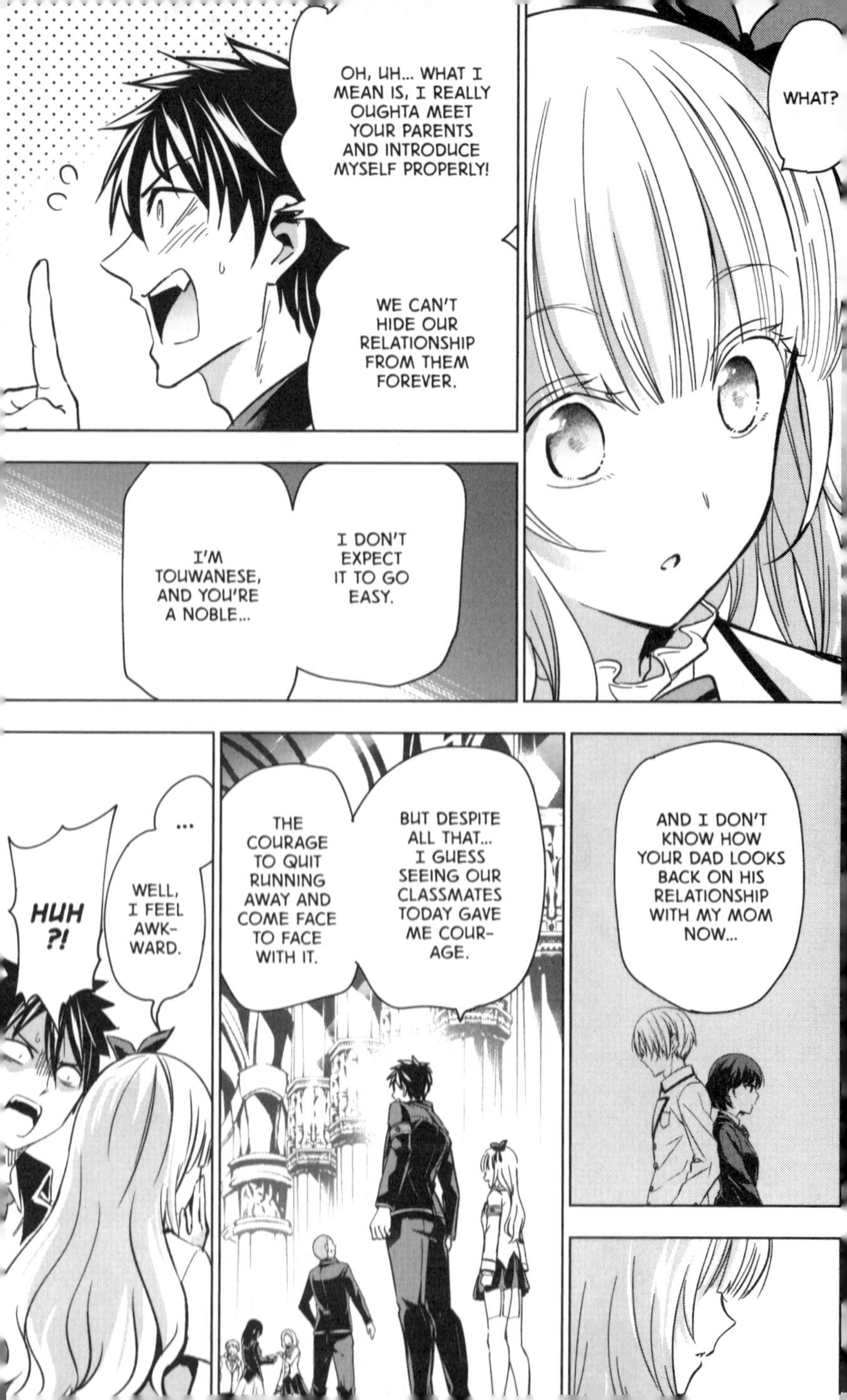
WHAT?
OH, UH... WHAT I MEAN IS, I REALLY OUGHTA MEET YOUR PARENTS AND INTRODUCE MYSELF PROPERLY!
WE CAN'T HIDE OUR RELATIONSHIP FROM THEM FOREVER.
I DON'T EXPECT IT TO GO EASY.
I'M TOUWANESE, AND YOU'RE A NOBLE...
AND I DON'T KNOW HOW YOUR DAD LOOKS BACK ON HIS RELATIONSHIP WITH MY MOM NOW...
BUT DESPITE ALL THAT... I GUESS SEEING OUR CLASSMATES TODAY GAVE ME COUR-AGE.
THE COURAGE TO QUIT RUNNING AWAY AND COME FACE TO FACE WITH IT.
...
WELL, I FEEL AWK-WARD.
HUH ?!

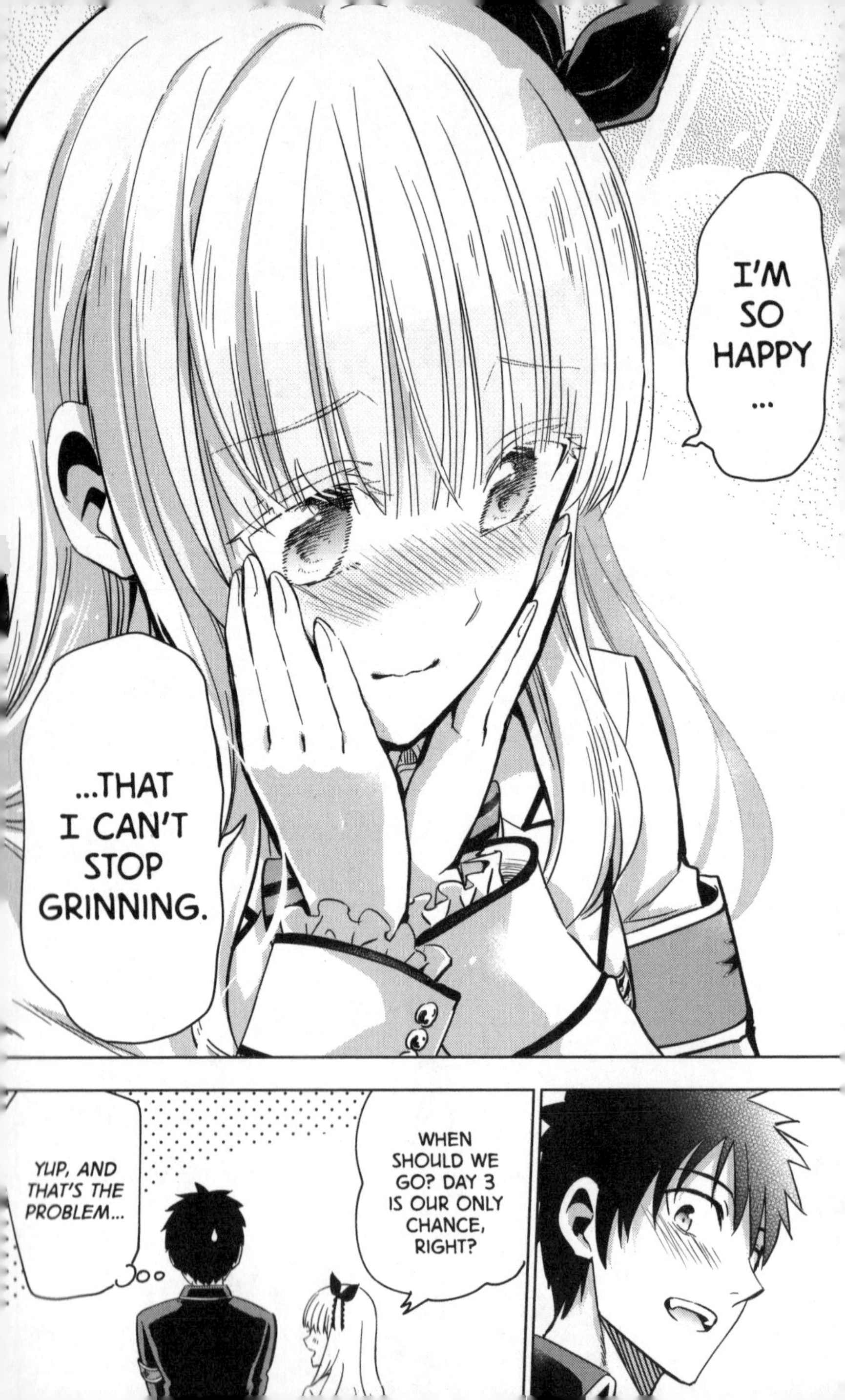
I'M SO HAPPY ...
...THAT I CAN'T STOP GRINNING.
WHEN SHOULD WE GO? DAY 3 IS OUR ONLY CHANCE, RIGHT?
YUP, AND THAT'S THE PROBLEM...

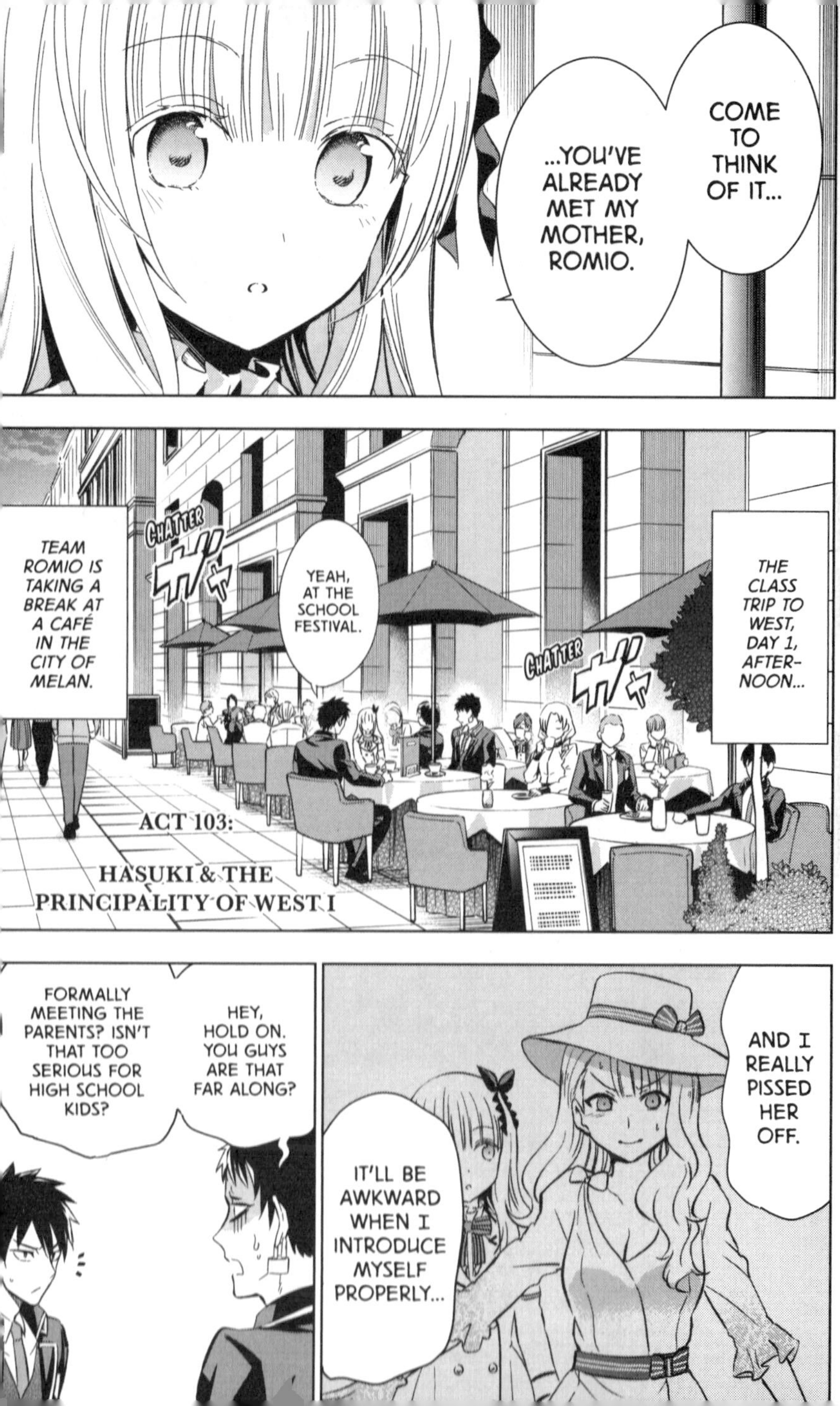
COME TO THINK OF IT...
...YOU'VE ALREADY MET MY MOTHER, ROMIO.
THE CLASS TRIP TO WEST, DAY 1, AFTERNOON...
CHATTER
ガヤ
YEAH, AT THE SCHOOL FESTIVAL.
CHATTER
ガヤ
TEAM ROMIO IS TAKING A BREAK AT A CAFÉ IN THE CITY OF MELAN.
ACT 103:
HASUKI & THE PRINCIPALITY OF WEST I
AND I REALLY PISSED HER OFF.
IT'LL BE AWKWARD WHEN I INTRODUCE MYSELF PROPERLY...
HEY, HOLD ON. YOU GUYS ARE THAT FAR ALONG?
FORMALLY MEETING THE PARENTS? ISN'T THAT TOO SERIOUS FOR HIGH SCHOOL KIDS?

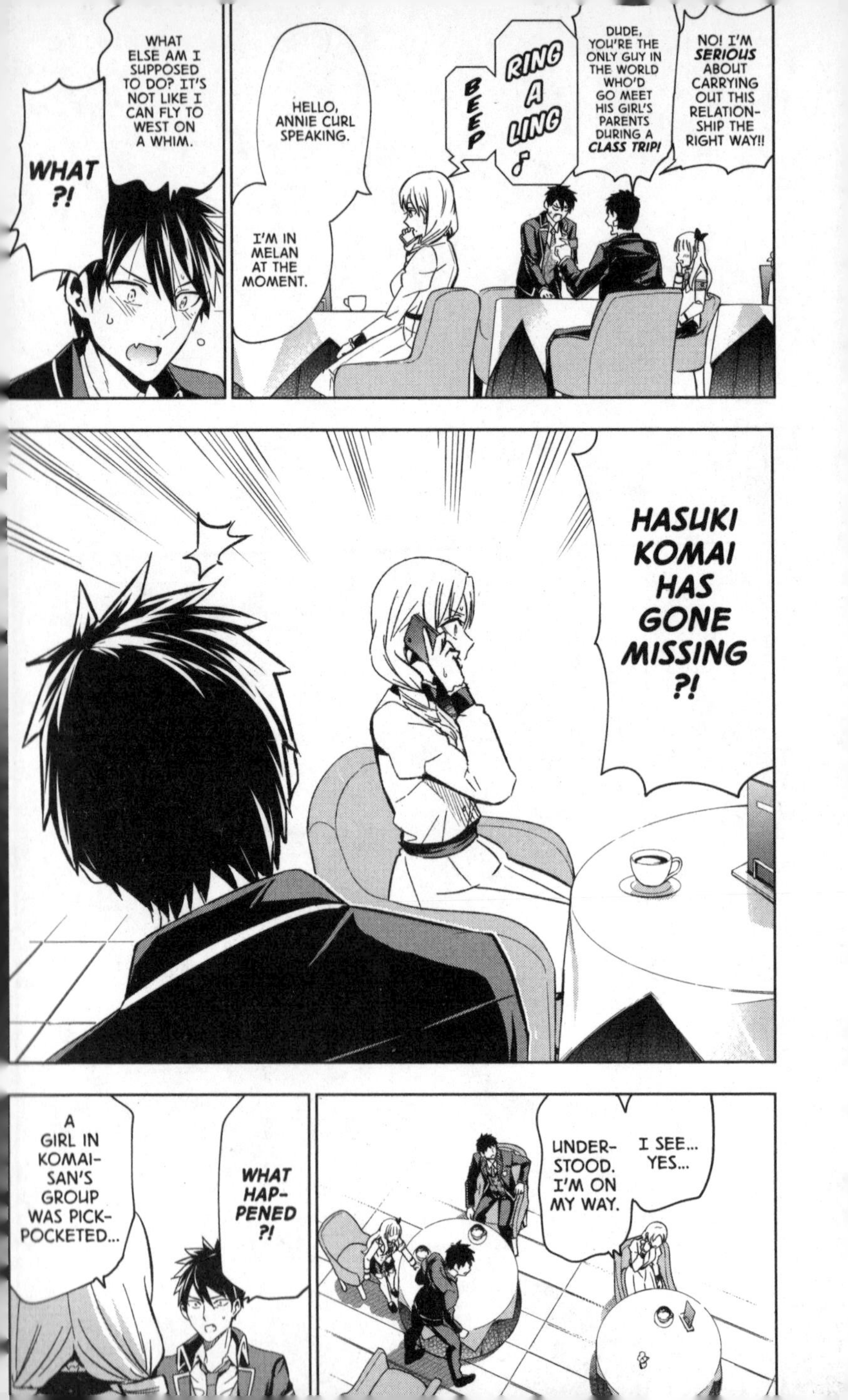
NO! I'M SERIOUS ABOUT CARRYING OUT THIS RELATIONSHIP THE RIGHT WAY!!
DUDE, YOU'RE THE ONLY GUY IN THE WORLD WHO'D GO MEET HIS GIRL'S PARENTS DURING A CLASS TRIP!
RING A LING
BEEP
HELLO, ANNIE CURL SPEAKING.
I'M IN MELAN AT THE MOMENT.
WHAT ELSE AM I SUPPOSED TO DO? IT'S NOT LIKE I CAN FLY TO WEST ON A WHIM.
WHAT ?!
HASUKI KOMAI HAS GONE MISSING ?!
I SEE... YES...
UNDER-STOOD. I'M ON MY WAY.
WHAT HAP-PENED ?!
A GIRL IN KOMAI-SAN'S GROUP WAS PICK-POCKETED...

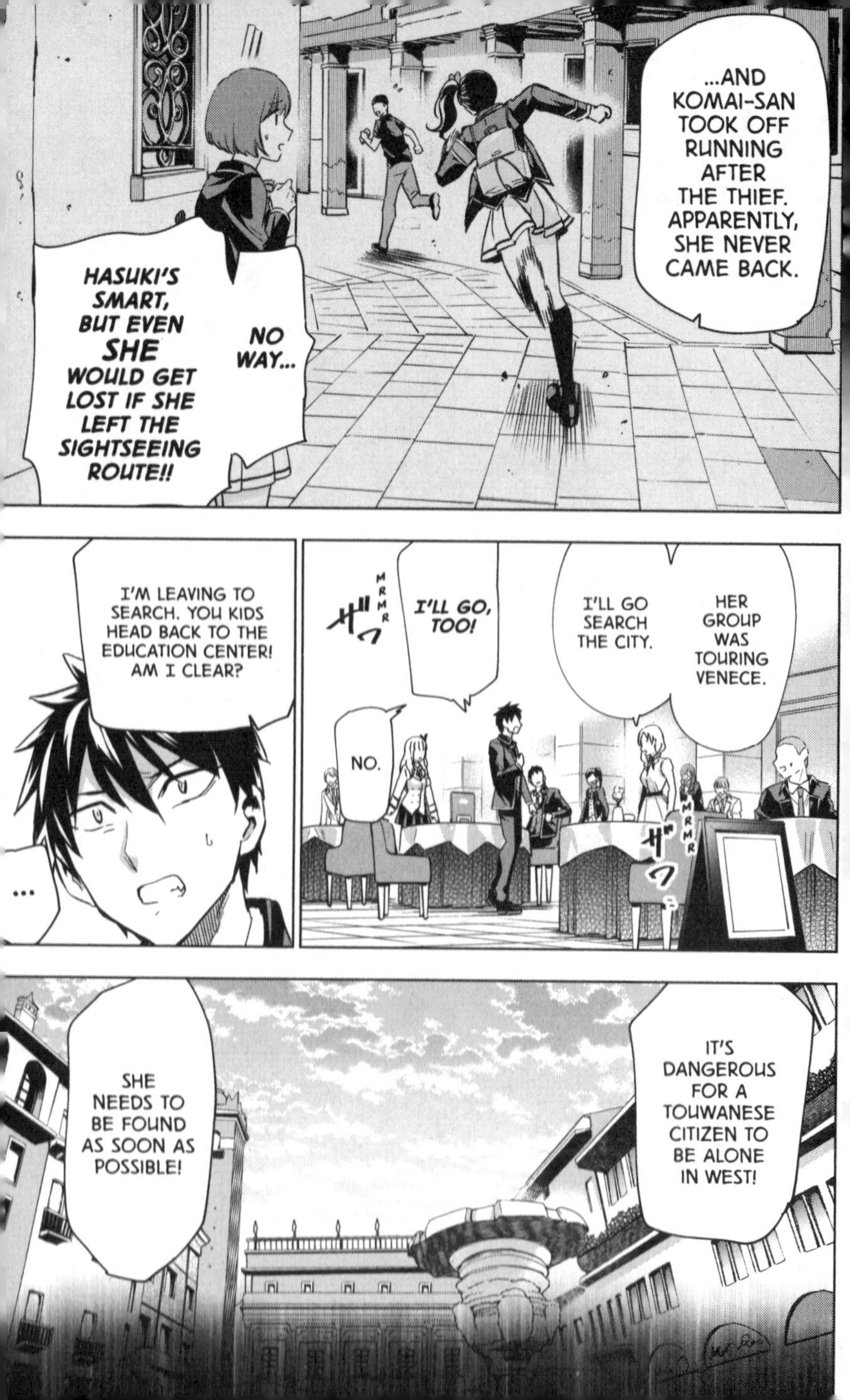
...AND KOMAI-SAN TOOK OFF RUNNING AFTER THE THIEF. APPARENTLY, SHE NEVER CAME BACK.
NO WAY...
HASUKI'S SMART, BUT EVEN SHE WOULD GET LOST IF SHE LEFT THE SIGHTSEEING ROUTE!!
HER GROUP WAS TOURING VENECE.
I'LL GO SEARCH THE CITY.
ザワ MRMR
I'LL GO, TOO!
ザワ MRMR
NO.
I'M LEAVING TO SEARCH. YOU KIDS HEAD BACK TO THE EDUCATION CENTER! AM I CLEAR?
...
IT'S DANGEROUS FOR A TOUWANESE CITIZEN TO BE ALONE IN WEST!
SHE NEEDS TO BE FOUND AS SOON AS POSSIBLE!

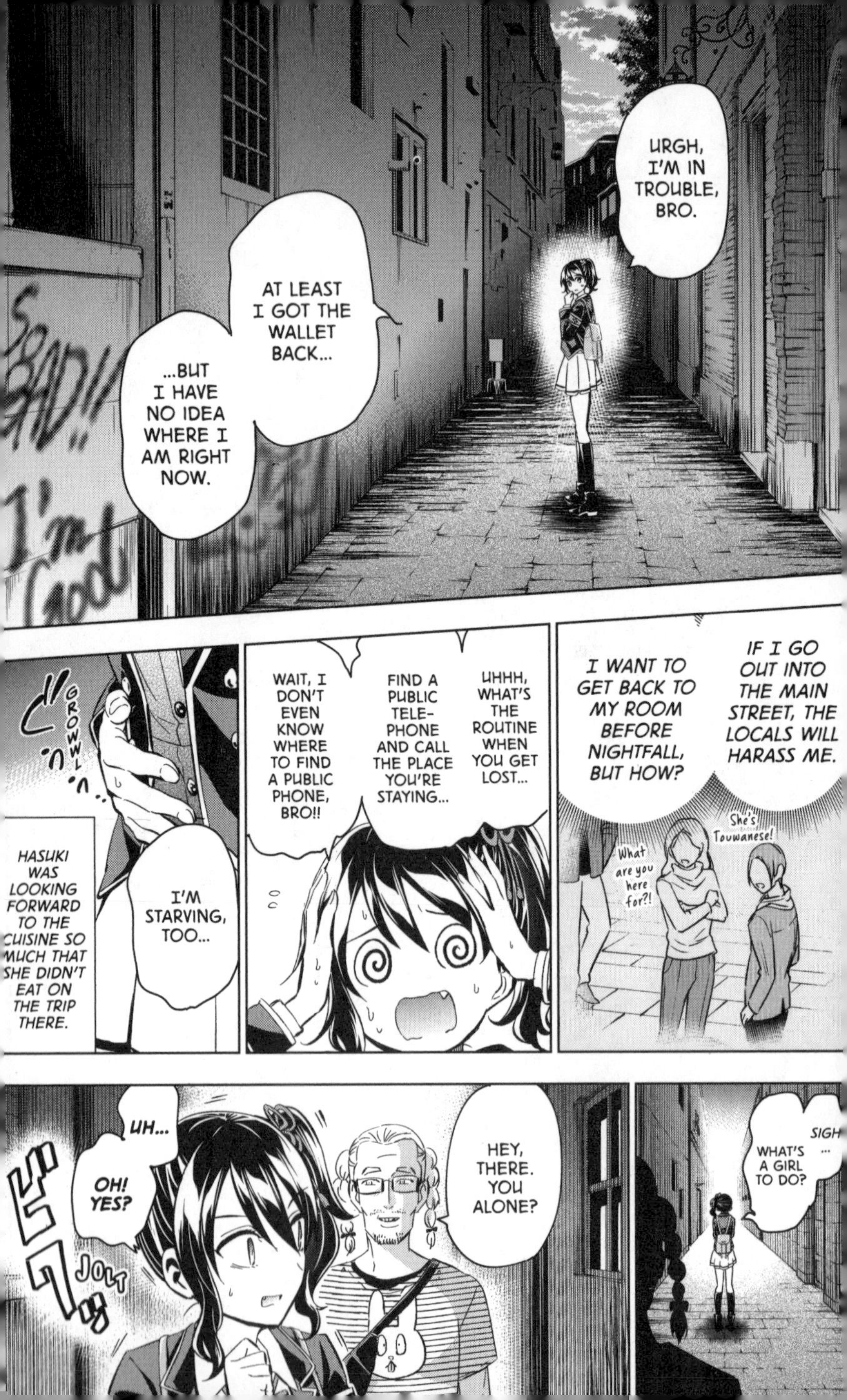
URGH, I'M IN TROUBLE, BRO.
AT LEAST I GOT THE WALLET BACK...
...BUT I HAVE NO IDEA WHERE I AM RIGHT NOW.
IF I GO OUT INTO THE MAIN STREET, THE LOCALS WILL HARASS ME.
I WANT TO GET BACK TO MY ROOM BEFORE NIGHTFALL, BUT HOW?
She's Touwanese!
What are you here for?!
UHHH, WHAT'S THE ROUTINE WHEN YOU GET LOST...
FIND A PUBLIC TELE-PHONE AND CALL THE PLACE YOU'RE STAYING...
WAIT, I DON'T EVEN KNOW WHERE TO FIND A PUBLIC PHONE, BRO!!
GROWWL
I'M STARVING, TOO...
HASUKI WAS LOOKING FORWARD TO THE CUISINE SO MUCH THAT SHE DIDN'T EAT ON THE TRIP THERE.
SIGH...
WHAT'S A GIRL TO DO?
HEY, THERE. YOU ALONE?
UH...
OH! YES?
JOLT

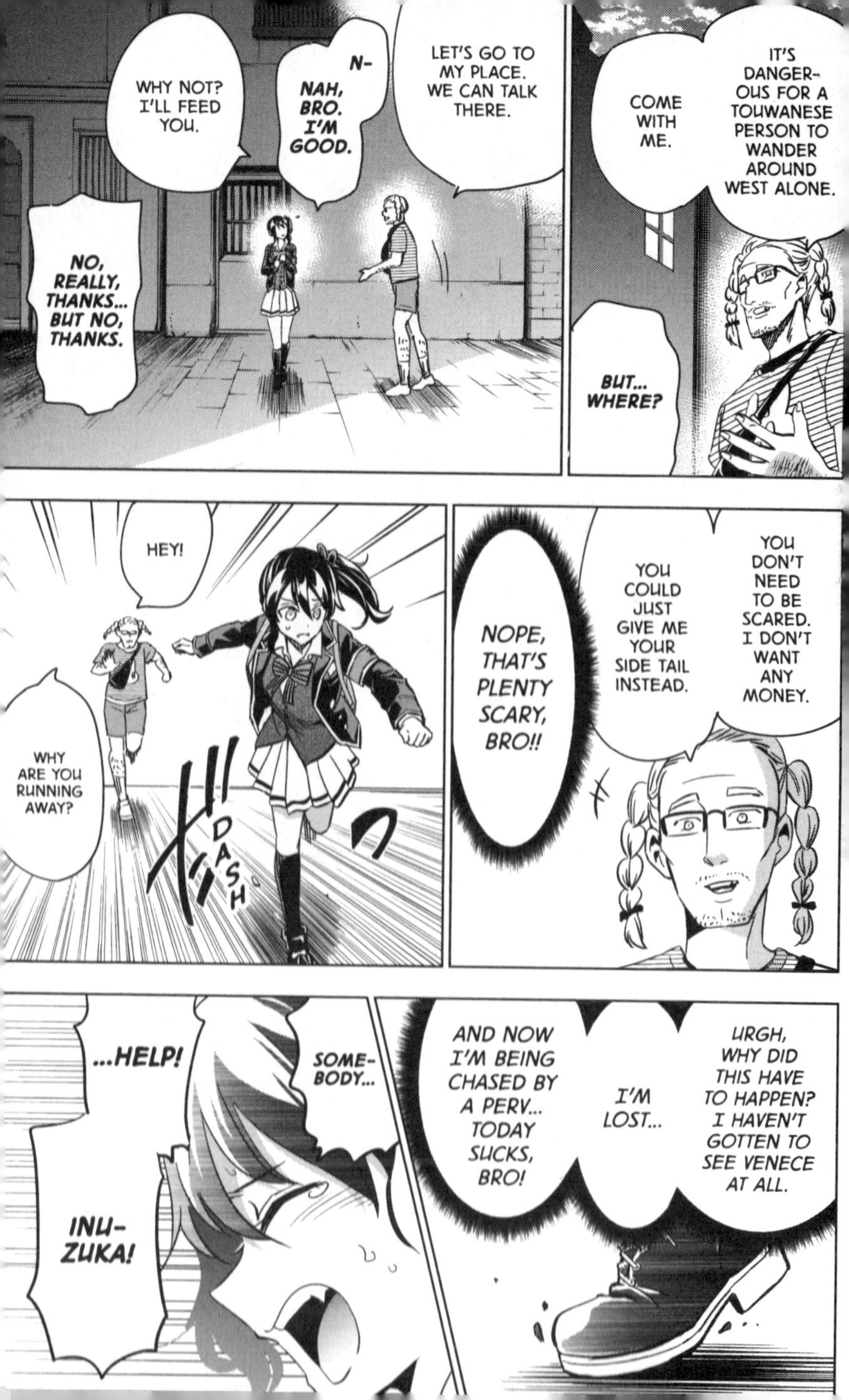
IT'S DANGEROUS FOR A TOUWANESE PERSON TO WANDER AROUND WEST ALONE.
COME WITH ME.
BUT... WHERE?
LET'S GO TO MY PLACE. WE CAN TALK THERE.
N- NAH, BRO. I'M GOOD.
WHY NOT? I'LL FEED YOU.
NO, REALLY, THANKS... BUT NO, THANKS.
YOU DON'T NEED TO BE SCARED. I DON'T WANT ANY MONEY.
YOU COULD JUST GIVE ME YOUR SIDE TAIL INSTEAD.
NOPE, THAT'S PLENTY SCARY, BRO!!
HEY!
DASH
WHY ARE YOU RUNNING AWAY?
URGH, WHY DID THIS HAVE TO HAPPEN? I HAVEN'T GOTTEN TO SEE VENECE AT ALL.
I'M LOST...
AND NOW I'M BEING CHASED BY A PERV... TODAY SUCKS, BRO!
SOMEBODY...
...HELP!
INUZUKA!

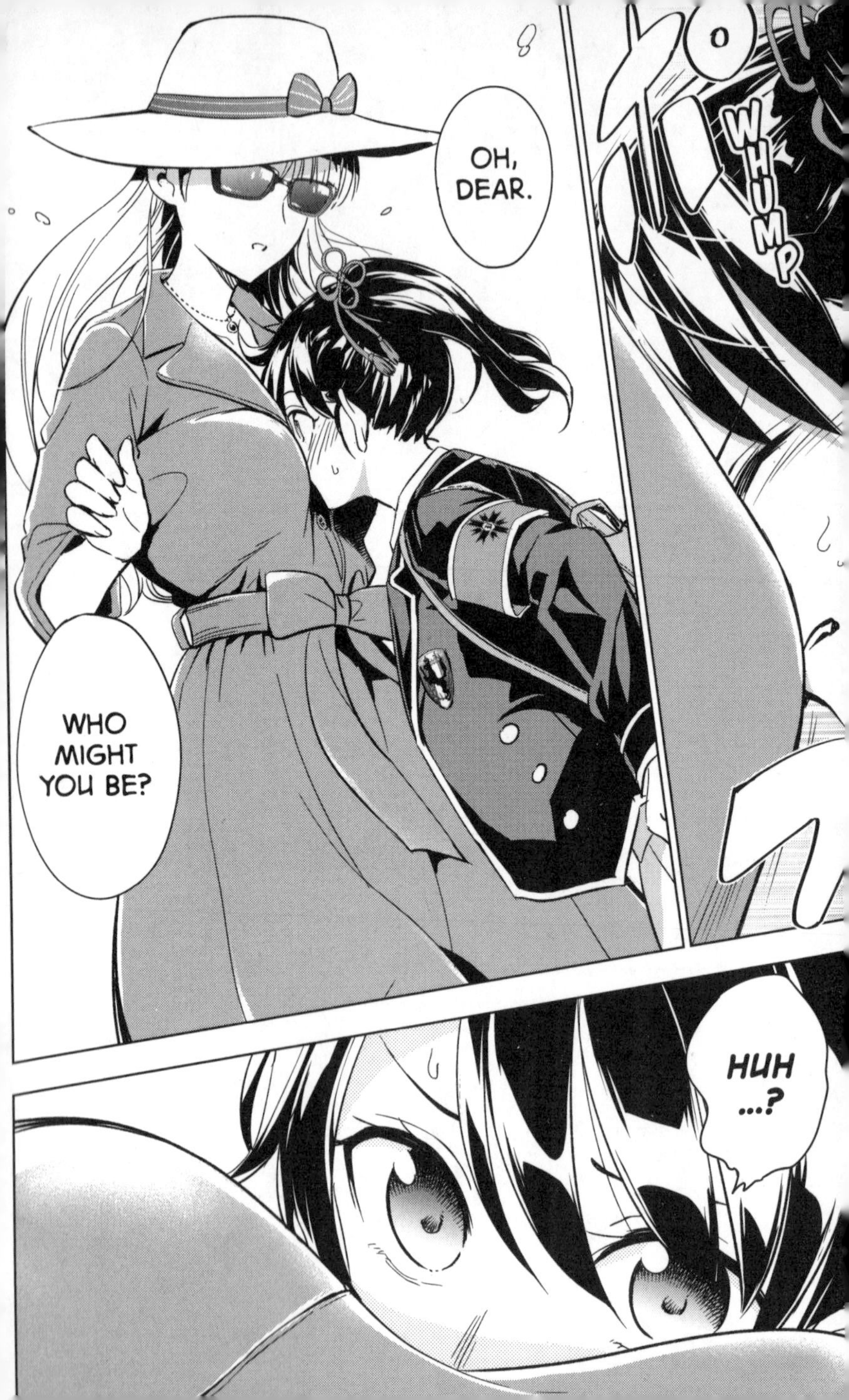
WHUMP
OH, DEAR.
WHO MIGHT YOU BE?
HUH ...?

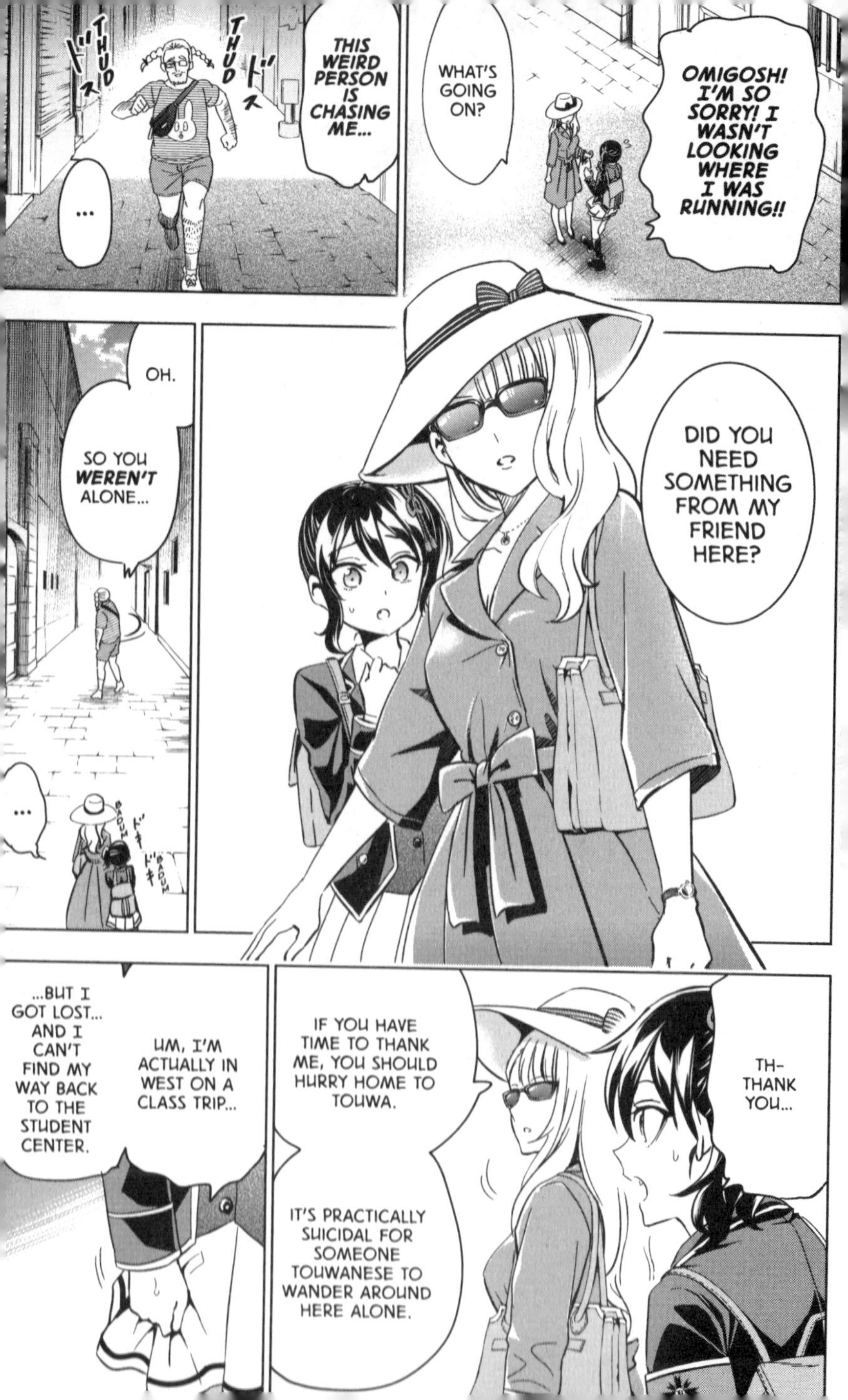
OMIGOSH! I'M SO SORRY! I WASN'T LOOKING WHERE I WAS RUNNING!!
WHAT'S GOING ON?
THIS WEIRD PERSON IS CHASING ME...
THUD
THUD
...
DID YOU NEED SOMETHING FROM MY FRIEND HERE?
OH.
SO YOU *WEREN'T* ALONE...
...
BADUM
BADUM
TH- THANK YOU...
IF YOU HAVE TIME TO THANK ME, YOU SHOULD HURRY HOME TO TOUWA.
IT'S PRACTICALLY SUICIDAL FOR SOMEONE TOUWANESE TO WANDER AROUND HERE ALONE.
UM, I'M ACTUALLY IN WEST ON A CLASS TRIP...
...BUT I GOT LOST... AND I CAN'T FIND MY WAY BACK TO THE STUDENT CENTER.

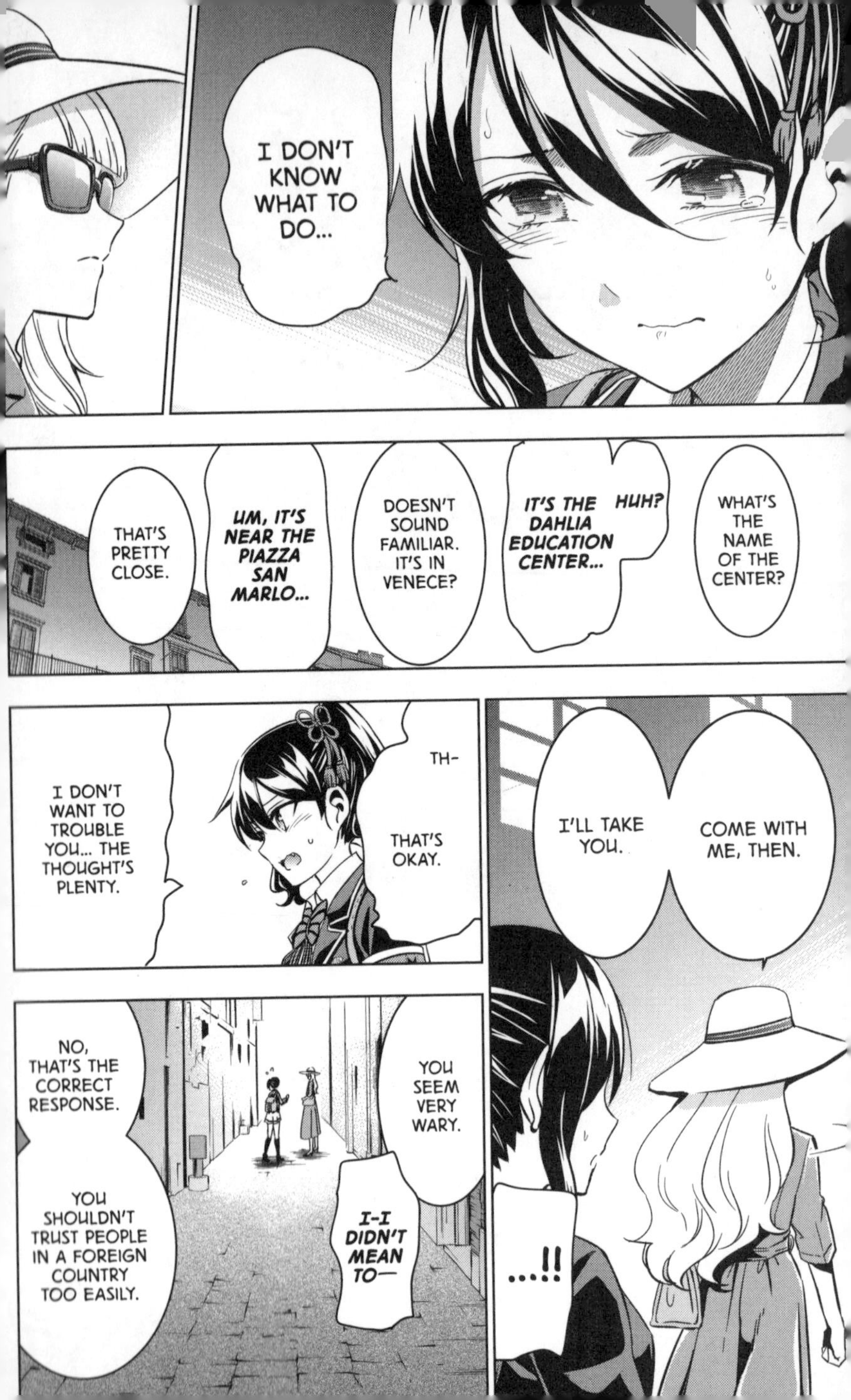
I DON'T KNOW WHAT TO DO...
WHAT'S THE NAME OF THE CENTER?
HUH?
IT'S THE DAHLIA EDUCATION CENTER...
DOESN'T SOUND FAMILIAR. IT'S IN VENECE?
UM, IT'S NEAR THE PIAZZA SAN MARLO...
THAT'S PRETTY CLOSE.
COME WITH ME, THEN.
I'LL TAKE YOU.
...!!
TH-
THAT'S OKAY.
I DON'T WANT TO TROUBLE YOU... THE THOUGHT'S PLENTY.
YOU SEEM VERY WARY.
I-I DIDN'T MEAN TO—
NO, THAT'S THE CORRECT RESPONSE.
YOU SHOULDN'T TRUST PEOPLE IN A FOREIGN COUNTRY TOO EASILY.

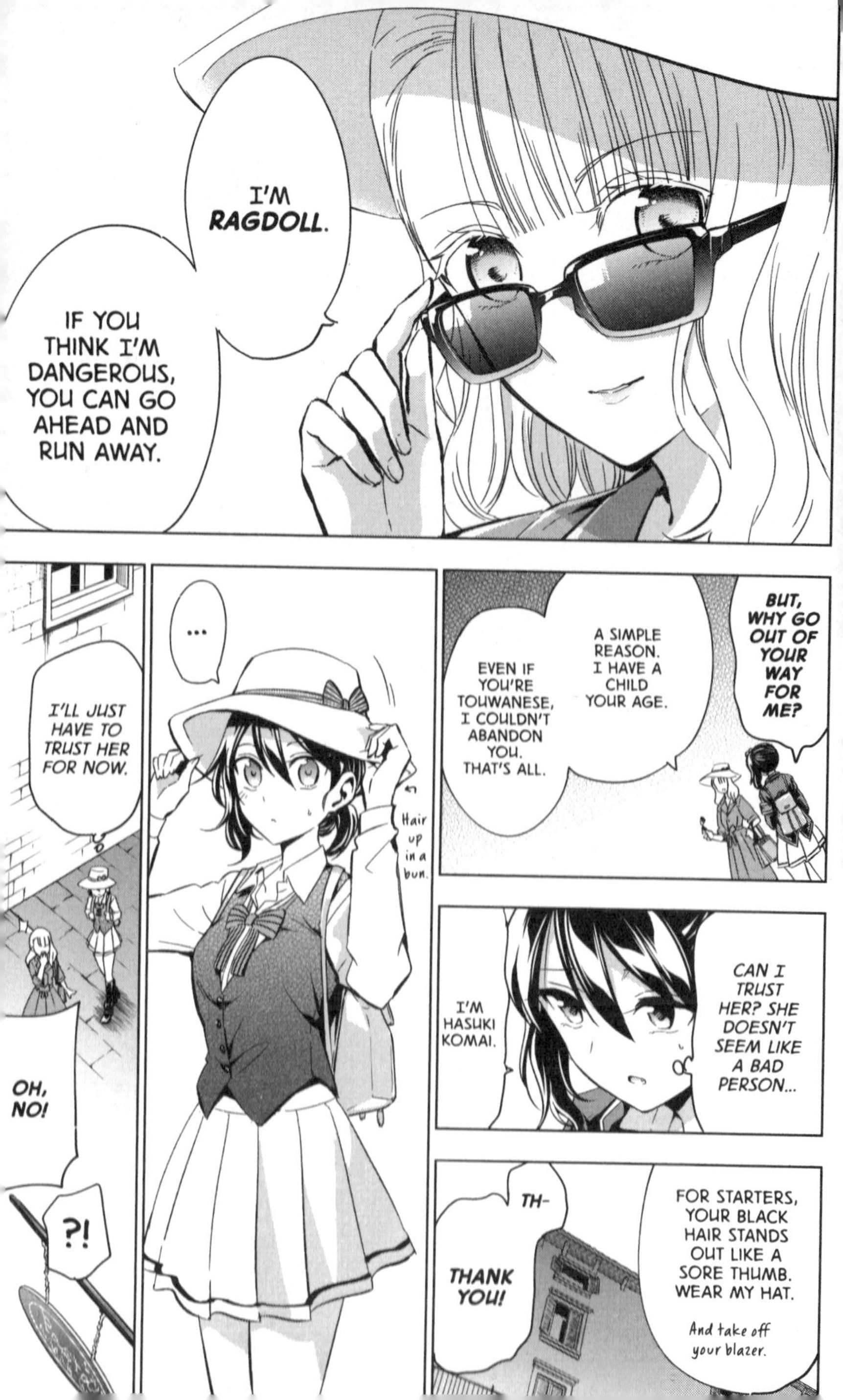
I'M **RAGDOLL.**
IF YOU THINK I'M DANGEROUS, YOU CAN GO AHEAD AND RUN AWAY.
*BUT, WHY GO OUT OF YOUR WAY FOR ME?*
A SIMPLE REASON. I HAVE A CHILD YOUR AGE.
EVEN IF YOU'RE TOUWANESE, I COULDN'T ABANDON YOU. THAT'S ALL.
*CAN I TRUST HER? SHE DOESN'T SEEM LIKE A BAD PERSON...*
I'M HASUKI KOMAI.
FOR STARTERS, YOUR BLACK HAIR STANDS OUT LIKE A SORE THUMB. WEAR MY HAT.
And take off your blazer.
TH-
THANK YOU!
...
Hair up in a bun.
*I'LL JUST HAVE TO TRUST HER FOR NOW.*
OH, NO!
?!

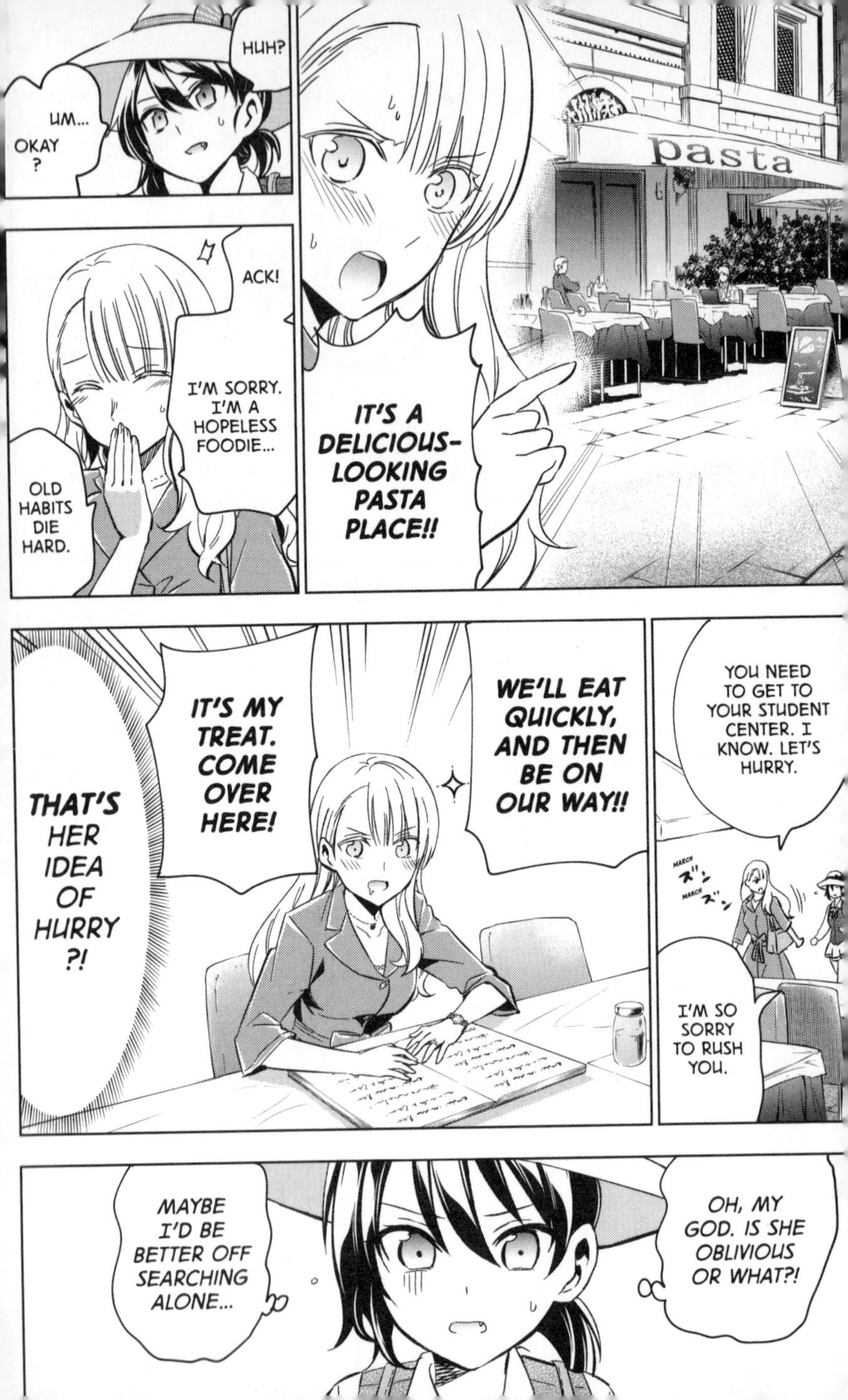

pasta
IT'S A DELICIOUS-LOOKING PASTA PLACE!!
HUH?
UM... OKAY?
ACK!
I'M SORRY. I'M A HOPELESS FOODIE...
OLD HABITS DIE HARD.
YOU NEED TO GET TO YOUR STUDENT CENTER. I KNOW. LET'S HURRY.
MARCH
MARCH
I'M SO SORRY TO RUSH YOU.
WE'LL EAT QUICKLY, AND THEN BE ON OUR WAY!!
IT'S MY TREAT. COME OVER HERE!
THAT'S HER IDEA OF HURRY?!
OH, MY GOD. IS SHE OBLIVIOUS OR WHAT?!
MAYBE I'D BE BETTER OFF SEARCHING ALONE...

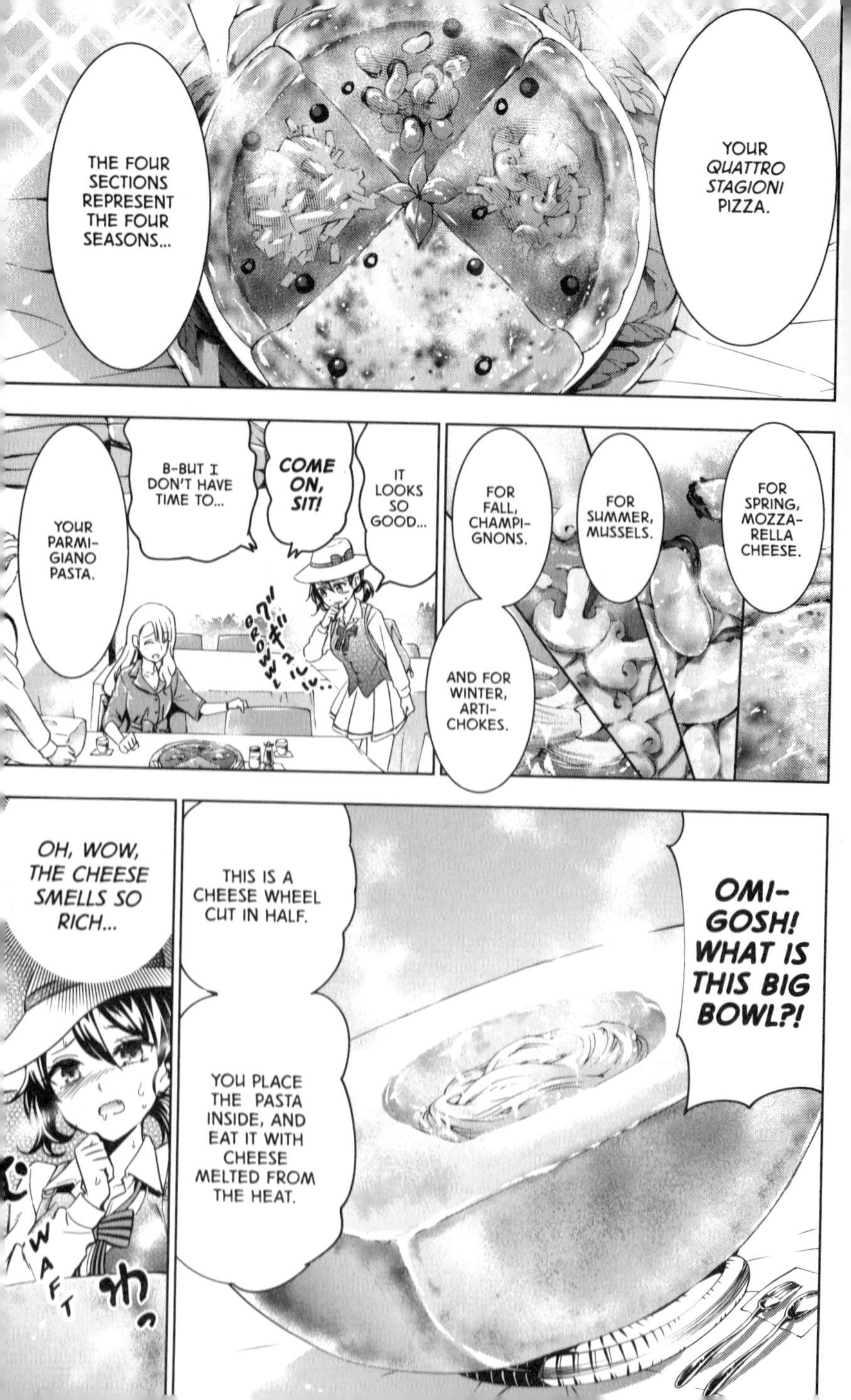
YOUR QUATTRO STAGIONI PIZZA.
THE FOUR SECTIONS REPRESENT THE FOUR SEASONS...
FOR SPRING, MOZZARELLA CHEESE.
FOR SUMMER, MUSSELS.
FOR FALL, CHAMPIGNONS.
AND FOR WINTER, ARTICHOKES.
IT LOOKS SO GOOD...
COME ON, SIT!
B-BUT I DON'T HAVE TIME TO...
YOUR PARMIGIANO PASTA.
GROWL
OMIGOSH! WHAT IS THIS BIG BOWL?!
THIS IS A CHEESE WHEEL CUT IN HALF.
YOU PLACE THE PASTA INSIDE, AND EAT IT WITH CHEESE MELTED FROM THE HEAT.
OH, WOW, THE CHEESE SMELLS SO RICH...
WAFT

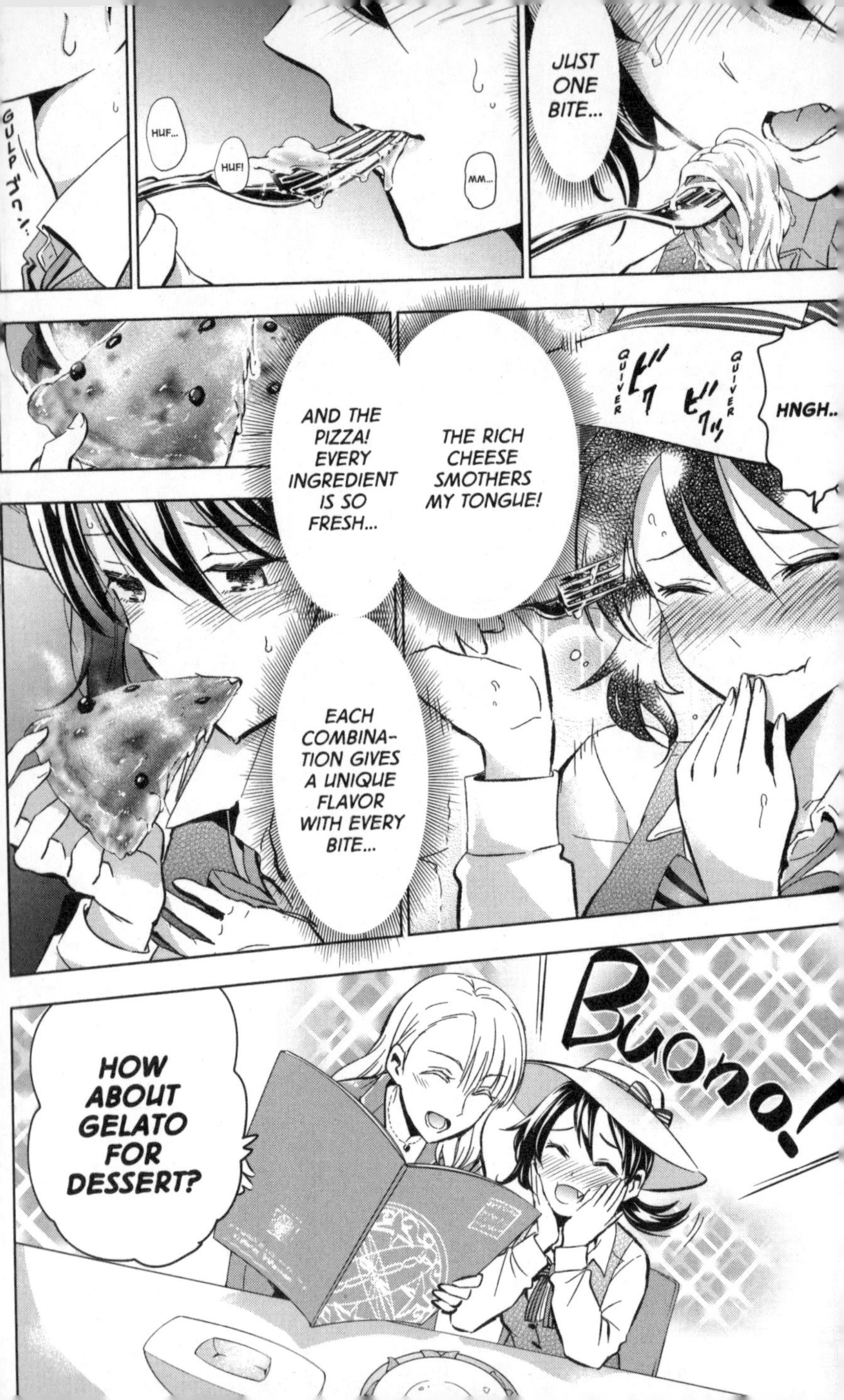
JUST ONE BITE...
MM...
HUF!
HUF...
GULP
HNGH..
QUIVER
QUIVER
THE RICH CHEESE SMOTHERS MY TONGUE!
AND THE PIZZA! EVERY INGREDIENT IS SO FRESH...
EACH COMBINA-TION GIVES A UNIQUE FLAVOR WITH EVERY BITE...
Buono!
HOW ABOUT GELATO FOR DESSERT?

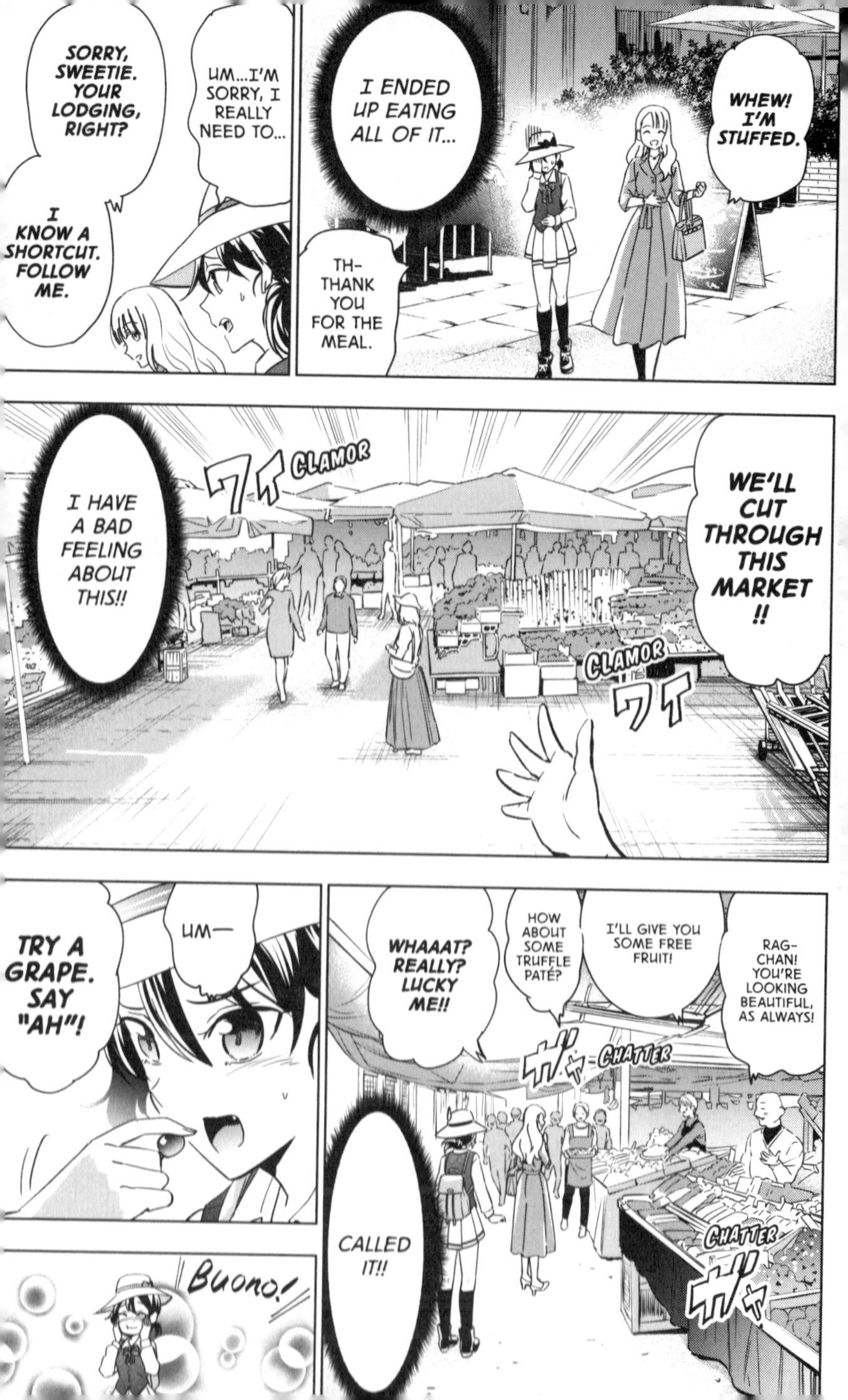
WHEW! I'M STUFFED.
I ENDED UP EATING ALL OF IT...
TH-THANK YOU FOR THE MEAL.
UM...I'M SORRY, I REALLY NEED TO...
SORRY, SWEETIE. YOUR LODGING, RIGHT?
I KNOW A SHORTCUT. FOLLOW ME.
WE'LL CUT THROUGH THIS MARKET !!
CLAMOR
CLAMOR
I HAVE A BAD FEELING ABOUT THIS!!
RAG-CHAN! YOU'RE LOOKING BEAUTIFUL, AS ALWAYS!
I'LL GIVE YOU SOME FREE FRUIT!
HOW ABOUT SOME TRUFFLE PATÉ?
WHAAAT? REALLY? LUCKY ME!!
CHATTER
CHATTER
CALLED IT!!
UM—
TRY A GRAPE. SAY "AH"!
Buono!

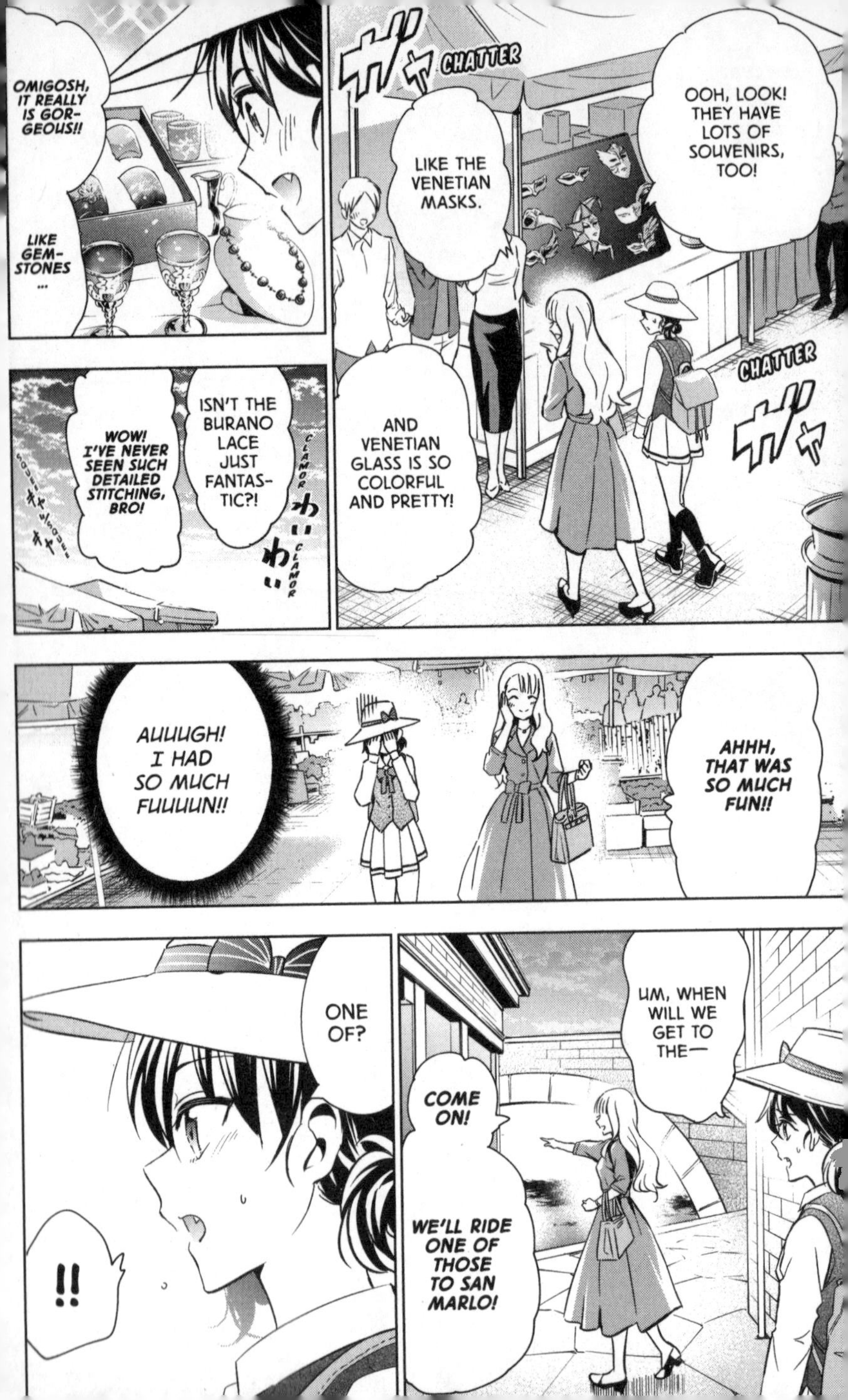
CHATTER
OOH, LOOK! THEY HAVE LOTS OF SOUVENIRS, TOO!
LIKE THE VENETIAN MASKS.
AND VENETIAN GLASS IS SO COLORFUL AND PRETTY!
CHATTER
OMIGOSH, IT REALLY IS GOR-GEOUS!!
LIKE GEM-STONES ...
ISN'T THE BURANO LACE JUST FANTAS-TIC?!
CLAMOR CLAMOR
WOW! I'VE NEVER SEEN SUCH DETAILED STITCHING, BRO!
AHHH, THAT WAS SO MUCH FUN!!
AUUUGH! I HAD SO MUCH FUUUUN!!
UM, WHEN WILL WE GET TO THE—
COME ON!
WE'LL RIDE ONE OF THOSE TO SAN MARLO!
ONE OF?
!!

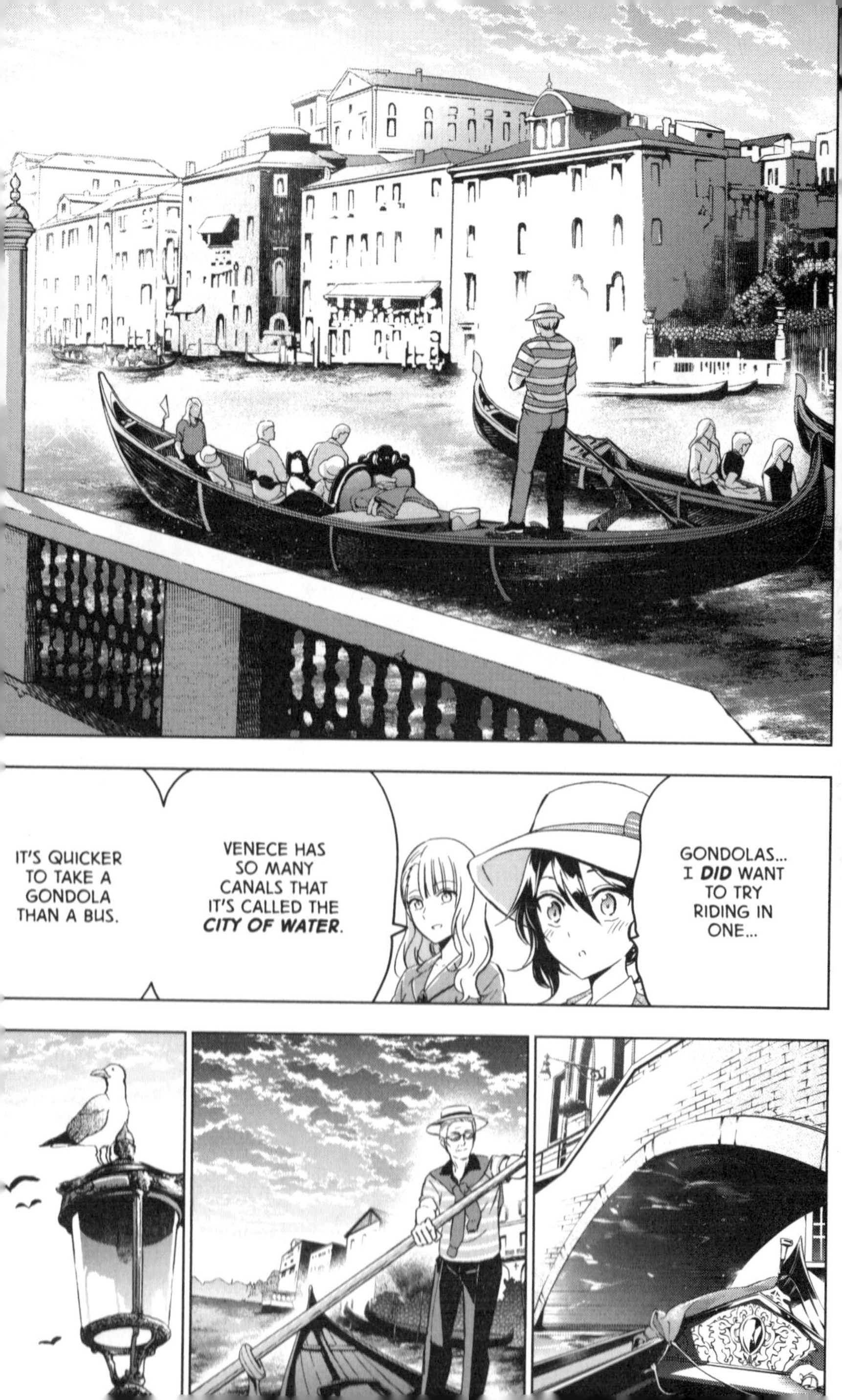
GONDOLAS... I *DID* WANT TO TRY RIDING IN ONE...
VENECE HAS SO MANY CANALS THAT IT'S CALLED THE *CITY OF WATER*.
IT'S QUICKER TO TAKE A GONDOLA THAN A BUS.

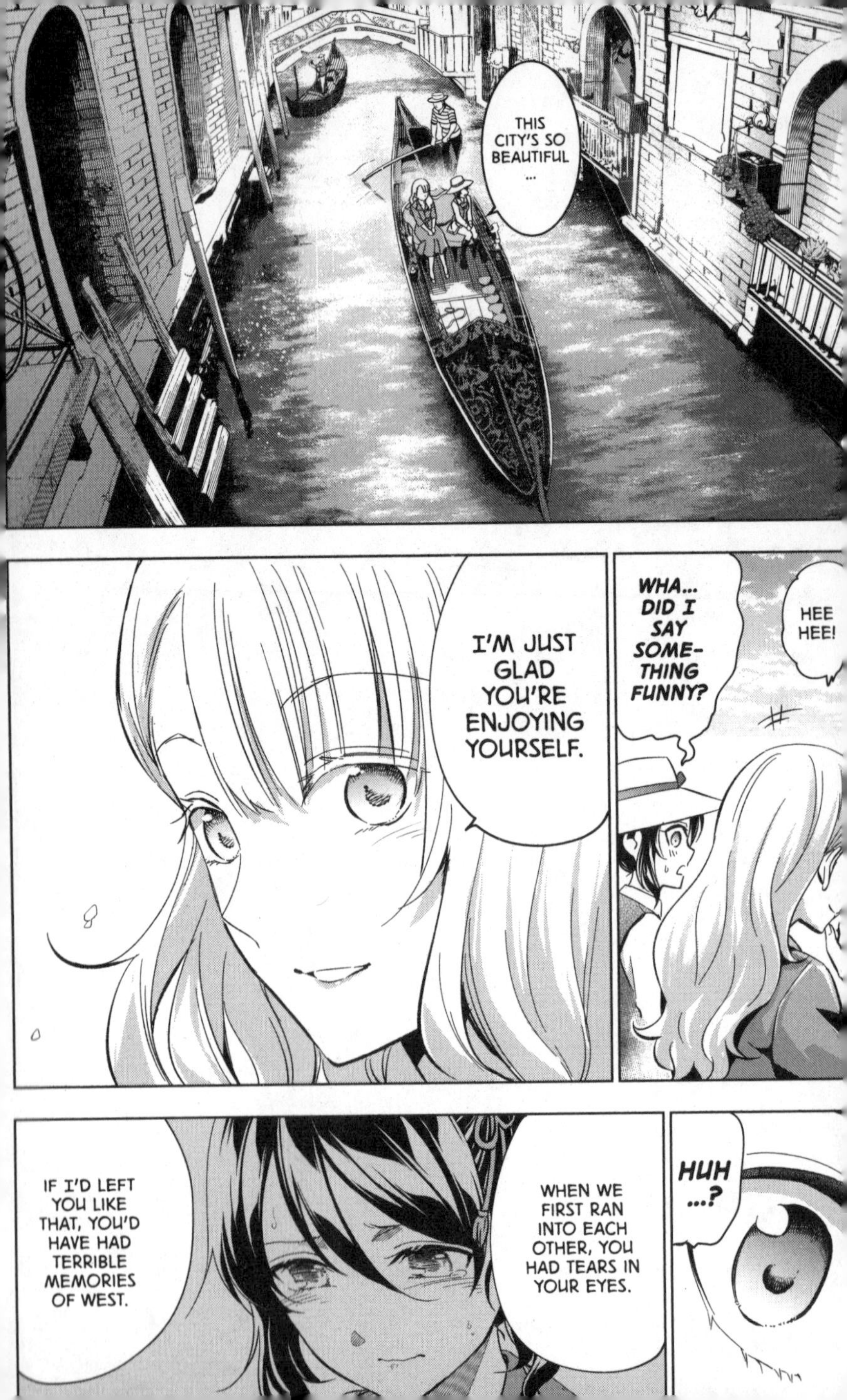
THIS CITY'S SO BEAUTIFUL ...
HEE HEE!
WHA... DID I SAY SOMETHING FUNNY?
I'M JUST GLAD YOU'RE ENJOYING YOURSELF.
HUH ...?
WHEN WE FIRST RAN INTO EACH OTHER, YOU HAD TEARS IN YOUR EYES.
IF I'D LEFT YOU LIKE THAT, YOU'D HAVE HAD TERRIBLE MEMORIES OF WEST.

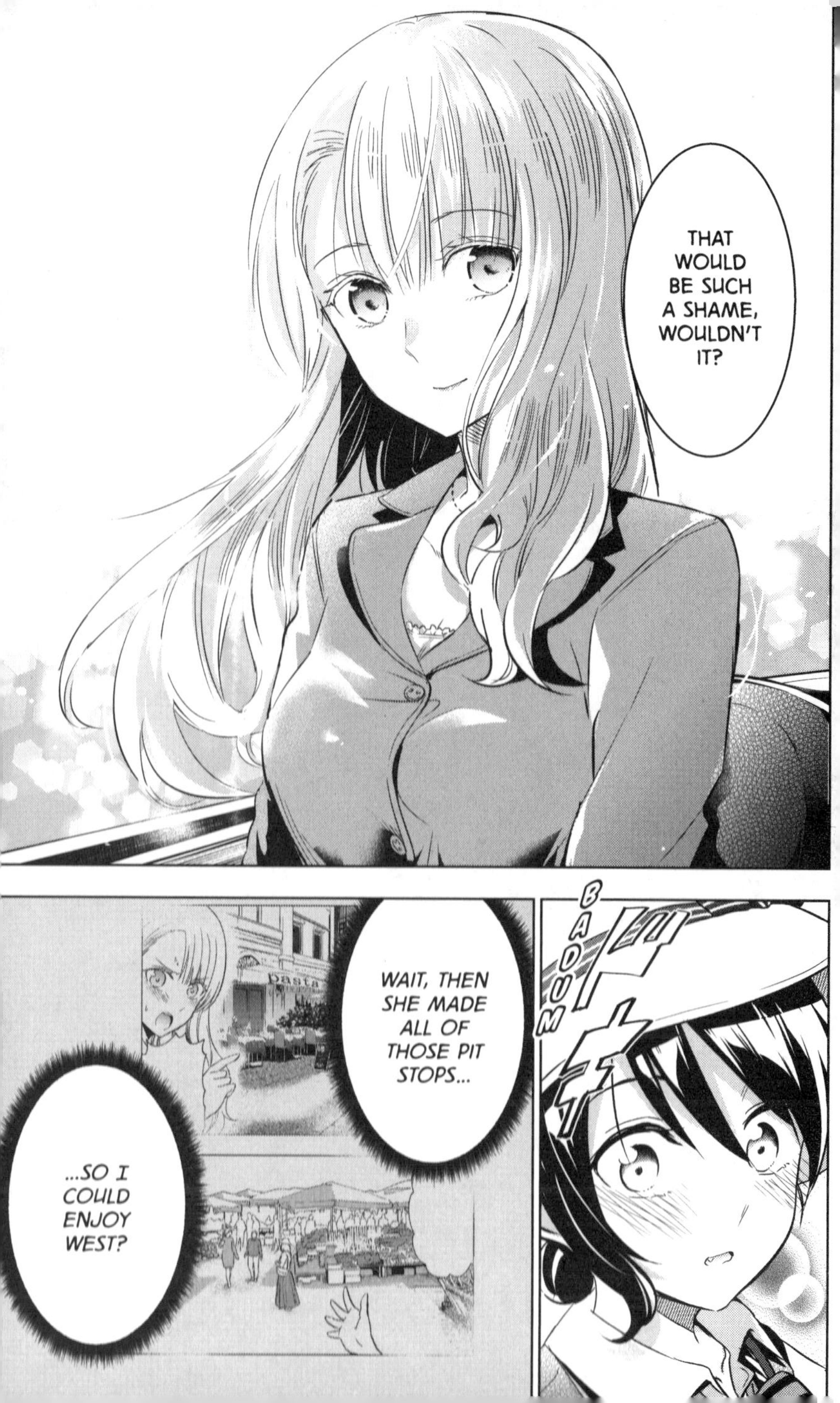
THAT WOULD BE SUCH A SHAME, WOULDN'T IT?
BADUM
WAIT, THEN SHE MADE ALL OF THOSE PIT STOPS...
...SO I COULD ENJOY WEST?
Pasta

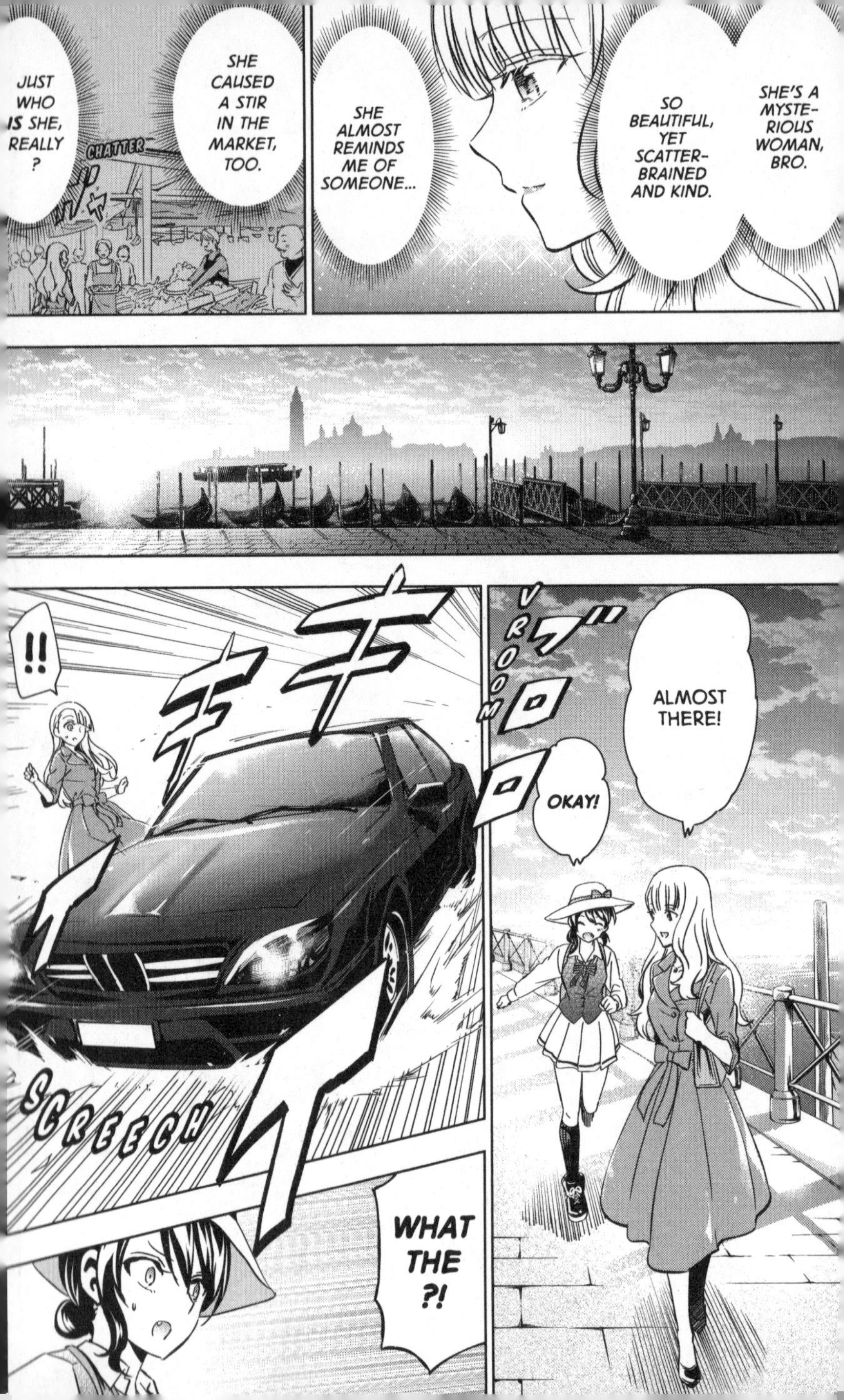
SHE'S A MYSTERIOUS WOMAN, BRO.
SO BEAUTIFUL, YET SCATTER-BRAINED AND KIND.
SHE ALMOST REMINDS ME OF SOMEONE...
SHE CAUSED A STIR IN THE MARKET, TOO.
JUST WHO IS SHE, REALLY?
CHATTER
VROOOM
ALMOST THERE!
OKAY!
!!
SCREECH
WHAT THE ?!

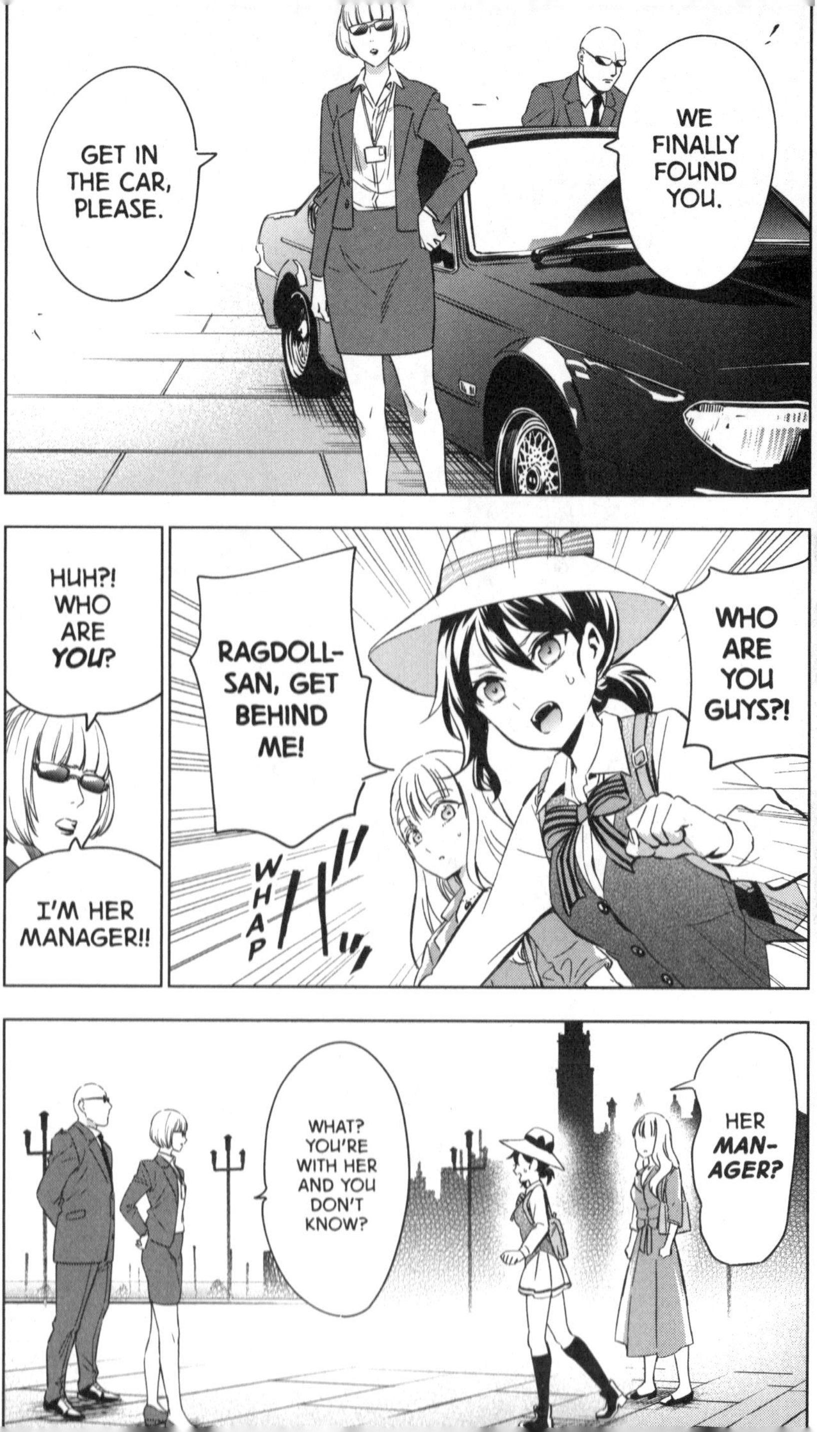
WE FINALLY FOUND YOU.
GET IN THE CAR, PLEASE.
WHO ARE YOU GUYS?!
RAGDOLL-SAN, GET BEHIND ME!
WHAP
HUH?! WHO ARE *YOU*?
I'M HER MANAGER!!
HER *MANAGER?*
WHAT? YOU'RE WITH HER AND YOU DON'T KNOW?

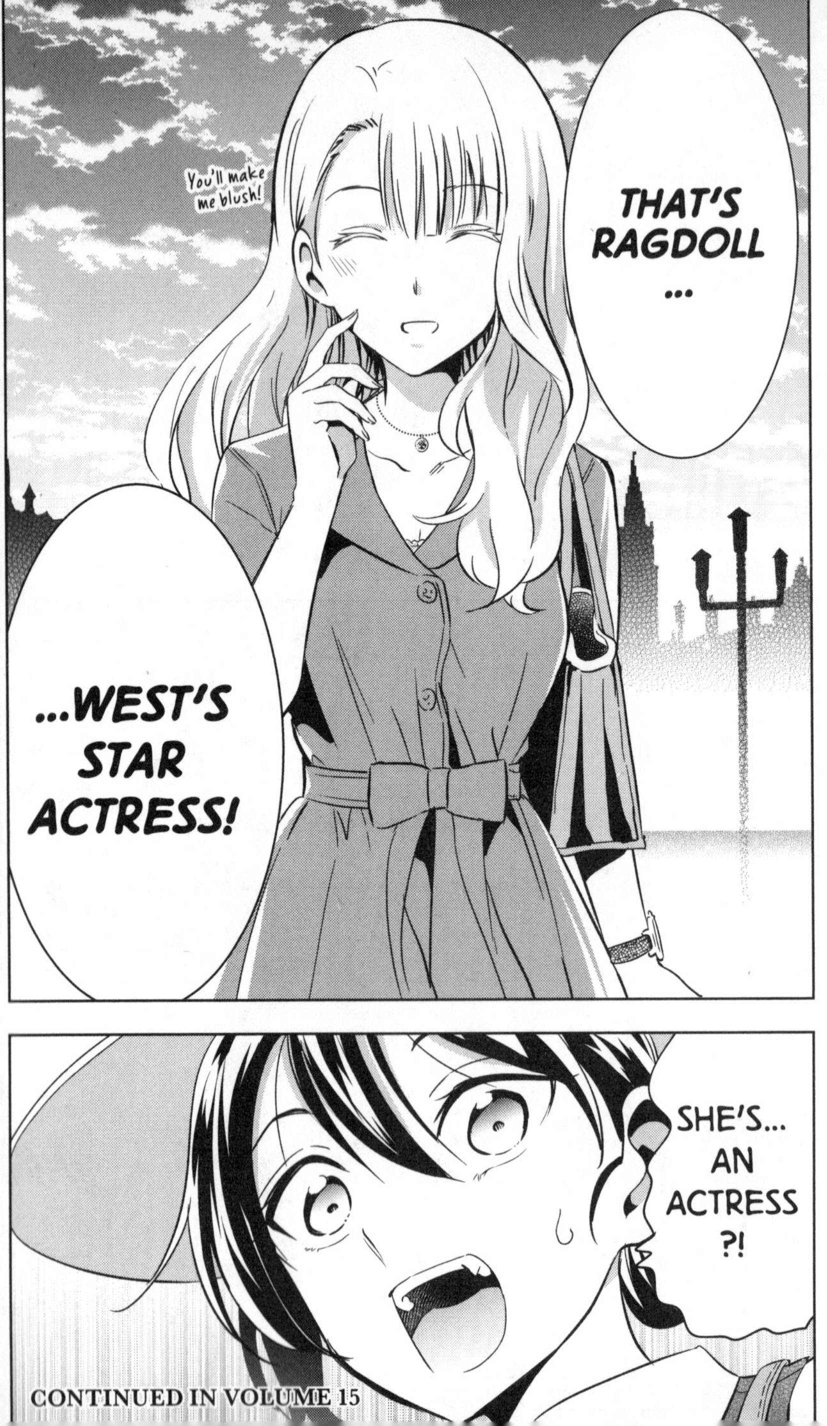
THAT'S RAGDOLL ...
You'll make me blush!
...WEST'S STAR ACTRESS!
SHE'S... AN ACTRESS ?!
CONTINUED IN VOLUME 15

# BONUS STRIP: COAT

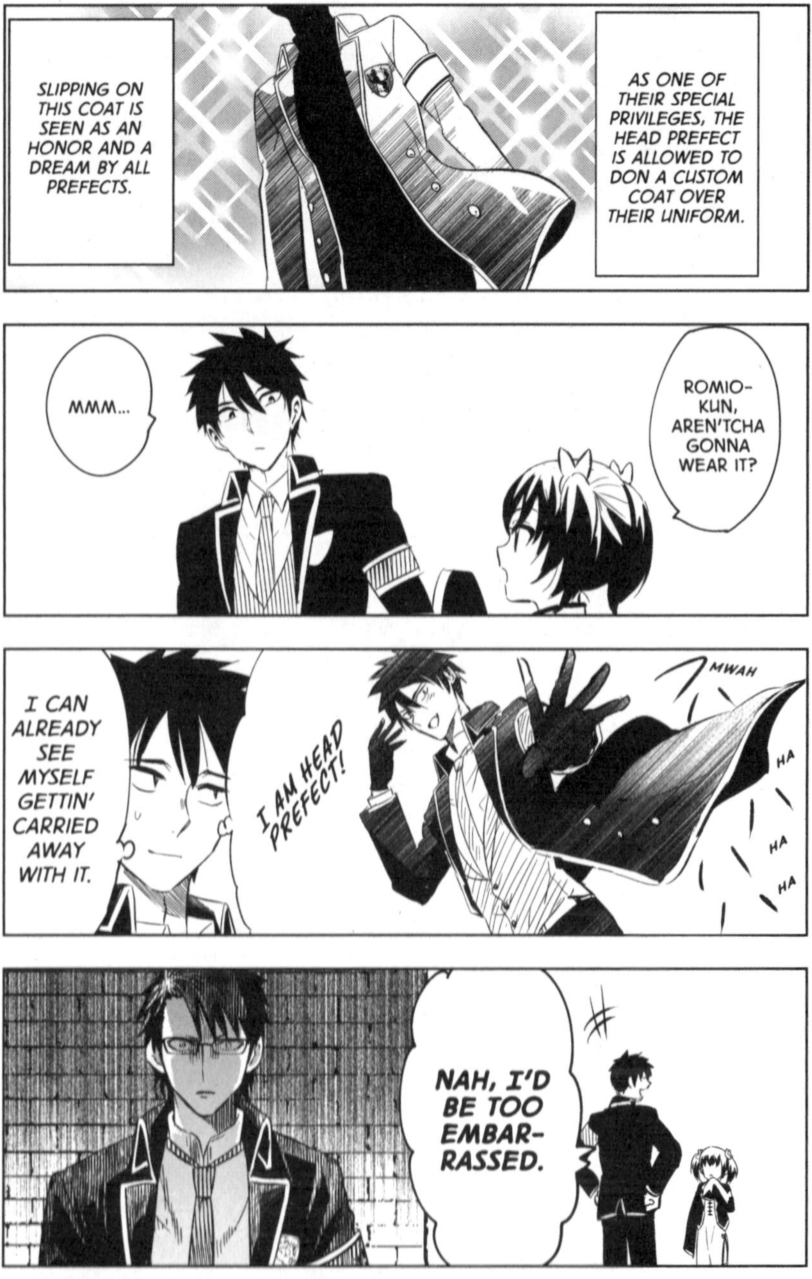
AS ONE OF THEIR SPECIAL PRIVILEGES, THE HEAD PREFECT IS ALLOWED TO DON A CUSTOM COAT OVER THEIR UNIFORM.
SLIPPING ON THIS COAT IS SEEN AS AN HONOR AND A DREAM BY ALL PREFECTS.
ROMIO-KUN, AREN'TCHA GONNA WEAR IT?
MMM...
MWAH
HA
HA
HA
I AM HEAD PREFECT!
I CAN ALREADY SEE MYSELF GETTIN' CARRIED AWAY WITH IT.
NAH, I'D BE TOO EMBARRASSED.

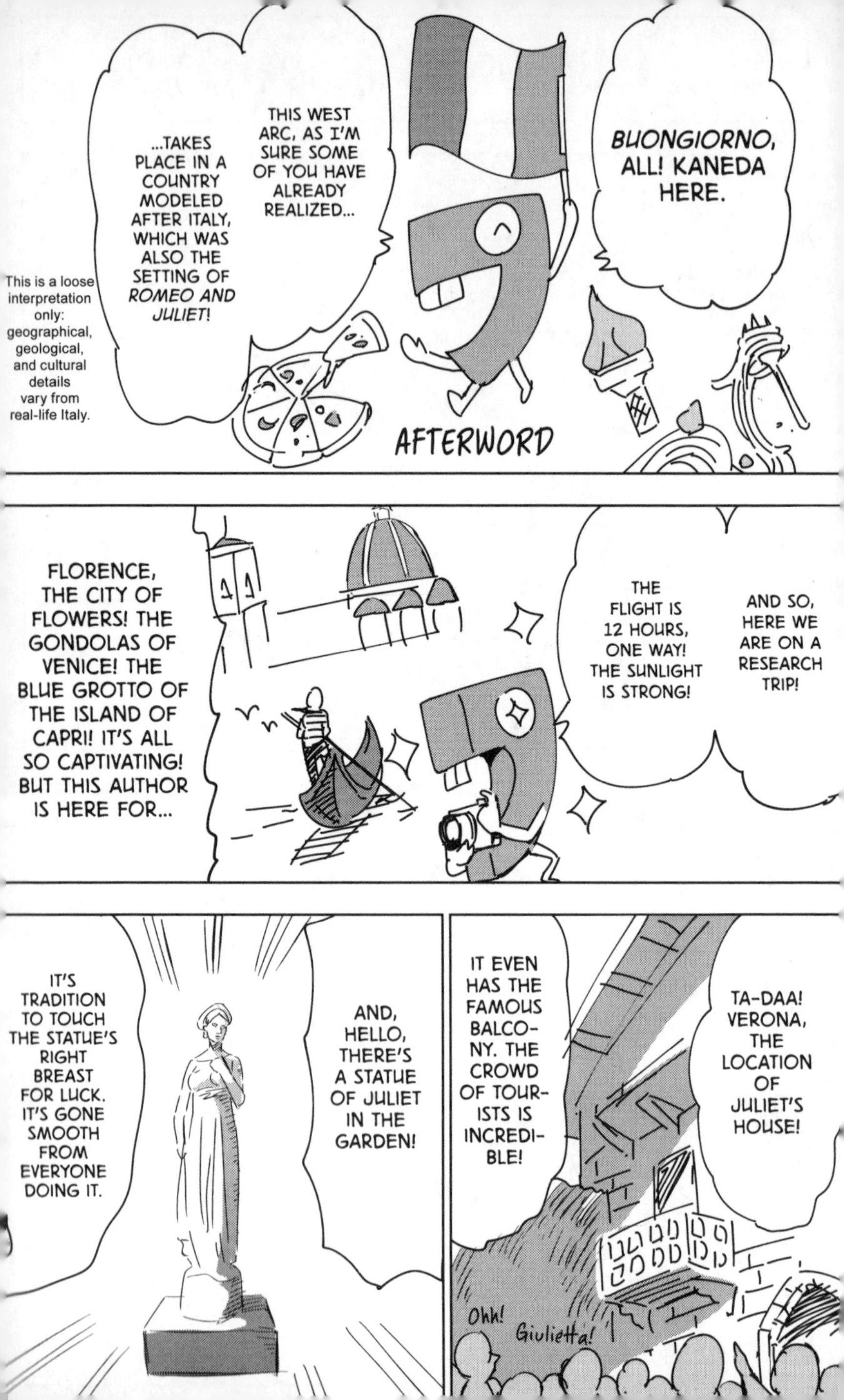

BUONGIORNO, ALL! KANEDA HERE.
THIS WEST ARC, AS I'M SURE SOME OF YOU HAVE ALREADY REALIZED...
...TAKES PLACE IN A COUNTRY MODELED AFTER ITALY, WHICH WAS ALSO THE SETTING OF *ROMEO AND JULIET*!
This is a loose interpretation only: geographical, geological, and cultural details vary from real-life Italy.
AFTERWORD
AND SO, HERE WE ARE ON A RESEARCH TRIP!
THE FLIGHT IS 12 HOURS, ONE WAY! THE SUNLIGHT IS STRONG!
FLORENCE, THE CITY OF FLOWERS! THE GONDOLAS OF VENICE! THE BLUE GROTTO OF THE ISLAND OF CAPRI! IT'S ALL SO CAPTIVATING! BUT THIS AUTHOR IS HERE FOR...
TA-DAA! VERONA, THE LOCATION OF JULIET'S HOUSE!
IT EVEN HAS THE FAMOUS BALCONY. THE CROWD OF TOURISTS IS INCREDIBLE!
Giulietta!
Ohh!
AND, HELLO, THERE'S A STATUE OF JULIET IN THE GARDEN!
IT'S TRADITION TO TOUCH THE STATUE'S RIGHT BREAST FOR LUCK. IT'S GONE SMOOTH FROM EVERYONE DOING IT.

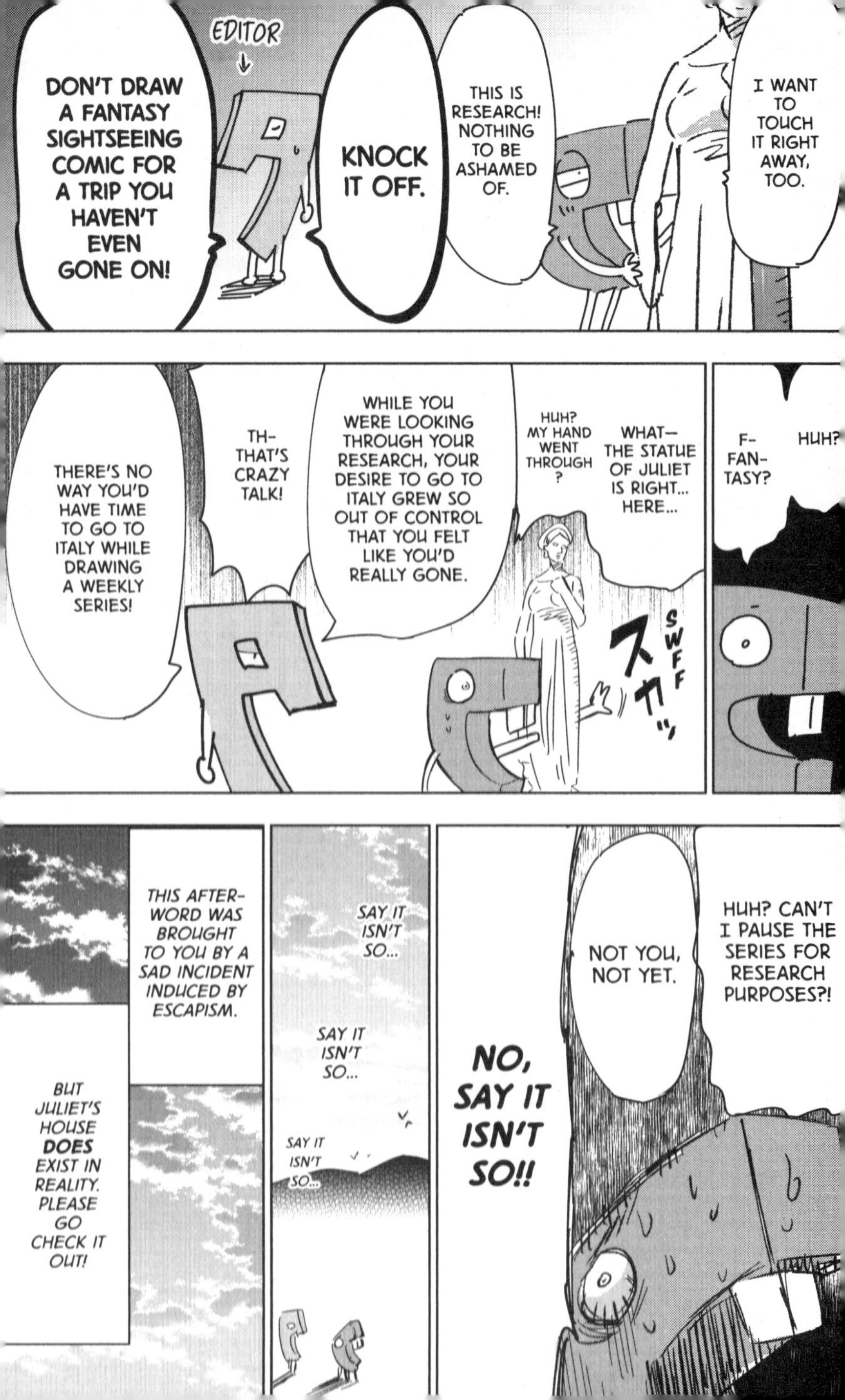
I WANT TO TOUCH IT RIGHT AWAY, TOO.
THIS IS RESEARCH! NOTHING TO BE ASHAMED OF.
EDITOR
KNOCK IT OFF.
DON'T DRAW A FANTASY SIGHTSEEING COMIC FOR A TRIP YOU HAVEN'T EVEN GONE ON!
HUH?
F-FAN-TASY?
WHAT— THE STATUE OF JULIET IS RIGHT... HERE...
HUH? MY HAND WENT THROUGH?
SWFF
WHILE YOU WERE LOOKING THROUGH YOUR RESEARCH, YOUR DESIRE TO GO TO ITALY GREW SO OUT OF CONTROL THAT YOU FELT LIKE YOU'D REALLY GONE.
TH-THAT'S CRAZY TALK!
THERE'S NO WAY YOU'D HAVE TIME TO GO TO ITALY WHILE DRAWING A WEEKLY SERIES!
HUH? CAN'T I PAUSE THE SERIES FOR RESEARCH PURPOSES?!
NOT YOU, NOT YET.
NO, SAY IT ISN'T SO!!
SAY IT ISN'T SO...
SAY IT ISN'T SO...
SAY IT ISN'T SO...
THIS AFTER-WORD WAS BROUGHT TO YOU BY A SAD INCIDENT INDUCED BY ESCAPISM.
BUT JULIET'S HOUSE DOES EXIST IN REALITY. PLEASE GO CHECK IT OUT!

# PERFECT WORLD

### Rie Aruga

A TOUCHING NEW SERIES ABOUT LOVE AND COPING WITH DISABILITY

An office party reunites Tsugumi with her high school crush Itsuki. He's realized his dream of becoming an architect, but along the way, he experienced a spinal injury that put him in a wheelchair. Now Tsugumi's rekindled feelings will butt up against prejudices she never considered — and Itsuki will have to decide if he's ready to let someone into his heart...

"Depicts with great delicacy and courage the difficulties some with disabilities experience getting involved in romantic relationships... Rie Aruga refuses to romanticize, pushing her heroine to face the reality of disability. She invites her readers to the same tasks of empathy, knowledge and recognition."
—Slate.fr

"An important entry [in manga romance]... The emotional core of both plot and characters indicates thoughtfulness... [Aruga's] research is readily apparent in the text and artwork, making this feel like a real story."
—Anime News Network

KC/ KODANSHA COMICS

Knight of the Ice

*Knight of the Ice ©Yayoi Ogawa*

Yayoi Ogawa

# SKATING THRILLS AND ICY CHILLS WITH THIS NEW TINGLY ROMANCE SERIES!

KC
KODANSHA
COMICS

*Boarding School Juliet* 14 copyright © 2019 Yousuke Kaneda
English translation copyright © 2021 Yousuke Kaneda

Published in the United States by Kodansha Comics, an imprint of Kodansha USA Publishing, LLC, New York.

Publication rights for this English edition arranged through Kodansha Ltd., Tokyo.

First published in Japan in 2019 by Kodansha Ltd., Tokyo as *Kishuku Gakkou no Jurietto*, volume 14.

Original cover design by Seiko Tsuchihashi (hive & co., Ltd.)

ISBN 978-1-64651-013-9

Printed in the United States of America.

www.kodanshacomics.com

9 8 7 6 5 4 3 2 1
Translation: Amanda Haley
Lettering: James Dashiell
Editing: Erin Subramanian and Tomoko Nagano
Kodansha Comics edition cover design by Phil Balsman

Publisher: Kiichiro Sugawara

Director of publishing services: Ben Applegate
Associate director of operations: Stephen Pakula
Publishing services managing editor: Noelle Webster
Assistant production manager: Emi Lotto, Angela Zurlo